Landmarks in Rhetoric and Public Address

LANDMARKS IN RHETORIC AND PUBLIC ADDRESS

David Potter, *General Editor*

Lectures Concerning Oratory

By JOHN LAWSON

Edited with an Introduction by

E. NEAL CLAUSSEN

and

KARL R. WALLACE

Foreword by DAVID POTTER

SOUTHERN ILLINOIS UNIVERSITY PRESS
Carbondale and Edwardsville

Feffer & Simons, Inc.
London and Amsterdam

Printed in the United States of America
by offset lithography
Designed by Gary Gore

International Standard Book Number 0-8093-0519-4
Library of Congress Catalog Card Number 78-156792

Contents

Foreword

By David Potter

A RENOWNED preacher, a dedicated academician, the first of his generation in Great Britain to publish his lectures on oratory, a classicist with a strong interest in the practical application of theory to the needs of a contemporary clergy, an early critic of mechanical means of teaching delivery, an eighteenth-century advocate of "animated Conversation," John Lawson on his merit warrants consideration in the twentieth century. And the neoclassical rhetoricians, of which he was an early and prominent member, have long deserved the careful analysis which editors Claussen and Wallace make available in their concise and readable introduction to this edition of *Lectures Concerning Oratory.*

E. Neal Claussen, Associate Dean of Liberal Arts and Sciences at Bradley University, is particularly at home among the Irish rhetoricians. Recipient of a grant from the National Endowment for the Humanities in 1968 to study at Trinity College in Dublin, he is presently engaged in further exploration of the treasures in the Trinity archives. Karl R. Wallace, for many years chairman of the Department of Speech at the University of Illinois, award-winning specialist in Francis Bacon, and internationally recognized for his contributions to British and American Rhetoric and Public Address, is currently Professor of Speech at the University of Massachusetts.

This edition of the *Lectures,* the first in two centuries, is a facsimile, reprinted by the offset lithography process, of the edition published in 1758 by Faulkner. No attempt has been made to correct the original; thus the pagination has been preserved although the folios of the Contents are i–xii and the following Dedication are iii–xvii. An error remains in the latter: folio vii is shown as v. But these are minor flaws in a handsome volume which should further establish the importance of Lawson and enhance the reputations of Claussen and Wallace.

Editors' Introduction

By E. Neal Claussen
and Karl R. Wallace

> [The writer] hath been induced to come forth from the Shade, uncalled; and to venture out from calm safe Obscurity into the Publick, a wide and stormy Sea, covered with Wrecks of unsuccessful Writers; sensible, at the same Time, that he is exposed to greater Inconveniences, than they who should publish under the proposed Regulation could encounter with. They would have Necessity to urge, a just Plea for Indulgence; he is a willing Adventurer: And more gallant Behaviour is expected from a Volunteer, than from one impressed into the Service. (xv)

YEARS before the publication of John Lawson's lectures, British universities had provided opportunities for the study and practice of oratory and belles lettres. Public lectures, such as those by Adam Smith and John Ward, and works on rhetoric, elocution, and grammar were not uncommon. The subject was elevated to esteem by the establishment of endowed professorships which proposed to perpetuate the study and reward the scholarly or oratorical achievements of faculty members. None of the holders of these prestigious chairs, however, had taken the venturous step of making his lectures available to critics and the general public. A new custom was established after the appearance of Lawson's *Lectures Concerning Oratory* in Dublin on November 7, 1758, and John Ward's *System of Oratory* a few months later. Thomas Sheridan, George Campbell, Joseph Priestley, Hugh Blair, John Witherspoon, John Quincy Adams, and others followed precedent, making public for wider audiences what they taught in university halls.

Without a model by which he could judge his work, Lawson was cautious and apologetic. His letter of dedication called the undertaking "unadvised" (viii), yet publication represented an honest but probably "unsuccessful Ambition" (xvi) to fulfill his office well. He also presented a rationalization for the regular publication of books, though some might be judged ordinary and insignificant; for publication would spur lecturers to greater efforts and be a test of ability for all to see. His close friends and literary advisors, William Dunkin and George Faulkner, probably had pressed him into a publishing agreement before his lectures completely satisfied his high standards of literary excellence. His long illness, culminating in his death only two months after the book was published, his lecturing, his frequent sermons at various churches in Dublin, his work with the poor, and his office of First Librarian of Trinity College undoubtedly precluded extensive rewriting. Lawson, nevertheless, was aware that revisions were necessary if his works were to "sustain the Examination of severe and penetrating Eyes" (xiii), and he sought the reader's indulgence.

His contemporary critics found little to praise. One assessment Lawson might have read before his death was the most vituperative. His argument in favor of enjoining professors to publish their lectures, regardless of their significance, came under special attack. "We know from experience that a man may be a very good teacher and a very bad writer; and we are afraid, that if every pedagogue, even *invita Minerva,* was obliged ex officio to commence author, the present fog of dulness that overspreads the land, would be thickened into an impenetrable gloom of worse [than] the Aegyptian darkness, and all taste for letters be swallowed up in universal disgust." [1] The reviewer described Lawson as "a cold, unanimated writer, both in prose and poetry," was convinced that no system could make an orator if a man were not already possessed of genius, and accused the author of laboring self-evident subjects. Particular disagreements were limited to three judgments Lawson expressed in his fifth lecture: Dante had not been excelled for sublimity of thought, lively description, strength, or poetic fire; Chaucer's verse was strong, smooth, and beautiful; and the Moors corrupted the Spanish tongue. The reviewer's general evaluation was more temperate: "On the whole, though we do not meet with anything very striking or new in this performance, we think the parts are well disposed, the lectures full and regular, the stile clear, correct, and pretty well adapted to the variety of the subjects, though in many places it sinks under them; the poetry cold, yet not inelegant; the observations generally just, and the author's erudition well displayed." [2] A similar appraisal was made by William Rose who considered the work repetitious of both ancient and modern writers without providing new insights and the style not well adapted to the dignity of the subject. "His language, though clear and strong, is sometimes inelegant; and his periods often harsh and unharmonious. His observations, however, are generally just; his method is easy and natural; and he has displayed no inconsiderable share of learning." [3]

Deeply saddened by his death and intensely irritated by such reviews, Lawson's friends set out to reestablish his literary reputation. At the insistence of Margetson Armar and George Faulkner, William Dunkin penned an inflated but touching poem which recounted Lawson's life and interests and lavishingly praised his verse and *Lectures*. In his dedicatory letter to the Earl of Chesterfield, Dunkin first flailed the "profound Pedants and shallow Critics" and then turned to his primary purpose. While Lawson's *Lectures* suffered minor imperfections, they should be considered the work of a dedicated genius who brought honor to his university and nation. His "exquisite Lectures . . . will remain the Standard and Criterion of sound Judgment, masculine Stile, and sublime Sentiment." [4] The final lines of the *Obsequies* were meant to put to rest petty criticisms by "Cob-web-weavers of high-flown Fustian":[5]

> Let Lawson's Labours, which Minerva spun,
> Burst into Day, and travel with the Sun:
> His Labours, which the Sister-Graces wove,
> Reserv'd as Incense for imperial Jove,
> Should only feel the great, the final Fire,
> Triumphant over Time, and with the Globe
> expire.[6]

One critic, somewhat placated, described the letter to Lord Chesterfield as "exquisitely humorous" and the *Obsequies* "an elegant poem." [7] Oliver Goldsmith reacted similarly but with less enthusiasm. He considered it inappropriate to append a festive letter to a mournful poem and was critical of Dunkin's stylistic affectations. The closing comments of Goldsmith's review are especially revealing because he was familiar with Lawson's *Lectures*[8] and may have studied under him at Trinity. Knowledgeable of the close friendship between Dunkin and Lawson, Goldsmith was caustically satirical of Dunkin's attempt to grant Lawson a position of importance.

> There is scarcely a trifling city or university in Europe which has not its great men; characters, who are taught by adulation, to fancy themselves figuring in the republic of letters, and leaving monuments of their merit to remote posterity. If there should happen to be two of this character in the same city, the compliments they mutually bestow on each other are pleasant enough; they attempt to raise each other's reputation by mutual flattery, and establish their little dominion within the circle of all their acquaintance.[9]

Further vindication of Lawson's reputation was attempted by a revision and translation by Dunkin and his son, James, of the Latin poem, *Irene,* Lawson had written and appended to his *Lectures*. Declining health had kept Lawson from refining the poem, and Dunkin therefore assumed the responsibility for correcting and enlarging it for posterity.[10] A comparison of the Lawson and Dunkin versions reveals that many inaccuracies of spelling, punctuation, word choice, and verb endings had been emended without changing much of the substance. Only occasionally were ideas embellished, most notably the last fifteen lines of the original poem; these Dunkin more than doubled to heighten the dramatic effect of the conclusion.

The final literary effort Lawson's friends made to assure an enduringly favorable memory of him was the publication of his sermons in 1764 and again in 1765 and 1776. As was the custom of the day, George Faulkner had printed several of these addresses in tract form,[11] but there was no compilation. Several of his friends had collected pamphlets and manuscripts over the years, and eventually one associate, still unknown, published them in London. The editor's rationale for carrying out this task was that since the sermons "may be justly ranked among the first Class of this Species of Composition . . . the

Suppression of them would be an Injury done to the Republick of Letters, to whom they are a very great Acquisition." [12] Perhaps as a tribute to his eminence in the pulpit, Lawson was never explicitly identified as the author of the volume. Even if one were unsure, little effort would have been required to make the proper disclosure, since the date and place of each sermon was provided. William Rose, whose review of the work was generally commendatory, correctly named the sermonizer and removed all doubt.[13]

Lawson's apologists, therefore, worked diligently to give his work a prominent place in literary history, but all their efforts could not keep his publications from obscurity. With minor exceptions, it was not until the twentieth century that Lawson was restudied, and then more because he was representative of a significant trend in rhetorical theory than because his lectures exercised much influence on contemporary or later scholars.

2

While little is known of Lawson's early life, several significant influences can be seen. His family, probably of English origin, had settled in Ulster and were loyal to the Established Church at a time when the state was moving toward enacting rigid controls over the lives of the Roman Catholic majority. Probably he was born in 1709 in Magherafelt, a small village in county Derry.[14] His father, Alexander, like several other relatives was a minister in the Anglican Church who served various parishes in Ulster until his death in 1718.[15] Undoubtedly influenced by his father and other members of the family, Lawson later began studies to enter the ministry. His mother, Katherine, sent him to live with relatives in Monaghan and to read with a Mr. MacMahon to prepare for entrance into Trinity College, Dublin. Since many of the College lectures were delivered in Latin and Greek, all entering students were required to pass examinations in those languages over prescribed classical texts. MacMahon evidently instructed him well, for Lawson was admitted to Trinity on June 1, 1727. His tutor was Vice-Provost Claudius Gilbert, a widely read cleric who bequeathed his library of thirteen thousand books to Trinity College.[16]

Lawson entered as a sizar, "his father's income and numerous family scarcely enabling him to bear the smallest expence."[17] He was thereby exempt from annual fees and charges for room and board. Within two years he had proven himself worthy of receiving a university scholarship. During this time he composed his first work of poetry to be made public. Sir Ralph Gore, Speaker of the House of Commons and a Lord Justice of Ireland, sponsored a competition for the best verse written in honor of the king's birthday. One hundred pounds were distributed to the winners, with Lawson's work judged the most meritorious. The poem is not extant, and the only reference to it is in Dunkin's elegy:

> High was the Subject, and as high the Song,
> Harmonious, ardent, vehement, and strong,
> The genuine Son confess'd the *Delphic* Sire,
> And rag'd with Homer's Heat, and Pindar's Fire.[18]

The object of the university was to produce well-mannered gentlemen of high taste who held European rather than national viewpoints.[19] It was primarily through classical studies that this goal was implemented for the five to six hundred students. Two characteristics in particular set undergraduate instruction at Trinity College apart from other British universities. The required entrance examinations ensured a fairly even level of attainment among the students; everyone had read the same works and possessed minimum capabilities in classical languages. In addition, the prescribed course of classical reading at Trinity "was probably a good deal more thorough than that provided in any other British university."[20] A deeper understanding, it was believed, resulted from studying the classics as literature rather than as exercises in foreign languages or as sources of ideas relevant to other university subjects.

The following sources approximate closely what Lawson was required to study for his bachelor's degree. Read in Latin in the first year was Sallust, all of the *Aeneid,* and Terence; in Greek were Dugard's Lucian, the first half of the *Ilaid, Hero and Leander,* and some Theocritus. Second year requirements were Juvenal, Caesar, Justin, Horace, the *Enchiridion* of Epictetus, the *Tabula* of Cebes, the remainder of the *Iliad,* and the first eight books of the *Odyssey.* Third year readings were the *Georgics,* Cicero's *De Officiis* or Pliny's letters, completion of the *Odyssey,* the *Cyropaedia,* more Lucian, Valleius Paterculus, and the first third of Livy. Mandatory in the final year were Longinus, Suetonius and Tacitus, the remainder of Livy, three plays of Sophocles, the speeches of Demosthenes and Aeschines on the Crown, and the *Philippics* of Demosthenes.[21]

The ancients were judged to have expressed sublime thoughts more eloquently than all other men, and their languages became both models for imitation and media for teaching other subjects. The emphasis was heavily on the humanities, with studies in literature, criticism, oratory, logic, ethics, metaphysics, history, and ancient and modern languages consuming most of the students' time and thought. But a growing body of knowledge and an evolving experimental attitude were beginning to reveal a scientific disposition. Hence students were instructed in mathematics and those subjects falling within what was called natural and experimental philosophy, such as anatomy, botany, chemistry, and physics. Professional studies, such as civil and canon law, theological controversies, and ecclesiastical history, occupied a minor position. Newtonian physics, Boyle's experimental philosophy, and Locke's metaphysics were said to prevail at Trinity at the time Lawson was there.[22]

Two other general requirements for the baccalaureate are particularly relevant to Lawson's education in rhetoric. Not only were students required to read ancient works on oratory, but they also attended lectures on the theory of this subject delivered by the Erasmus Smith Professor of Oratory and History and received practice and criticism by declaiming and disputing before their tutors. In order to graduate, each student had to declaim once and dispute publicly on philosophical questions, twice as respondent and twice as opponent. Private disputations were also required.[23] Only first year students were excused from disputations, presumably because they had not yet learned to argue syllogistically. Such requirements evince the respect paid to oral argumentation and the appropriateness of the subject to the concept of a well-educated man in the eighteenth century. Religious obligations were also imposed upon the students. Each candidate for a degree had to attend religious services in the College Chapel, to take an oath denying the temporal supremacy of the Pope in the British dominions, and to declare against transubstantiation.[24] No conjecture is needed, therefore, to understand what kind of theological education contributed to Lawson's strong anti-papist viewpoint which he later expressed in his sermons and *Lectures*.

Lawson's higher education was obtained entirely at Trinity College,[25] and its influence is plain. Foremost is the wide and thorough acquaintance he gained from the best of Latin and Greek literature. His *Lectures Concerning Oratory* stemmed directly from this background, so much so that one of Lawson's critics described it as a "treatise that adhered more or less slavishly to classical doctrine." [26] It could more accurately be said that Lawson had an immense fund of classical rhetorical knowledge, and this he modified as he thought appropriate to his day. More will be said on this point later. Second, the direct practice and evaluation of his speaking, the lectures he heard on rhetorical theory, and his attendance at chapel services laid the foundation for a practical understanding of oratory which he put into effective use both as a professor and a leading sermonizer of his day. Third, he acquired an avid interest in languages and became adept in Latin, Greek, Hebrew, French, Italian, and Spanish. A substantial part of his own one thousand volume library contained books in Latin and French.[27] Reading works in their original tongues enabled him to draw authoritative judgments about modern eloquence in poetry, drama, novels, and oratory. Such evaluations appear throughout the *Lectures,* although they occur principally in the fifth lecture. His interest in foreign languages was sustained throughout his life, partly because as professor and head librarian he had ready access to Trinity's fine library. Another influence stemmed from his studies in natural and moral philosophy. While literature and poetry were his first interests as a student, he became intrigued with the sciences after attending the lectures on natural philosophy delivered by Richard Helsham, first Erasmus Smith professor of this subject, 1724–38. William Dunkin described this turn of interests poetically.

> His growing mind, extended, and unfurl'd
> Beyond the flaming Limits of the World,
> Launch'd into Regions, whither *Newton* soar'd,

. . . .

Exploring Nature's universal Laws
And tracing from Effects the distant Cause,
By Reason steering to the Port of Truth,
He prov'd the mental Manhood of his Youth:
And mix'd acknowledg'd in these envious Days,
Minerva's Ivy and *Apollo's* Bays.[28]

Other studies led him to read Locke, Bacon, Descartes, Fenelon, Melbranche, Berkeley, and Hutcheson in particular. The broad understanding of man's mind, passions, and values he obtained from these authors was eventually reflected in his *Lectures* and his charity sermons.

By the time he graduated, Lawson had decided to continue his studies at Trinity and to try for a fellowship rather than follow his father's example in the ministry. Having earned the master's degree and passing examinations lasting four days in logic, mathematics, natural philosophy, morality, history, languages, and Latin composition, he procured "the grand object of his wishes." [29] He was co-opted Fellow in 1735 in the place of Robert Shawe, Professor of Oratory and History from 1732 to 1738. Then began a lifelong career at Trinity where he served in various academic and administrative capacities. In his first years as "morning lecturer" and assistant to the Senior Greek Lecturer, he conducted ordinary disputations, commonplaces, and other exercises, but was charged with greater responsibilities after being named Senior Fellow in 1743. He was then appointed head librarian, a post he evidently held until his death, and later Lecturer in Hebrew and Greek. After receiving the Doctor of Divinity degree in 1745, he became Archbishop King's Lecturer in Divinity, an annual appointment for one of the Senior Fellows. In 1750 he was named the Erasmus Smith Professor of Oratory and History and two years later Professor of Divinity. He held both these offices until his death.[30] Other posts were assumed at various intervals: Junior and Senior Dean, catechist, registrar and auditor, College preacher, bursar, senior proctor, and acting Vice-Provost.

Evidence is limited, but Lawson appears to have excelled as a teacher. The anonymous editor of his sermons described Lawson's instruction of the young men at Trinity as "efficacious, by Precept and Example exciting them to pursue their

Studies to Advantage."[31] If Dunkin was not exaggerating, Lawson was especially respected when he "grac'd the Critic's Chair" and was generally popular with the students.

> Self-pois'd, attractive with collected Force,
> He could inform, and moderate their Course:
> High as her Head celestial Science rears,
> He reign'd the Center of their lucid Spheres,
> Infusing Life and Motion through the Whole,
> Like his own *Plato*'s universal Soul.[32]

The Erasmus Smith chair which Lawson held for about nine years has historical significance to the development of rhetorical theory. It was one of the first professorships endowed for the specific purpose of instructing university students in oratory. It has been in continual existence for almost two and a half centuries, even though its original intent has long been ignored. The chair was established in perpetuity upon the recommendation of the board of governors of the Erasmus Smith Schools and by act of the Irish parliament in 1723. Smith (1611–91) was a wealthy London businessman and owner of vast amounts of land in Ireland who desired to use his money to educate the children of his estates. He particularly wanted to have them instructed "in the fear of God, and good literature, and to speak the English tongue."[33] Various elementary, grammar, and high schools in Ireland have been established from his benefaction as well as lectureships, fellowships, and exhibitions at Trinity College. Two chairs were inaugurated simultaneously in 1724, one in Oratory and History and the other in Natural and Experimental Philosophy. Regulations were the same for each. The original statutes outlined a procedure requiring candidates for these lectureships to pass competitive examinations and those best qualified to be approved by the board of governors. Subject matter of the lectures and arrangements for the instruction were to be determined by the Provost and Senior Fellows. Those appointed were required to deliver four public lectures a year, two of which were to be presented to the governors for publication if they approved.[34] Of the fifteen professors who held the Erasmus Smith lectureships from 1724 to the present, only Lawson and his successor, Thomas Leland, published works in oratory.[35] Whether others had submitted lectures to the governors for approval and were rejected, we can not discover. In Lawson's time the lectures were intended primarily for divinity students, though others attended.[36] Regulations for the first Professor of Oratory and History limited the scope of his subject to "such parts of Oratory as conduce to . . . improvement in elocution." [37] Lawson later went beyond elocution and included the Aristotelian view of rhetoric for the Trinity students.

Lawson lectured on oratory at a time when much attention was paid the subject in the classroom and the literary journals and when parliamentary debates and sermons were followed closely by the well-educated. Some students were concerned enough about the art that they themselves devised a form of practice and study which they could not get from lectures and faculty controlled exercises. About three years before Lawson assumed the Smith chair, Edmund Burke and other undergraduates formed the first debating society in the United Kingdom, the Academy of Belles Lettres. According to Burke, it sought "the improvement of its members in the more refin'd, elegant, and useful parts of Literature, these seeming the most likely means for attaining the great end in view—the formation of our minds and manners for the functions of a Civil Society." [38] The Academy was the predecessor to the Historical Club, founded October 24, 1753, and the College Historical Society, formed March 21, 1770. These organizations along with frequent visits to the Irish House of Commons deepened the students' interest in political issues and were valuable adjuncts to university instruction in oratory.[39]

Lawson performed his duties thoroughly. He was conscious of the need for reforming the conduct of his office and outlined some revisions in his letter of dedication. Rather than delivering a public lecture at the end of the terms as required by statute, he apparently devised a regular series. Whether or not all twenty-three lectures were delivered within a single year is not clear, but it is likely, for many are continuations of the same topics. This "perpetual discourse" was meant to provide a theoretical framework which included principles of criticism. The younger students also met for weekly declamations so that "they may be exercised in the useful Art of just, distinct Pronunciation" (xi); upper classmen were assigned readings from classical works on oratory. Written compositions were required for improvement in expression. As a Senior Fellow, Lawson's responsibilities did not include hearing declamations or reading essays. Frederick Haberman was correct in saying that as a lecturer he "appeared only in the auditorium, never in the rehearsal hall."[40] But as a Junior Fellow Lawson heard exercises and gave individual instruction. That he took his office seriously is further demonstrated by his arranging to have the lectures published, something his four predecessors apparently had not considered. Lawson's dedication to his position grew out of the high value he placed in his subject for its usefulness to all men and clerics in particular and for the beauty it created.

Lawson's academic background made him a competent rhetorical theorist and critic. His preaching proved he was a successful practitioner of the art, and doubtless stimulated reader interest in the *Lectures*. The hundreds of sermons he delivered as one of the most popular ministers in Dublin from about 1745 until his death fall into three categories. Chapel services at the college were occasions for explaining such theological tenets as the Trinity, the fall of Adam, and the appearance of the Messiah, and for exhorting the young men to appreciate their education more and to lead better lives. Similar subjects were used in Sunday sermons at various churches in Dublin. Lawson also preached on special occasions such as the consecration of the Lord Bishop of Cloyne in 1753, before the House of Commons the same year for the anniversary of the 1641 Irish Rebellion, an official visit to Trinity by the Lord Lieutenant of Ireland in 1757, and the funeral of Richard Baldwin, college provost, in 1758. On the last two occasions, the sermons were in Latin. But his exhortations in support of charity schools and hospitals gained him the greatest renown. As the editor of his sermons said, Lawson's "Reputation in the Art of Preaching caused the churches to become crowded, and it was unfashionable not to be able to recollect some of the Doctor's persuasive Arguments in Behalf of those truly Christian Institutions . . . on which Occasions he successfully exerted his Powers to the real Ornament of our Language, and to the Advancement of Christian Eloquence."[41]

Lawson's devotion to charity was in keeping with the times,

for the educated and aristocratic classes believed that caring for the poor was their humane and religious duty. The existence of a vast population of poor and ignorant people "shamed constituted authority and challenged the moral and religious idealism of the age."[42] Charity schools were established as a safeguard against vice, irreligion and Popery, and subversive tendencies. But the schools were evidence that the poor were subordinate and not sharers in the society, for children were vocationally trained for subservient jobs. Since the schools were associated with and controlled by parishes, they were supported by legacies, endowments, and voluntary contributions. The annual charity sermon was an occasion which demanded the presence of a leading clergyman who was immediately identifiable with the cause and who could appeal effectively for funds. Lawson was such a man. For example, it was reported that when the Lying-in-Hospital was opened in 1757, Lawson's eminence had induced the governors to invite him to preach, since he was "the only person who could effectually recommend their cause to the government and the nation."[43] How many sermons of this nature he delivered was impossible to learn, but the Dublin newspapers frequently printed announcements of forthcoming sermons and reported the sum of money each had raised. Lawson limited his work for the poor principally to Dublin and only on rare occasions, such as journeying to Oxford or London, did he travel for that purpose.

Although this is not the place for a detailed analysis of Lawson's sermonizing, the reader of the *Lectures* should at least be aware of the power of his speaking and of the chief ways it was felt. He was moved deeply with sympathy and compassion for the poor and conveyed his sincerity effectively to his audiences, who generally were from the wealthy and noble classes. He had a firm grasp of the most successful ways appeals to reason and emotion could be utilized. As one of his contemporaries observed, "The weakness of his Voice was fully compensated by the Energy and *Pathos* of his Addresses, striking at once the Reason and affecting the Passions of his Auditors."[44] Reason was satisfied by respecting the ideas of the scriptural text and by meeting the rational standards of explication. The explication usually incorporated arguments implied or expressed. Its course often culminated in an appeal, as may be seen in a plea for funds he planned to use in connection with the Lying-in-Hospital:

> When the Sight of exquisite Misery strikes our Eyes, or it's Cry sounds in our Ears, we are melted at once, and hurried away before reflection with a Zeal to relieve. He who can listen to the Complaints, count over the Groans, behold the Tears streaming down the Cheeks of the Wretched unconcerned, unmoved; what is he? What do we account him? A Savage, a Monster, not a Man. And after we have removed or soothed Misery when we reflect upon it, what Pleasure do we feel? Human Nature knoweth not such pure, exquisite, heartfelt Delight: But if the selfish Principle hath prevailed, we are conscious, uneasy, and filled with Remorse.[45]

Emotion would be served by applying the exposition to the passions apparent in the circumstances of the occasion and in those feelings associated with the duty and obligations of Christians. Sometimes the strength of feeling seemed to overpower reason, as Lawson realized in the following excerpt. He was developing an appeal in narrative form in the words of the patients when he applied sudden restraint:

> "what Hazards must we run? We! Alas! What Hazards must they, which Nature hath Made most dear to us, our wretched Infants run? Shall we then become Mothers, but to lament the Loss of our Children? Alas! Dearest Babes, do we bring you into Life, only that ye should feel the Pain of losing it? O! Ye, whom God hath blessed with Plenty, assist, preserve; so may Ye be happy Parents. . . ."
>
> But I trangress. I would not, I ought not to move your Passions. Consult Reason, severest Reason.[46]

Lawson was remembered affectionately in Dublin for his energetic support of projects to help the poor. For that reason he was admitted into the Dublin Society for the Improvement of Husbandry, along with such other dignitaries as the Earl of Chesterfield, the Duke of Bedford, and the Lord Archbishop of Dublin. He was especially honored by St. Bride's church, a wealthy and generous parish and his most frequent pulpit outside the college. Upon his death the church determined to erect a bust of him in gratitude for the 111 discourses, many of them charity sermons, he delivered there.[47]

Lawson was so immersed in the functions of the college and church that little time was left for socializing, something for which he had little temperament anyway. He was not as active as some of his contemporaries in soliciting patronage from the elite and fell into the circle of literati more through the efforts of two friends than by his own doing. William Dunkin (1707–65), described as a clergyman "of rollicking character," [48] was Lawson's longest and closest friend. Dunkin depicted their association in this way:

> It was my peculiar Happiness to have lived, and conversed with him for the Course of many Years, under the most familiar and unreserved Degrees of Intimacy, not without those mutual Attatchments [sic], which unite Persons, addicted to the same Studies and Amusements, and indeed it was impossible to know him well, and at the same Time not love, and esteem him thoroughly.[49]

Dunkin received his baccalaureate degree in 1729, his master's in 1732, and his doctorate in 1744. During the time he ran a school in Dublin after his graduation, he became well acquainted with Jonathan Swift, Alexander Pope, the Earl of Chesterfield, George Faulkner, and other notables. It was Chesterfield, then Lord Lieutenant of Ireland, who appointed Dunkin to the mastership of Enniskillen Royal School in 1746, a position he held till his death. There he formed a close relationship with Margetson Armar, a wealthy landowner who commissioned Dunkin's eclogue to Lawson.[50] Dunkin wrote many poems and had them published as tracts or in newspapers and journals; after his death, they were collected and published in two volumes. His approach was to write a Greek poem on a subject, then translate it into Latin, then into English blank verse, and finally into heroic rhyme "so that he gave you the same joint dressed in four different ways, and you might feed upon that which best suited your palate." [51] Swift thought highly of him as "a gentleman of much wit and the best English as well as Latin poet in this kingdom." [52]

Close ties also existed between Lawson and his publisher, George Faulkner (1699–1775). The only formal education Faulkner received was from Dr. Lloyd, esteemed as the best instructor in Ireland at the time. Yet he became the editor, critic, publisher, and confidant of several prominent writers.

The success of his *Dublin Journal,* begun in 1728, attracted the notice of Swift who frequently supplied it with his writings. Faulkner's fame as a book publisher came after he printed the first collected edition of Swift's works. The Dean called him "the prince of Dublin printers," a title which still denotes Faulkner. The *Journal*'s shop, only a few blocks from the college, "became the rendezvous of the friends of Ireland, and of the most distinguished in literature."[53] Doubtless it was there that Lawson met and conversed with such men as Swift and Chesterfield. Faulkner, a self-important person who uninhibitedly passed judgment on authors, often made changes in manuscripts or showed how something ought to have been written. Dunkin described his bumptiousness in book 3 of "The Poetical Mirror":

> He, big with Phoebus, and from early years
> Imbu'd, imparts his sentiments unask'd
> To pregnant authors in their teeming throes,
> Benignly candid, nor disdains to point
> The lapses relative beneath each page
> With inky stars, apply his healing hand,
> And lick the crude conceptions into form,
> Mature impress'd, that, elegantly bound
> In oxen-hide, and polish'd, they may view
> The radiant Sun, and flutter through the world.[54]

Faulkner made some of these kinds of alterations in the second and third printings of the *Lectures*. His eccentricities were ridiculed in the character of Peter Paragraph in Samuel Foote's play, *The Orators,* which was first produced in 1762 to satirize Thomas Sheridan, the prevailing passion for oratory, and the popularity of debating societies.

Several other names of friends and associates appeared in comments on Lawson, such as Robert Johnson, Bishop of Cloyne, but the only other of importance was Edward Maurice, Bishop of Ossory (1689?–1756). He and Lawson were both excellent preachers and occasional poets. Among the things Maurice's will left to his "good friend" were his translations of the *Iliad* and *Odyssey* in the manner of Milton and other original manuscripts.[55] Lawson dedicated an historical poem to Maurice in the *Lectures* (202–9), and the inference has been drawn that that portion of the *Iliad* appearing on page 297 was Maurice's.[56]

Lawson had long been ill, and his full schedule of activities as lecturer, librarian, and preacher must have been enervating. He died in his forty-ninth year on the morning of January 9, 1759, "of a tedious and painful Illness" [57] and was interred privately in the college chapel on January 12. His *Lectures,* published only two months before, were remembered favorably in all the notices of his death. But the public grieved more for the loss of the leading advocate for the poor:[58] "He was their Charity-Sermon Preacher, a Champion for the helpless Orphans; and ever engaged himself in that religious Service with a Chearfulness and Condescension that marked the Piety of his Disposition." [59]

3

The works of Lawson and Ward, the leading examples of restatements of classical doctrines of rhetoric, appeared near the end of a period marked by an intense interest in Greek and Roman societies and a veneration of such literary figures as Homer, Aristotle, Cicero, Quintilian, and Longinus. The new age certainly would not totally abandon classicism, but would move away from primary reliance upon ancient theories and ideals. The pillars of the Augustan period were shaken by the new generation's relativism, sentimentality, and acquisitive ethic, by its concept of art as "an end-product of self-expression," and a "lower-middle-class prudential religious 'enthusiasm'" that threatened authority and tradition.[60] As for rhetorical theory, Lawson and Ward bridged the rigid and attenuating Ramistic dichotomies and the innovative rhetorical concepts of Blair, Campbell, and Whately. As Douglas Ehninger has put it, "though later writers may have departed from classicism, unless the full scope of the classical rhetoric had been firmly established they hardly could have advanced beyond it." [61] It cannot be said that Lawson was aware that his work would perform this transitional role. On the contrary, any major shift away from classical theory would have been incompatible with his philosophy. The reasons for his strict adherence to ancient thought can be disclosed by a more penetrating look at the foundations of the Augustan age in which he was educated, taught, and wrote.

Paul Fussell provides a valuable summary of the dominant characteristics of the eighteenth-century humanist mind as revealed in the works of such conservatives as Johnson, Swift, Burke, Reynolds, and Pope. The characteristics also give insight into Lawson's rhetorical theory. (1) Human nature is historically unchanged; innovation is, therefore, incongruous to man's permanence and uniformity. "It is this idea in the eighteenth century that sanctions the orthodox conception of the permanence of the literary genres, each of which is thought to address itself to one unchanging element of the human consciousness." [62] (2) Human problems are insoluble, but man possesses nobility and dignity since only he can contrive situations so complex. (3) Literature is revered because it results from the uniquely human attribute of symbol-making. (4) The humanist is obsessed with evaluation and ranks everything.

> This *libido aestimandi* is naturally accompanied by hierarchical rather than egalitarian expectations about society and politics; about literary genres and techniques, some of which are conceived to be in the nature of things "better" than others; about periods of history, some of which are assumed to be more "noble" than others; and even about the assumed elements of the human psyche, which is still imaged by the eighteenth-century humanist in a very seventeenth-century way—with "will" in a position of almost military "command" at the top, "reason" or "judgment" in the middle, and the senses or "passions" as servants at the bottom.[63]

(5) Past experience has been tested and proven and is, therefore, elegized. (6) Ethics and expression are fused so that one must be virtuous before he can write well; good literature is an index of high moral attainment. (7) Above all, man must seek to settle moral questions; a description of the external world is irrelevant and perhaps dangerous. (8) Man is incurably blemished because of original sin or the decay of nature, but he has dignity because he perceives his defects. Satire, a common literary form at this time, understandably follows from self-distrust. (9) The physical world teaches man little if anything about his moral existence. (10) Simplistic explanations of man's nature, e.g., he is entirely rational, are viewed suspiciously. (11) Man's need for redemptive assistance requires that the principal use of expression be didactic. "The eighteenth-century humanist is given to uttering and re-

uttering the classical commonplace that the office of literature is to teach, but to teach through the agency of aesthetic delight." [64] (12) Man is unique among all creatures because only he can exercise free power of choice over environmental or physical determinants and achieve acceptance or happiness.

Each of these characteristics is related to Lawson's concept of rhetoric, but several stand out as more significant than others and deserve comment. What influenced Lawson to compose a series of lectures based almost exclusively upon classical precepts can be deduced from Fussell's remarks. Much faith was placed in the ancients because their works on rhetoric accurately and fully revealed the methods of attaining eloquence, had allowed Greek and Roman poets and orators to become sublime in thought and style, and had withstood the tests of time so that they were as relevant to man in the eighteenth century as in the time of Aristotle or Cicero. Early in the *Lectures* Lawson exhorted his students:

> First and principally, seek after Wisdom and Virtue; For Elevation of Soul can alone support Sublimity of Genius. Next, Be unwearied in tracing back Eloquence to it's true Source, the Monuments of pure Antiquity, of those Heroes whom you have lately seen. Imitate their Solidity, their Method, their Justness, their Purity, their Force, their Sublimity. (71)

He was reflecting what James Johnson called the "prime neo-classical belief: that a knowledge of the past provides an infallible insight into the affairs of the present." [65] Edmund Burke had expressed it this way: "In history a great volume is unrolled for our instruction, drawing the materials of future wisdom from the past errors and infirmities of mankind." [66] If one holds, as Lawson did, that little improvement can be made upon the classicists, he is forced to look back to gain an authoritative, valuable, and tested understanding of eloquence or rhetoric. Formulating new theories would be audacious and tenuous.

The concept of imitation is basic to Lawson's teaching. He recommended the practice throughout the work and did not hesitate to rank the poets, historians, orators, and languages most deserving emulation. His seventh lecture was devoted specifically to the theory and the particular methodology he recommended. Lawson was thus following a common literary form. Men of letters, particularly poets, in the first half of the eighteenth century had settled upon the moralistic and stately literature from the time of Augustus for models; works of Cicero, Livy, Virgil, and Horace were favored. The neo-classicist sought to be like his predecessors in their efforts "to stem the increasing tide of degeneracy, venery, and immorality" [67] and aimed at a comparable mode of expression marked by "grace, high style, urbanity of tone, meticulousness of form, and morality of theme." [68] The rules of art espoused by the ancients became the established guidelines for composition and evaluation.

> The aesthetics based on symmetry, proportion, and fulfillment of function; the supremacy of the judgment over the imagination; the emphasis on realism; the attempt to find a universal foundation for taste; and effort to re-establish the Rules on the basis of reason are all more or less intimately connected with the basic temper of the Age of Reason.[69]

So pervasive was this imitative impulse that Oldham, Etherege, Dryden, Pope, Johnson and almost all the major authors were translators and followed one of two courses. The "pure" translation corresponded to classic poems faithfully, but substituted modern allusions, places, and names for ancient and foreign examples and illustrations. The aim was to imitate the form of the model and communicate its thoughts to the contemporary reader who likely was unfamiliar with the work. The "independent" or "creative" translation demanded familiarity with the source. "In this form the poet incorporates much or all of a specific older model into his own poem, self-consciously parallels the works and, in varying degrees, creates a new poem, one in which the focus is on the living (or domestic) rather than the dead (or foreign) author." [70] Pleasure, it was believed, derived from the comparison of the texts. An interesting example of an "independent" translation relevant to the study of oratory is Robert Dodsley's *The Art of Preaching; In Imitation of Horace's Art of Poetry,* first published in London in 1738. Dodsley took Horace's work as the base and provided excerpts from the Latin for comparison. What resulted, however, was a criticism of the preaching of the day, an issuance of instructions for improvement, and a commendation of the style and thought of such moderns as Tillotson, Butler, Clarke, and Atterbury. Even Lawson was caught up in this practice. Two of his own translations were included in the *Lectures* (314–24) not because he considered them worthy of being preserved but because they demonstrated how one could elevate his "Fancy and Stile" by borrowing "some Sparks of poetic Fire" (312).

Lawson's advice on imitation was not unlike the translator's object and means. His detailed discussion of imitation followed five lectures which traced the history of eloquence from the earliest time to the present, provided brief summaries of the major classical works on rhetoric, commented on the most eloquent orators, and critiqued modern languages and writers. The scheme was purposeful, for imitation follows easily and naturally from acquaintance with the best writers and orators. To Lawson, the value of imitation rested in its "being a great and compendious Method of arriving at Eloquence" (108) and in transforming the student into the likeness of the ancients.[71] It is inescapable, he argued, for all who have excelled in any science or art started from the materials of others, not from their own knowledge. Man is unable "by the Power of his own Genius, to carry on Art from its first Rudiments to Perfection" (112). His prescribed rules for imitation were intended to produce a result analogous to an "independent" translation. The best model and the one most suitable to the individual should be chosen with good judgment. Servile copying of the model orator should be avoided because it leads to stiffness. Instead, the imitator should give his model a new turn or apply it in a new way in order to make it his own. Following only one model was considered confining and dangerous since it often led to awkward resemblances. The imitator was also instructed to adapt his copy to the present time, place, and occasion. "He is not a *Demosthenes,* who can copy with the utmost Exactness any, even the most shining Passage in his Orations; but He is, who can speak or write as *Demosthenes* would have done in a parallel Conjuncture" (122). Lawson's final rule was to refrain from mere borrowing. "It is not enough, that you can imitate well the best Writer; you must likewise add somewhat of your own" (123). Imitation, then, meant the acquisition of the spirit, skill, and form of the original, not the words and examples, and should produce a new work which resembles the model and which is itself worthy of imitation. The other major neoclassical rhetorician, John Ward, offered almost identical advice, although his methodology was far more specific.[72]

Lawson understood the value of precept as well as imitation. His precepts, of course, were drawn from the greatest of ancient works. Modern thought could not surpass the masters' concepts which had given "Law to the whole Earth" (vi). Lawson's aim, however, was not to present merely a repetition of classical doctrine. Like the student orator, the theorist should produce something of his own. His goal was "to clear the Road marked out by the Antients, to smooth and open it; perhaps in some Places to strike out new and shorter Paths" (3). An examination of the list of books Lawson had in his library indicates he was familiar with some of the more important modern French works relevant to rhetoric and logic, particularly works by the Port-Royalists. He owned two copies of *La Logique, ou L'Art de Penser;* one was a 1723 English translation by John Ozell, and the other was in Latin. Also in his possession was *Grammaire Generale et Raisonnée* by Antoine Arnauld and Claude Lancelot, *Systéme des Reflexions, . . . ou nouvel Essai de Logique* by Jean Pierre de Crousaz, *Dialogues sur l'Eloquence* by Fenelon, *La Rhetorique, ou l'Art de Parler* by Bernard Lamy, *Traitté de l'Action de l'Orateur, ou de la Prononciation et du Geste* by Michel Le Faucheur, and *Traité de la Maniére d'Étudier et d'Enseigner les Belles-Lettres* by Charles Rollin. For the most part, however, he disregarded many of the newer ideas found in these works and relied upon the classics. His dismissal of modern thought is apparent in his discussion of aids to invention. First, he ignored the distinction Francis Bacon, his cited authority, had drawn between topics and commonplaces and proceeded to define topics as Bacon had used commonplaces:[73] "a Number of Observations on all common Heads, digested into convenient Order; which should be ever ready at Hand, that the Orator may have Recourse to them; and draw from them, as from a general Store, Materials on all Occasions" (127–28). Lawson was concerned that "the Moderns have not only neglected, but despised this whole Matter; it seems not with good Cause" (128). Yet he failed to give full treatment of the specific kinds of topics. Instead, he encouraged students to read Cicero and Quintilian to become acquainted with the precepts. In so doing, he was criticizing Lamy, Fenelon, and the Port-Royalists for their hostility to categories, predicables, and places[74] and advocating a return to classical doctrine.

Lawson's disapproval of elocutionists is another notable example of his reaction against modern developments. He expressed firm disagreement with any system that purported to create art by mechanical and simplistic means while ignoring nature and genius. The marking of words and syllables with musical notations was disapproved of. Lawson argued that tonal patterns in speech are far too complex to be recorded accurately and thoroughly, that learning this marking system is an insuperable task, that it is a waste of time for a preacher who had more important things to learn, and that the speaker's inner conviction is more influential than the emphasis and cadence of his voice (423–26). For Lawson, the strongest opposition came from Cicero and Quintilian who had not even hinted that such mechanical techniques existed or were of value. Again, the ancients remained the best authority. The supposition may be advanced that Lawson was referring to Thomas Sheridan's concepts of elocution, for Sheridan had been lecturing on the subject in Dublin while Lawson was discoursing at Trinity. But Lecture Twenty-two is explicit about one source which had recommended the musical notation system: *Reflexions sur la Poesie, la Peinture, et la Musique* (424). This work by Abbé Jean-Baptiste Dubos first appeared in 1719 and was reprinted many times. Lawson owned a copy of the 1732 edition. It advanced Dubos's theory of the arts, including declamation, even though he had no practical experience with any of them. In the debate over the value of classical studies in modern times, Dubos generally favored the ancients. Lawson indicted Dubos for lack of information and misinterpretation. Lawson's denunciation of the elocutionists' methods was one of the first expressed in the eighteenth century. His understanding of classical rhetoric provided a broader perspective of the orator's art.

Another instance of Lawson's reluctance to accept contemporary ideas was his position in the dispute over taste as a faculty of the mind. In his first lecture, he included genius and application as the qualities necessary to form an orator and excluded taste. Genius was considered a natural ability that one either had or did not have. If a person possessed an inherent propensity for oratory, he could improve himself by studying the best works of the best speakers and by frequent practice. Probably referring to Francis Hutcheson and Anthony A. C. Shaftesbury,[75] he objected to the frequently stated assumption that taste was a distinct faculty of the mind and determined aesthetic excellence in the polite arts. Neither could he agree that taste was a sentiment that operated independently of understanding. To refute these theories, he first turned to the ancients and found that they had not used the term in the context moderns had applied to it. Further substantiation for his objections, as Vincent Bevilacqua has noticed, came from two Newtonian axioms concerning simplicity in causes and sufficient causality.[76] Because "no more Causes are to be admitted, than such as are real, and sufficient to produce the Effect" (17), genius, guided by firm understanding and improved by application, was enough to account for the judgmental powers attributed to taste. In Lawson's estimation, nothing in the arts was produced by anything but genius and understanding. These faculties were known "to be real Causes, existing in Nature, and we find them to be sufficient; what then is Taste? Conceived as a Faculty distinct from them, is it any Thing, but a meer Name?" (18) The vagueness of the term, his third objection, was the source of much confusion. For the word to be used to connote anything but a result of the exercise of genius and application, "a distinct precise Notion of it" would have to be fixed (21). In these ways, Lawson again chose the more settled position. But this time he was more cautious because of a possible conflict of merits: in "restoring the ancient Simplicity . . . the Danger is, that as Custom hath established firmly the present Notions, the antient may be deemed new; and the desire of bringing them back looked upon as a Zeal for Innovation" (20). As Lawson's criticisms of the mechanistic methods of teaching delivery failed to damage the growth of the elocutionary movement, so his opposition to treating taste as a faculty failed to gain wide acceptance. The concept of taste became an integral part of Henry Home's *Elements of Criticism* (1761), Hugh Blair's *Lectures on Rhetoric and Belles Lettres* (1783), and many other works in the belletristic movement.[77] Lawson chose to emphasize Cicero's divisions of rhetoric, commenting on these and related matters as his own interests and best judgment dictated. For the student who knows classical rhetoric and the rhetorical doctrines of Lawson's contemporaries, the interpretations and comments are often insightful. All but seven of the lectures were addressed specifically to invention, arrangement, style, and delivery. Memory was referred to briefly as a faculty of the mind (218). Ray Keesey's thorough study of these sixteen lectures disclosed Lawson's chief sources.[78] Aristotle's *Rhetoric* provided the framework for the discussion of invention. Lawson translated Aristotle's definition of rhetoric as "the Art of finding out on all Subjects what is fitted to perswade" (45) and believed that the orator's chief goal was to convince. Therefore, it followed that logical proof was considered the most important. Topics, enthymemes, and examples were recommended for use, but meager explanation of each was provided. Instead, Lawson gave more emphasis to "the Science which seems most conducive to instruct an Orator in the Art of Reasoning," geometry (131). As he used the term, it meant a plan of arriving at general truths from simple elements or, conversely, particular truths from theorems. The special value of the geometrical method was that it led to a clear and precise test of the argumentative structure of a discourse (133). Aristotle's nonartistic proofs were treated as means of amplification in the lecture on arrangement. Later he dismissed laws, facts, and evidence because they were more relevant to forensic and deliberative oratory. Pulpit speaking concerned weightier matters (372).

Aristotle was also relied upon for advice on the use of pathetic proof, which need not be repeated here. It is significant, however, that the discussion of pathos was preceded by a critique of unnamed modern moralists, rhetoricians, and metaphysicians for separating the faculties of the mind unrealistically. "Examine closely into the opinions usually entertained about them, you will find that they are looked upon as several independent Principles, distinct Beings, grafted as it were into the Mind, and acting by their own Force" (153). Undoubtedly influenced by John Locke,[79] Lawson expressed opposition to this explanation of behavior and took a more gestaltlike position. He theorized that the "whole Soul" determined response and that each "Mode of Apprehension" was the act of the "Soul" exercising the faculties (154). He was unwilling, then, to accept completely the assumption that various functions of the mind act independently and have the power to account for distinguishable actions. Passion, an act of the will, was a necessary "Spur within the mind incessantly rouzing it from Sloth" (157), but restrainable by the mind. It is susceptible to "two original Emotions . . . Desire and Aversion, or as they are commonly stiled, Love and Hatred; Love of Happiness and Hatred of misery" (156), the genera of all other passions. The implications of these viewpoints upon oratory were laid down philosophically before turning to Aristotle's more practical suggestions. Because Lawson believed the passion of fear was more powerful than love, he advised that pleasure would result from effective appeals to the audience's sense of tragedy, pain, misery, and the like. He reasoned that if one were threatened, relief would come from knowing how to remove or avoid the distresses. Not only were appeals to the passions means of gaining success through discourse, but they were necessitated by the nature of man: "As the End of Eloquence is Persuasion, and strictly speaking, all Persuasion ought to be founded in Conviction alone, it must be acknowledged, that all Address to the Passions is grounded in the Imperfection of Mankind; it is faulty if not necessary" (165). Men are not so completely rational and unprejudiced that they will accept truth through exposition; one must use all the skill at his disposal to accomplish that goal. Lawson's understanding of man, as revealed in his discussion of the faculties of the mind, distinctly reflects the dominant characteristics of the eighteenth-century humanistic philosophy, particularly as he assumed that passions were the servants of the mind, that man is universally and incurably imperfect, and that man can exercise control over his difficulties and attain happiness.

If Lawson had followed Aristotle closely, ethos, a third mode of artistic proofs, would have been treated along with reasoning and emotional appeals. Rather, comments about the speaker's character appear throughout the lectures and specifically as they related to the preacher in Lecture Nineteen. This is not to say Lawson underestimated the force of ethical proof, for he asserted that "nothing contributes more to Persuasion, than a Belief of Sincerity in the Speaker" (354). Appropriately, Quintilian was Lawson's major source on this topic. A preacher must possess two qualities, and if he could not acquire them, he must quit the profession. First, he must be virtuous and love religion and piety. Just as a wicked man who uttered sacred truths would stimulate indifference or aversion to his words, an unbeliever who talked about religion would raise doubts. Second, he must be knowledgeable and broadly and liberally educated. Acquaintance with the Scriptures was especially important, and Lawson believed that ability to read them in Hebrew and Greek would prevent unwarranted interpretations. The writings of philosophers and moralists and a background of polite literature were also necessary as was knowledge about the world and man. Lawson recognized, however, that one might have the required qualities and not be persuasive. Therefore, he encouraged the speaker to cultivate a manner of delivery which would make the audience sense his authority:

> But this *Authority,* if obtained, will make up abundantly for whatever may be wanting in your Genius, or defective in their Conceptions. It sets every Thing you say in a favourable Light, hiding Imperfections, and doubling the Value of what is good. It giveth Spirit to your Diction, Force to your Arguments, Strength and Weight to your Advice. It rendereth you beloved and reverenced, and by Means thereof, useful; indeed, a publick Blessing. (431)

Were it not for the exacting prerequisites Lawson established for the art and the speaker, this advice might lead to deception. Keesey's conclusion about Lawson's consideration of ethos is apt: "The *Lectures* are permeated with the ethical teachings of the devout preacher who preaches as much as he lectures, even to the students in his classes." [80]

Lawson treated arrangement primarily in Lectures Nine, Twenty, and Twenty-one and relied on Quintilian as his principal source of instruction. Wisely recognizing that arrangement was integrally involved with invention, Lawson taught that skill in arranging arguments was part of the reasoning process and seemed to follow upon discovering the ideas and materials of proof. The present-day reader will find familiar directions for selecting, ordering, and adapting ideas for a given situation. Of special interest is Lawson's criticism of such notable preachers as John Tillotson, Samuel Clarke, Jacques Bénigne Bossuet, and Thomas Sherlock. His library was replete with collections of sermons by most of the major modern English, Irish, Scotch, and French preachers, and his reading enabled him to form perceptive judgments of their methods of developing arguments. Lawson's own long and reputable experience in the pulpit served to confirm the advice he offered.

Lawson's thoughts on style were in keeping with the commonly held beliefs of his day, especially the reliance upon time-tested rules, the emphasis on the imaginative and symbol-making powers of the mind, and the tenet that expression should instruct pleasingly. The subject was developed in Lectures Twelve through Seventeen and the beginning of Eighteen and Twenty-two. Lawson drew heavily from Aristotle, Cicero, and Quintilian and, to a lesser extent, Homer, Longinus, and Dionysius. Thus, his suggestions are not new or innovative. His aim was not to develop a theory of style nor to issue detailed instructions on how one achieved eloquence; students were referred to the ancients for such assistance. Rather, Lawson sought to make clear what features characterized the proper use of the elements of style and what faults should be avoided. The fact that he devoted more lectures to style than to the other three divisions of rhetoric should not be misconstrued. Beautiful expression unrelated to substance was not the end which he proposed. Lawson was adamant about the perspective which ought to guide the orator. Early in Lecture Twelve he stated that the "great End of Language" was "to Communicate our Sentiments for the Instruction or Perswasion of other Men" (187), and then he became more specific by declaring that more than clear instruction was necessary.

> For what avails it to be clear, unless I can make you think it worth your while to attend? However intelligible I be, importeth not; for you will not understand unless you listen, and you will

> rarely listen if I be no more than intelligible. The Oratory must therefore *please* and *move*. (191)

He continued this line of thought in the following lecture and refuted an opinion held by many that ornament was superfluous to an orator whose object was to prove (214–15). Lawson's arguments in favor of the proper use of stylistic elements are both a reaction against the austere sermons of his day and a warning against the excesses of the seventeenth-century stylistic rhetoricians.[81]

Almost as an afterthought, Lawson's definition of style appeared at the conclusion of his lengthy exposition of the concept. Style is "An Assemblage of Words considered with regard to Propriety of Signification, and Arrangement in Sound" (325). The three classes of expression recognized were those of Homer: the concise and nervous, the copious and sweet, and the vehement and sublime. Three of the characteristics of acceptable style discussed by the classicists were recommended by Lawson: clarity, purity, and ornament. Clarity was called "the first and most necessary property" (187), but he dealt with it and purity as parts of each other. Various faults of obscurity, such as equivocal expression and obsolete words, were mentioned as qualities to be avoided. Ornament was that which "maketh Rhetorick an *Art:* All other Parts whereof may be attained by meer Felicity of Nature, but without Discipline, without much Study and Experience you cannot arrive at the Perfection of Ornament" (211). This aspect of style was divided into composition and figures. Composition involved the "due Arrangement of Words with Regard to Signification and Sound" (227) and differed from Lawson's definition of style by emphasizing the arrangement of words and ideas. Thus, rules were stated governing the order of words in sentences, sentence length, and relationships between sentences. Figures were treated in Lecture Fifteen under three headings, the number, the kinds, and the application. A distinct resemblance to ancient rhetorical doctrines is apparent in Lawson's instructions on style.

Also evident is the influence of faculty and associational psychology on his concept of style. Lawson traced the source of ornament to the nature of man. The faculty of reason entailed man's awareness of his existence and the ability to respond with feeling, and the mind allowed him to discriminate. The mind also possessed the power of memory, or recollecting images from another time. Memory is called the "Storehouse of the Soul" (218) because it accumulates ideas and experiences and becomes the source of learning. But it is imagination, "a Kind of intermediate Faculty" (217), which enables man to sift, sort, and associate recollections to form new ideas in pleasing ways. The value of imagination was related to the other faculties: "If Reason makes Discourse convincing, Passion vehement, a fine Imagination, renders it beautiful and charming" (219–20). These abilities were not shared by all men in the same degree. Style was the product of natural genius which could not be learned. The person with little talent could only hope to be preserved "from gross Errors; and thus advance to Mediocrity" (327). The person with genius, on the other hand, should be taught to judge style, not be overwhelmed with rules. Such views are better understood as they are related to the tenor of the eighteenth century when the humanist normally made much of man's symbol-making ability and the set nature of man.

One last point that needs to be made about Lawson's views on style is the relationship he saw between the arts of the poet and the orator. Having an extensive background in poetry through his schooling and having tried his hand at the art several times, his fondness for the subject never diminished. He saw its relevance to other manners of discourse, a belief held by the classicists, as he made obvious by quoting from Cicero and Quintilian (276). The prevailing view in the *Lectures* is that the study of poetry can give force and grace to truth. As was the case throughout his discussion of style, the goal was not to please the ear. Embellishment was a way of capturing audience attention and making ideas more appealing to the mind. It was one of the available means of persuasion. Lawson made it abundantly clear in his first lecture that he would make frequent references to poetry. His rationalization was that examples from either oratory or poetry extended to the other because the two arts were closely related, that examples from poetry were more usable in the lectures because they were shorter, and that poetry used bolder ornaments and made better illustrations (22). He did not fail to fulfill his word. Besides the usefulness of poetry to oratory, other advantages as these appeared at various intervals: poetry laid the foundation of true eloquence (107) and allowed one to acquire "Classical Taste" (439). Three lectures were specifically assigned to this matter. Sixteen and Seventeen consisted of a hypothetical dialogue in which Eubulus refuted Philemon's arguments about the dangers and irrelevance of orators utilizing the poet's skills. Lawson's last lecture was a defense of his opinion stated previously that writing verse in native languages was preferable to composition in Latin. His position seemed contrary to common practice and had aroused much criticism. He believed that poetry was not widely read when written in the language that only a few knew well, that too much was unknown about the precise use of Latin, and that the honor of the country was better served when native languages were used. At the same time, he justified Latin poesy because it was the "Source of Elegance in every Language" (440), it enabled students to use a greater variety of expression, it was a polite study well suited to the educated man, and it stimulated acquaintance with the best authors. To prove his devotion to the art and his ability, he included an example of his own work at the end of the lectures.

The point that Lawson tried to make was that oratory and poetry were branches of the same gift, eloquence, and therefore were separable only by the ends they served, not the means they used. Vincent Bevilacqua described this position as a "belletristic view that the various modes of discourse . . . are not independent species, but essentially related forms of discourse commonly rooted in style." [82] He made it known in his first two lectures that he would not treat rhetoric or oratory alone. His subject was eloquence, the "Cloathing of Reason" (6). This viewpoint encompassed history, drama, novels, or any other literary forms, as seen in his lectures on the history of eloquence and most vividly illustrated in his assessment of Aristotle's *Rhetoric*. Lawson warned the reader that this work was limited to public speaking. "Hence, the Poet, the Historian, the Philosopher, are not to search here for Rules useful in their particular Studies and Kinds of Writing; which although contained in the general Extent of Eloquence, belong not to the Scheme of our Author" (51). Finally, because eloquence was more refined and required higher standards than conversational speech, it required close semblance to the best models: "Writers should endeavour to preserve, to bring back the Form of Writing, to that which was used by the best Authors of the best Period; the Nature of Mankind being such, as rather than not to change, to change for the Worse" (103).[83]

Delivery was discussed in Lecture Twenty-two as it related to the preacher. Following Cicero and Quintilian, Lawson saw the subject as pronunciation or voice and as action; he repeated many of the instructions found in classical works. Since most of the training in delivery was left to weekly exercises, the *Lectures* were not the place to establish specific directions. Instead, Lawson set forth criteria for judging effective delivery and faults to be avoided. While it is true that he again adhered to ancient principles, two significant ideas appeared in this lecture. Lawson undertook one of the earliest criticisms of mechanical methods of teaching delivery. This we commented on earlier. The other important idea was his advocacy of what he termed "animated Conversation" (418). He began with an illustration of two people first conversing and then debating, and projected one of them before successively larger audiences until he was found delivering a sermon. Lawson observed that while volume had to be increased and greater variety would be used, the same tone, pronunciation, and emphasis would characterize the speaker's voice. The similarity of this example to the one James Winans used in his *Public Speaking* has already been noted by several writers.[84] Lawson's belief that conversational delivery was superior to the pompous and feigned expressions by some preachers led him to advise the students to eschew reading or memorizing sermons.

> As that extemporary Discourse, which approacheth most to a studied one in Regularity of Composition and Purity of Stile, is the best; in like Manner, among studied Discourses that undoubtedly excelleth, which is composed with the easy Air, and pronounced with the unaffected Warmth and Fluency of the Extemporary.[85] (418–19)

In sum, Lawson rightly recommended naturalness whether in voice or action, coupled with a sense of gravity appropriate to the pulpit.

Perhaps Lawson's greatest departure from classical doctrine was the absence of a detailed analysis of the three major kinds of oratory. It was not a matter of Lawson being unaware of what the ancients had said concerning forensic, deliberative, and epideictic speaking, for the material was part of the abstract he presented of Aristotle's *Rhetoric* (45). The omission was a matter of expedience and appropriateness. Lawson conceded that he knew little about courtroom and senate speaking, which he had viewed only from a distance (353). His mature life had been spent in the classroom and pulpit where he was at home and knowledgeable. Besides, only a few of the students attending the lectures were preparing for the bar or politics. Most of them were destined for the ministry. Nevertheless, the present-day reader wishes Lawson had elaborated upon the few criticisms he made of the speaking in parliament and the courts. For example, he observed that, as in ancient Athens and Rome, liberty balanced with power flourished under the English constitution. Consequently, deliberative speaking had been perfected: "modern Times can shew few Pieces of Eloquence equal to many, that are to be met with in the Debates of the British Senate" (93). In contrast, Lawson was displeased with courtroom pleading, which he said was marked by detailed references to a multitude of laws and by a lack of ornament. Concentrating, then, on pulpit speaking, he spent four lectures adapting much of what he said previously about invention, arrangement, and style to that platform and not differing greatly from what other modern authors had said about these subjects as they related to preaching.[86]

In summary, eight characteristics of the *Lectures* stand out. (1) Lawson clearly associated himself with the philosophy and literary forms of the Augustan humanists. (2) He relied doggedly upon the time-tested standards of the classicists, but did not present as full a restatement of them as did John Ward. Rather than summarizing classical doctrines at length, Lawson encouraged his students to read the works in the original languages. (3) Lawson abhorred mechanical rules for any aspect of the art. His own "rules" more closely approximate general criteria to be followed or faults to be avoided. He also realized that diligent practice without constraining limitations was more valuable than memorizing long lists of specific directions. (4) To Lawson, oratory was only one branch of the larger study of eloquence. Poetry was a sister art and could supply the speaker with examples of stronger oranamentation. (5) The *Lectures* were firmly established upon faculty psychology, but only as it was consistent with ancient usage. (6) Lawson was emphatic throughout that imitation of the best works by the best authors was the road to excellence. (7) Invention, arrangement, style, and delivery were not wholly separable skills. They were all needed by one who would persuade. (8) Finally, the *Lectures* were formulated for divinity students and only meagerly referred to the classical kinds of oratory.

Appearing only a few months before Ward's more complete neoclassical rhetoric, Lawson's volume immediately met a formidable competitor. Later, both works were superseded by the new directions set by Campbell, Blair, and Whately. Also, attention to Lawson and Ward was diverted by the rapid increase of interest in elocution, as exemplified by the books of Sheridan, Burgh, Bayly, Steele, Enfield, Walker, and Austin. Thus, the effect of Lawson's *Lectures* upon rhetorical theory was limited. One would expect Lawson's successors to the Smith lectureship to have been the most strongly influenced by his thinking, but there is little evidence that significant agreement existed. Francis Staughton Sullivan was appointed to the position in 1759 soon after Lawson's death, but he published no works in rhetoric or oratory. If he delivered lectures on the subject, they are not now extant. A jurist, Sullivan was the first nonclergyman to occupy the Smith chair and ought to have been able to communicate different impressions and judgments about the art. The custom of appointing clerics to the lectureship was resumed in 1761 when Thomas Leland was elected. He had published *The Philippic Orations of Demosthenes* in translation and with notes in 1754 and prepared his lectures on eloquence for printing in 1764. Few similarities of outlook can be found between Lawson and Leland. In publishing his lectures, Leland stated that they were not originally intended for the reader but simply to fulfill an office. He then may have been referring to Lawson, Ward, or Sheridan when he wrote:

> If they are now submitted to the censure of the world, it is not from any ambition of appearing in a Contest with a writer of distinguished Eminence; but principally from a deference to

> their Opinions, who thought that the liberties taken with such a Character, and the examination of his Opinions should be strictly *public:* and that to confine them to a small Circle, might appear equally disingenuous, with secret and clandestine Censure, in Common Life.[87]

Despite their acquaintance, Lawson's name never appeared in Leland's *Dissertation,* even though the *Lectures* were only a few years old when Leland was writing. Like Lawson, Leland had a thorough acquaintance with the ancients; he frequently cited Plato, Aristotle, Cicero, Quintilian, and Longinus. But Leland was much more restrictive in viewpoint; he regarded rhetoric "as principally a matter of style" [88] and did not develop invention. To him, "perfect Eloquence is, and must be, the expression of TRUTH," and a man must persuade "by the real excellencies, the engaging and conciliating qualities of speech." [89] Leland's was a much less practical treatise than Lawson's, for Leland was actually responding critically and theoretically to the treatment of style and composition of the New Testament by William Warburton, Bishop of Gloucester, in *The Doctrine of Grace* (1762).[90] None of Lawson's other successors to the Smith chair wrote on rhetoric.[91]

The *Lectures* were readily available in Britain in the last half of the eighteenth century, for they were reprinted three times, twice in Dublin and once in London. They appeared while Campbell was writing his *Philosophy of Rhetoric* and while Blair was lecturing in Edinburgh. They were easily accessible to Whately as he made revisions of his *Elements of Rhetoric* while Archbishop of Dublin. Yet none of these authors referred to Lawson specifically. Campbell might have been thinking of him when commenting on the contributions the ancients made to rhetorical theory:

> I must acknowledge that, as far as I have been able to discover, there has been little or no improvement in this respect made by the moderns. The observations and rules transmitted to us from these distinguished names of the learned world, Aristotle, Cicero, and Quintilian, have been for the most part only translated by later critics, or put into a modish dress and new arrangement.[92]

Only Joseph Priestly acknowledged he was familiar with Lawson.[93] The familiarity may have strengthened Priestley's faith in sincerity, extempore qualities, and naturalness in delivery.[94] Though scholars might have read Lawson's work, the mainstream had changed. The period for reviving classical works and restoring ancient concepts to rhetoric had passed. Men such as Campbell, Blair, and Whately could then build upon the foundation Ward and Lawson had helped to lay.

Neoclassicism came later to America and reached its apex with the establishment of the Boylston chair at Harvard. The *Lectures* were imported to this country not long after publication and were accessible at Harvard by 1767 and at Brown by 1782.[95] In 1791, Yale's library listed them as one of eight titles classified under Rhetoric and Belles Lettres, along with works of Quintilian, Demetrius, Ramus, Vossius, Farnaby, Ward, and Blair.[96] Ota Thomas Reynolds may have been correct when she wrote that the *Lectures* were "readily available for student use" in colonial times.[97] When John Quincy Adams began preparing his lectures for the classically oriented Boylston professorship, his reading included not only the ancient works but modern French and English rhetorics. While no record was found that Adams was acquainted with Ward's *System,* which presumably was the major source used to derive the rules for the chair, J. Jeffery Auer and Jerald L. Banninga discovered from Adams's diary that he was familiar with Lawson's *Lectures*. The diary revealed that Adams "accepted the writings" of Lawson, but not as fully as Blair's and that Blair was judged to have "borrowed too freely" from Lawson.[98] In Adams's opinion, Lawson's *Lectures* "'are in a degree methodical, but the arrangement is not well made,' and that 'Mr. Lawson's verse is somewhere near the level of mediocrity.'"[99] Adams's successor, Joseph McKean, was also acquainted with Lawson's work, but the only specific citation made by McKean is Lawson's definition of oratory.[100] As in Britain, Lawson's influence on American rhetorical theory was limited. The works of Campbell, Blair, and Whateley were used more widely in the classroom and by scholars of rhetoric in the nineteenth century. In this century, interest in Lawson's *Lectures* stems from their position in history, between the fractionized Ramean and stylistic rhetorics and the works of the psychological-epistemological movement.

When the view of rhetoric contained in the *Lectures on Oratory* is compared with the views of mid-eighteenth-century rhetoricians, Lawson does not seem to be signally innovative. In a period marked by the creativity of Kames, Hume, Shaftesbury, Priestley, and Campbell, not everybody could be in their company. Lawson's strength was in making rhetoric clear to his listeners and readers. This he accomplished in part by locating sources of imprecise thought. The concept of taste, he asserted, was vague and could be dispensed with. Amidst much talk of his contemporaries about the sentiments, affections, and passions, he pointed out that the special character of these remained dim and could not be separated from understanding and will. In his chapters on the passions, he tried to characterize concisely the faculties of man, and his attempt deserves the attention of the modern student. Artificial schemes of teaching delivery were cast aside since they seemed apart from a speaker's personal nature and his ideas. The style of animated conversation, reflecting knowledge, sincerity, and conviction, was the model of delivery. Knowing that classical subjects, including classical rhetoric, were under fire, Lawson pinpointed what he thought was intelligible and valuable in the older tradition and requisite to the moralistic culture in which he lived. In a word, he endeavored to make rhetorical sense to practical speakers. Perhaps for this reason, his book was in the small collection of rhetorics in Yale's library in 1791, and Campbell's *Philosophy of Rhetoric* was not.

4

While Lawson's *Lectures Concerning Oratory* exerted only limited influence on the teaching and study of rhetoric in his day, the demand for the volume was great enough to warrant four printings. George Faulkner published three of them: the first on November 7, 1758, the second on August 4, 1759, and the third in August 1760. He labeled the latter two "editions," but the advertisements in his newspaper referred only to the continued appearance of "The Second Edition." [101] A fourth printing was produced in London in the summer of 1759 by William Bowyer for sale by Lockyer Davis and Charles Reymers. Faulkner and Bowyer were two of the most important publishers in Britain at the time and, in all probability, were well acquainted. S. Austin Allibone described Bowyer's reputation this way: "It may well be supposed that the amiable character and remarkable erudition of Mr. Bowyer gathered around him a host of devoted friends. We venture the assertion that no man in any age ever had a larger circle of distinguished literary acquaintances." [102] Bowyer was known as "the learned printer" since he was also an author, editor, translator, and pamphleteer.[103] He was the printer for the House of Commons, the House of Lords, the Royal Society, and the Society of Antiquaries. Faulkner may have influenced Bowyer to publish the *Lectures* in order to help Lawson's reputation in England.

Here in facsimile is the only version of the *Lectures* which Lawson prepared. All others appeared posthumously and contain numerous alterations which, while minor, were not of his plan. None of the printings altered the substance of the lectures, but both publishers, especially Bowyer, frequently used their editorial privileges on such grammatical matters as punctuation, capitalization, and spelling. Faulkner corrected all but two of the errata noted in the original edition. The instruction to place a comma after "Applause" on page 329 was not observed; the page was probably a misprint for 349. The change of punctuation requested for page 449 was not followed; Faulkner used a comma instead of a colon. Bowyer complied with the latter but not former direction and ignored the changes requested for pages 51 and 248. While these emendations were made, new typographical errors, such as in pagination and spelling, occurred in all subsequent versions. Faulkner used the same type-set throughout the book in all three printings, but Bowyer used a more compressed type for two of Lawson's poems, "The Judgment of Plato" and "Irene," and thereby slightly reduced the total number of pages. Comparison of the various printings also revealed that Bowyer consistently modernized Lawson's spelling of such words as *style, persuasion, epigrammatic,* and *you.* Faulkner allowed *stile, perswasion, epigrammatick,* and *ye* to stand. Because the text remained with only minor changes through its publication history, all issues after the first should be regarded as reprints, not editions.

A final textual matter deserves attention. On page 297 Lawson offers a "Translation of a Friend" of a passage from the *Iliad.* Who was the translator? The argument has been advanced that Lawson was in fact quoting his own translation but implying it was Bishop Edward Maurice's. The anonymous eighteenth-century critic who held this conviction called the translation in the *Lectures* "incorrect and insipid"; "indeed scarcely can anything be so wretchedly bad." For comparison, the critics cited the following passage from Maurice's translation he had found in Trinity College's library:

> Thus under arms upon the brink of fight,
> Elate in thought, with many a fire around
> Them blazing all the night, strict watch kept they.
> As when around the silver queen of night
> Through the calm cloudless sky the stars appear
> With lustre undiminish'd; every hill
> And cliff and forest standing out to view.
> When not one light is lost, so wide and vast
> The heav'ns are open laid: the shepherd's soul
> Sweet transport strikes: so not in number less
> Nor less in brightness shone the Trojan fires.[104]

The critic praised this version and believed it was superior even to Cowper's. Whether or not Lawson meant to imply that he was quoting Maurice's translation is questionable. Since it was widely known that the Bishop had willed his manuscript of the *Iliad* to Lawson, the connection was understandable. It is conceivable, however, that Lawson may have used a translation from another close friend, possibly William Dunkin. Whether the passage in the *Lectures* was Englished by Lawson is not yet known.

The editors wish to express their appreciation for the generous assistance received from various sources. Bradley University granted a release from summer teaching responsibilities and provided funds for the purchase of two copies of the *Lectures* through the Committee on Faculty Research and Creative Production. A grant from the National Endowment for the Humanities in 1968 made it possible to study unexamined material relating to Lawson in various British libraries. Mrs. Kaye John and Mrs. Vincent Bevilacqua were valuable research assistants.

NOTES

[1] *The Critical Review,* 6 (November 1758), 387.

[2] Ibid., p. 402.

[3] *The Monthly Review,* 20 (January 1759), 63–64.

[4] *An Epistle to the Right Honourable Philip Earl of Chesterfield; to which are added, Lawson's Obsequies: An Eclogue* (Dublin, 1759), p. 32. This work was reprinted in London the same year and again in Dublin in 1760. It also appeared in the second volume of Dunkin's *Select Poetical Works* (Dublin, 1769–70, and 1774).

[5] Ibid., p. 21.

[6] Ibid., p. 57.

[7] *The Monthly Review,* 22 (February 1760), 175.

[8] See the review of John Ward's *System of Oratory* in *The Critical Review,* 7 (April 1759), 367. For evidence of Goldsmith's authorship, see Arthur Friedman, "Goldsmith's Contributions to the *Critical Review,*" *Modern Philolophy,* 44 (August 1946), 38–39.

[9] *The Critical Review,* 9 (March 1760), 235. See also Friedman, p. 32.

[10] *Irene: Carmen Historicum* (Dublin, 1760), p. iii.

[11] See, for example, *A Sermon Preached in St. Andrew's, Dublin, Before the Honourable House of Commons on Wednesday the 18th of December, 1745, Being the Day Appointed for a General Fast* (Dublin, 1745); and two "editions" of *A Sermon Preached in St. Andrew's Dublin, Before the Honourable House of Commons; On Tuesday, the 23rd of October, 1753* (Dublin, 1753).

[12] *Occasional Sermons . . . Written by a late eminent Divine of the Church of England* (London, 1764), pp. iii–iv.

[13] *The Monthly Review,* 32 (April 1765), 270. A century later, there was some confusion over the authorship. The rector of Swanscombe in Kent was also named John Lawson and was inaccurately cited as the sermonizer. See the correspondence in *Notes and Queries,* 3rd series, 6, October 8, 1864, 310–11; October 22, 1864, 340; November 12, 1864, 401; and November 26, 1864, 439.

[14] George D. Burtchaell and Thomas U. Sadleir, eds., *Alumni Dublinenses* (London, 1924), p. 486. Gordon Goodwin, in the *Dictionary of National Biography* (Cambridge, 1949–50), XI, 736; Alfred Webb in *A Compendium of Irish Biography* (Dublin, 1878), p. 286; and various other sources record his birth as 1712 in Omagh, county Tyrone.

[15] James B. Leslie, *Supplement to "Armagh Clergy & Parishes"* (Dundalk, 1948), p. 35. Leslie presented confusing information in an earlier book. He reported that Alexander was the son of Thomas, had entered Trinity College in 1708, was married to Rebecca, was the curate of Monaghan 1717–20 and Donacavey 1721–54, and died in 1758. This Alexander was likely John's cousin. See *Clogher Clergy and Parishes* (Enniskillen, 1929), p. 155.

[16] Constantia Maxwell, *A History of Trinity College, Dublin, 1591–1892* (Dublin, 1946), p. 92. Gilbert also bequeathed 500 pounds

to provide for busts of eminent men of learning which are now housed in the Long Room of the old Trinity Library. One of these is Lawson's bust completed in 1759 by Patrick Cunningham. See W. G. Strickland, *A Descriptive Catalogue of the Pictures, Busts, and Statues in Trinity College, Dublin . . .* (Dublin, 1916), p. 60.

[17] "Biographical Notices of Eminent Irish Writers, from the Year 1745; John Lawson, D.D.," *Anthologia Hibernica,* 2 (December 1793), 410.

[18] Dunkin, *Lawson's Obsequies,* p. 37.

[19] Maxwell, p. 106.

[20] M. L. Clarke, *Classical Education in Britain 1500–1900* (Cambridge, 1959), p. 160.

[21] Ibid., p. 161.

[22] Maxwell, p. 149.

[23] John W. Stubbs, *The History of the University of Dublin* (Dublin, 1889), pp. 44–45.

[24] Graham Balfour, *The Educational Systems of Great Britain and Ireland* (Oxford, 1903), p. 261.

[25] He was awarded the B.A. in the spring of 1731, the M.A. in the summer of 1734, and D.D. in the spring of 1745.

[26] Clarence Edney, "English Sources of Rhetorical Theory in Nineteenth-Century America," in *A History of Speech Education in America,* ed. Karl R. Wallace (New York, 1954), p. 102n.

[27] *A Catalogue of Books Being the Library of the late Revd. John Lawson . . .* (n.p., 1760).

[28] *Lawson's Obsequies,* p. 39.

[29] *Anthologia Hibernica,* p. 410.

[30] Statutes had established the Professor of Divinity as an officer of the university, thereby providing him with special chambers and relieving him of ordinary duties of instructors.

[31] *Occasional Sermons,* p. iv.

[32] *Lawson's Obsequies,* pp. 40–41.

[33] *Dictionary of National Biography,* XVIII, 442.

[34] *Chartae et Statuta Collegii Sacrosanctae et Individuae Trinitatis, Reginae Elizabethae, juxta Dublin* (Dublin, 1768), pp. 108–12.

[35] Leland's work was entitled, *A Dissertation on The Principles of Human Eloquence* (Dublin, 1765).

[36] See *Lectures,* pp. 8, 352–53.

[37] Hely Hutchinson, "History of Trinity College, Dublin" (unpubl. typescript in Trinity Library), II, p. 298.

[38] Quoted in Maxwell, p. 142.

[39] Robert M. Post, "Forensic Activities at Trinity College, Dublin, in the Eighteenth Century," *Central States Speech Journal,* 19 (Spring, 1968), 23–24.

[40] "The Elocutionary Movement in England, 1750–1800," Diss. Cornell 1947, p. 395.

[41] *Occasional Sermons,* pp. v–vi.

[42] S. E. Frost, Jr., *Historical and Philosophical Foundations of Western Education* (Columbus, Ohio, 1966), p. 299.

[43] *Anthologia Hibernica,* p. 410.

[44] *Occasional Sermons,* p. v.

[45] *A Sermon Intended to have been Preached at the Publick Opening of the Chappel of the Lying-in-Hospital* (Dublin, 1759), p. 15.

[46] Ibid., pp. 28–29.

[47] *The Public Gazetteer,* No. 47 (February 27–March 3, 1759), p. 366. See also W. G. Carroll, *Succession of Clergy in the Parishes of S. Bride, S. Michael le Pole, and S. Stephen* (Dublin, 1884), pp. 44–45.

[48] Richard R. Madden, *The History of Irish Periodical Literature* (London, 1867), II, 48.

[49] *Lawson's Obsequies,* p. 30.

[50] See Earl of Belmore, *The History of the Two Ulster Manors of Finagh and Coole* (London, 1881).

[51] *The Monthly Review,* 50 (May 1774), 355.

[52] Quoted in *Dictionary of National Biography,* VI, 203.

[53] "Authentic Memoirs of the late George Faulkner, Esq.," *The Hibernian Magazine* (September 1775), p. 505.

[54] *Select Poetical Works,* I, 262–63.

[55] Henry Cotton, *Fasti Ecclesiae Hibernicae* (Dublin, 1848), II, 286n.; James B. Leslie, *Ossory Clergy and Parishes* (Enniskillen, 1933), p. 29.

[56] Detailed comments on this matter appear in section four of this essay.

[57] *The Dublin Journal,* No. 3306, January 9–13, 1759, p. 1.

[58] See the two elegies written about Lawson in *The Dublin Journal,* No. 3307, January 13–16, 1759, p. 1; and No. 3313, February 3–6, 1759), p. 1.

[59] *The Public Gazetteer,* No. 33, January 9–13, 1759, p. 258.

[60] Paul Fussell, *The Rhetorical World of Augustan Humanism* (Oxford, 1965), p. 21.

[61] "John Ward and His Rhetoric," *Speech Monographs,* 17 (March 1951), 16.

[62] Fussell, p. 4.

[63] Ibid., p. 6.

[64] Ibid., p. 9.

[65] "The Meaning of 'Augustan'," *Journal of the History of Ideas,* 19 (October 1958), 516.

[66] *The Works of Edmund Burke* (London, 1883), II, 211–12.

[67] Johnson, p. 518.

[68] Ibid., p. 512.

[69] Francis Gallaway, *Reason, Rule, and Revolt in English Classicism* (New York, 1940), p. 18.

[70] Howard D. Weinbrot, "Translation and Parody: Towards the Genealogy of the Augustan Imitation," *English Literary History,* 33 (December 1966), 434.

[71] Lawson's treatment of imitation is similar to Quintilian's and Cicero's, especially the former. See Donald Lemen Clark, "Imitation: Theory and Practice in Roman Rhetoric," *Quarterly Journal of Speech*, 37 (February 1951), 11–22.

[72] See Ward's lectures 53 and 54.

[73] Karl R. Wallace, *Francis Bacon on Communication and Rhetoric* (Chapel Hill, N.C., 1943), p. 56.

[74] Wilbur Samuel Howell, *Logic and Rhetoric in England, 1500–1700* (New York, 1961), pp. 353–57; and his translation of *Fenelon's Dialogues on Eloquence* (Princeton, 1951), pp. 41–42.

[75] Lawson was acquainted with these authors. Some of their works in his library were Shaftesbury's *Characteristicks of Men, Manners, Opinions, Times* (London, 1733); and Hutcheson's *An Essay on the Nature and Conduct of the Passions and Affections* (London, 1728), *An Inquiry into the Original of Our Ideas of Beauty and Virtue* (London, 1713), and *A System of Moral Philosophy* (Glasgow, 1755).

[76] "Two Newtonian Arguments Concerning 'Taste'," *Philological Quarterly*, 47 (October 1968), 585–90.

[77] See Herman Cohen, "Hugh Blair's Theory of Taste," *Quarterly Journal of Speech*, 44 (October 1958), 265–74; and John Waite Bowers, "A Comparative Criticism of Hugh Blair's Essay on Taste," *Quarterly Journal of Speech*, 47 (December 1961), 384–89.

[78] Ray Keesey, "The Rhetorical Theory of John Lawson," Diss. Ohio State 1950; "John Lawson's Lectures Concerning Oratory," *Speech Monographs*, 20 (March 1953), 49–57.

[79] Keesey, dissertation, pp. 35–36. Works by Locke in Lawson's library were a collection of essays (1734), *Some Thoughts Concerning Education* (1693), *Of Civil Government* (1728), and a commentary on St. Paul's epistles (1738).

[80] *Speech Monographs*, p. 50.

[81] In warning of stylistic extravagancies, Lawson was echoing the admonition of Anthony Blackwall in his *Introduction to the Classics* (London, 1728), p. 187. A copy of this work was in Lawson's library.

[82] "Philosophical Influences in the Development of English Rhetorical Theory: 1748 to 1783," *Proceedings of the Leeds Philosophical and Literary Society, Literary and Historical Section*, 12, Part 6 (April 1968), 198.

[83] Unlike the most notable authors of his day, Lawson believed the "Best Authors of the best Period" were not the Romans, but the Greeks. See pp. 39–43, 68, 107, 174–75, 188, and 228. Thus, Lawson's commendation of Latin poesy as an instructional aid appears to be a concession to a common practice of his time.

[84] Keesey, *Speech Monographs*, p. 54; and Harold F. Harding, "English Rhetorical Theory, 1750–1800," Diss. Cornell 1937, p. 40.

[85] Earlier in the *Lectures*, Lawson observed that extemporary discourse would result in defective style. See pp. 171–72.

[86] Keesey, dissertation, pp. 162–63.

[87] Leland, p. iii.

[88] Harding, p. 81.

[89] Leland, pp. 21, 85.

[90] The second edition of Leland's *Dissertation,* 1765, more than doubled in size by including a critical letter from Richard Hurd and Leland's response.

[91] The history of this chair shows how the importance of oratory diminished at Trinity so that today it is vestigial. The professorship was divided in 1762, forming a new lectureship in modern history and Leland occupying the original foundation in oratory. His successors to 1852, John Kearney, Richard Graves, Philip Cecil Crampton, and Richard MacDonnell, were all clergymen. The office was again given a dual role from 1855 to 1867 when it existed as a professorship of Oratory and English Literature. John Kells Ingram held the post during this period; he wrote many works in English and classical literature, mathematics, economics, positivism, and poetry, and later became the first editor of *Hermathena.* In 1867, the chair was renamed Professor of Oratory and History and was held by Edward Dowden, a literary critic and poet. "Since 1914 the Professorship of Oratory and the Professorship of Modern History have, although formally maintained as distinct offices, been held by the same person." Two historians of Ireland have occupied the position from that time. Edmund Curtis served from 1914 to 1939. Theodore William Moody is his successor. See *Trinity College Record Volume* (Dublin, 1951), p. 73.

[92] *The Philosophy of Rhetoric,* ed. by Lloyd F. Bitzer (Carbondale, Ill., 1963), p. li.

[93] *A Course of Lectures on Oratory and Criticism,* ed. by Vincent M. Bevilacqua and Richard Murphy (Carbondale, Ill., 1965), 287–88.

[94] Ibid., pp. xlix–lii.

[95] Keesey, dissertation, pp. 206–7.

[96] *Catalogue of Books in the Library of Yale-College* (New Haven, 1791), pp. 10–11.

[97] "The Teaching of Rhetoric in the United States During the Classical Period of Education," in *A History of Criticism of American Public Address, ed.* by W. N. Brigance (New York, 1943), I, 202. Whether or not Lawson's volume was used as a textbook, as claimed by Anthony Faulkner Blanks, could not be determined by research for this study. "An Introductory Study in the History of the Teaching of Public Speaking in the United States," Diss. Leland Stanford Junior Univ. 1927, p. 14.

[98] "The Genesis of John Quincy Adams' Lectures on Rhetoric and Oratory," *Quarterly Journal of Speech,* 49 (April 1963), 124.

[99] Ibid.

[100] Paul E. Ried, "Joseph McKean: The Second Boylston Professor of Rhetoric and Oratory," *Quarterly Journal of Speech,* 46 (December 1960), 422.

[101] See *The Dublin Journal* from August through September 1760.
[102] *A Critical Dictionary of English Literature*, (Philadelphia, 1891), I, 230.
[103] *Dictionary of National Biography*, II, 991.
[104] *Anthologia Hibernica*, 1 (January 1703), 18.

LECTURES

CONCERNING

ORATORY.

Delivered in

TRINITY COLLEGE, DUBLIN,

By JOHN LAWSON, D. D.

LECTURER in ORATORY and HISTORY, on the Foundation of ERASMUS SMITH, Esquire.

Videmus quid deceat, non assequimur.

CICERO de Oratore.

DUBLIN:

Printed by GEORGE FAULKNER in Essex-street.

M DCC LVIII.

CONTENTS.

EPISTLE DEDICATORY.

LECTURE THE FIRST.

LECTURE THE SECOND.

Containing an Account of the Rise and Progress of Eloquence among the Antients.—Plan of the following Lectures.—Oratory why first cultivated. Why in free States? Why not in the East? Why most in Greece? Principally why in Athens? PERICLES. *Of the Sophists. Of the two great Historians. Character of* Isocrates. *Of* Demosthenes. *Two Remarks upon the History of Eloquence among the Romans. Why Poesy cultivated before Prose. Why it survived Prose. Two Causes of the Decay of Eloquence among the Greeks. Similitude in it's decaying among the* Romans. *Comparison of the* Greek *and* Roman *Eloquence.*

Preference given to the former.—For four Reasons.

LECTURE THE THIRD.

Containing an Abstract of the two most famous Treatises concerning this Art, remaining from Antiquity.

Of Aristotle's *Rhetorick. Two Remarks useful to the right understanding of this Treatise. First, it was written to remove two general Mistakes. Secondly, Caution not to expect more in this Work than the Author intended. Advantages arising from the Study of it. Two mentioned. Design and Method of the Treatise* de Oratore. *Comparison of these two.*

LECTURE

LECTURE THE FOURTH.

LECTURE THE FIFTH.

LECTURE THE SIXTH.

LECTURE THE SEVENTH.

LECTURE THE EIGHTH.

LECTURE THE NINTH.

LECTURE THE TENTH.

LECTURE

LECTURE THE TWENTIETH.

LECTURE THE TWENTY-FIRST.

LECTURE

LECTURE THE TWENTY-THIRD.

TO THE

Moſt Reverend, the Right Hon. *&c.* the Governors of the Schools of ERASMUS SMITH, Eſq;

MY LORDS,

THE Wiſdom of our Anceſtors thought fit to eſtabliſh Profeſſors, and injoin publick Lectures to be delivered in all Seats of Learning, as Means highly conducive to the right Inſtruction of Youth: Which End they were deemed to anſwer, obtained Place in all Countries, and have been held in general Eſteem almoſt down to the preſent Times. But in late Days, at leaſt among us, a Diſlike of this Inſtitution hath been inſenſibly growing up, and ſeemeth now pretty widely to prevail: It being in the Nature of Mankind to become tired of old Cuſtoms, and ſeek after new Inven-

A tions

tions, miſtaking too often meer Change for Improvement.

It is likely indeed, that this Inſtitution doth not now anſwer the good Purpoſes it might, and actually did. Miſmanagement may have crept in: For render a Thing unfaſhionable, it muſt decline. But we ought not to charge on the Deſign Abuſes thereof, nor confound the Effect with its Cauſe. Thus, general Diſregard occaſions Failure in Execution; but that Failure ſhould not be alledged as an Argument to juſtify this Diſregard; although when eſtabliſhed, it keepeth up and encreaſeth it. Negligence is at firſt the Effect of Contempt, afterwards a Cauſe.

I would not however be underſtood to aſſert, that this Plan of Inſtruction is perfect, that all Objections offered againſt it are groundleſs. On the contrary, it is urged with much Shew of Reaſon and ſome Truth; "That the conti-
" nued Diſcourſe of a Profeſſor, however judi-
" ciouſly compoſed, cannot convey ſufficient
" Knowledge of any Art or Science; to the
" Attainment of which, Care, Attention, and
" the Slowneſs of gradual Progreſs are neceſſa-
" ry. That this eſſential Defect hath farther
" an

" an evil Tendency, accuſtoming young Per-
" ſons to content themſelves with ſuch ſuper-
" ficial Knowledge as they can glean up from
" hearing looſe general Eſſays, and to conſider
" this as a competent Fund of Learning; from
" whence uſually ſpring Conceit and Pedantry."

If we were to trace up the Diſlike of this Article of Academic Education to its Source, I fear, that we ſhould find it cloſely connected with, or rather a Branch of ſomewhat, more momentous, of a Prejudice againſt the Whole; a Plant, the Seeds of which have been of late induſtriouſly ſown in the Mind, have taken Root, and been artfully cheriſhed there; until at Length it hath grown to mighty Size and Strength, extending its Branches far and near; and hath well nigh covered the Land.

And yet, upon weighing the Matter, one is at a Loſs to aſſign for this Averſion any tolerable Appearance of Reaſon. Setting aſide Revelation, are there any Writings, which preſent Goodneſs in ſo amiable a Light, which recommend the nobleſt and moſt generous Virtues, Juſtice, Friendſhip, the Love of our Country and of Mankind, in ſo warm and ſtrong a Manner, as the Volumes tranſmitted to us from

Greek and *Roman* Antiquity? Any, that give an higher Idea of the Dignity of human Nature; or any, that contribute more to ſtrengthen and elevate the Mind, to raiſe and unfold all its Talents? Where are there offered to us more beautiful Models of true maſculine Eloquence, finer Sentiments, exhibited in all the Grace of pure and unaffected Ornament?

Do not they place us amid the buſieſt, the moſt ſplendid Scenes; lay before us the greateſt Characters; acquaint us with the moſt private Tranſactions, and bring us into the Converſation and Intimacy as it were, of the moſt extraordinary Perſons; who, joined to the Advantages of Letters, conſummate Experience of the World; ſome of whom moved in the moſt exalted Sphere, and gave Law to the whole Earth?

AND can it be imagined, that ſuch Ideas, ſuch Scenes, ſuch Patterns and Companions muſt not be highly beneficial to Youth?

ESPECIALLY, what can equal our Surprize when we enquire into the End propoſed from that Form of Education, to which this hath been condemned to give Place; "A Know-"ledge

"ledge of modern Languages and of the "World?"—For ſurely the beſt Foundation of the former is an Acquaintance with the Antients; Excellence of Stile even in one's native Tongue, is beſt learned from their admirable Models; ſince what is eſſential in Eloquence is common to all Languages. And the latter, to a Mind rude, unlettered, unprincipled, is uſually the greateſt of Misfortunes; it becometh Knowledge of Vice and Folly.

BUT it is not my Deſign at preſent to enter into ſo large a Field: The Branch of this Prejudice I ſet out with, which has led me inſenſibly into theſe Reflexions, in my Opinion deſerveth our careful Attention; eſpecially in this Place, bearing, as it doth, a particular Relation to your Lordſhips TRUST.

IT was allowed, that the Objection beforementioned hath ſome Force; but the Inference does not ſeem juſt. We ought not to condemn from a View of one Side. The Queſtion is, are there not Advantages which greatly leſſen, which do more than counterballance the Evils objected? And may not Methods be found of procuring ſtill farther Advantages?

"THE

" THE continued Diſcourſe of a Profeſſor " cannot convey ſufficient Knowledge of a Sci- " ence."—True: Yet that hinders not, but that it may do a great deal, and profit much.

THE more diligent Hearers, who join with their Attendance upon ſuch regular Courſe, a Peruſal of the beſt Authors on each Article, may receive from it great Benefit; becauſe a Man of Genius and good Capacity may comprehend in thoſe, however ſhort Compoſitions, the principal Points; may open more general Views; and by abridging, ſupplying, explaining, ſet Things in a new and fuller Light. On the other Hand, the Careleſs who do not read, may yet derive from thence ſome Knowledge, likely to prove uſeful afterwards, at leaſt ornamental; certainly preferable to total Ignorance.

AGAIN, Diſcourſes coming from the Mouth of an eſteemed Perſon naturally make an Impreſſion upon the Minds of the Audience, turn their Thoughts to the Matters treated of, are made the Subjects of Converſation, probably of Debate; which cannot fail of engaging them in Diſquiſitions and Enquiries concerning the Things talked of: And among many Perſons, it muſt happen, that ſome will perſiſt in theſe

Searches,

Searches, and be led inſenſibly from a ſimple Deſire of knowing ſome one Point into an Acquaintance with, it may be a maſterly Comprehenſion of the whole Science For the Seeds of Curioſity are ſtrong in every young Mind, however frequently kept dormant by the Love of Pleaſure or Force of Faſhion; but if ſtirred up by an apt Occaſion, they become quickly full of Life and Motion, ſhoot out, and ſoon produce fair and valuable Fruit; eſpecially, when warmed by the animating Ray of Emulation, the Principle, which above all in human Nature, contributes to the Growth and Flouriſhing of every uſeful Art.

ANOTHER Conſideration of no ſmall Moment is, That among very numerous Performances of this Kind, ſome there will be of a better Stamp and Frame than the reſt, which ſhall draw publick Notice and Applauſe, which ſpreading beyond the narrow Sphere of academic Inſtruction, ſhall bring Honour to the Society abroad, it may be to the Country, and enrich with new Treaſures the Commonwealth of Letters. Experience confirms this Hope; and it would be eaſy to cite many celebrated Productions, which owe their Birth to Occaſions of this Sort.

THUS

Thus it ſeems to me, that the Objection mentioned in the Beginning hath been fully anſwered: And perhaps we may add ſomewhat, and anſwer yet more fully; a Method perhaps may be found of improving the uſual Form, and of opening thereby new Benefits.

In this Manner of lecturing by perpetual Diſcourſe, there is a manifeſt Diſadvantage, that the Stream of Words paſſing away in a rapid Flow, makes a ſlight Impreſſion; they glide ſwiftly by with unbroken Current, and little remains in the Hearer's Mind.

Upon other Occaſions of Inſtruction there is a different Form employed: Wherein the young Perſons are directed to ſtudy with Exactneſs ſome approved Book; a certain Portion of which they are to give an Account of in the Way of Examination. Here, the regular alternative of Queſtion and Anſwer, the gradual Opening of the Underſtanding by the clearing up of Doubts, and rectifying of Miſtakes, the Traces engraved in the Memory by frequent Repetition, by Conjectures, Meditation, paſt Errors, Endeavours of Recollection, muſt beſtow a diſtinct and laſting Comprehenſion of what is learned. But this Manner is laborious, is leſs pleaſing than the other; neither doth it give Riſe to any laſting Work, which may diffuſe its Influence and Luſtre beyond the preſent Circle, illuminate the literary World, and poſſibly may extend the Ray down to Poſterity.

Now ſuppoſe theſe two Plans of Inſtruction combined, and properly united: In this Caſe, we might reaſonably hope for the Advantages of both, free from the Inconveniencies of either ſingle; which Scheme ſeems to bid fair for Perfection.

NEITHER is this a viſionary Project. It actually ſubſiſteth; and has been in a great Meaſure executed in the Plan of the preſent ORATORY-LECTURE, under your Lordſhips' Inſpection.

HERE the Profeſſor is enjoined, at certain Seaſons, to pronounce according to the firſt-mentioned Form, a perpetual Diſcourſe. At all other Times, the young Perſons are inſtructed in the latter Way: They are required to read aloud ſome Paſſage of an Hiſtorian or Orator, to the End that they may be exerciſed in the uſeful Art of juſt, diſtinct Pronunciation: To which, as they advance farther, is added

the

the Perusal of some among the celebrated Treatises concerning Oratory, remaining from Antiquity. Thus are they instructed betimes in the Principles of just Criticism, are taught to think, to cloath their Thoughts in apt Expression, and to utter these with Propriety and Gracefulness. Whilst at the same Time Composition is encouraged, the Curiosity of the Hearers is raised, their Emulation kindled: And it is hoped, that they may have proposed to them a fit Model of good Writing in the Performances of their Professor; some of which may possibly, in Length of Time, remain an Ornament to the Community that produced them, and, spreading abroad their Fame, may contribute to the Honour or Advancement of Letters.

FARTHER Improvements, I doubt not, may be thought of: Some were not long ago proposed by a Person of publick Spirit and enlarged Views. One there is, which if I might be allowed to hint at any such, I would mention, as following naturally from the Observations just now laid down.

" PROFESSORS should not only read at cer-
" tain Seasons, as they are now obliged to do,
" original Discourses; but they should be en-
" joined

" joined to publiſh a fixed Number of ſuch,
" within a limited Time."

THIS Neceſſity would take away the Plea, real or pretended, of Modeſty, and Delicacy about Reputation; would overcome that great Enemy even in the beſt Capacities to Excellence, the Love of Eaſe; and would compel the Writers to exert their whole Force, to weigh with Caution, and poliſh with Labour, Works, which they know muſt go abroad, muſt ſuſtain the Examination of ſevere and penetrating Eyes. The Want of which uſeful Compulſion hath, I believe, been felt among us; and is the Cauſe that the preſent (I fear unadviſed) Undertaking is here, even at this Day, a new, and, as I think, yet unattempted Eſſay.

I AM not ignorant, that a Propoſal of this Kind is likely to be treated with Contempt or Ridicule. " The World, it is ſaid, abounds " with bad or ordinary Books; why ſhould " we ſeek to augment the Number?" To which I think the Anſwer not difficult.

A GOOD Book, (and ſometimes a good one may be hoped for) is well worthy of being purchaſed at the Price of enduring many bad or or indifferent, an Evil which falls only upon willing Sufferers; eſpecially, as theſe cannot be laſting Incumbrances; for ſuch are publiſhed, juſt talked of, ſlightly looked into, condemned; and then turned into ſome Corner of a Library, there to moulder amidſt Worms and Duſt in undiſturbed Oblivion. Even bad Books, in the Caſe before us would have one good Effect; they would ſhew the Inability of the Writers for the Poſt they hold, and give timely Warning to diſplace them; a Diſcovery, which, it were to be wiſhed, could be rendered univerſal.

WE may add, that theſe Performances, however in themſelves inſignificant, would afford a probable Argument of Diligence in the Writer: For one who ſhews this Attention in the Diſcharge of no eaſy Article of his Duty, cannot well be ſuſpected of great Remiſſneſs in the others.

THEY bear a Similitude in this reſpect to the Prudence of that Inſtitution in Cities, which enjoins the Watchmen to go their Circuit and proclaim the Hour, not ſo much for the Sake of informing the Inhabitants in a Point little needful, as becauſe ſuch periodical Vociferation furniſheth a Proof, that theſe Guardians of

midnight

midnight Order do attend, and watch, whilst others sleep.

THIS, Diligence, hath its Praise; and the Discourses annexed may, it is hoped, entitle the Speaker to that humble Merit. He walketh his Rounds; and if he call out in no tuneable Voice, nor utter any useful Admonition, yet he thereby proves himself to be on his Station, and awake.

WITH this View, he hath been induced to come forth from the Shade, uncalled; and to venture out from calm safe Obscurity into the Publick, a wide and stormy Sea, covered with Wrecks of unsuccessful Writers; sensible, at the same Time, that he is exposed to greater Inconveniencies, than they who should publish under the proposed Regulation could encounter with. They would have Necessity to urge, a just Plea for Indulgence; he is a willing Adventurer: And more gallant Behaviour is expected from a Volunteer, than from one impressed into the Service.

THE Nature likewise of this Design, and the Subject, lay open to peculiar Hardships.

ITS Nature admits not a Criterion, whereby to judge; whence one can never hope to ſatisfy all. And in Difference of Opinion, few make befitting Allowances, or even afford to the oppoſite one an impartial Hearing.

AGAIN, continual Criticiſm diſguſteth. Seek by digreſſing to relieve; you offend againſt the Rules of your Art; thus are thought tireſome, or trifling.

IF you be plain, you repeat; if nice, you refine; you are vulgar, or viſionary.

THIS likewiſe is a Subject, which all underſtand, or think they do; hence all are Judges: And among ſo many, there muſt be Cenſurers.

THESE, however, are counterballanced by chearful Conſiderations on the other Side.

IT is pleaſing to have endeavoured well; to have given ſome Mark of Care, and permit me ſo to name it, of an honeſt, although it is too likely, unſucceſsful Ambition.

BESIDES, I am perſwaded that there is in the collective Body of the Publick a Fund of Candour, which never fails in the End to caſt

the

the Ballance. Passion, Prejudice, Temper, Fashion, may for a while carry with them the publick Suffrage, but they shall at last subside; and Truth and Reason be listened to, speaking in the Voice of the Majority always just; rather indeed mild and indulgent, inclined to favour those who appear desirous of deserving well from them.

WITH these Thoughts, relying on the Merit of a good Intention, I seek to encourage myself; hoping, in the mean Time, to obtain Pardon for the Liberty I take, of INSCRIBING to your Lordships the following Lectures, the FIRST-FRUITS of an Office, derived from your Appointment, and held under your Approbation.

LET them, so long as they may happen to be remembered, remain a TESTIMONY of the Author's RESPECT for your Lordships, and a MEMORIAL of his GRATITUDE.

E R R A T A.

Page 51, Line 10, dele *that.*
103, Note, read MAFFEI.
161, Line 12, for *atatch* read *attach.*
163, Line 20, read *Exercise.*
167, Line 18, for *push* read *pusheth.*
248, Line 22, dele *a.*
192, Line 1, dele *from.*
305, Line 26, read *himself.*
308, Line 24, place a *Comma* after *Pert.*
324, Line 14, *World, a Full-stop* instead of *a Comma.*
329, Line 12, *Applause*, place *a Comma* after.
361, Line 3, instead of *himi n*, read *him in.*
410, Line 2. *Oyle itself*, place *the Comma* after *Oyle*,
442, Line 8, for *Semitam*, read *Callem.*
449, Line 5, put *a Colon* after *fragore.*
454, Line 14, for *conditio*, read *sors aspera.*

LECTURES

CONCERNING

ORATORY.

LECTURE the Firſt.

INTRODUCTION.—*Praiſe of Eloquence.—Difficulty of it.—Prejudices removed.*

IT is not without much Diffidence and Sollicitude of Mind that I enter upon the preſent Undertaking, this of delivering to you Diſcourſes, concerning the Nature, Precepts, and Method of Oratory. I ſhall not as a Ground of ſuch Diffidence, however real, urge my own Inability; ſuch Pleas being commonly offered, and ſeldom regarded as ſincere. The Difficulty of the Work itſelf is a ſufficient Ground, comprehending ſo wide a Circuit, and abounding with Points ſo various, ſubtile, and delicate.

WHICH Difficulty becomes not a little encreaſed, by the Multitude of Writers upon this Subject. For, in ſuch Circumſtances, how ſhall one proceed? Have you nothing new to offer? Perpetual Repetition diſguſts. Beſide, if that be the Caſe, why do you write? Do you ſeek to inform Men of what they know already? On the other Hand, have you made any Diſcoveries? The Probability is, that the Love of Novelty hath led you into Miſtakes. At beſt, you will have eſtabliſhed Opinions and Prejudices, no weak Enemies, to encounter with: Wiſe Men will ſuſpect you, the vulgar at once condemn. To which I may add, that the frequency of Writing and Diſcourſe on this Kind of Subjects, indiſpoſeth Men to the whole Kind: The Ground hath been ſo traverſed and beaten, that they have no Hope of ſpringing new Game, and follow thoſe who would lead into it, with Reluctance.

SUCH is the forbidding Aſpect of my preſent Undertaking: But it may be conſidered in more pleaſing Lights, which take off from theſe Diſcouragements. One of theſe is, the Neceſſity laid upon me from the Situation in which I am placed, of making ſome Attempt; and Neceſſity renders even Mediocrity excuſable.

I SHOULD mention as a *Second*, the Candour and Indulgence of my Hearers, who would rather approve and profit by what is right, than ſearch for Errors or Defects, and condemn. But waving this as a Point of too much Delicacy to be inſiſted on; I am not a little comforted

by

by a Reflexion which I often make, that notwithſtanding the numberleſs Treatiſes before-mentioned, it ſeems that the Subject is not exhauſted; new and uſeful Obſervations may be ſtill added. My Reaſon for thinking ſo, is this: Of the infinite Multitude of rhetorical and critical Compoſitions, Accounts of which are ſent down to us from Antiquity, ſome, Works of the moſt celebrated Authors, ſcarcely a Dozen remain at this Day. How then ſhall we judge; that among the innumerable Treatiſes which have periſhed, there were not any, which contained ought valuable or peculiar? You cannot believe, you will not ſay it. But if they did contain ſuch; may not the ſame or like Thoughts occur at this Time; and Eloquence be ſtill enriched by new Inventions? At leaſt, we may hope to clear the Road marked out by the Antients, to ſmooth and open it; perhaps in ſome Places to ſtrike out new and ſhorter Paths.

THESE Reflexions help to animate: But my chief Encouragement is the Hope, that theſe Lectures imperfect as they are, may do ſome Good.

THEY may at leaſt turn your Attention to the Subject upon which they are raiſed: An Effect, which (pardon the Remark) ſeemeth at preſent needful to us. Sciences are cultivated not unhappily, Languages are ſtudied, polite Authors are read and underſtood among us: But a Spirit of imitating them is not ſufficiently high. Content to know and admire, who ſeeks to resemble? Reason is more exercised than Invention. Attached to what is solid, we neglect Ornament. Now the treating publickly of this latter, the hearing much concerning it, will unavoidably make it the Subject of your Thoughts and Discourse: And, if it hath, as certainly is the Case, much of real Value in it, will naturally introduce a Fondness for it, will recommend it to your Study and Care.

I AM the more at Liberty to hope for this Consequence, as the Trial is new; as Lectures on the present Argument have been long disused; or rather have never been carried on in a continued and regular Course.

THAT this, ELOQUENCE, is a Possession highly valuable, an Art worthy of your utmost Application, seemeth not to require Proof. The Histories ye read daily, the Writings of those whom ye justly admire, abound with Evidences of its Power, and Praises of its Dignity. There is not any Nation so barbarous, so uncultivated by Arts, so foreign from all Humanity, in which there may not be found Traces of its Influence, although in its rude and imperfect State. And in those happier Climates where Reason was improved, wheresoever the Beams of Arts and Knowledge were extended, Eloquence obtained likewise Admission, met with proportional Advancement, and flourished together with them. If there be more of Worth in Science, if it be more estimable to find out Truth than to impart it when

when found, to think deeply than to ſpeak well; yet is there not leſs Utility in this latter; becauſe, it is abſolutely neceſſary to the obtaining in any conſiderable Degree, the Advantages of the other. For of what Importance is the Diſcovery of Truth, if it cannot be communicated? What avails the moſt improved Underſtanding, if incapable of conveying properly its own Notions?

Prometheus is ſaid by the Poets to have ſtolen Fire from Heaven, beſtowing which to Mankind yet wretched and ſavage, he rendered Life comfortable, and prepared the Way for all the beneficial Arts afterwards invented. Such we may eſteem Eloquence; a divine Ray, which gave Life and Warmth to all the Faculties, teaching them to impart the Fruit of their Operations to others; by this Means diffuſing Humanity, Knowledge, Politeneſs of Manners.

For Mankind, however Curious and Lovers of Truth, will ſeldom give Admiſſion to her, if preſented in her own native unadorned Shape. She muſt ſoften the Severity of her Aſpect, muſt borrow the Embelliſhments of Rhetorick, muſt employ all the Charms and Addreſs of that, to fix, conquer, and win over the Diſtractions, Prejudices, and Indolence of Mankind. If becauſe Reaſon is natural to Men, they were to be left to the Power of ſimple unaſſiſted Reaſon, the Minds of the Multitude would be in a State as deſtitute as their Bodies, if abandoned equally to Nature alone, without Raiment, without Houſes. Eloquence we may therefore ſtile the Cloathing

Cloathing of Reaſon, which at firſt coarſe and plain, a Defence meerly againſt the Rigour of the Seaſons, became at Length a Source of Beauty, defendeth, preſerveth, adorneth it.

LET us not then attempt to ſeparate two Friends thus happily united. Ye do rightly without Doubt in cultivating Science; it is the only firm Foundation. But, if you ſtop there, you leave your Work imperfect: Add to Science this Gift of Eloquence, which, if in the Order of Nature inferior, is equal as I ſaid before, rather indeed preferable, in Uſe and practical Advantage; is more forcible, more ſplendid, more univerſally powerful. Conſider it not in the Light of philoſophical abſtracted Severity, but according to the Rank it actually holdeth in the World; for we ſhould be guided in our Choice by Reality, not Speculation: What is there more to be deſired, what more admirable, than for one, a private Perſon, by Means hereof, to fix the Attention of a large Aſſembly; notwithſtanding their different Tempers, Views, and Diſpoſitions, to inſpire alternately, Joy, Sorrow, Indignation, Compaſſion, Love, Averſion; to keep every Motion of their Minds ſuſpended as it were on his Words; and in the Concluſion, to leave them pleaſed, convinced, perſwaded? Reflect, in what grand Images do the Writers of Antiquity repreſent the Orators of their Days. [*a*] Sometimes they

[*a*] Vehemens ut procella, excitatus ut torrens, incenſus ut fulmen, tonat, fulgurat, et rapidis eloquentiæ fluctibus cuncta proruit, et proturbat. CICERO.

they are Torrents, that rolling with impetuous Fury, bear down every Thing before them. Again, they are Lightnings, that dazzle and ſtrike blind, that pierce and diſſolve. At another Time, they are Tempeſts, that rage and thunder, that rend, ſcatter, overturn.

In one Place, you ſee a mighty People diſſolved in Luxury and Indolence, effeminate, corrupted, terrible only to thoſe who would reform them; [*b*] the Orator layeth before theſe their true State; he ſhews them from without a powerful Enemy deceiving, and ready to enſlave them; Traitors ſelling them within; their Allies inſulted, their Territories mangled and alienated, their Armies uſeleſs, their Trade deſtroyed, their Fleets bafled and idle; themſelves in the mean while buried in Sloth, devoted to Shews and Spectacles, the Contempt of *Greece*: Which affecting Picture he contraſts with that of their Anceſtors, Lovers of their Country, patient of Labour, intrepid, victorious over the innumerable Hoſts of the *Perſian* Monarch, the Defenders of Liberty and *Greece*, Patriots honoured with immortal Fame.—Lo! this degenerate People are rouzed, kindled, fired; the Orator's Voice recals the Spirit of their Anceſtors; they ruſh with Emulation to Arms; they fight and fall, although unſucceſsful, yet glorious, on the Plains of *Chæronea*.

In another Place, ſee a [*c*] Tyrant trampling on the Laws and Liberties of his Country, in other

[*b*] Demosthenes. [*c*] Julius Cæsar.

other Respects the most accomplished of Mankind: Behold him determined to inflict Death upon an [*d*] Enemy now in his Power! [*e*] One offereth himself to plead for this illustrious Criminal, and the Usurper, although resolved to condemn, assenteth to hear. He seateth himself on his Tribunal, holding the fatal Decree prepared beforehand: He listeneth, his Curiosity is engaged; as the Advocate goeth on, he is moved, affected, his Compassion is raised, he turns pale, he trembles, the Decree drops from his Hand; he forgives [*f*].

" BUT these Wonders have ceased: No " such Effects have been wrought in modern " Times."

TRUE:—Yet they are still possible; and is it not worth while to cultivate an Art which may possibly lead to such? At least, we cannot doubt, that somewhat resembling these, may be still hoped for.

BUT, there remains a Consideration of more Importance, " This Art will enable us to do " much Good."

IN the several liberal Professions, for which all who now hear me are intended, the Power of Speaking-well qualifies the Possessor to be eminently useful. Whether you deliver your Sentiments concerning the Measures most beneficial to your Country, and seek to abrogate hurtful, or enact wise Laws: Whether you do right to injured Innocence, or bring Guilt to due

[*d*] CAIUS LIGARIUS, [*e*] CICERO.
[*f*] PLUTARCH in the Life of CICERO.

due Puniſhment, recover or defend Property uſurped or attacked: Or whether laſtly, you lay before Men their Duty as reaſonable Creatures and Chriſtians, paint the Charms of Religion and Virtue, or diſplay the Horrors of Infidelity and Vice: In all theſe important Offices, of what mighty Efficacy is Eloquence? Without this, Knowledge proceedeth faintly, ſlowly, like unaſſiſted Strength in manual Works, which may at length obtain its End, but with much clumſy Labour: Oratory we may compare to the mechanical Arts, which, by furniſhing Engines, and well adapted Inſtruments, produce the ſame Effects with Eaſe, and finiſh with Elegancy.

THOSE who underſtand the Nature of Society will not, I believe, eſteem it a Paradox, if we aſſert, that the Orator, who employeth his Talent aright, is one of the moſt uſeful Members of the Community, infuſing Principles of Religion, Humanity, and virtuous Induſtry in all who hear him, contributing to preſerve Peace, Juſtice, and Harmony among Men.

WE may therefore lay it down as acknowledged, that this Art is excellent. At the ſame Time it ſhould not be concealed, that it is difficult; and cannot be obtained by meer Approbation and indolent Wiſhes. This we might fully prove, by a bare Recital of the many Endowments of Mind, which beſide outward Qualifications of Perſon, Voice, Action, are requiſite to the forming a great Orator: An Aſſemblage rarely met with; and where met, ſtill inſufficient without Care. For Nature hath dealt with the Mind of Man as with the Earth about him, which produceth not Grain, unleſs ſhe hath before ſown the Seeds in it, and Culture be afterwards added.

THIS Remark points out the two great Articles, of which are formed, as it were, the Root and Stem of this lofty Tree of Eloquence, from whence the leſs Parts, like Branches, quickly ſhoot. Theſe are GENIUS and APPLICATION. Concerning which, as ſome Obſcurity hath ariſen, allow me to add a few Words in Explanation of them.

THE Air and Features of every Individual in the human Species are different: Not leſs Diverſity is obſervable in their Minds: Their Diſpoſitions, their Likings, their Powers alſo are altogether different. Take any Number of Perſons, you will find them inclined to different Studies; each capable of ſucceeding well in his own, yet averſe from, and uſually unable to make a Progreſs in that choſen by another. Nothing is more commonly met with. Here is one, who in early Youth reads the Poets with Pleaſure, learns with Eaſe to imitate them, but can ſcarcely be brought to comprehend the firſt Elements of Geometry: While this other young Perſon can hardly be dragged through a Page of *Homer* or *Horace*, who yet runs over *Euclid* with Rapidity. As again, others there are, utterly inept for Letters, who become good Mechanicks, or raiſe a Fortune by Commerce.

THIS

THIS Distinction is essential; it gives to Life its whole Colour and Character. If a Man set out in the Path, to which Nature pointeth, he will go on easily and swiftly to his utmost Degree of Perfection; for there are Limits to all: But, if by wrong Influence or Choice, he be forced or seduced into another Road, he will meet with Difficulties at every Step, go on struggling and stumbling, and if he have Resolution to persevere, will arrive in the End, to Mediocrity. *RICHLIEU*, the greatest Statesman of his Age, had an immoderate Ambition to be admired as a Poet, and became in that Respect ridiculous: Somewhat of the same Kind we see in *Machiavel*; and perhaps in *Cicero*. Even the most versatile Mind, that which can best suit itself to different Things, confesseth still this Power of *Nature*: For, though it may perform tolerably well in a foreign Province, yet it doth far better in its own. [g] Every Circumstance and kind of Life, saith the Poet, became *Aristippus*; yet we cannot imagine, that stoical Severity suited him so well, as his own soft voluptuous Philosophy.

IF I might be allowed to borrow a Comparison from Science, I would liken such *Nature*, to a Body placed in a Ray separated by passing through a Prism, which appeareth always of the same Colour of that Ray; but is much brighter, more luminous, when beheld in Light of its own natural Colour. *Boccace* hath left behind

[g] Omnis ARISTIPPUM decuit color, & status, & res. HOR.

behind him some serious Writings which are deservedly neglected; take up his *Decameron*, you must be pleased: What comick Wit and Humour! What Delicacy, yet Simplicity of Stile and Sentiment! He is a Model in this Kind: It was his *Genius*. *Milton*'s Sublimity transports, astonishes; his Attempts of Humour move Pity.

" UNIVERSAL Genius may seem an Exception."——This, like universal Conquest, is chimerical, sought after by many; always with ill Success, and to the Prejudice of the Seeker. No Man seemeth to have fairer Pretensions to it, than Lord *Bacon*. What Depth of Thought! What vast Extent of Learning! What grand Ideas! Yet when he aimeth at Ornament, as he doth not seldom, how doth this great Person fail! He becomes forced, unnatural, obscure. Nature hath fixed the Bounds. Some exalted Souls have a much wider Range to move in; within which, they seem to be more than human; beyond, are but as common Men: They are *Sampson, shorn of his Strength*; *Anteus*, held up aloft in Air. Where the impulse is strong, it cannot be mistaken; divert, cover, overwhelm it, still it will send out Sparks, if it cannot blaze. *Mallebranche*, an Enthusiast in the Cause of Truth, inveigheth against all rhetorical Embellishments, as Instruments of Falsehood; and Nature breaks out, betraying him in every Page; he is unawares an Orator, and a fine one.

IN the general Course of Mankind, the Difference

ference is much less strongly marked; but it always is. As no Man is alike fit for every Employment, so there is not any, unfit for all.

The Sum is; in the original Frame of our Souls, there is a Difference proceeding from the Hand of the great Maker, by which, every Man is enabled to make a better Progress in some one Thing, Study, or Art, or Handicraft, than in another; which natural Ability we name GENIUS. Sometimes it comprehendeth a wide Circuit; is sometimes confined to one Science or Art, or even to one Branch of each: But the most extensive is bounded; the narrowest hath open to it its peculiar Path. The Usefulness or final Cause of which Disposition is manifest, that Men thus differently qualified, should stand in Need of, and be benefited by each other; thus all mutually obliged and obliging, whilst each moveth in his own peculiar Sphere, should conspire to promote the Good of the Whole.

Let us now bring home these Observations to the Point before us. The first Article to be regarded in one destined to the Study of Oratory, is this, GENIUS. It is the Foundation of all; to this, all subsequent Improvement must be proportional; without some Degree of it all Attempts are vain, no Progress can be made; in which Case, the Attention should be turned some other Way.

This precious Gift being supplied by the Hand of Nature, you then proceed to the second Article mentioned as necessary to perfect the

the firſt; this was ſaid to be APPLICATION, which conſiſteh of two Parts, STUDY and PRACTICE.

YOU muſt read the Works of the moſt eminent Speakers; read not ſlightly or tranſiently, nor ſo as meerly to apprehend the Senſe, but with Care, Intentneſs, Aſſiduity; with an [*b*] Earneſtneſs nearly equal to that of Writing. Make yourſelf Maſter of their Subject. Obſerve the Method they have choſen. Follow them through every Tranſition. Attend to their Reaſoning. Take Notice, of the Addreſs with which they prepare Things; how they guard againſt Prejudices, prevent or ſolve Objections; how they paint, move, amplify, contract; where abound in Images and Figures, where aſſume a plain ſimple Stile: Penetrate into the ſeveral Reaſons for this Variety. Having arrived thus far, learn to diſtinguiſh the Genius of each Speaker; which being known, you will trace it through every Variety ariſing from Occaſions, Circumſtances, Conjunctures, Imitation: This is the principal Form; the Key, which gives the Tone to the reſt.

FURNISHED with this Knowlege, you are to compleat all by adding the ſecond Branch of Application, PRACTICE.

YOU ſhould by frequent Trial, make yourſelf acquainted with the Bent, Strength, Limits of your own Genius; that having learned the proper Cultivation of it, you may lay out your utmoſt

[*b*] Legendum eſt pene ad ſcribendi ſollicitudinem.
QUINT.

utmoſt Efforts in that Way; and by obſerving, correcting, and guarding againſt Faults, raiſe it gradually to the utmoſt Perfection, of which it is capable. For as Exerciſe forms the Body, maketh it ſtrong, pliable, and docile; ſo doth Practice the Mind, giveth to it Firmneſs, and Force, and Eaſe, a Readineſs and Gracefulneſs, not otherwiſe attainable.---But as the enſuing Lectures are to turn chiefly upon Articles relative to theſe, STUDY and PRACTICE, I ſhall ſay no more of them at preſent.

One Thing however it ſeems, that I ought not to paſs over: It will probably be aſked, "Among the Qualities requiſite to form an "Orator, why is *Taſte* omitted? The general "Opinion gives it a high Rank among them."

I ACKNOWLEGE it. In Writings and Converſations upon this and the like Subjects, no Word occurs more often: All Excellence in Compoſition and Judgment is reſolved into it. But hath this Term a clear Idea annexed? Aſk for an Explanation of it; you meet with various Opinions, much Confuſion and Controverſy. Let us then conſider the Point: Let us, if we can, fix the Value and preciſe Meaning of the Term.

The firſt Thing which occurred to me in enquiring upon this Subject was to aſk, In what Senſe was this Word uſed in *Greece* and *Rome*, the two great Fountains of that Elegance, which Moderns expreſs by *Taſte*? I could not recollect to have met with the Word applyed at all in this Manner, in any *Greek* or

Roman

Roman Author. And yet, there is a Multitude of Places in the Works of *Cicero*, and not fewer in those of *Quintilian*, where the Subject led them unavoidably to a mention of this Term, if such had been at that Time used.

IN this latter, a remarkable Expression occurreth [*i*]; speaking of Judgment as connected with Invention, he sayeth. " that Precepts are here useless [*k*], it can no more be delivered by " Art than Taste and Smell;" and he adds, " must be placed in the same Rank with the " Senses, which cannot be taught:" A Proof, I suppose, that the present fashionable metaphorical Sense of this Word was not then known. To the same Purpose we may cite the Question of *Horace* [*l*]; " Whether Excel- " lence in Poesy springeth from Nature" (that is Genius) " or Art:" To which, he determines, that, " it is necessary both should conspire:" He seemeth to have no Conception of any third Faculty.

What then? Do we not rightly infer from hence, that this Term, since unknown among those Nations who excelled all others in the fine Arts, is not necessary; that there is no Thing essential in those Arts which may not be exprest without it? Where and when therefore shall we fix it's Origin?

IT seemeth to me the most probable Conjecture, that it's rise is to be dated from the Time of

[*i*] Lib. 6. cap. 1.

[*k*] Nec magis arte traditur quam gustus aut odor. Referatur oportet ad sensus qui non docentur.

[*l*] De arte poeticâ.

of the Revival of Letters; and that it's native Country was *Italy*, the great Scene of that Revival. In this Conjuncture Men applied themselves to Statuary, Painting, and Poetry, with an Ardour that rose to Enthusiasm; and thus overflowing as they were with Fondness for these Arts, and unable to express worthily their Rapture of Admiration, they searched on all Sides for Words adequate to their Ideas; when among others, this metaphorical Name *Gusto* or *Taste* was introduced; and being judged apt and emphatical, spread together with these Arts, was transfused, and by Degrees incorporated into the several Languages of *Europe*.

" What then," you will say, " do you re-" ject, would you abolish as useless, a Word " so universally received, and deemed of such " Energy?"---By no Means. Let it be still used; I mean only to guard against the Abuse of it: For in my Opinion the unskilful and uncertain Use of it hath given rise to Mistakes of ill Consequence. If I understand rightly the Authors who treat of it, they represent it as a distinct Faculty of the Mind: That as the Understanding judgeth of Truth and Falsehood in Science, so doth Taste, of what is beautiful or otherwise in the polite Arts; it is here the Umpire and sole Judge. Now it hath been laid down as an Axiom, and is not I think disputed, that no more Causes are to be admitted, than such as are real, and sufficient to produce the Effect. If then, the known Faculties of the Mind suffice to this End which is ascribed to

Taſte, why ſhould we ſuppoſe the Exiſtence of this latter? We muſt reject it as altogether imaginary.

AND that they do thus ſuffice, I apprehend to be clearly the Caſe. For Proof of which, run over in your own Minds the ſeveral Arts, Poeſy, Eloquence, Muſick, Painting, Architecture; then aſk, "Is there any Thing in theſe, "which I may not conceive to be produced by "*Genius*, directed by a good Underſtanding, "improved in the Manner above-mentioned; "by judicious Application?" I know not any: Proportion, Harmony, Variety, Novelty, Beauty, and if there be any other Excellence, may be all accounted for from theſe Cauſes. *Genius* and Underſtanding we know to be real Cauſes, exiſting in Nature, and we find them to be ſufficient; what then is Taſte? Conceived as a Faculty diſtinct from them, is it any Thing, but a meer Name?

If theſe, Genius and Underſtanding have produced, it follows, that they ſuffice to judge of theſe Arts. Diſtributed in different Degrees, they produce and judge: A great Degree of Genius makes the excellent Artiſt; a leſs, joined with good Underſtanding, forms the accurate Critick. From whence you ſee the Reaſon, why the deepeſt Mathematician, however juſt his Underſtanding, may be a very incompetent Judge of Poeſy, or Eloquence: Genius is wanting: Which Reaſoning may be extended to the other Arts.

It deserveth particularly to be noted, that this realizing the imaginary Faculty of Taste, began indeed in the Arts; yet it did not remain confined to them; the Infection spread farther, was received into the Affairs of common Life, into Modes and Dress; nay it caught even the Philosophers; it became the great Standard of Manners; and we have seen a certain inward Sense, a moral *Taste*, made the Source of Duty and Obligation; it may be feared with worse Effects; as it is more dangerous to resolve *Manners*, the Art of Living well, than other Arts, into chimerical, at least refined metaphysical Principles.

My Answer then to the Question proposed, " Do I allow of the Use of the Term *Taste*," is direct. I do, as a complex Term, expressing the Result of " Genius and Understanding, " improved by due Application;" in which Sense you see it is the same with the Qualities before mentioned; but in what I take to be the usual Supposition, as a distinct Principle from the Understanding, as an independent Legislator, I cannot see any Reason for admitting it's Existence, and I think the Use of it hath caused much Obscurity, and some Mistake.

" But *Taste* is represented as a *Sentiment*; " not as an Act of the Understanding, but a " Feeling of the Heart [*m*]." Another Mistake,

[*m*] In this metaphorical Sense only, as a *relish for*, or *liking*, do I find the Word used by the Antients; as, " Gustus veræ laudis; gustus virtutis:" never as a Talent, or Power of excelling or judging in any Art.

take, as I imagine: For what are all these, distinguished by the fashionable Name of *Sentiments?* The Understanding approveth or disapproveth: To those Acts, Nature hath annexed certain Degrees of Pleasure or Pain: But these Consequences follow so closely, that we cannot distinguish between them and their Causes; and the *feeling* being the stronger Impression, we drop the preceding Act of the Understanding, and name the whole, *Sentiment*.

I hope, that I shall be pardoned for this little Excursion into Metaphysicks; the Subject required it. What I have said may appear new, perhaps false; but let it be considered, that I deliver it only as an *Opinion*. In Matters of such Nicety, where Enquirers must probably disagree, it becometh us to temper Judgment with Humanity, to chuse the best Opinion, without greatly condemning the others.

SURE I am, that an Attempt of restoring the antient Simplicity ought not to be discouraged: But the Danger is, that as Custom hath established firmly the present Notions, the antient may be deemed new; and the desire of bringing them back looked upon as a Zeal for Innovation.

IF, after all, any Person should still insist upon the Use of this Word *Taste*, in a Sense different from, and additional to Genius and Application, (for we dispute not about mere Words or Sounds) I shall not contend with him: This only I would propose as necessary to avoid Confusion and Mistake; let him fix a distinct a distinct precise Notion of it; for I confess myself, after much Reflexion, utterly unable to form any such.

I HAVE proceeded thus far in some general introductory Observations, which I thought fit to be premised, as useful in giving Light to what shall follow. In my next Lecture, I propose to enter upon my main Design, and to lay before you the Plan of the ensuing Discourses. At present, I shall only beg your Indulgence to make one or two Remarks, relative to the Manner I have chosen.

First, IT may be necessary to make an Apology for the Language, which in Academical Lectures, it is thought, should be *Latin*. "Why, it may be asked, do you depart from "an established Rule?"

IN answer to which Question, without entering into the comparative Merits or Demerits of writing in a dead Language, which would carry me too far, I shall only observe, that on the present Occasion at least, our own Tongue is preferable: Because, the End now proposed is Improvement in Eloquence; And how is this Eloquence to be exerted? In our own Tongue. Thus it is, we are to speak at the Bar, in the Senate, in the Pulpit. To it therefore must our Rules principally relate, and from those who have written in it, we must draw Citations and Examples: Which we cannot perform properly in a learned Language; for although Custom hath rendered familiar the Introduction of *Latin* Passages in *English* Dis-

 course;

courſe; yet *Engliſh* interwoven in a *Latin* Compoſition would, I ſuppoſe, appear abſurd and monſtrous.

Secondly, IT may give Ground for Objection, that Rules and Remarks concerning Eloquence are here illuſtrated, very much by Inſtances, taken from the Poets. "Would it not be "more uſeful as well as pertinent, to draw "them from the Orators? Why are we at eve-"ry Inſtant checked in our Courſe, and hur-"ried into another Art?

FOR three Reaſons. *Firſt*, Becauſe, the Connexion between Poeſy and Eloquence is ſo cloſe, that in moſt Caſes, Examples from the one extend equally to the other.

Secondly, BECAUSE Poetical Examples are ſhorter; thus more ſuited to the Nature of theſe Lectures, and eaſier to the Memory.

Thirdly, BECAUSE the Poets, leſs ſtudious of concealing Art, uſe bolder Ornaments, and more ſtriking; for that Reaſon fitter to illuſtrate and exemplify.

BESIDES, Verſes interſperſed form a Variety, which may enliven; and relieve the Attention. In which laſt View it is, that I have ventured to intermingle ſome few original Performances of the poetical Kind; not as Patterns propoſed to your Imitation, for I am ſenſible how ſlender, if any, my Vein is in that Way; but merely as Change to diverſify, and Novelty to entertain.

Laſtly, WE all know, that the chief Deſign propoſed in the Eſtabliſhment of the preſent Lecture,

Lecture, was to teach the Art of Speaking, the Rules of distinct, proper, graceful Pronunciation; yet this Article hath but small Share in the Discourses I am about to deliver: "How is "this to be justified?"

BECAUSE, this Art of speaking cannot be taught with any good Effect in a continued Discourse [*n*]. General Precepts avail little to this End, without Experience; their Use lieth in the practical Application, in frequent Trials, wherein an attentive Hearer may interpose occasionally, remark Errors and Defects, give the due Tone and Cadence, and point out and exemplify the right Manner. Hence in the following Lectures I have chosen a Subject more capable of being treated in this general Way; yet I hope not wholly without Advantage; such as may contribute to form your Judgments to a Knowlege of true Eloquence; leaving to our usual weekly Lectures the Care of Pronunciation; entreating you at the same Time, in this last important Article, to follow my Judgment, rather than Example [*o*].

[*n*] See ARIST. Rhetor. Book iii.

[*o*] Quasi non ea præcipiam aliis, quæ mihi ipsi desunt. CIC. de Orat. lib. ii.

LECTURE

LECTURE the Second.

CONTAINING,

The History of the Rise and Progress of Eloquence, among the Antients.

THERE is not any Art, which hath been more frequently and amply treated of than this of Rhetorick; a Proof at once of its Worth and Difficulty. Discourses prepared for this Audience, cannot be supposed to comprehend so mighty an Object, as this whole Art, a Work as disproportioned to their Nature to which Conciseness is essential, as it is superior to the Abilities of the Writer. Their Aim is much more humble; to chuse out such Parts as have been less accurately handled, or such as seem likely to furnish the most useful Observations; which Observations shall be thrown together, without that exact Regularity necessary in a formed System, or elaborate Treatise; yet not without Regard to Order; for even Essays have their Method. That ye may see as much of this as appeareth requisite, and have some View of the Course through which ye are to be led, I begin here with a short Sketch of my Design.

IN

IN this Lecture, I propose to treat of the Rise and Progress of Eloquence among the Antients. [a] Next, I shall give some Account of the most celebrated Treatises concerning it, which remain to us from Antiquity. [b] Afterwards, shall follow its History in modern Times, together with some Reflexions upon it. This leadeth to some Thoughts concerning [c] Imitation. We shall then proceed to consider Eloquence in the various Respects it beareth to Man, as it addresseth itself first to his [d] Reason: Secondly, to his [e] Passions. Thirdly, to his outward Senses; under which last Head, we shall discourse of [f] Stile or Elocution, as it comprehendeth Ornament, Composition, Figures. Lastly, I shall endeavour to direct these Observations, this Art, to practical Use and Advantage, applying them to our Improvement in one [g] Profession, which almost all my Hearers are destined to engage in.

THIS View openeth to us a large Field to expatiate in. But, I shall contract what I have to say, touching lightly on many Particulars, that I may dwell on the Principal, avoiding as far as I can, to repeat trite Remarks; yet not studious to seek for such as are singular: As proposing to inform without tiring, and, if possible, to entertain without misleading.

THE

[a] Lect. 3 & 4. [b] Lect. 5 & 6. [c] Lect. 7. [d] Lect. 8 & 9. [e] Lect. 10 & 11. [f] Lect. 12, 13, 14, 15, 16, 17, 18. [g] Lect. 19, 20, 21, 22.

THE Faculty of Speech was given to Mankind for excellent Ends, for communicating our Wants, and transacting Business; to be the Instrument of conveying Instruction, Advice, Exhortation, and Comfort to each other. This, like all other natural Powers, is observed to exert itself with different Degrees of Efficacy in different Men. Some, therefore, excelled originally in the Use of this Faculty, and by this Superiority, were distinguished from the rest; being enabled hereby, to contribute much more than the others, to the Advantage and Pleasure of those, with whom they conversed. Now, this Distinction must have been more conspicuous in Society, than among scattered Individuals, or small Families: Most conspicuous in those Societies, which had risen to some Degree of Grandeur: For, as in these latter, the Variety of interfering Interests is greater, more numerous and nicer Affairs are to be transacted, Excellence of this Kind becometh of Course more useful, and the Person thus excelling more eminent.

IN Societies where Freedom was established, this was likely to be the Case, more than under despotick Government; because, in this last, Force rules, in the other, Perswasion: And where shall you expect to find the Art of Perswasion most cultivated, but there, where it hath the strongest Influence?

HENCE we are not to look for it in any great Degree of Perfection in the East, although it is probable that Letters first flourished there; because caufe that Part of the Globe was early and almoft univerfally fubject to arbitrary Sway. It is eafy to fee, that in mentioning the Eaft I except the People of the *Jews*, whofe facred Monuments abound with Strains of the moft fublime Eloquence: But thefe were of a divine Original, and fall not within my prefent Argument, which is confined to Effects purely human.

NEITHER are we to look for Eloquence in *Egypt*, although the Fountain of Arts. The Spirit of Myftery which prevailed, the hieroglyphical Characters in which all their Erudition was couched, were mortal Enemies to all Improvement of this Sort: Intent only on painting their Thoughts, they were carelefs about the Manner of fpeaking them. At leaft there are no Monuments remaining which may induce us to think that they applied themfelves with any Care to cultivate this Art. On the contrary, many Caufes confpired to render this Art flourifhing among the *Greeks*.

LIBERTY, the Nurfe of all Arts and Sciences, in a particular Manner the Parent of Eloquence: The Number of independent States in *Greece*, from whence muft have arifen perpetual Difputes, Treaties, and Alliances, which gave continual Exercife to the Talent of Speaking: Commerce early attended to, which enlarges the Knowledge, Views, and Intercourfe of Men: The great Council inftituted by *Amphictyon*, in which the Interefts of the feveral States were difcuffed, and all Differences fettled; and it is evident, that where Debate is allowed, with Exclufion

Exclusion of Force, the Art of Speaking must be improved.

WE have no History of the first Rise and gradual Advancement of this Art in *Greece*: But we are certain, that it had made a considerable Progress in the Time of *Homer*, as he hath characterised three principal Kinds of it in three of his Heroes: The short, clear, and unadorned in *Menelaus*: The diffuse, insinuating, and pathetick in *Nestor*: The strong, animated, and vehement in *Ulysses*. There are also many Passages in his Poems, in which he mentioneth with high Praises the Art of Speaking, and the Esteem in which they who excelled in it, were held even in those early Times. And, as he is supposed to have drawn with Exactness the Manners of the Age of which he wrote, we may conclude from hence, that Eloquence was known and valued in the Time of the *Trojan* War. Agreeably to which, we learn from PAUSANIAS, that the first School of Oratory in *Greece* was opened under the Reign of *Theseus*, in the Generation preceding this War.

AMONG all the States of *Greece*, *Athens* however it was, that carried this Art to its highest Perfection. To which the Genius of the People, the Form of its Government, and its Laws, more especially contributed.

First, THE Genius of the People favoured its Improvement: For they were valiant, Lovers of Liberty, addicted to Commerce, quick of Apprehension, vain, exceedingly Curious, inconstant, fond of Novelty; Qualities, fit to render

der them Admirers and Encouragers of thoſe, who could ſpeak plauſibly, elegantly, and artfully.

THEIR Form of Government had alſo the ſame Tendency. All Affairs relating to the State were propoſed in the Senate of Five-hundred: From thence, if approved, were carried before the Council of Five-thouſand. And in Points of an extraordinary Nature, every Citizen had a Right to give his Suffrage. Were not theſe different Scenes of Debate, the Audience enlarging in each, ſo many Schools as it were, to initiate, and perfect an *Athenian* Senator in Eloquence?

THE whole Turn of their Laws likewiſe contributed to produce the ſame Effect. Of this Sort was the fundamental Law, which ordained every Perſon who had been Magiſtrate, or exercіſed any public Truſt, to give Account of his Adminiſtration before the People.

SUCH likewiſe was the Law, which puniſhed with Confiſcation of Goods and Baniſhment the Accuſer, where the accuſed was abſolved by more than two-thirds of the Suffrages.

NO Perſon likewiſe was permitted to ſpeak in publick, who was under a certain Age, or who was proved to be guilty of any great Crime, of publick Immorality, Effeminacy, or Extravagance.

WHOEVER alſo propoſed a new Law, if it were rejected, and appeared wrong or pernicious, was liable to be called to a publick Account,

count, and if condemned, ſeverely fined. All theſe Laws, and many others of a like Kind might be recounted, evidently tended to promote the Study of Oratory.

I AM likewiſe inclined to paſs the ſame Judgment on that Law of the *Areopagus*, which made it highly penal for an Advocate, to attempt in his Pleading to move the Paſſions of the Judges: For, although a great Part of Eloquence doth conſiſt in the pathetick, yet is the Abuſe hereof, the quitting the Point under Debate, and appealing to the Paſſions, a prime Cauſe of corrupting Eloquence: And it ſeemeth not improbable, that to this wiſe Law may, in a great Meaſure, be attributed the cloſe, correct, reaſoning Manner peculiar to the Orators of *Athens*.

FROM theſe concurring Cauſes it came to paſs, that Eloquence was the chief, almoſt the only Way of opening Acceſs to Honours in the State. It became more remarkably ſo, from the Time of *Pericles*, who governed *Athens*, notwithſtanding its Love of Liberty, for many Years, with almoſt abſolute Sway. To which Height he was raiſed, and ſupported in it, by many great Qualities; above all, by his ſingular Eloquence, wherein Hiſtorians agree, that he far excelled all who lived before him. He is deſcribed in his Harangues, as Thundering and Lightening, from whence we may conclude, that his Manner was forcible and vehement.

ABOUT his Time, *Greece* abounded with extemporaneous Orators, named *Sophiſts*, who profeſſed

fessed the Art of defending all Causes, of speaking without Preparation on any Point proposed, and rendered themselves greatly admired for these extraordinary Talents. By the Fragments which remain of these Persons, it appears, that however inaccurate and vain-glorious they might have been, yet they had great Abilities, and contributed not a little to the polishing and perfecting of the *Greek* Language.

Socrates, the great Improver of human Reason, was also an Improver of Eloquence, ridiculing the false Ornaments of these Sophists, as well as confuting their false Reasonings. And his Disciple *Plato*, by Example as well as by Precept, carried Oratory nearly to its Height. But, concerning him, we shall take an Opportunity of speaking more at large hereafter [*i*].

ABOUT the same Time, History which had hitherto appeared in a mean Dress, arrayed herself in all the Charms that Eloquence could bestow; pure, easy, flowing in *Herodotus*; in *Thucydides*, elaborate, deep, sublime. This latter, beside the extraordinary Spirit of his Narration, hath interwoven many admirable Speeches, written with the utmost Brevity and Force, which render his Work peculiarly fit for the Study of one who would speak in publick: For all whom, he is an excellent Model, with some Variation in one particular; his Manner is exceedingly close and compact, fitter for the Closet than a large Audience: As abundant in Sense as frugal of Expression, he hath equalled Sentences

[*i*] Lecture 18.

Sentences to Words; whence Difficulty then, now Obscurity [*k*].

I OUGHT not on this Occasion to omit *Isocrates*, who although not in the first Rank of Orators, was highly Instrumental in the Advancement of the Art. Born with an easy and fruitful, although not elevated Genius, of sweet Temper, and gentle Manners, he opened a new Track suitable to his Disposition, soft and flowery. He first perfected Composition; taught the Periods to fall with tuneful Cadence; and Prose hitherto wandering in harsh Licence, he first restrained by certain Feet and harmonious Measures [*l*]. Having also lived to extreme old Age, and remained very long at the Head of a famous and flourishing School, he filled *Greece* with his Disciples, who spread every where the Politeness and Elegance of his Manner.

AT length, forming himself upon these Models, chiefly upon that of *Plato*, whom he had heard in his Youth, and that of *Thucydides*, whose History he is said to have transcribed eight Times that he might impress it the more deeply on his Memory, *Demosthenes*, raised Eloquence to the Summit of Perfection: Uniting the Elevation and Majesty of the Philosopher, to the deep Sense and Conciseness of the Historian, he added to both, the Fire and Vehemence of *Pericles*, thus equally fitted to instruct, to affect, to

[*k*] Verborum prope numerum sententiarum numero consequitur. De orat. lib. 2. Subobscurus THUCYDIDES. Idem. [*l*] CICERO de claris oratoribus.

to convince. Examine his Orations attentively; you find nothing superfluous, nothing idle, no glittering Points, no affected Turns, no false Sublime, no studied Pathetick; but all seemingly artless, plain, and simple; yet under that apparent Simplicity, Energy, Vehemence, Sublimity, Passion irresistable. Is he to compute, to provide for the Expences of a necessary War? No Geometer more exact, more methodical. Is he to relate a Transaction? He is pure, distinct, perspicuous. Is he to cite the Example, and commend the Behaviour of their Ancestors? What Pomp, what Grandeur, what Magnificence! The Verses of *Homer* scarcely flow with more Copiousness and more Harmony. Is he to reproach the Degeneracy of the present Race of *Athenians*? What Ardor! What Keeness! mingled with Strokes of Tenderness and Concern!

" [m] BEHOLD then, O *Athenians*, your " true State; to what Height of Insolence this " Man hath arisen; so as not to leave it in " your Power to chuse Action or Tranquillity. " He menaceth, he speaks with Arrogance; " and not contented with the Places he hath " subdued, is continually aiming at more; and " while we sit careless and at Ease, is drawing " over our Heads a mighty Net. When there- " fore, O *Athenians*, will ye do what ye ought? " When something shall have happened! " When there is a Necessity? What Judgment " then

[m] See first PHILIP, chap. 4.

" then ſhall we form of what hath been al-
" ready done, for I think the greateſt Neceſſity
" to ingenuous Spirits, is the Shame of their
" own ill Management. Will ye compleat
" your own Diſgrace? Will ye perſiſt in run-
" ning through the public Aſſembly, aſking
" each other, Is there any News? What can
" be more new than a Man of *Macedon* ſub-
" duing the *Athenians*, and governing *Greece*
" at his Pleaſure? Is *Philip* dead? No in
" Truth, but he is ſick. What importeth it
" to you, which be the Caſe; for ye will ſoon
" make to yourſelves another *Philip?*"

O GREAT and exalted Genius! Prince, I had almoſt ſaid God of Eloquence! Thou haſt pointed out the true Path to Perſwaſion. We labour ambitious to tread in thy Foot-ſteps, although at an infinite Diſtance, convinced, that even a faint Reſemblance of thee excelleth every other Original.

BUT I return to the Courſe of my Narration. After the Death of *Demoſthenes*, Eloquence quickly declined, at length totally vaniſhed from *Greece*. At the Diſtance of many Years, we behold her reviving in *Rome*, which having ſubdued *Greece* by Arms, laboured to force from her the Praiſe of Arts likewiſe. But here, although triumphant, and ſcarcely diminiſhed in Luſtre, ſhe made but a ſhort Abode: For ſoon declining, after now and then ſome feeble Efforts, ſhe at laſt ſunk in the Inundation of Barbarians with the Empire itſelf: Thus, to uſe the

the Comparison applied to the [n] State and Fall of that Empire, resembling the *Rhine*, which long a great River, then flowing divided through separate Channels, is diminished, at length entering into vast Sands, is absorbed and lost.

HOWEVER, from the History of Eloquence among the *Latins*, there are two Remarks which I would make. The first, which I shall have Occasion hereafter to mention more than once, is that Poesy was brought to some Degree of Maturity, long before Eloquence. For *Ennius*, *Terence*, and *Plautus*, had raised the Glory of the *Roman* Muse very high, before the Name of an Orator was heard of. As far as we can judge, the Case was the same in *Greece*, and we have no Cause to think, that there had appeared a single Piece of good Prose, when the *Iliad* displayed Poesy in its meridian Glory. And I believe the Observation is true in general.

I WOULD account for it in this Manner. Men just coming out of Ignorance are struck most by what is extraordinary; they are fond of the marvellous, and do not approve except where they admire. Hence Poesy, recommended by Harmony of Numbers and Stateliness of Expression, claiming somewhat supernatural, and speaking in a Stile singular and strange, pleased, charmed, and was cultivated. Time and Experience, and Reflexion were necessary to mature the Judgment, and form it to

[n] Considerations sur les causes de la grandeur, &c. des Romains.

a Relish of Truth in its plain, natural Dress. This Account is confirmed by an Observation of *Aristotle* [o], that the first Orators affected a poetical Stile; at length, a better Judgment taught them to descend to one more simple: Wherein saith he, they had the Example of the Poets themselves to instruct them; among whom, they, who writing for the Stage were obliged to give their Fictions an Air of Probability, thought it necessary to bring their Expressions nearer to those of Conversation.

A SECOND Remark is, That Poesy long survived Eloquence. For this latter fell with *Cicero*, before the former had attained to its Summit: And, late in the Empire, when Oratory had been long extinguished, the *Roman* Muse appeareth in the Writings of *Claudian* with many Charms, although lessened in Purity and Majesty. The Reason whereof seems to be this: The absolute Power of one, suppose him to be a polite and generous Prince, may encourage and cherish, perhaps better than a Commonwealth, a Poetick Genius: But Freedom is the only Parent and Nurse of Eloquence: The Soil of Liberty, is the only one, from which her Lawrels can be gathered. A farther Instance of which I think, may be drawn from a neighbouring Nation on the Continent, which governed by one absolute Monarch, hath produced some, indeed excellent Poets; but few Orators, and none by any Means equal in their

Kind:

[o] Rhetor, Lib. 3.

Kind: As you may prove by reading the most admired Pieces, delivered in their Academy, and from their Pulpits.

To return to *Greece*, from whence on this Subject it is scarcely possible to depart, we may assign two Causes for the Decay of Eloquence. One is, the Loss of Liberty; for the *Greeks* had passed successively under the Yoke of *Macedon* and of *Rome*. From henceforth the Love of their Country turned into private Faction; their Eloquence was lost in slavish Panegyrick and mean Adulation; their Learning became a vain, wordy, disputative Philosophy.

ANOTHER Cause was; the Multitude of foreign Persons and Customs, which after *Alexander*'s Conquests in the East, poured in upon them; corrupting their Morals, infecting them with Luxury and Effeminacy; and introducing into their Speech and Writings the *Asiatick* Manner, which had been always opposed to the *Attick*; being pompous, swelling, and redundant; whereas the other was pure, neat, and nervous.

IT may be worth while, in this Place, to remark, the Similitude of Degrees, by which this Corruption proceeded in *Athens* and in *Rome*. After the Death of *Demosthenes* and *Phocion*, this Degeneracy appeared early in the Writings of *Demetrius Phalereus*, one of high Rank and great Virtues; but the Man, who is recorded to have [*p*] first stripped Eloquence of her plain manly Dress, and to have cloathed her in effeminate

[*p*] CICERO Orator.

minate Gaiety. He first sought after Ornaments, pointed Turns, glittering Expressions, affected Oppositions, with all the little Prettinesses and Elegancies, which may adorn an Epigram, but are unbecoming of Truth and good Sense. [q] *Timeus Siculus* added an Affectation of Novelty, and the florid Stile. At length we see as it were the last Glimmerings of Eloquence, about the Time of the Emperor *Julian*, in the Writings of *Libanius* and the other Sophists, which are high, tedious, pompous Declamation. Thus Eloquence in its old Age, as in a second Infancy, endeth just as it set out, in a flowery poetick Stile.

How like to this was its gradual Declension in *Rome?* You see its first Corruption just appearing in *Velleius Paterculus*; more strongly in *Seneca*, whose Writings abound with the little Beauties before-mentioned, studied Oppositions, and sparkling Conceits: Which Manner was followed by *Lucius Florus*; and carried to the most refined Height by the younger *Pliny*. Even the superior Genius and profound Sense of *Tacitus* could not wholly escape the Infection; who, probably to enliven the Dryness of his Subject, of which he expresseth his Sense, and Apprehension that it would disgust, added to this short affected Point, the foreign Mixture of poetick Expression. *Ausonius*, and the other late Panegyrists, from this Corruption sunk yet lower,

[q] LONGINUS gives this Account of him, and produceth an Instance.

lower, into cold, frothy, prolix Declamation: Until at length, after this long duſky Evening, the Night of Barbariſm, *Goths* and *Vandals*, overſpreading all, put out every Spark of Learning and Eloquence.

FROM theſe Obſervations we might draw Leſſons inſtructive to ourſelves, which is the nobleſt Uſe of Hiſtory: And, if I might be permitted to digreſs, I think, that I could ſhew among us ſomething not very unlike this Succeſſion of Changes. It is to be hoped indeed, that we have not yet ſunk far into the Decline of Letters: But, one Symptom there is of the Decay of Eloquence very conſpicuous: We have ſeen the Age of Points, Turns, and flowery Expreſſion; Faults, which all, young Perſons eſpecially, cannot be too earneſtly warned againſt. But we ſhall have a fitter Opportunity of diſcourſing hereafter on this Subject.

I HAVE purpoſely deferred hitherto, meaning to conclude with it, a Point much agitated, and variouſly decided by learned Men, "A "Compariſon of the *Greek* and *Roman* Elo-"quence;" concerning which, I ſhall hazard a Conjecture or two.

IF we ſhould ſuppoſe the Genius of each Nation to have been equal, which may be much doubted, yet there ſeem to be Reaſons, why the Advantage ſhould have lain on the Part of the *Athenians*. *Firſt*, Becauſe Eloquence was not at all ſtudied in *Rome* during the beſt Age of the Commonwealth, the Age of Virtue and Liberty: This we may determine

to

to have been, the Time from the Defeat of *Pyrrhus* until the entire Conqueſt of *Carthage* by the younger *Scipio*; during which Space, no Orator of Note is mentioned. Afterwards, little more remained than the Form of a Commonwealth; for the Struggles that enſued were not ſo properly Contentions for Freedom, as who ſhould be the Tyrant. In this latter Seaſon it was, that Eloquence began to appear, and grew up; a Seaſon too ſtormy for ſo tender a Plant. For, although diſturbed Times contribute often to confirm Eloquence, ſharpening the Wits and rouzing the Spirits of Men, yet this ſhould be an Eloquence already far advanced, ſtrong enough to reſiſt Difficulties, and which may gain new Strength by the Contention; if it be in its Infancy, ſuch tumultuous Seaſons nip it in its Bud, at leaſt keep down its Growth. This was the Caſe in *Rome*. For *Antony* and *Craſſus*, the firſt Orators of Note, and after them *Hortenſius* and *Tully*, flouriſhed in the moſt unſettled and corrupt Times of the Republick. In the Writings of this latter, we ſee the Struggles of dying Liberty; and with his laſt Groans expired together Freedom and Eloquence. In *Athens* it was otherwiſe. For, in the moſt glorious Age of that City, from the Time of *Themiſtocles* until the Death of *Phocion*, Eloquence and the polite Arts were no leſs eagerly attended to, than Arms. From whence it is reaſonable to conclude, that they muſt have been cultivated here more ſucceſsfully than

than in *Rome*, where they fell upon a general Dissolution of Manners, and a declining Government.

Secondly, The Time, during which Eloquence was cultivated in *Rome*, was also much shorter than in *Athens*; from whence its Improvement should seem to have been less. For, as we have just now said, *Antony* and *Crassus* were the first celebrated Orators among the *Romans*, and they were but the Generation before *Tully*, the last: Whereas, we may compute the Age of Eloquence at *Athens*, from *Solon* and *Pisistratus*, down to *Demetrius Phalereus*, which contained about 280 Years.

Thirdly, It seems, that the Language of the *Greeks* gave them great Advantages over the *Romans* in this Respect. The great Variety of Inflexions; the Number of different Terminations in which it aboundeth, many of them Vowels; the extraordinary Copiousness of the Language; its Harmony; the Ease of varying Expressions in it; of making new and more significant Words by Composition; the Number and Distinctness of its Particles, useful both for Emphasis and Perspicuity; were all important Advantages, which enabled the *Greeks*, on every Subject to cloath their Thoughts in a Dress easy and graceful. Whereas, the Language of the *Romans* being less rich, less harmonious, less pliable, they were compelled to have Recourse to Art; and, in order to supply these Defects, fell into such harsh Transpositions, as give an Air of Stiffness and Constraint

to

to their Writings; often occasion Obscurity; and tire the Ear by an uniform Cadence of the Periods.

Lastly, IF we rest the Merit of both Nations upon two Champions as it were, it seemeth to me that we shall be confirmed in the same Judgment. We cannot deny the *Roman* to have been possessed of the most extraordinary Endowments. Where do we meet with such Fruitfulness of Fancy? Sentiments so delicate, yet so just? Such Richness of Expression with so much Purity? In Panegyrick, such Pomp with Chastity of Stile; such Elegance without Affectation; such Abundance without Superfluity; so much Address in gaining the Affection and Attention of his Hearers; such Art in moving the Passions, those especially of the softer Kind, as Pity and Sorrow, in which he hath not any Rival? On the other Hand, it must be acknowledged, that the *Athenian* Orator is defective in some, inferior to him in most of these. But are not these, if they be real Wants, much more than compensated by a Crowd of Excellencies; Strength, Closeness, Vehemence, Rapidity inconceivable? What Clearness, what Conciseness, what Argument, what Energy, what Grandeur, what Fire, what divine Enthusiasm! The one winneth your Attention; this other commandeth it. One windeth about artfully until he gaineth you to his Purpose; this other forceth you to his. That is a soft gentle Stream, that gradually undermineth its Banks, and worketh a Passage as the

the Ground favours; the other is an impetuous Torrent, that bearing down all before it, rusheth on in a straight Course, and teareth to itself a Channel. The one entertains, sooths, perswades; the other convinces, terrifies, transports. In reading *Tully*, you admire the Orator, you are ever ready to cry out, "How "artful, how delicate, how touching this Sen-"timent! What an accomplished Speaker!" Read *Demosthenes*; you instantly lose Sight of the Man, and are engrossed by the Subject; you are every Moment ready to cry out, "Come, let us snatch up Arms, let us march "out against this *Philip*, this Tyrant, this "treacherous Invader of our Country." You catch the Speaker's Flame; you are *Athenians*; you are each, a *Demosthenes*.

LET us therefore, Gentlemen, diligently consider and consult these two great Models of Eloquence, both excellent, although different: Him especially, the Glory of *Athens*, whom *Tully* himself proposed as his Model, in whom if any Thing be wanting, it seemeth wanting not to the Artist, but to the Art. Let us read, let us study, let us commit to Memory, let us if we can, imitate him; assuring ourselves, that we then begin to have a Relish for true Eloquence, when we become pleased with his Writings [r].

[r] Ille se profecisse sciat, cui CICERO valdè placebit. QUINT. lib. 10. cap. 1.

LECTURE the Third.

Abstract of ARISTOTLE'*s Rhetorick.---Of* CICERO'*s Treatise concerning the Orator. Comparison of these two Tracts.*

I PROCEED now, according to the Method laid down in my last Lecture, to offer some Remarks upon the most celebrated Treatises concerning Eloquence, which remain to us from Antiquity. I do not mean to present you with large Abstracts of these, or a compleat Criticism upon them; an Undertaking of too great Length for the present Occasion, neither as it seemeth to me, very useful, as the Originals themselves deserve, and will, I hope, obtain your careful Perusal. My Design is no more, than to lay before you some Observations, which may induce you to make yourselves acquainted with these Writings, and may be of Use to you in the Study of them.

ARISTOTLE is the only one among the *Greeks* who hath written a general Treatise on this Art, which hath come down to us entire. Those who are accustomed to read the Essays of modern Criticks, consisting too often of a few superficial Remarks set off with some Embellishments of Fancy, are apt to be discouraged at first

first Entrance into this Book; which being the Result of long Study and Observation, tracing Things back to their Causes, and from thence descending to unfold the several particular Effects, demandeth continued Attention in the Reader: From hence, at first Sight, it wears a severe forbidding Aspect, presenting us with Toil, where we may have come with hope of Amusement. Yet be not deterred hereby; for ye may be assured, that if ye will bestow upon it the Care it deserveth, your Trouble shall be fully recompenced in the End. The Author's general Plan is this:

HAVING defined Rhetorick, to be the Art of finding out on all Subjects what is fitted to perswade, he sheweth it's Affinity to Logick; being like it, founded in the Nature of Man; and proposing to itself an End, Instruction or Conviction, by like Means, which are *Proofs*. From whence he proceedeth to deduce the Usefulness of the Art; especially to the Generality of Mankind, who cannot comprehend, or will not listen to strictly logical Reasoning. He then considers the different Kinds of it, the Deliberative, the Judicial, and Demonstrative. The End of the Deliberative is to prove that which is useful, or the contrary; to compare the Value of two Goods, or weigh what is honourable against that which is profitable. The End of the Judicial is to defend Property or Character when attacked, or attack where others defend. The End of the Demonstrative is to praise Virtue or blame Vice. In all which, the Author sheweth

ſheweth at large, what previous Knowlege the Orator ſhould have, in order to ſpeak well in each Kind; and he pointeth out with much Brevity, the Sources, from which he may derive Arguments in each.

THUS far he treateth of Rhetorick as an Art purely rational. But becauſe the Paſſions of Mankind do neceſſarily interfere in all Cauſes of Moment, and therefore the Orator who would perſuade muſt gain over theſe alſo, he goes on in his ſecond Book, to diſcourſe of them: Shewing diſtinctly: "Who are the "Men liable to each Paſſion: From what "Cauſes it ſprings: And towards what Kind "of Perſons it is directed." To which he addeth, an Account of the Varieties, that ariſe in the Manners of Men from the difference of Ages, Rank, and Fortune. This Part of his Work comprehends that which rendereth Eloquence generally moſt admired and ſucceſsful; and is the Product of deep Thought and exquiſite Diſcernment. Accordingly, it hath been always eſteemed a Maſterpiece; and although imitated by innumerable Writers, never equalled.

IN his laſt Book, he treateth of *Elocution*, or *Stile*; the Virtues of which he reduceth to Purity, Clearneſs, Propriety, and Ornament. Under this laſt Head he conſiders *Figures*, and *Compoſition* or the Arrangement of Words: Concluding the Whole, with a ſhort Account of the ſeveral Parts which make up a perfect Oration, namely the Exordium, Narration, Proof,

and

and Peroration; of the Design and proper Use of each Part.

In order to your reading this Work with Advantage, and forming a right Notion concerning it, there are two Remarks, which I would recommend to your Attention.

First, The Constitution of *Athens*, and the Disposition of the Inhabitants was such, that the Power of Eloquence grew exceedingly great, and became of mighty Importance, we may say Necessity, in opening the Way to all Dignities of the State. By Eloquence, were new Laws recommended; Magistrates elected or deposed; Treaties of War and Peace concluded: Even the Soldiery was to be harangued into Courage; and the Art of Speaking was requisite in a General scarcely less than the Art of War. These Advantages accruing from Eloquence made it very desirable, and much studied: From whence it came to pass, as it almost always happens where the Torrent of Fashion runs violently one Way, that many Pretenders to this Art appeared; undertaking, however unqualified, to instruct others therein; and all *Greece*, as we learn from the Writers of those Times, was over-run with numberless bad or ordinary Performances on that Subject. Hence those who spoke in Publick, were induced to leave the Road of plain Sense as a beaten Track, endeavouring to surprize and please by somewhat uncommon. And although at the Time in which our Author wrote, Eloquence had arrived to it's height in *Demosthenes*, yet

even

even then, a falſe Taſte had ſpread itſelf widely, and the Minds of Men were drawn away from a Love of Simplicity and Truth. Two Miſtakes prevailed very generally.

ONE was, a ſcrupulous Attachment to Elocution, to the Graces and Harmony of Stile, which were preferred before Strength of Argument and Energy of Diction. This Abuſe had its Riſe from the great Admiration, which had been for many Years, and was then, paid to *Iſocrates*, and had introduced an injudicious Imitation of his Manner. Perhaps he himſelf, who had grown old in poliſhing Stile, in weighing Words, and diſcovering Rules for harmonious Cadence, carried this Attention to Exceſs; being pure indeed, and elegant, yet as appears by his Writings, ſtill extant, Feeble and not without Affectation. This we have Cauſe to think was the Judgment paſt upon him by *Ariſtotle*, who wrote his Rhetorick profeſſedly in Oppoſition to this celebrated Teacher. For he was wonted to ſay, “ When *Iſocrates* teacheth “ Oratory, it is ſhameful for me to be ſilent.” Accordingly, his firſt and great Care is to lay a ſolid Foundation to Eloquence, to fix the Attention upon Things not upon Words: And having once eſtabliſhed this main Point, he delivereth ſuch Inſtructions concerning Language, as are conſiſtent with Nature and Reaſon.

A SECOND, and no leſs general Error was, The Cuſtom of Speakers addreſſing themſelves almoſt entirely to the Paſſions of their Judges.

In

In which, ſays our Author, they are encouraged by the univerſal Conſent of Writers concerning Rhetorick, who make this whole Art conſiſt in gaining over to their own Side, the Affections of their Hearers; and to this principal End direct all their Precepts: A Proceeding contrary to the Reaſon of Mankind; and even to the Laws of the beſt regulated Societies, which in Trials of great Importance forbid all Attempts to move the Paſſions [a].

HOWEVER, as this Method was moſt likely to be ſucceſsful where a whole People was the Judge in Cauſes of the greateſt Moment, it became the moſt admired Way of Speaking in *Athens*. As an Inſtance how far this pathetick Manner muſt have been abuſed, obſerve the Concluſion of the Oration againſt *Cteſiphon*, by *Eſchines*, who appears to have held the next Rank among Orators to *Demoſthenes*, and to have contended even with him for the Prize. "And now," ſaith he, "O Earth, and Sun, "and Virtue, and Prudence, and Learning "by which we diſtinguiſh Things excellent "from baſe, I have ſaid, I have aſſiſted the "Commonwealth. If my Accuſation hath "been juſt and worthy of the Commonwealth, "I have ſpoken as I deſigned; if defective, as "I could. Do ye, from what hath been ſaid "and admitted, pronounce Judgment, as may "be beſt and moſt honourable for the State."

WHICH Paſſage, his great Adverſary not undeſervedly derides [b], as a vain ſwelling Decla-

 mation,

[a] ARIST. Rhet. Book i. [b] DEMOST. pro Corona.

mation, fitter for a Tragedy, than a ſerious Cauſe, in which the Characters of two conſiderable Perſons were to be examined into, by an accurate ſtating of Facts, and impartial Reaſon. Now, if a Speaker of ſuch Experience and diſtinguiſhed Eminence as *Eſchines* was, could err in this groſs Manner, at the Concluſion of a very noble Oration, I believe we may aſſume it as certain, that the Exclamations of the vulgar Sort were highly abſurd and outrageous.

IT is therefore with a View to correct this great Abuſe, that our Author in the Treatiſe before us, ſets out with declaring, that the Firſt great Aim of an Orator ſhould be to perſuade by convincing the Underſtanding; that to this Purpoſe, he ſhould make himſelf Maſter of his Subject, and furniſh himſelf with rational Arguments on all Topicks; that Ornaments and Addreſs to the Paſſions ſhould be only an inferior and ſecondary Care. And even herein, he preſcribes to make Reaſon our Guide, teaching us not to attempt working upon the Paſſions by extravagant Figures and vague Exclamations; but from a perfect Deſcription of their Cauſes, Effects, and Motions, he lays down clear and unerring Principles concerning the Treatment of them.

A SECOND Remark which I propoſe to make is:---That we ſhould not expect more than the Author intended in his Work: The Ground of which Precaution is this. He wrote it ſolely for the Inſtruction of thoſe, who were to ſpeak

ſpeak in Publick, in the great Council, or before the Aſſembly of the People, concerning Matters relating to the State, or judicial Cauſes. Hence the Poet, the Hiſtorian, the Philoſopher, are not to ſearch here for Rules uſeful in their particular Studies and Kinds of Writing; which although contained in the general Extent of Eloquence, belong not to the Scheme of our Author.

NEITHER are we to imagine, that becauſe he doth not among the neceſſary Qualifications of an Orator mention Virtue, that he therefore thought ſlightly of it. He adheres to his particular End, The Art of Perſuaſion: And the Language and Appearance of Virtue, being alone neceſſary to that End, them he preſcribes; the Reality is the Care of another Science. It is his Buſineſs to prepare his Combatant for the Battle, to furniſh him with Arms of Proof, to teach him the Uſe of them; but he leaves to the Moraliſts to direct him in the Juſtice of his Caſe.

AFTER what hath been ſaid, it is needleſs to add any Thing in Praiſe of this Work. It is, however, worthy of Obſervation concerning it, that beſides its profeſſed Intention of inſtructing in the Rules of Eloquence, there are two Advantages attainable from the Study of it, which render it peculiarly uſeful to young Perſons.

ONE is, that it is a perfect Model of good Order; by attending to which, they may learn to range their Thoughts methodically. Every

Part is ſo diſpoſed as to prepare the Way for that which ſucceeds, the ſucceeding gives Strength to that which went before, and in it's Turn introduceth what is to follow; ſo that the whole Book is one firm, regular, well-compacted Piece, without Flaw or Inequality: Whereas in moſt Performances, even in thoſe abounding with what is good, one meets with ſome Things ſuperflous, others miſplaced, which raiſe in the Hearer, Diſtaſte or Confuſion.

A SECOND Advantage is, that from hence they may learn to expreſs their Thoughts with Brevity. There is much Shortneſs in all the Writings of *Ariſtotle*. In this Treatiſe particularly, no Expreſſion is idle, every Word hath meaning; which gives Vivacity, Force and Spirit, is a great Perfection in all Kinds of Writing, in a peculiar Manner is the Life and Soul of the Didactic. For Precepts ſhould be ſhort, that they may be attended to and remembered.

THERE is farther an Excellence rarely found with Conciſeneſs, yet the moſt neceſſary of all, Clearneſs; which two we find here reconciled. Whatever Difficulties occur, ariſe manifeſtly not from the Diction, throughout ſingularly ſtrong and proper; but ſometimes from Depth and Subtilty of Thought: Sometimes from the Mixture of Logical Terms. For as this Philoſopher had very much improved, and as it were invented a new Logick, he continued always to ſhew a great Fondneſs for it, and introduceth it upon all fit Occaſions: So that if we would underſtand his Writings perfectly, we ſhould

ſhould read his Logick in his own Language: A Study, which if it was for ſome Ages over-rated, hath been of late too much deſpiſed, and, it ſeems, raſhly exploded. Which however, if it were for this Reaſon only, that it is neceſſary to the right Knowlege of the beſt antient Philoſophers and Criticks, ought certainly not to be neglected. If they refined formerly, and ſubtilized too much, we are in danger from a Fault perhaps worſe, an empty ſuperficial Elegance.

AMONG the *Romans*, *Tully* wrote many Things concerning Eloquence, of which a conſiderable Part hath periſhed, but the moſt celebrated Treatiſe remains, His three Books concerning *The Orator*. This Work he hath thrown into a Form entirely different from that of *Ariſtotle*, chuſing in Imitation of *Plato*, the Manner of Dialogue. One Advantage of this Form is, that it renders the Work more entertaining. The Fame of the Perſonages introduced, uſually of high Conſideration; The Deſcription of their ſeveral Characters and Manners; The Contraſt of theſe expreſt and kept up in the Diſcourſe attributed to each; The Variety of Opinions, and friendly Contention of well conducted Controverſy exhibit to the Mind a Kind of dramatick Entertainment; by theſe Means taking off from the Dryneſs which almoſt always attends upon a long Courſe of Precepts.

BUT on the other Hand, it hath this great Diſadvantage, that it lengthens the Diſcourſe, ſometimes

ſometimes to a Degree of Prolixity. The Prefaces, the Characters of Perſons, their mutual Praiſes or Apologies, with Interruptions of Argument neceſſary to keep up the Spirit of Converſation, every where breaking in upon, and ſuſpending the main Deſign. To which you may add the Genius of *Tully* himſelf, leſs cloſe and acute than that of *Ariſtotle*. Hence thoſe many Digreſſions; A Panegyrick upon Eloquence; Whether an Orator ought to be acquainted with the whole Circle of Science; Whether it be neceſſary that he ſhould be ſkilled in the Civil Law; Whether Eloquence or Philoſophy ſhould be preferred: All which are as it were *Epiſodes*, having a Relation to the Subject, rather than being properly Parts of it. Theſe employ the greater Share of the Firſt Book. Beſide which, it contains ſome Remarks on the three Kinds of Eloquence above-mentioned; on the Parts of a Diſcourſe; with ſome Rules for Pronunciation; and concludes with mentioning thoſe Sciences, the Knowlege of which is moſt conducive to form a juſt and ſolid Eloquence.

THUS far *Craſſus* is the principal Speaker. To whom *Antonius* ſucceeding in the Second Book, treats more at large of the different Kinds of Cauſes; of the Parts of an Oration, their Scope and Uſe: Then proceeds to diſcourſe of the Paſſions: In all which he followeth *Ariſtotle* with little Variation. Afterwards, he enlarges more copiouſly on a Topick ſcarcely touched upon by the *Greek*, engaging *Cæſar*

to

to discourse concerning Facetiousness and delicate Raillery; an Art, oftentimes of the greatest Use in publick Pleading; but one of the most difficult to conduct well: And he concludes with some Remarks upon Memory.

In the Third Book, *Crassus*, who resumes the Discourse, treats of Elocution or Stile. The whole Art hereof he makes to consist in two Things; In Ornament, which gives Majesty and Grandeur to Discourse: And, *Secondly*, In speaking suitably to the Subject. For he distinguisheth two Kinds of Ornaments. One, which extendeth itself over the whole Discourse, which giveth to it Ease and Dignity, commands the Attention, and raises the Admiration of the Hearer. The other consisteth in the right Use of Figures, which are to be placed only in certain Parts. To set off and compleat the Whole, he recommends great Care in the *Composition:* Under which Head he considereth with the utmost Accuracy, the Ranging of Words, the Turning of Periods, and Harmony of Cadence. He closes the Whole, with some Directions concerning just, animated, and graceful Action, a Care of the greatest Importance.

This is the Substance of the last, and in my Opinion, if I may venture where all is excellent to give the Preference to one Part, the best Book; as indeed it was natural to expect that it should be so; That *Cicero*, who himself excelled all Mankind in the ornamental Part of Eloquence, should excel most in treating of that Part.

It

IT muſt be an agreeable Sight, to behold two of the greateſt Perſons of Antiquity engaged in the ſame Career, and to compare the Effects of very excellent, yet different Talents, exerted on the ſame Subject. If we were to draw a Parallel between theſe two celebrated Performances, perhaps we ſhould form ſome ſuch Judgment as the following.

IN each of theſe Tracts, we behold ſtrongly expreſt the Character of the Writer. The *Greek* ſpeaks itſelf the Work of an Author turned to Speculation, one of ſevere Study, and intenſe Thought, a Genius ſubtile, penetrating, and profound. The *Latin* diſcovers the Hand of a Writer long in high Office, poliſhed by Converſation and Commerce with the Great, a Genius rich, agreeable, and delicate. The one is ſtrong, grave, and cloſe: The other eloquent, eaſy, and copious. That addreſſes himſelf to Reaſon alone: This calleth in the Aſſiſtance of Imagination. You may liken *Ariſtotle*'s Book to a vaſt Magazine, compleatly furniſhed with all Materials and Inſtruments uſeful to an Orator, all diſpoſed in the moſt exact Order; yet their very Abundance produces a ſeeming Diſorder; and in this Profuſion of Treaſure, where no Space remains unpoſſeſt, Things moſt valuable ſeem piled up negligently, as if vulgar and ordinary: *Cicero*'s is a much ſmaller Store, and for the moſt Part ſupplied from the other; but he has poliſhed every Thing to ſo high a Luſtre, and hath ranged them with ſuch Skill, that they appear in the moſt advantageous Light,

and

and even Trifles in him are Things of Value. The one excelleth in Energy; the other in Beauty.

Ariſtotle never dwelleth upon a Thought, giveth ſhort, and here and there ſeemingly imperfect, but bold and maſterly, Strokes: *Cicero* carrieth every Thought to its utmoſt Perfection; and you ſee his whole Work finiſhed with Touches of the moſt patient and exquiſite Art. As *Cicero*, when writing of Philoſophy, by enlivening and adorning the Dryneſs of his Matter diſcovers the Orator; ſo *Ariſtotle*, treating of Oratory, diſcovers the Philoſopher, traceing Things back to their firſt Cauſes, and reducing all as far as may be, to fixed Principles. This latter engages your Attention by gratifying your Curioſity; you are ſtill pleaſed, becauſe ſtill learning: *Cicero* hath little new, but ſo embelliſheth the old as to give it the Charms of Novelty. Reading the former you are in the State of one travelling through a ſtrange Country, always pleaſed, becauſe every Step opens a new Proſpect: The other, it is true, leads you through a Country already known, but ſo Beautiful both from Nature and Art, that no Repetition maketh it tireſome; you ſee indeed what is familiar, but in ſuch Lights that it is always charming.

THE *Roman* it is owned hath this Advantage, that writing of Oratory, himſelf a moſt excellent Orator, he exemplifieth his Precepts in his Diſcourſe, at once Teacher and Pattern: On the

the other Hand, in Strength of Reaſon, in manly Brevity, in Depth of Thought, in ſolid Reflexion, and capacious comprehenſive Genius, the *Athenian* is undoubtedly ſuperior. If you are not capable of Improvement in Eloquence, from reading *Cicero*'s Work, you reap no Advantage: Whereas with Reſpect to *Ariſtotle* we may pronounce, that every attentive Reader cannot but receive much Benefit, from the vaſt Fund of good Senſe, the great Inſight into human Nature, and the curious Obſervation, which form the peculiar Praiſe of this judicious, weighty, accurate Treatiſe. There remain other Rhetorical Writers of Note, whom I ſhall proceed to conſider in the next Lecture.

LECTURE

LECTURE the Fourth.

The Temple or Palace of ELOQUENCE, A VISION.

I PROPOSED to carry on in this Lecture the Scheme begun in the last, and to lay before you in the same Manner, some Account of other celebrated Treatises concerning Rhetorick, remaining to us from Antiquity, those especially of *Quintilian* and *Longinus*. But reflecting, that the latter of these is very familiar to you, that the other is both extremely useful throughout, and very easy, I doubted, whether Abstracts of the like Kind were fitting in this Case, and whether it were not better to refer you to the Originals themselves.

WHILST I was revolving this Point in my Mind, Accident threw into my Way a little Work, which as it is probably unknown to you, as the Manner of it is altogether different from that which I have hitherto employed, and the Subject, if not the same, very nearly connected with this before us, I judged that it might answer the same End, and prove more entertaining. It is a Poem written in *Greek*, by an Author whose Name is not preserved, about the

the ſeventh Century, as may be conjectured from ſome hiſtorical Alluſions contained in it; in a Stile too much indeed infected by the Barbariſm of the Age, but upon a Plan worthy of Notice. I ſhall here give you an Abridgment of it, ſtripped of thoſe Ornaments and Digreſſions which it weareth in its poetical Dreſs.

As I walked in the great Portico of the Temple of *Minerva*, and looked down upon the City of *Athens*, I could not help deploring the great Decay of Arts and Sciences, particularly of Eloquence, for which ſhe had been renowned over the whole Earth: An Art, to which indeed I had long applied myſelf with much Induſtry, but with little Encouragement, or Hope of Succeſs. Whilſt I was wrapt up in Contemplations of this Sort, a Perſon deſcending as it ſeemed, from the Heavens, ſuddenly alighted before me. By his Form, by the Wings on his Heels, and the Caduceus in his Hand, I knew him immediately to be the God *Mercury*. He addreſſed himſelf to me in the following Manner.

I AM not unacquainted with the Subject of your preſent Meditations, with your Doubts, and Perplexity. Think not that the Degeneracy of this Age in all good Arts, in Eloquence eſpecially, which is almoſt wholly extinguiſhed, ariſeth from a Change in the Genius of Mankind, the Cauſe to which you ſeem inclined to aſcribe it. No: Human Nature is ſtill the ſame; the Difference ſpringeth from the different Uſe and Application of its Talents: At preſent

present the Methods of Education and Study are totally wrong; consequently the whole Form and Model of Speech have been corrupted. To give you a more distinct Conception of this Matter, added he, pointing upwards with his Finger, look yonder.

RAISING my Eyes at these Words, I was surprized to see a high Mountain, with a magnificent Structure on the Summit. Its Foot was covered with thick Woods, cut into a Variety of Paths, in which wandered a Multitude of People. That Edifice, said he, is the Palace of Eloquence, the Daughter of Liberty. Those, whom you behold scattered over the low Grounds, are they, who flattering themselves with the Hope of attaining easily to it, wander at the Foot of the Mountain, through Paths, which engage them in endless Delusion. But come, I will lead you thither.

THE Road by which we were to ascend, was very steep and narrow; barred at the Entrance by a great Gate. The Keeper of which, an aged and venerable Person, whose Looks gave Indications of extraordinary Penetration and Sagacity, examined with much Strictness all who sought for Admission, and rejected far the greater Number. His Name, said my Guide, is *Genius*, without a Passport from whom, no Man can arrive at the Mansion of Eloquence.

HE made me observe during our Ascent, that the Road toward the Mountain-top grew much wider and smoother, having been opened and levelled by the Labour of several excellent Men in antient Times; but was now in a great Degree overgrown with Brambles and Weeds, as it had been for ſome Ages almoſt wholly unfrequented. For even thoſe few who were admitted at the Gate, impatient of the Slowneſs, and extreme Severity and Harſhneſs of *Induſtry*, who is appointed the Guide to conduct them, ſoon quitting the ſtraight Road, turned into ſome one of the By-paths, that ſtruck off from it, and ſeemed far more eaſy and pleaſant.

I SHALL not detain you with a Deſcription of the Temple itſelf, which is given at full Length by our Poet. It may be ſufficient to obſerve, that it joined to the utmoſt Magnificence great Simplicity, its Ornaments being ſuch, that while they beautified the Fabrick, they ſeemed neceſſary Parts of it.

UPON entering, we found the firſt great Apartment adorned with Pictures of the moſt celebrated Poets. For, as my Conductor took Notice on the Occaſion, in all Nations, Poeſy was the firſt Effort of Eloquence, opening the Way by Degrees for a more juſt and natural Stile.

IN the next, we obſerved the Portraits of the moſt famous Hiſtorians, and of thoſe who recorded the Actions and Sayings of great Perſons.

IN the third, which was by far the moſt ample and grand, were placed the Statues of excellent Orators; ſuch as by Means of their Eloquence chiefly, had governed great States, who obtained a Sovereignty over the Minds of Men

Men more powerful and lasting, as well as far more glorious, than Force can confer, or Policy ensure. Among these I distinguished *Pericles* and *Phocion*, the younger *Gracchus* and *Julius Cæsar*.

As my Guide was pointing out some of these Persons to me, one who appeared of Dignity by his Air and Train of Attendants, in passing saluted him with a profound Respect. Upon my enquiring, who this was; You are to know, answered he, that all who propose to excel as Orators, endeavour to gain Admission into this Temple, that they may be here presented to the Deity, and receive her Approbation; the Consequence whereof is, that they are immediately admitted into familiar Conversation with all the famous Orators of Antiquity, who abide here for ever in the Palace of their great Patroness. From whence, after a certain Time, returning to Earth, they are assured of obtaining the highest Honours among Mankind, and their Writings are consecrated to Immortality.

Now such as have conquered the Difficulties of the Ascent, are directed to address themselves to this Person concerning whom you enquire, who is the celebrated Critick *Quintilian*; that he may examine into their Qualifications, and lead such as he approveth of, into the inner Part of the Temple. You may read much of the Character of the Man in his Form and Air. You see he is grave in his Aspect, plain in his Dress, composed in all his Motions. His peculiar Excellence as a Critick is, that he descendeth to the

the loweſt Elements of Rhetorick, leadeth from thence by the Hand as it were, to the higheſt and moſt refined. He is every where ſtrictly methodical, perſpicuous, and ſimple, entereth into the moſt minute Detail, yet is never tedious, dry, or inſipid, animating the Whole with a lively, yet well-governed Fancy. Fallen upon an Age when Eloquence had for ſome Time declined, you may indeed diſcover in him, ſome little Taint of the general Infection, from which even his exquiſite Judgment could not wholly preſerve him [*a*]; yet he ſet himſelf firmly to withſtand the growing Corruption; and laboureth above all Things to eſtabliſh a true manly Taſte, joining with the familiar Exactneſs of a Teacher the Spirit and Elevation of an Orator.

BUT his Charge doth not extend ſo far, as to give immediate Admiſſion to the Preſence of the Deity. He delivers thoſe committed to his Care over to another, to the Perſon, whom you behold yonder. He ſeemeth to be far advanced in Years, and appeareth as fixed in profound Thought; yet obſerve what Penetration, what Fire in his Eyes. This is the Sage of *Stagira*. He it is, that hath unfolded all the ſecret Treaſures of Eloquence, who teacheth to pierce into human Nature, to know the Heart, and by Means of that Knowledge to obtain an abſolute

[*a*] See the Preface to the ſixth Book. And he very frequently cloſeth his Paragraphs with a pointed Sentence; many of which have too much of the brilliant Oppoſition, himſelf condemneth.

absolute Government over it. The most subtle and learned of Philosophers, he is likewise the most judicious of Criticks.

THE Candidates delivered to him he consigneth to two thin shadowy Forms you behold near him, *Silence* and *Study*. Having afterwards fully instructed them, he at length presents them to the Goddess. On which Occasions, one of the Antients, Orator or Critick, who are suffered to abide here in her Presence, pronounceth an Harangue, containing usually, with some Commendation of the admitted, Admonitions useful to be observed by him hereafter in the Course of his Studies and Conversation among Men.

FEW Occasions of this Kind have happened of late. But fortunately just now falleth out one. For *Marcus Rufus*, a *Roman* Senator, not unknown to you, a worthy Imitator of the Antients, is about to be presented. You see the Crowd pressing inward towards the Center of the Fabrick: That is the Cause; and I know that the Critick *Longinus* is to pronounce the Oration. Follow me; I will give you the Opportunity of a very pleasing Spectacle.

So saying, he led me forward into the Midst of the Temple. It was a spacious Dome; towards the upper End of which, was placed the Goddess, upon a Throne of pure Gold. Behind her, stood the Genius of *Athens*, known by her Olive-branch and the Bird of *Pallas*. On the other Side, towards the left Hand of the Throne, the Genius of *Rome*; leaning on her

 Shield,

Shield, grasping a Spear in her Hand, and bearing an Eagle on her Helmet.

ON the Steps of the Throne, sat Contemplation, with her Eyes fixed on the Ground, and her Arms folded. Near her, stood Perswasion in the Attitude of one speaking, with her Arm stretched out, Fire in her Eye, and irresistable Magick in her Tongue. Below, were placed the *Passions*, each with her proper Symbols, Handmaids of the Goddess, always attending to obey her Orders. In the Countenance of the Goddess there was somewhat inexpressibly charming; the Tone of her Voice bewitched the Heart.

BEFORE her lay open a vast Book, upon which she ever and anon cast her Eye, as making it the Rule of her Judgment and Conduct. This is named the Volume of Nature. She held in her Hand a Mirror of transcendent Brightness, to which she applied all Compositions that were presented for her Approbation: Whatsoever was not of the right Standard this immediately reduced to Ashes: Where it did not consume the Whole in this Manner, yet it never failed to destroy some, oftentimes the greater Part, leaving that which was pure, alone untouched. This, my Instructor informed me, was named the Mirror of Truth.

HERE my Author proceeds to describe the whole Ceremony of presenting the new Orator. He gives also the Oration pronounced by *Longinus*, much too long to be translated on the present Occasion: It is besides chiefly an Abstract

Abſtract of the Treatiſe concerning the Sublime, probably little known in thoſe Days of Darkneſs, but with which ye are all well acquainted: The general Heads are theſe.

HE begins with congratulating *Rufus* upon the Choice he had made, upon his Perſeverance and good Progreſs in the Study of Eloquence; upon which, he makes a ſhort, but lofty Panegyrick. From this general Eulogy, he deſcends to one particular Branch of it; the *Sublime*. This he ſhews to be the greateſt Excellence, that human Compoſitions can attain to: That it may be, if not acquired, yet improved by Art and Precept. He proceeds to diſtinguiſh the ſeveral Fountains from which it flows: Points out the right Uſe of it; and warns againſt ſuch Faults as are moſt oppoſite to it. It dwells not, ſaith he, with Correctneſs; faultleſs Sublimity is unattainable to Mortals. But, then it atones abundantly for ſuch little Specks as are unavoidable; it charms, it elevates, it tranſports. It is a Torrent rapid, irreſiſtable; a Conflagration conſuming every Thing around; a Thunderbolt breaking, tearing, conſuming whatever is oppoſed to it.

NATURE, adds he, hath given to you, *Marcus Rufus*, Talents for this Sublimity, this Perfection of Eloquence. Labour inceſſantly in cultivating them. Elevate your Mind by the Contemplation of heavenly Things; by the Study and Practice of Virtue. Make the Writings of uncorrupted Antiquity familiar. Eſpecially bend all your Force to reſemble theſe Heroes, whom you behold now encircling the Throne of our Goddeſs. After your Return to Mortals, conſider theſe when you are about to write or ſpeak, as they are at this Hour, your Spectators and Hearers; and endeavour to produce nothing unworthy of ſuch Judges, as *Homer*, *Plato*, and *Demoſthenes*, the moſt ſublime of all Mankind [*b*].

I LISTENED, continues my Author, with Attention and Delight to this Diſcourſe, remarking through the Whole, though the Stile, as my Guide obſerved to me, wanted the Simplicity and Purity of old *Athens*, high Inſtances of that Sublimity, which the Speaker recommended. Immediately turning towards my Conductor, with Intention to expreſs my Pleaſure and Admiration, how greatly was I aſtoniſhed, to find the whole Scene I know not how, entirely changed!

I FOUND myſelf in a Place altogether different from the former, though I could perceive a Similitude in certain Reſpects, as in the Figure and firſt Appearance. In all the new Objects preſented here to my View, there ſeemed induſtriouſly aimed at a Reſemblance of the former, amidſt the ſtrongeſt real Unlikeneſs. The Fabrick itſelf was a huge Pile of Gothick Architecture. I beheld in every Part a Superfluity of Ornaments, crowded without Unity of Deſign or Elegance; fitted by the Help of Varniſh and Gilding to dazzle the unſkilful Eye. The Deity adored in this Temple was ſeated on a Throne,

[*b*] See the Treatiſe of LONGINUS.

Throne, which, as well as the Garments ſhe wore, ſeemed all on Fire with what appeared to be precious Stones; for all their Luſtre was counterfeit. Her own Beauty likewiſe was artificial. Her Face glowed with Paint. Her Behaviour, her Looks, Geſture, the Tone of her Voice, were affected and unnatural.

SUITABLE to their Queen were her Attendants. On one Side ſtood ſquint-eyed Error. On the other, Ignorance, with her Head wrapt in perpetual Fogs. There was Flattery, painting the Viſages of her Votaries, and at the ſame Time covertly beſmearing them with Filth all over. Yonder was Imagination, in a Dreſs of Rainbow Colours, ſtrowing half-withered Flowers on barren Rocks, or over Beds of Snow. Here you might ſee *Bombaſt* ſtrutting with the Airs and Stature of a Giant, but ſurveyed more accurately he is found to be a Dwarf mounted upon tall Stilts. There you might behold *Declamation*, roaring aloud with indefatigable Lungs; while *Nonſenſe*, a many-headed Monſter, prompted him: And *Sleep* followed behind, diffuſing Numbneſs and Inſenſibility over the yawning Multitudes.

I VIEWED theſe, and many other like Monſters with Surprize and Horror. "Where am "I? How have I changed the moſt beautiful "Objects in Nature for the moſt ſhocking? "Speak, O divine Inſtructor, explain this "Myſtery." This, anſwered he, you may eaſily perceive to be the Palace of falſe Eloquence. Here it is, that all the Roads which

you

you observed in our Ascent to branch off from the great one, do at last terminate. Men are flattered into them from their appearing Ease and Openness; and enchanted by the false Glories of this Place, when they have arrived here, imagine themselves possessed of all they wished for. While the Temple of Eloquence is almost deserted, behold how this is crowded! Multitudes hourly pour in, and kneel by Thousands before the Throne, praying to be admitted into the Train of this pretended Divinity. Such at present is the Blindness of Mankind. Hither *Greece* and *Rome* send all their Sons. Princes, Consuls, Senators, Priests, Patricians, and People, all fall down before her Footstool. The Road traced out by illustrious Antiquity is become unfrequented.

BEHOLD there, among other Suitors, many well known to you; some already renowned amongst you; others who are soon to be admired for rhetorical Compositions. Sophists, who creep in long, tedious, cold Declamation: Speakers, who delight in Oppositions, in sparkling Conceits, and make every Period an Epigram: Declaimers, who soar in Hyperboles, and lose Sight of despised Reason: Advocates and Haranguers, who on the most serious Subject profusely scatter the faded Flowers of puerile Imagination. For such at present are the Persons honoured with Applause, who bear the rare and valuable Title of Genius, and are set up as Governors of the publick Taste.

YET

YET plunged in Darkneſs as the preſent Age is, darker ſhall ſucceed. A thick Cloud of Ignorance ſhall cover the whole Earth. Error and falſe Eloquence ſhall reign abſolute over Mankind. But deſpair not, this State of Barbariſm ſhall not laſt until the End. I ſee Truth and Eloquence return. Their pure Luſtre though for ever baniſhed from forſaken *Greece*, once more illumines their favourite *Italy*. It ſpreads beyond the *Alps*; It enlightens the adjoining Continent: I behold their Beams extending Weſtward,---beyond the Limits of *Albion*, over *Iſlands* yet ſcarcely known to Fame.

IN the mean Time, O Mortal admitted to the View of Secrets, hidden from all others of the human Race, fail not in applying this Knowlege to thy own Advantage, ſince thou can'ſt not at preſent to the Publick;---for the Fates forbid as yet the Converſion of a deluded World. Firſt and principally, ſeek after Wiſdom and Virtue; For Elevation of Soul can alone ſupport Sublimity of Genius. Next, Be unwearied in tracing back Eloquence to it's true Source, the Monuments of pure Antiquity, of thoſe Heroes whom you have lately ſeen. Imitate their Solidity, their Method, their Juſtneſs, their Purity, their Force, their Sublimity. Hope not however, though you ſhould ſucceed well in this noble Ambition, to obtain the Applauſe of your Fellow-Citizens; neither be diſcouraged by their Cenſures: Leave them to their own depraved degenerate Taſte.

HERE

HERE he ceafed to fpeak. Tranfported with Delight and Gratitude, I was about to throw myfelf at the Feet of my great Inftructor, when looking round, I perceived him no more. Together with the God, the whole Scene, Goddefs, Votaries, and Temple vanifhed, like a Dream from the waking Eye. I found myfelf as at firft, in the Temple of *Minerva*, and beheld only the City of *Athens*, the Summits of whofe Houfes were now gilded by the Rays of the fetting Sun.

I RETURNED homeward, meditating deeply on what I had feen, much delighted, and as it feemed, not a little inftructed.

LECTURE the Fifth.

History of Eloquence among the Moderns.—*Concerning Languages*;---*particularly* English.

WE have now taken a ſhort View of the Riſe and Progreſs of Eloquence, and have given a Sketch of the moſt celebrated Treatiſes concerning it, which remain from Antiquity. It may not be uſeleſs or unentertaining to proceed a little farther. Caſt your Eyes nearer Home, and obſerve what the Induſtry of modern Ages hath performed in this Way. That this Speculation may be of ſome Advantage, I propoſe,

Firſt, To lay before you ſome Remarks on the State of Eloquence ſince the Reſtoration of Learning in *Europe*:

And then, To point out the Uſe which is to be made of theſe Reflexions.

Italy claims our firſt Notice, as it had the Merit of being the firſt in the Revival of Letters, after a long Interval of Ignorance and Barbariſm. We ſhall find confirmed by what happened there, an Obſervation made before concerning *Greece*, that Verſe was cultivated, and brought near to Perfection, ſooner than Proſe.

Dante

Dantè flouriſhed about the End of the 13th Century, when as yet there were no Writings of Note in Proſe. Although the Plan of his Poem be faulty, and many of his Expreſſions are now become obſolete, yet for Sublimity of Thought, for lively Deſcription, for Strength and poetick Fire, he hath not been excelled by any, who followed him.

AFTER him, at no great Diſtance, came *Petrarch*; who although inferior in Taſte and Sentiment, yet improved upon his Numbers; and ſeems thus early to have brought Verſification to it's Perfection.

MUCH about the ſame Time with this latter, appeared *Boccace*; the firſt who applied himſelf with Succeſs to poliſh and refine Proſe; excelling in familiar Narration, as writing in a clear, eaſy, and pure Stile. It received not till near two Centuries after, it's laſt finiſhing, acquiring Strength and Harmony from *Machiavel* and *Guicciardino*; what Changes it hath ſince undergone, being eſteemed rather for the worſe: About which Time alſo we may fix the moſt flouriſhing Æra of Poetry, in *Arioſto*, who hath adorned the wildeſt, moſt extravagant Plan, with all the Charms of Diction and Harmony of Numbers.

QUICKLY after this Period, the true Manner began to decline in both Kinds of Eloquence. A Love of Points and Turns, or as they named them *Concetti*, ſoon after almoſt univerſally prevailed. This was introduced, at leaſt was rendered faſhionable (for the original of them may

be

be referred to *Petrarch)* by the fertile and beautiful Genius of *Tasso*: Is yet much stronger in *Guarini*: And *Marini* [a], for a long Time the most admired of their Poets, is over-run with it. And the same Infection was spread through the co-temporary Writers of Prose.

If we pass the *Alps*, we shall behold nearly the same Course of Things. Long before any tolerable Orator appeared in *France*, *Marot* flourished. His Verse in many Respects, particularly for Ease and Simplicity, or as they chuse to name it *Naiveté*, is much celebrated at this Day. Succeeding Writers indeed lost the Vein he had opened: yet it was not till after it had been recovered, and Poesy much cultivated and refined by *Racan*, and principally by *Malherbe*, that *Balzac* and *Voiture* began to improve and polish Prose, as yet irregular and rude: And *Corneille* had carried poetical Eloquence to it's Height, before Prose-writing had received it's last Perfection from *Bossuet*, and *Bourdaloue*.

From thence, as we observed it to have happened in *Italy*, a Change in Manners began to take Place; the florid and affected, which exist indeed at all Times, but are kept down and vanquished in the Days of true Genius, began openly

[a] See the *Adonis*; of which *Milton* gives the following very just Character:

Qui canit Assyrios divum prolixus amores,
Mollis, & Ausonias stupefecit carmine Nymphas.

Luxuriant in his Strain, of am'rous Themes
Luscious and soft, he sings; *Italian* Dames
Admire his sparkling Song, and catch the pleasing Flames.

openly to prevail. Recommended by a Perſon of admired Talents, one of lively Imagination and pure and harmonious Stile, *Flechier*, it throve apace, and ſpread widely; being ambitiouſly purſued by all the Writers of middle Rank; and infecting in no ſmall Degree ſome of the higheſt, as *Fontenelle*, who valuable as he is, indeed excellent in many Reſpects, yet aboundeth with theſe falſe Brilliants: At this Day their moſt admired Genius, who hath excelled ſcarcely leſs in Proſe than in Verſe, ſhews a manifeſt Fondneſs for theſe ill-judged Ornaments. And they are ſcarcely any where more conſpicuous, than in Pieces delivered from the Pulpit, where they are certainly moſt unbecoming.

FROM this Account, I cannot help ſtopping to repeat one Obſervation: That whenever Eloquence hath arrived to it's Height in a Country, the firſt Step towards Declenſion is generally this Epigrammatick Taſte. One Cauſe of which may be, That the firſt Places in Reputation being already poſſeſt, Writers of Genius labouring to open for themſelves new and untrodden Paths to Fame, ſtrike off from the Road choſen by the others: And as this pointed Way of Writing hath the Appearance of diſtinguiſhed Excellence, being quick and ſparkling, they readily fall into that: Which coming thus recommended, ſoon gaineth Admirers, and groweth the reigning Faſhion; the more ſpeedily, as up to a certain Degree, it is perhaps one of the moſt eaſy Kinds of Writing to a Perſon of lively

lively Imagination; in which State of Things, the more Wit a Man hath, he runs the greater Hazard of being involved in this epidemic Contagion. It is with Unwillingneſs that I add, Is not this in ſome Sort the Caſe of a late Writer [b] of that Nation, who joining very extenſive Knowlege to profound Senſe and extreme Vivacity, could not yet wholly avoid this Temptation of Points and Oppoſitions, and ſeemeth juſtly chargeable with Affectation, Refinement, and Obſcurity?

If we turn our Eyes homeward, we ſee ſtill the ſame Order. *Engliſh* Proſe, which was written three hundred Years ago, is not now intelligible: Yet how finely did *Chaucer* write in Verſe long before that Time? Unequal, it is true, often unmuſical, yet how ſtrong, how ſmooth, how beautiful frequently are his Lines! Every where happy in Imagination, and that Enthuſiaſm which forms the Eſſence of Poeſy, he is very often not inferior in Elocution, and often far ſuperior, to all who have attempted to tranſlate him into a modern Dreſs, even although *Dryden* is one of that Number. Succeeding Times of national Confuſion and Miſery ſtopped all Progreſs of Letters. In the Reign of *Henry* the Eighth, being encouraged in the ſouthern Parts of *Europe*, they revived in *England* alſo. The *Latin* Language was written with great Elegance by Sir *Thomas Moor*, *Linacer*, *Aſcham*: And we find at the ſame Time the Dawn of Eaſe, Harmony, and Politeneſs

[b] Monſ. *de Monteſquieu* in, L'Eſprit des loix.

nefs in the Mufe of Lord *Surrey*, who feems to have been the firft that wrote in Blank Verfe, at leaft with any Degree of Elegance: As *Triffino* about the fame Time introduced the Ufe of it into *Italy*, in an Epic Poem and a Tragedy; fince the Time of which latter, *(Sophonifba,)* it hath kept Poffeffion of the Drama. The *French* Tongue is of a Frame too feeble to fupport Verfe without Rhime.

DURING Queen *Elizabeth*'s aufpicious Reign, all Branches of Literature were happily cultivated. Yet *Spencer* had raifed Verfification to its utmoft Perfection in the peculiar Stile of Poefy which he chofe, before Profe had met with equal Improvement from the Pen of a *Hooker*, and a *Rawleigh*; whofe Writings will remain for ever the Model of a ftrong, pure, and mafculine Stile. It hath been juftly doubted, whether the Alterations made in later Times have improved their Manner, yet I think it muft be acknowledged, that their Stile is not faultlefs, being hard, long, and cloudy.

THE Language was in a great Meafure new-moulded by the Writers in *Charles* the fecond's Days. Their Manner refembles the Humour of the Times, abandoned wholly to Pleafure; it is eafy, and flowing, but loofe, and carelefs, and irregular.

SUCCEEDING Authors have in fome Degree corrected thefe Faults; but it may be queftioned, whether they have not fallen into, and encouraged others equally wrong. Even in *Addifon*, however worthy of Refpect on Ac-

count

count of the Cause, being that of Virtue, in which he was engaged; however pleasing for the Beauty of his Genius and Exactness of his Judgment; however amiable for the Vein of pure and original Humour running through all his Writings; yet it seems, that a critical Eye may spy some Defects, in this Article of Language: If I might be allowed to hint at any Thing amiss in this excellent Person, I would ask, Is there not too much of laboured Elegance in it? Are there not too frequent Oppositions? Periods measured out into equal corresponding Members, and falling with too uniform a Cadence? In short, too much of Art and Study; exquisite Beauty, if not too nicely and sollicitously adorned?

SWIFT appears to have approached nearer to uncorrupt Antiquity and Nature; easy in his Language, pure, simple, unaffected: But his Stile wanteth that Fire and Elevation, sometimes necessary to an Orator. Indeed, the Subjects he chose, and his Manner of treating them, did not admit of such, being taken usually from common Life; and thrown into the familiar or humourous Manner, in which Nature had given to this Writer great Talents: Let him therefore be esteemed a Model in his own Way: But powerful and perswasive Eloquence must soar higher.

CONFORMABLY to what we have taken Notice of in other Countries, here also, Conceit and Epigram have had their Turn of reigning; happy, if it were yet ended. One sees in many late

late Productions a Similitude of that Manner for which Dr. *Sprat* was distinguished in Prose; and more lately an eminent Satirist in Verse, short, sententious, and pointed; in the former, mingled with the florid and declamatory: In which latter Way particularly, many ingenious Persons, who profess themselves Imitators of *Milton*, have contributed to hurt the Language, soaring beyond the Bounds of Propriety, and tumid where they should be sublime.

THIS little History of modern Eloquence naturally leads into some Remarks on the Languages themselves. If we compare them with those of *Greece* and *Rome*, we must acknowledge them to be much inferior. The great Variety which the Inflexions of the Verbs and Nouns afforded to the *Greek* and *Roman*, by Means of which every Word became as it were multiplyed; and the different Length of their Syllables composing different Feet, whence their Periods were made capable of great and ever-varying Harmony, are Advantages peculiar to those Languages, not to be equalled, nor compensated by any Thing in the modern. We may add a third, flowing from the former of these; the Power of transposing their Words; which enabled the Orator to consult Harmony without injuring the Sense; whereas the Moderns are confined to a much narrower Range, being bound down nearly to the natural Order of the Words, by the Frame of their Language.

YET allowing, what I look upon as evident, and if we would judge impartially, as undeniable,

ble, this Superiority; we should not for that Reason limit ourselves to write in those learned Tongues only. A Fashion which prevailed exceedingly at the Revival of Letters, and greatly retarded the Improvement of modern Languages: Nay, so strong and of such long Continuance was this Prejudice, that both Father *Paul*, who is notwithstanding, esteemed defective in Purity of Stile, and *Davila*, doubted and remained long undetermined, whether they should not write their Histories in *Latin*; which, if they had done, their Country, indeed all Posterity would have suffered, in being deprived of such noble Performances: For it cannot be imagined, that in this Way they could have outdone their Countryman *Paulus Jovius*, one of the most admired among the modern Latinists; yet, how far short of theirs doth his Work fall at present? But, not to dwell upon Instances, of which we might produce many, in a Point so clear, I believe we may take it as granted, that every Man who maketh Use of his native Tongue, notwithstanding it's confessed Inferiority, shall excel any Composition he can produce in a dead one; because here, writing from Books alone, after all possible Care, he must often be at a Loss, must err, must want or forego pure Expression, or which is yet worse, must cramp his Thoughts, and cut and pare them to the Dimensions of Classical Phrase; by which Means, he either alters the Truth, or delivers it imperfectly, he becomes barbarous or obscure, tortures himself with needless Labour, and gives Pain to his Readers.

IF we proceed in comparing modern Tongues, not with the antient, but with each other, we shall find Cause to be contented with our own. If it hath not the Musick, the Softness, the liquid Lapse, if I may so speak, of the *Italian*; yet is it more bold, more manly, more strong. It hath not perhaps the Ease, the Clearness, the Pliableness of the *French*; but it abundantly compensates by superior Force, Energy, Conciseness.

GRANTING this to be the Case, we must however acknowlege, that our Tongue hath not been improved with the same Care as the others; and even our best Writers have not been very solicitous to preserve it's Purity. The Poets are particularly faulty herein. These Gentlemen, under the Excuse of I know not what poetical Licence, scruple not to break through the Frame and grammatical Construction of the Language. Such Licence is in Truth a meer Fiction, the Invention of ignorant Criticks, who would in this Way account for what they do not understand; or of Poets, who abuse their Art, and shelter their own want of Care under a vulgar Error.

I WILL mention a very few Instances of this Kind of Transgressions against the Grammatical Purity of the Tongue, which I chuse to take from the most correct and excellent of our modern Poets. If such, even small Negligences find place in HIM, though rarely, how often may

may we expect to find the like or much greater, in Writers of the common Rank?

Grows with his Growth and strengthens with his
Strength [*a*].

Strengthens, a Verb active is here used as, Neuter.

Bliss is the same in Subject or in King,
In WHO *obtain Defence, or* WHO *defend* [*b*].

Instead of, In them who obtain Defence, &c.

SPEAKING in Praise of Virtue, he says,

And but more relish'd as the more distrest,
Good from each Object from each Place acquir'd,
For ever exercis'd yet never tir'd [*c*].

In the second of which Lines, all Connexion is lost with that which goes before, and that which follows.

DESCRIBING the Life of a certain Person in Trade, he says,

His Compting-house employ'd the Sunday-morn.
Seldom at Church, 'twas such a busy Life,
But DULY SENT *his Family and Wife* [*d*].

Instead of *he* duly sent.

TALKING of *Voiture* he hath this Line,

Still with Esteem no less convers'd than read [*e*].

Is it that he read as he convers'd with Esteem? But what is *reading with Esteem?* Is it that he was read with Esteem as he conversed, equally

 liked

[*a*] Essay on Man, Epist. i. [*b*] Essay on Man. Epist.
[*c*] Essay on Man, Epist. [*d*] Abuse of Riches.
[*e*] Epist. with Works of VOITURE.

liked as an Author and Companion? In this Sense, the Expression is very faulty: at best obscure in either Way.

IN the Dunciad, the Heroe is introduced saying,

E'er since Sir Fopling's *Perriwig was* PRAISE [*f*].

That is, was praised and applauded.

AGAIN,

But Fool with Fool is barb'rous civil War [*g*].

Instead of the War of Fool with Fool is barbarous.

IN the same Work,

Spoil'd his own Language and acquir'd no more [*h*].

That is I suppose no other Language.

IN the Imitation of *Horace* he says of one,

----*With more than Harpy-Throat indu'd* [*i*].

Indued is applied to Gifts of the Mind, as indued with Wit or Sense: We do not say, indued with a Face or Shape,---or Throat.

AGAIN, the poor Man says,

Prefer a new JAPANNER *to their Shoes* [*k*].

Which is a low Expression.

HE says of his Prince,

Wonder of King.------ [*l*]

BUT if we should allow these, and still greater Licences to Poets, who may be entitled to Indulgence,

[*f*] Dunciad Book i. [*g*] Dunc. Book iii. [*h*] Dunc. Book iv. [*i*] Satire ii. of 2d Book. [*k*] 1st Epistle of 1st Book. [*l*] 1st Epistle of 2d Book.

Indulgence, fettered as they are by Rhyme; we have Cause to expect, to insist upon Accuracy from the Writers of Prose: Among whom we shall not however find it. The common Sort abound with the grossest Mistakes, and Barbarisms; nor are the best free from Errors.--- I will mention a few Instances from one of the first Rank, particularly celebrated for Purity of Stile; which Instances I have also chosen from his most finished Work, (in Point of Stile,) I mean the Travels of *Gulliver*.

In the Voyage to *Lilliput* occurs this Passage, "Mistakes committed by Ignorance, in a vir-"tuous Disposition, would never be of such "fatal Consequence, as the Practises of a Man, "whose Inclinations led him to be corrupt, and "HAD *great* Abilities to manage, multiply, "and defend his Corruption [*m*]."
That is, and who had great Abilities, *&c.*

In another Place we meet with this low Expression, *Rowing for Life* [*n*].

"I durst not stay, but RUN as fast as I could." Instead of *ran*.

"When they were sat down [*o*];"----instead of when *they had sat* down.

"On each Side the River [*p*];"---for on each Side OF the River.

"Put himself upon A FOOT with the great-"est Persons of the Kingdom [*q*];"---a low Expression. As again,

"What

[*m*] Page 58 of the *Dublin* Edition in Octavo. [*n*] Page 88. [*o*] Page 95. [*p*] Page 125. [*q*] Page 141.

"What Share of Knowlege they had, and "how they *came by it* [r]."

THE following is an Expreſſion entirely ungrammatical:

"Refunding themſelves for the Charges and "Trouble they were at [s]."

"The King when higheſt provoked [t],'--- for moſt highly.

"Found the Natives VERY HARD TO BE-"LIEVE [u]."

"I had ſeveral Men *died* in my Ship [w]."

"Civility and Cleanlineſs, Qualities altoge-"ther ſo oppoſite to thoſe Animals [x]."---- What are *Qualities* oppoſite to *Animals?*

"Becauſe *their* Wants and Paſſions are few-"er, *than among us* [y]."

"Fall together *by the Ears* [z]."

"This I filled with the Feathers of ſeveral "Birds I had taken, *and were excellent Food* [a]."

I MIGHT go on to ſwell this little Catalogue conſiderably; but Remarks of this Sort, I would barely mention, not inſiſt upon; it being an invidious and diſagreeable Taſk, to ſearch for trifling Overſights in Works of conſpicuous Merit. But the Uſe to be made of theſe Remarks is, that we ſhould attend to, and endeavour to avoid even ſuch Overſights: If we cannot equal the Flight of great Genius, let us make what little amends we can, by more exact Correctneſs.

FARTHER,

[r] GUL. Trav. p. 149. [s] Page 150. [t] Page 204. [u] Page 255. [w] Page 267. [x] Page 284. [y] Page 294. [z] Page 319. [a] Page 314.

FARTHER, In tracing after this Manner the Hiſtory of Eloquence, it is natural to reflect upon the different Kinds of Productions, in which each Country appears to have excelled.

AMONG the Moderns it ſeems beyond all Doubt, that the Prize for Hiſtory is due to *Italy*. No other Country can ſhew Writers equal to *Machiavel*, *Guicciardino*, Father *Paul*, and *Davila*. Yet ſurely, he muſt carry to a ſtrange Height his Partiality in Favour of theſe, who can prefer any one of them, as Lord *Bolingbroke* doth, before *Thucydides*:---But that Writer affected ſingular Notions: Happy! if all had been as innocent as this.

France hath it is true, produced two or three voluminous Hiſtorians, who although by no Means contemptible, do yet fall ſhort not only of the antient Models, but of theſe juſt named. Some detached Pieces of Hiſtory indeed, *A Revolution of Portugal*, *A League of Cambray*, *A Conſpiracy of Venice*, the moſt compleat of all, if it were as truly as it is finely written, ſhe may boaſt of, as compoſed with much Spirit and Art: But the three great Hiſtories, two of her own Affairs and one of our's, muſt be acknowleged to be very defective. The Branches of Eloquence, Poeſy excluded, in which *France* ſeemeth to excell, are Memoirs, Familiar Epiſtles, Dialogues, to which we may add Panegyricks, with ſuch other little Works, where Elegance is ſought rather than Strength.

IN Hiſtory, *England* can claim but the third Place. Lord *Verulam*'s, however valuable, is not worthy of the great Author. Lord *Clarendon*'s, which is the beſt, indeed a great Work, hath yet many important Faults, in the Manner, and perhaps in the Matter. Biſhop *Burnet*, with a great Stock of Knowlege, with a rich and lively Imagination, is yet a careleſs, looſe, inaccurate Writer.

BUT it ſeems, that, In Remarks of this Kind, we ſhould not omit a People, whoſe Language, though little known to us, may vie with any of the others; I mean that of *Spain*; which is expreſſive, ſonorous, and is affirmed to be the moſt copious of all: In Proof of this laſt Quality, *Spain* boaſteth of five Novels, of moderate Length, in each of which, one of the five Vowels is wanting throughout; which hath not been performed, it is urged cannot, in any other modern Tongue: Somewhat indeed of a ſimilar Nature is related of *Tryphiodorus*, a *Greek* Writer, who in a Poem conſiſting of 24 Books, is ſaid to have omitted every Letter of the Alphabet ſucceſſively, one throughout each Book; and he we know, wrote in a Language remarkably copious.

IT is amuſing to obſerve, how far a Zeal for the Glory of one's Country even in ſuch Points as this, carryeth wiſe Men. A late [b] Writer of *Italy* deſervedly eſteemed, hath advanced a ſingular Opinion concerning the *Italian* Tongue. Not enduring that it ſhould be deemed *Latin* corrupted by the Barbarians who ſubdued the Country, he aſſerteth it to be the ſame, which was

[b] SCIPIO MAFFEI, *nella Verona illuſtrata.*

was spoken by the Peasants and Persons of low Rank, in the flourishing Time of the *Roman* State; who unable or unwilling to observe the Nicety of Conjugations and Cases, made use as we Moderns do, of Articles and auxiliary Verbs: An Opinion, which notwithstanding the very ingenious Arguments brought in it's Support, doth not seem likely to meet with general Assent.

THE *Spanish* Tongue varyeth not more from *Latin*, than doth the *Italian*: Yet the Royal Academy of *Madrid* hath not set up such Pretensions; but ingenuously acknowlege it as their Sentiment, that their Language is derived from *Latin*; which through the long Dominion of the *Romans* had become universal in *Spain*. The *Goths* first, afterwards in a greater Degree, the *Moors*, who possessed for some Centuries almost the whole Country, corrupted this by blending with it their own Speech: And the whole Mixture forming in the Beginning a rude ill-mingled Mass, was by Degrees digested into some Order; in Times of Peace became softened, and polished into the present Language: which this Society hath laboured by their Dictionary to fix and render perpetual; with what Success, Time will shew.

AT the Revival of Letters, the Light which filled the adjoining Continent, extended it's Rays to *Spain* also: Where after the first Dawning, which was bright and promising, Letters made not a proportionable Progress: Not as I suppose through any Defect in the Genius of the People,

People, but from many incidental Causes, some of which allow me just to touch upon.

ABOUT this Time *America* was discovered: The vast Empires of *Mexico* and *Peru* were conquered with surprizing Rapidity, and great Quantities of Gold imported daily into *Spain*: From whence the whole Nation became possest with a Rage of growing rich, incompatible with Study.

NEITHER were the Times immediately succeeding favourable to it; the State being engaged in a long, bloody, and disgraceful War, in which the *Low Countries* were dismembered from it.

THE Disposition likewise of the Nobles, and in Proportion of the Gentry, was adverse to Literary Improvement; being high, haughty, attached to received Customs and Opinions, and averse from every Thing new: And *Mariana*, in the Dedication of his History to *Philip* the 3d, King of *Spain*, expressly complains, that there was not any Encouragement for Letters or learned Men.

THE extreme Bigotry of the People also made them unwilling to engage in Studies, grounded on Heathen Rites and Authors.

BUT above all, the Inquisition reigning here with absolute Tyranny, discouraged all Freedom of Thought and Speech, and with them all Science: Or at best, permitted only the Weeds and Tares of Learning to spring up, scholastick Philosophy and Theology, and a vain and dangerous *Casuistry*.

HENCE

HENCE Miſtakes, which ſoon after the Birth of Letters prevailed here as in other Places, were not corrected here, as in them; but ſpread and took deep Root, and infected almoſt all the *Spaniſh* Writers. Their Proſe was either vainly or extravagantly Swelling, as appears in their Romances and early Hiſtories; or was affected, abruptly and obſcurely Sententious, as in *Gratian*, and others of the ſame Time. Their Poeſy had more univerſally the ſame Errors: It more eſpecially abounds with Refinements, with ſubtile Metaphyſical Sentiments, diſpoſed into ſuch a Variety of laboured Oppoſitions, that their fineſt Sonnets have the Appearance of Riddles: And it was not until of late that they have ſeen, and laid aſide this unnatural Manner.

PERHAPS there may be ſome Propenſity in the national Diſpoſition to theſe Miſtakes; ſince we find Inſtances of them among the Antients, in *Lucan* and *Seneca*, who were both *Spaniards*: Both endowed with fine Genius, in ſome Reſpects both excellent Writers: But the one tumid in Verſe to the Confines of Bombaſt; and the other prepoſterouſly decking out the ſevereſt Form of Philoſophy with the gay Flowers of juvenile Fancy.

YET to do Juſtice to this People, we muſt acknowlege, that the Genius of the Nation ſtruggled nobly with all theſe Impediments; and we ſee it burſting through the thick Cloud that covered it, in ſome very bright Inſtances. Hiſtory appears with much Gravity, with a ſtately

ſtately and pure Majeſty, in *Mariana*; with much Spirit and Luſtre though too romantick an Air, in *De Solis*; with Simplicity and good Senſe in *Herrera*. The Diſcourſes of *Lewis of Granada* are lively and eloquent. There is a fine Spirit of Satire, with much Wit and a Vein of peculiar Humour, in the Allegories of *Quevedo*. *Lopè de Vega* wrote a vaſt Number of Comedies, all indeed except four or five as himſelf owns, irregular; yet the Criticks who condemn him in this Reſpect, allow to him the Praiſe of a moſt fertile Imagination, and a true comic Vein. And it is remarkable, that the two firſt good theatrical Performances which appeared in *France*, one of each Kind, a Tragedy [*c*] and Comedy [*d*], were both Imitations from *Spaniſh* Writers. *Cervantes* is an original Genius, hardly to be matched in any Age. And the Care ſince taken to aſcertain their Language, the Kind and Caſt of ſome later Productions in it, render it probable, that it will make the Figure it deſerveth in polite Literature.

IT might be expected from the Conſtitution of *England*, in which, Liberty is ſo happily ballanced with Power, that Eloquence ſhould flouriſh here, as it did in *Athens* and *Rome*, the Form of her Government being in this Reſpect equally friendly to it.

ACCORDINGLY, we find that Sort of it, which floweth from and more immediately dependeth upon Liberty, hath arrived here to great

[*b*] The *Cid*, imitated from DE CASTRO.
[*c*] The *Menteur*, from LOP'E DE VEGA.

great Perfection: I mean, The Speaking in Publick, in Defence of, or in Opposition to Laws proposed, or with Relation to Measures used in the Administration of national Affairs: In this Article, the Advantage is manifestly on her Side; and modern Times can shew few Pieces of Eloquence equal to many, that are to be met with in the Debates of the *British* Senate.

NOT few likewise worthy of high Commendation are the Growth of the Bar. If we consider only the Fame and Ability of the Pleaders, we might expect more of this Kind: But whoever examines into the Matter will find two Causes, that fully account for this Rarity. One is, The Form and Nature of our Laws; which being greatly multiplied, and descending to the minutest Circumstances, do necessarily engage the Advocates in a dry and unpleasing Detail.

ANOTHER Cause seems to arise from the *Pleaders*, who give themselves up so entirely to the Study of our Laws, their more immediate important Business, that they neglect to lay those general Foundations, on which alone a pleasing and powerful Eloquence can be raised. Confining themselves to what is necessary, they overlook what appears to be ornamental only: A wrong Way of Proceeding; for undoubtedly one Part is defective without the other: And although it would be altogether unpardonable in one who professeth himself to be a Lawyer, to be ignorant of the Laws; yet it is true on the other Hand, that the Knowlege of them would

acquire

quire many real Advantages from Skill in the ornamental Part: Nay, if you consider him as a Pleader, must be imperfect, must lose much of it's Power and Use, without it.

WHAT maketh this Omission the less excuseable is, that there is not any Person, who has been well and regularly educated, that may not in the Intervals of Business or necessary Study, acquire Knowlege of what is named the politer Kind; somewhat which may be of Use to adorn and enliven the dry Deductions, which meer Skill in his Profession must for ever engage him in; some Muscles, as it were, and Flesh, to cover that uncomely and bare Skeleton of Usages and Statutes.

HEREIN it is more especially, that an early Acquaintance with the great Writers of Antiquity, an Intimacy contracted with them and such Moderns as resemble them, in the happy Hours of Childhood and Youth, before the Interruptions of Cares and Business come on, appeareth in it's true Light, of being highly useful and beneficial. It will then bestow to the Arguments of the learned Advocate not only Grace and Beauty, but render powerful and effectual that solid Erudition which is afterwards built upon it. It may be compared to those Friendships which are formed with valuable Persons in the Dawn of Life, grounded indeed upon Sports and Plays; but afterwards, when we become Actors in the World, they are often unexpectedly found to be of the greatest Advantage.

LECTURE the Sixth.

A Continuation of the Foregoing.

IN the Eloquence of the Pulpit it is, that *England* ſeems to ſtand alone, with manifeſt unrivaled Superiority. I am not ignorant, that the Countries mentioned have produced many admired Preachers; but it doth not appear to me from what I have read of them, and ſome of the moſt celebrated I have read with Attention, that any among them have given Proofs of ſo juſt and maſterly an Eloquence, as ſome of our own have done. It is true, we are apt to be partial to our own Language and Country, and in comparing them with others, to give them an unjuſt Preference: But on the contrary, I know that we are alſo prone to admire foreign Things and foreign Faſhions, and to ſet them above our own: It is the Buſineſs of Reaſon to ſteer equally between both Extremes, to conquer ſuch Prejudices, and weigh both Sides in the Scale of Truth and unbiaſſed Judgment.

COMPARISONS of this Nature ſhould never be made in order to gratify Pride, Paſſion, or mere Curioſity, but may be applied to real Uſe: For wherever we fall ſhort of our Neighbours,

bours, we may learn of them to ſupply the Defect, not by borrowing their Thoughts, but by catching their Air and Manner. Something of which Sort, where the Correſpondence is intimate, will unavoidably happen: Accordingly, in the laſt Century, our Writers were benefited by an Acquaintance with the *French*, deriving from them more Exactneſs, ſounder Criticiſm, Method, and a certain Grace and Poliſh; The *French* have ſince that Time, drawn not leſs Advantage from their Commerce with us; and one may with Certainty trace the *Britiſh* Genius in the Strength, Solidity, and Conciſeneſs of ſome late Performances in that Language.

IN this way then of national Compariſon, it is with good Cauſe, that in the Article mentioned, Precedence was given to our own Writers; I ſpeak according to my own beſt Judgment. For that perpetual Addreſs to the Paſſions, that Air of Declamation, which runs through all the foreign Productions of this Kind that I have met with, cannot I think, ſuppoſing it perfect in its Way, vie with the clear, ſolid, rational, yet ſufficiently animated Diſcourſes, which abound in our own Tongue. On this Occaſion, one cannot help aſking, how it hath come to paſs, that we have excelled ſo much in this Particular? And I have often thought the following no improbable Account of the Matter.

THE great Liberty allowed by the Laws, and Gentleneſs of the Government in *Britain*

to

to Unbelievers of all Sorts, however verging perhaps towards Excess, and certainly hurtful in some Respects, may have contributed to produce this good Effect: Inasmuch as their bold and open Attacks have given Rise to the best Treatises in Defence of Religion natural and revealed, that ever appeared in the World; the immediate Consequence of which Controversy, carried on as it was by the best Heads in the Nation, and wrought up on both Sides with the utmost Industry, must have been, the Production of a regular, close, reasoning Eloquence, which thus exercised continually and improved, must, from the Nature of the Subject, have been quickly transferred into, and hath shone with conspicuous Lustre in the Pulpit.

THIS Solution openeth an Answer to a Question relating to our Neighbours on the Continent; whence is it, that in this Article, they have sunk below their other Performances; for that I am persuaded is the Case.

THIS Effect is to be attributed to the Form of Religion established amongst them. Their Church lays Claim to Infallibility: Whatever therefore she declares to be an Article of Faith, is by that Declaration made such: Proofs are needless where Contradiction is not allowed. Nay, they may be worse than needless: The very Attempt to prove certain Points before a common Audience may be esteemed dangerous, as it is an Appeal from the sacred Tribunal of Authority to that of Reason, an unfriendly

Power. Thus ye ſee, that the Preachers of this Church, are in the moſt important Points of Doctrine, in a great Meaſure ſhut out from Argument; the want of which they cannot otherwiſe ſupply than by addreſſing themſelves to Imagination and Paſſion. They employ their whole Force and Skill in affecting and adorning; which however right and pleaſing in a certain Degree, cannot by the utmoſt Power of human Genius be ſo wrought up, as alone to form true Eloquence. In Confirmation of which, we may obſerve, that the [a] Writers in that Language, of the reformed Religion, although perhaps in other Reſpects inferior, do yet excel the Catholick Preachers herein; they are more inſtructive and rational.

BUT however this may be, for in Points of general Criticiſm it is not expected that all ſhould agree, I believe, that in our own Language, we may juſtly propoſe the Sermons of Archbiſhop *Tillotſon*, as Models of good Preaching. In Clearneſs of Method, Juſtneſs of Obſervation, Strength of Argument, at the ſame Time in chaſte and manly Ornaments, they have few, if any Equals. I do not mean, that all his Diſcourſes are alike. His poſthumous Works, ſome few excepted, are much inferior to the others: They are indeed for the moſt part, rude Draughts and Sketches, rather than finiſhed Performances; you ſee every where the great Strokes of a Maſter-hand, but the Grace

[a] Meſſ CLAUDE, DALLE, La PLACETTE, WERENFELS, SAURIN, &c.

Grace of Colouring, the laſt Touches are wanting. Neither in the moſt finiſhed of them, ſhould we expect abſolute Perfection; as indeed in what human Performance may it be expected? In thoſe which he himſelf publiſhed, admirable as they are, may I be allowed to ſay, that a critical Eye may diſcern ſome Specks? Doth he not ſometimes indulge too much to Fancy? He is often ſublime and pathetick; but doth he never paſs the due Limit? Although a great Maſter of our Language, tho' bleſt with an eaſy, copious, and flowing Stile, yet is he not ſometimes faulty in this very Article? Is not his Stile ſometimes looſe in the Compoſition, diffuſive, and redundant? And have you not remarked in him low Phraſes and Expreſſions?

" But the great Author ſaw and choſe " theſe, as fit in popular Diſcourſes, more in- " telligible, and better adapted to the Liking " and Apprehenſion of the Hearer." Perhaps ſo; I am willing to believe, that it was in ſome Meaſure the Caſe: Notwithſtanding, it does not appear to me, that his Example herein ought to be followed. The greateſt Clearneſs of Language is undoubtedly conſiſtent with the utmoſt Propriety; and you may be familiar without being low. At leaſt, in elaborate Compoſitions delivered to the World as ſuch, the Publick hath a Right to inſiſt upon more Care and Exactneſs; and you are not to offend the Ear of a well-bred Perſon by mean Language, that you may render your Senſe plain to the Ignorant; however at the Time of pronouncing a Diſcourſe, the Occaſion, Circumſtances, or Quality of an Audience may juſtify, or rather make excuſable, ſuch Licence and Inaccuracy. The Ear is a merciful Judge; a Reader is ſevere, and inexorable.

BUT it is Time that I ſhould cloſe this Part of my Deſign, and conclude this little Hiſtory of the antient and modern State of Eloquence: And becauſe I have recited Facts, only as I thought they might furniſh uſeful Remarks, ſuffer me to fill up the remaining Part of this Lecture with the Uſes, following naturally from the Obſervations before mentioned.

FROM this Survey of the preſent State of Eloquence, we ſee, that in our own Language there wanteth not Encouragement, ſufficient to induce us all to apply ourſelves with Care. Compare it with thoſe of our Neighbours, compare our Writers with theirs; and without giving any partial or invidious Preference, this Concluſion at leaſt, I am ſure we may fairly draw from ſuch parallel; that our Tongue is capable of admitting great Excellency; that many have excelled in it, ſome very highly: Yet not ſo, but that there is ſtill left room for new Attempts. In the Regions of Eloquence we have ſeen, that there are whole Tracts yet untouched, or ſlightly attempted by the *Engliſh* Genius. If our Talents do at all lead this Way, the Scene is open. Even in thoſe which it hath poſſeſſed, which it hath cultivated more ſucceſsfully than any other Nation, remain Vacancies,

cancies, into which with proper Care we may gain Admission. In the most compleat Writers are little Blemishes, which we may avoid; and though we cannot arrive at their Excellence, we may out-go them in faultless Correctness, which is some Degree of Praise. Every one may with some Hope of Success say, and it ought to be the Principle of all

[b] *I also must attempt myself to raise*
From Earth, and soar upon the Wings of Praise.

Secondly, We have seen from the concurring Practice of all, especially of the wisest and most polite Nations, what their Perswasion was concerning the Power of Eloquence: What Care they took of instructing young Persons in it: What Honours they conferred upon those who excelled in it. From all which it appears, that their universal Belief was, That this Eloquence, is an Art, which may be learned; certainly a natural Ability for it may be much improved by a due Attention to Rules, and by continual Exercise. We should not therefore rashly assent to those who despise all such Rules, who assert the Study of Rhetorick to be vain and useless, who exhort us to trust entirely to Nature, as if she, having endowed us with the Faculty of Speech, wherever Thoughts are, will quickly furnish Expression. But all Art is no more, than a Method of employing most effectually the Powers of Nature,

[b] Via Tentanda est, quâ me quoque possum
Tollere humo, victorq; virûm volitare per ora. VIRG.

Nature, reduced into Rules by long Obſervation and Experience: And whoſoever rejecting the Aid of theſe in Oratory, chuſeth to abandon himſelf to uninſtructed Nature, acteth with the ſame Kind of Prudence, as doth the Man, who in a dangerous Diſeaſe, perſiſteth in refuſing the Aſſiſtance of Medicine, and leaveth the Cure to the ſole Force of Nature; which ſucceedeth ſometimes, where all Remedies might have failed, but much more frequently faileth, where Remedies would have ſucceeded.

A third Conſequence is. Study moſt carefully, the Writers of the beſt Ages, of every Country. Obſerve what it is, that formed the Character of Eloquence in that Period; wherein it differeth from the Age which preceded or followed. Take particular Notice of the ſeveral Steps by which it declined. Learn accurately to diſtinguiſh all Infuſions of foreign or corrupt Manner, as they began to be introduced, until at length they became the eſtabliſhed Faſhion. This Care would ſerve effectually to guard us againſt the like Faults.

WE obſerve in a neighbouring Country, the Inhabitants of which are diſtinguiſhed by their Love of Novelty, a perpetual Flux of Language and Stile, notwithſtanding their publick, laborious, and laudable Attempts to fix a certain unchangeable Standard. And herein we are, as in other Things, but too much diſpoſed to follow them. Now this Kind of Inconſtancy we ſhould firmly reſiſt. Politicians ſay,

that

that a Form of Government, if become Irregular, can be ſet right, only by reducing it to its firſt Principles: In like manner, Writers ſhould endeavour to preſerve, or bring back the Form of Writing, to that which was uſed by the beſt Authors of the beſt Period; the Nature of Mankind being ſuch, as rather than not to change, to change for the Worſe.

ESPECIALLY, we at this Time ſhould do well to guard againſt the Uſe of Conceits or Points before mentioned; a Fault, which ſeems of late to have gained Ground among us, and has uſually attended the Decline of Letters. This Plant, naturally the Product of fertile but neglected Soil, ſpreads apace, and fails not if encouraged, to end in total Barrenneſs, or at beſt in Crops of glittering uſeleſs Weeds, Soon after the Reſtoration of Letters it ſprung up in the rank Soil of *Italy*, where it flouriſhed long, and notwithſtanding the commendable Endeavours of ſome [*c*] late judicious Writers, is not likely to be rooted out. From thence, the Infection paſſed the *Alps*; hath been alternately cheriſhed and ſuppreſſed, admired and condemned; and at preſent ſeemeth among us in a thriving State, which if we may judge from the Hiſtory of Letters juſt recited, is an evil Symptom.

I DO not deny, that theſe *Points* where moderately uſed, may have a good Effect: But they are grounded in partial Conceptions of Things, and involve, or almoſt always betray into

[*c*] SCIPIO MAFFEI, and GRAVINA.

into, falſe Thoughts; and where they are true, yet Exceſs in them is very faulty. Becauſe Jewels ſkilfully diſpoſed, may on ſome Occaſions become, and ſet off Beauty to Advantage, Writers of this Kind cover their Muſe all over with them, and deform by Ornament. Many of theſe fanciful Embelliſhments, the fineſt perhaps in their Kind, might be pointed out in our [*d*] Engliſh *Homer*: I do not recollect to have obſerved a ſingle one in the whole Original.

NOTWITHSTANDING the Rule laid down, I acknowledge, that the Authors of corrupt Times may be ſometimes read with Improvement; but herein much Caution ſhould be uſed. The beſt of ſuch may be compared to Fields producing Plants of all Kinds, Weeds and Flowers, healthful and poiſonous; and Readers are too apt to gather theſe latter,

Miſeros fallunt aconita legentes.

Fourthly. As the Study of Eloquence was ſo

[*d*] As theſe following:
And hiſſing fly the *feather'd Fates below*. B. ii. L. 68.
And o'er the Vale deſcends the *living Cloud*. ii. 116.
Decay'd our Veſſels lie, ii. 164.
And ſcarce enſure *the wretched Power to fly*.
That worſt of Tyrants an uſurping Crowd. ii. 242.
Now vaniſh'd *like their Smoke the Faith of Men*. ii. 407.
Our Ears refute the *Cenſure of* our Eyes. iii. 288.
With Spears erect a *moving Iron Wood*. iv. 323.
Glittering Terrors from his Head unbound. vi.
The troubled Pleaſure *ſoon chaſtis'd with Fear*.
Then in the Gen'ral's Helm the *Fates are thrown*. vii. 212.
And ſhoot a *ſhady Luſtre* o'er the Field. viii.
with many others of the ſame Kind.

ſo univerſal in the States of *Athens* and *Rome*, as it was the only Gate which opened the Way to Honours in both Commonwealths, and the Treatiſes written among them concerning this Art, were almoſt without Number, it is natural to enquire, how cometh it to paſs, that of ſo many Thouſands who applied themſelves to this Study, ſo very few have excelled? The vaſt Deluge of Time hath ſwept away Multitudes admired in their own Age, and few, very few remain at this Day above the Flood [*e*]. Now wherein conſiſteth the peculiar Excellence of theſe few? Let us conſult their Works, examine, reconſider: And this ſurely is Matter of juſt Curioſity; ſince they muſt have been poſſeſſed of very ſingular Merit: For all Men, of different Countries, Ages, Tempers, and Paſſions could not have conſpired to beſtow upon them undeſerved Praiſe. Farther, can we ourſelves catch any Spark of this Fire, which hath rendered their Works immortal? This is a noble Ambition, and worthy of our utmoſt Toil and Induſtry fully to gratify.

BUT it was before obſerved, and allow me for the Importance of the Point, to repeat it; That our Admiration of the Productions of *Greece* and *Rome* however juſt, our Study of them however prudent, ſhould not lead us into a Fondneſs of emulating their Writers in their own Language; which we know was the Aim and faſhionable Purſuit of the Reſtorers of Learn-

[*e*] Apparent rari nantes in gurgite vaſto. VIRG.

Learning, at that Time even in its Excess and Enthusiasm, perhaps useful; but it remained too long, and by dressing up all the Learned in foreign Habits, prevented the Establishment and Growth of Manufactures of their several Countries.

ANOTHER Disadvantage of which Practice is, that in such Attempts the Success never can be proportional to the Labour: The utmost Worth the best of us can arrive at, is that of a faint and faulty Resemblance. No; we should aim higher. We should endeavour to raise ourselves to the same Kind of Merit with them, to express their Ease, Strength, and Solidity, not creep servilely after Words and Phrases; to transfuse into our Writings their Spirit not Sound. Instead of resembling some among our young Gentlemen, who bring Home from their Travels, for their whole Improvement, the Dress, Grimace, and Phrase of Foreigners; let us rather follow the Example of those judicious Travellers, who retaining the outward Habit and Forms of their own Country, return with that Politeness and graceful Freedom, which is the Fruit of large Experience, and much Conversation, conducted by good Sense and Reflexion. Without this Care, we might write *Latin* like *Cicero*, and not deserve to be read; or compose Verses that may seem to have the Cadence and Harmony of *Virgil*'s, and merit little Regard. The writing in dead Languages I acknowledge is not altogether without its Use: It should be

injoined

injoined as an Exercise to young Persons, because it is not possible rightly to understand such a Language, without accustoming ourselves to write in it; so that otherwise, you cannot become acquainted with the Idiom, with the Frame, and Turn, much less with the more delicate Graces of that Language; nor consequently, have a true Relish for the Compositions in it, which are most excellent.

AND let me by the Way observe, that the Neglect of this Part of Discipline in our Education with regard to *Greek*, is injudicious, and hath an ill Effect. For not being at all exercised during our early Years in speaking or writing in this Tongue, whatever Pains we may take to understand it when we are grown up, it is hardly possible, to attain to such exact Knowledge of it, as to distinguish Varieties of Stile, to become skilfull Criticks in it, and catch the peculiar Shades and Colourings, that characterise the Work of each Master-hand in it. And yet there are obvious Reasons, which prove, that this Kind of Knowledge would be valuable; nay, I think it might be proved, if this were the Place for entering into such Points, that it would be more Useful towards the laying a Foundation of true Eloquence, than the like Skill in *Latin*, which is however so much cultivated in Schools, or at least so strongly recommended, and supposed to be cultivated.

HOWEVER this may be, undoubtedly it is not by using the same Words, or even Sentiments, with the Antients, that we shall become like

like to them: It is by the grafting upon a Fund of Knowledge and good Senſe of our own, their general Air and Manner; it is by viewing a Subject in the comprehenſive Light which they did; by chuſing out like them the moſt important Circumſtances, and diſpoſing them in the like juſt Order; and laſtly, by giving to the whole Work that inimitable Poliſh and Luſtre, which the more cloſely we ſurvey their Productions, appeareth the more clear and bright. But I am unawares anticipating Points, which ſhall be treated of more fully hereafter, in their proper Places. This now touched upon, *Imitation*, being a great and compendious Method of arriving at Eloquence, deſerveth indeed diſtinct Conſideration: Nor can I think of a more apt Place for it than the preſent, in which it followeth the Hiſtory of Eloquence, and of thoſe who moſt excelled therein.

LECTURE the Seventh.

Concerning IMITATION.

ONE of the beſt Fruits ſpringing from a frequent and careful Peruſal of the Works of the Antients is, that we are thereby led to imitate them, and by Degrees may be tranſformed as it were into their Likeneſs.

BUT as ſome Prejudices lye againſt Imitation in general, and as they who acknowledge its Uſefulneſs, are yet liable to err in the Application; it ſeemeth a proper Employment, and peculiarly ſuitable to the Courſe of Obſervations in which we have been engaged, to make ſome Reflexions upon this Subject; ſuch as may ſhew the Uſefulneſs of it; and afterwards, to point out the *Rules* of good Imitation.

THE Arguments by which we prove the Uſefulneſs of Imitation, are drawn from two Sources; Experience and Reaſon. Let us briefly unfold ſome of each.

LOOK back on former Ages: What hath been the Practice of Mankind? How have they who excelled in any Science or Art proceeded? Did they ſet out upon their own ſingle Stock, or did they borrow from the Fund of others? The Point is eaſily decided. It is a Fact

Fact not to be controverted, that the most eminent Persons in all Kinds of Literature, owe their first Materials to the Discovery of others; nay, and derive from Example a great Part of their Skill in the Management of those Materials.

CONCERNING *Homer*, it seems probable, not only from the Perfection of his Writings, but also from the loose Traditions and obscure Accounts of the Times preceding him, that there were Models, which he followed and improved upon. Such we may justly suppose to have been *Orpheus*, and *Linus*, and *Amphion*, and *Musæus*; Names which, however faintly, do still shine through the Darkness of Fable, and appear to have been renowned for Skill in Poesy and Musick. But as all Monuments of those very antient Times are now lost, we cannot determine this Point with any Degree of Certainty.

LET us therefore allow him the Honour of original Genius, to which his Antiquity hath perhaps contributed not a little to render his Title indisputable; it remaineth, however, undoubted, that the whole Multitude of Writers who flourished since, have been much indebted to him. The Criticks agree in this Observation; and ye may yourselves with little Difficulty confirm it by Instances from all the Authors of *Greece*. In the unaffected Simplicity of the first Historian; in the Strength of the second; in the Sublimity of this Philosopher; in the Ease and Sweetness of that other, and in in the expreſſive Brevity of a third, you may trace the Genius of *Homer*, his Sentiments, nay his very Words, taken by them, and fitted to the Contexture of their own Proſe; which they ſought not to conceal, as Thefts, but were open and ambitious in their Imitation; looking upon his Works as of a Rank above human, as a vaſt Treaſure left in common, from which it was allowable for all, who were capable of performing it rightly, to transfer a Gem to enrich and adorn their own Productions.

NEXT after the Poets, this Treaſure was moſt uſeful to the Orators, who found here an inexhauſtible Store of noble and lofty Images; and to none was it more uſeful than to *Demoſthenes*, who having applied himſelf from the Beginning to acquire a Reſemblance of this Poet and of *Thucydides*, hath happily united the Clearneſs, Abundance, and Elevation of the one, to the Weight, Nerves, and Brevity of the other; thus ſublime without ſwelling, and cloſe without Dryneſs.

IT would be tedious and unneceſſary to extend this Obſervation to the *Romans*; to ſhew particularly, that it was the Caſe of *Tully* and *Livy*, of *Virgil* and *Horace*; and the reſt of thoſe extraordinary Perſons, who were the Ornaments of the *Auguſtan* Age; of whom it is acknowledged, that they profeſſedly formed themſelves upon the Models of the Antients, eſteeming it ſufficient Honour, that they brought home to their own Country the moſt precious Treaſures of *Greece*.

IF

IF I ſhould go one Step farther, and aſk you, who among the Moderns have excelled, they who relied upon their own ſingle Force, or they who made a judicious Uſe, and trod in the Steps of antient Wiſdom? The Anſwer will decide the Queſtion; and this muſt be the Anſwer, "Almoſt all ſuch have been in ſome "Meaſure *Imitators*."

THUS Experience is on the Side of Imitation. The ſecond Source of Arguments on this Head is *Reaſon*. Let us next conſult her: She bids us firſt apply ourſelves to human Nature. Are Men ſo formed, that a ſingle Perſon is able, by the Power of his own Genius, to carry an Art from its firſt Rudiments to Perfection? Do we not ſee how gradual Improvement hath been in every Nation? That Arts and Sciences have always had their Infancy and Manhood as it were, no leſs than the human Race; weak and rude at their firſt Dawning, they received Strength and Growth by Degrees, and at laſt aroſe to Maturity. Doth not this Obſervation evince, beyond Controverſy, the Uſefulneſs of Imitation? Men aſſiſt each other. Some lucky Hit, or happy inventive Genius, opens the right Source; others, following his Steps, collect and guide the Waters in proper Channels. For ſuch are the Weakneſs and Indolence of Man, ſo limited are his Talents, ſo many the Accidents to which he is liable, and his Life at the utmoſt ſhut up within ſo narrow Bounds, that it is ſcarcely poſſible for the ſame Perſon to light upon the right Vein, to purſue it ſteadily, and trace it to its fartheſt Limit: No, this muſt be the Work of many Hands, imitating and improving each upon the other, for the moſt Part of Generations, labouring in Succeſſion. Whoever peruſeth the Hiſtory of Knowledge, will find this to have been the Fact almoſt without Exception. The Temple of Arts, if we may ſo ſpeak, cannot be raiſed by one Perſon, ſeldom in one Age; Generation after Generation worketh upon it, each mounting upon the Labours of the foregoing. Nor is it ſo perfect at this Day, but that it may admit of Addition; ſomewhat is ſtill wanting in Extent and Ornament.

The Hiſtory of the famous Painter *Raphael* affordeth a ſtrong Inſtance of uſeful Imitation. His firſt Manner was like that of his Maſter [*a*], dry and cold: Upon ſeeing ſome Paintings of *Leonardo de Vinci*, he altered this Manner, and gave to his Figures new Life and Grace: But after he had fixed his Abode in *Rome*, by a continual Study of the beautiful Monuments of Antiquity, of Statues, Coins, and Bas-reliefs; and more particularly, as Hiſtory relates, by obſerving privately the Stile of *Michael Angelo* his Rival, he opened a new Way, and raiſed himſelf to that animated, noble, and lofty Manner, which ſo glorioully diſtinguiſheth his lateſt Performances.

It is urged, in Oppoſition to what hath been advanced, "That an Original is much "more valuable than any Copy; that Nature

[*a*] Pietro Perugino.

"is the best Guide; that Men should resign "themselves to her only: Whereas Imitation "cramps and confines them in the Trammels "of Authority and Example."

THIS is partly true, "Nature is the best "Guide:" But will every Man, left to himself, follow her as far as she can lead him? Is she not to be conducted by Art? And how may this Art be so well acquired, as by judicious Imitation? But to come closer to the Point.

FIRST, An excellent Original, one who by the mere Force of his own Abilities hath struck out every Thing from himself, is exceedingly rare. Look back through the whole Annals of Time, how few, how very few are there, who have in this Manner wrought out from their own unborrowed Stock, and finished, any great Invention? Some rare and happy Spirits there may have been, who by their own Vigour have taken Flight, and soared aloft; who, imitating none, are also inimitable. But from such exceedingly few Instances, no Conclusion can be drawn; we cannot reason from them to the Generality of Mankind.

SECONDLY, Even these few Originals must be imperfect, and Instruction and Example would have been useful to them: Such is the Condition of frail Mortality. Invention is one of the rarest Gifts of Heaven, and the most liable, without great Care, to betray into Faults. No Writer seemeth to have a better Title to this singular Character of original Genius, than our *Shakespear*. What Richness of Imagination!

tion! What Loftiness of Thought! What amazing Command of the Passions! Yet how totally different is he from every other Writer? There is scarcely a Line of his that doth not bear impressed his peculiar Genius. In Tragedy and in Comedy he is alike new, as uncommon in his Vein of free and flowing Humour, as in the highest Soarings of Imagination. Accordingly, he reigns over us with equal Power in both Extremes; throws us into Fits of Laughter, or calls from our Eyes Streams of Tears. Notwithstanding which, we cannot but see and acknowledge his strange Inequality. It is impossible not to be displeased with the Irregularity of even his best Pieces, with the Falshood of his Thoughts, and the Affectation and Obscurity of his Stile; Faults which, though they should not lessen our Admiration, yet take away from the Delight we should otherwise have in reading, or seeing his Pieces represented; which, if he had been acquainted with the good Models of Antiquity, he would undoubtedly have avoided: And, in that Case, would probably have carried dramatick Poesy to a Height of Excellence yet unknown.

GIVE me Leave to add an Instance in a Sister-Art. In Painting, the Title of Original is with great Justice given to *Correggio:* who poor, without any Instructor, having never even seen a good Picture, attained to great Eminence. Carried on by a Happiness of Nature altogether without Example, for Grace and Delicacy of

Pencil he vyed with, if not ſurpaſſed, the foremoſt. But Criticks obſerve him to be alſo ſtrangely unequal, to fail mightily in Compoſition and Deſign: Why? Principally, becauſe he had not the Advantage of great Models to conſult and copy from.

THUS it appears evident, that Imitation is in ſome Meaſure neceſſary, is at leaſt very uſeful. Experience tells us, that all thoſe who have excelled in Arts did imitate; and Reaſon aſſureth us, that it is beyond the Power of human Nature to arrive at Perfection without its Aſſiſtance. I acknowledge at the ſame Time, that it may likewiſe hurt, and that it hath miſled, as well as ſet right. But we are not therefore to reject it; we are to regulate. To which Purpoſe, Rules may be delivered worthy of Attention.

FIRST, "Propoſe to yourſelves the beſt Pattern for Imitation." This is ſo plain, that it ſhould ſeem needleſs to mention it, if Men did not very often neglect, or tranſgreſs it. We daily ſee Perſons chuſing the Manner of *Ovid* and *Seneca*, rather than that of *Virgil* and *Salluſt*; and it is manifeſt, in the Works of a great Tragick Poet (*b*), that he preferred the *Pharſalia* as a Pattern, before the *Eneid*. For which prepoſterous Choice we may aſſign two Cauſes:

EITHER they want Diſcernment, and approve the worſe; or they find this more attainable. It is therefore requiſite, firſt "to acquire and eſtabliſh a good Judgment." Genius,

[*b*] CORNEILLE.

nius, the Groundwork of the Whole, is indeed the Gift of Nature; but where there is any Ray thereof, Attention and Study will ſtrengthen and brighten it.

NEXT, "Seeing thus what is good, aim at "that, or write not at all." Chuſe your Models like your Company, the beſt; Acquaintance will bring on a Likeneſs.

THE proper Limitation of this Rule, produceth a ſecond: Among theſe Good, ſome may be more ſuitable to your Nature than others. "Select theſe."

MEN differ widely in their Diſpoſitions and Talents. We know that they are often forced into Oppoſition with theſe, and may acquit themſelves indifferently well in Undertakings for which Nature had not deſigned them; but it is paſt Doubt, that he will go on with much greater Speed, and proceed farther, who followeth the Impulſe and Direction of Nature.

YOU ſhould conduct yourſelf, as a ſkilful Deſigner doth an Improvement; who attempts not to force the Ground to a fixed preconceived Plan, though it be abſolutely the beſt, but rather conforms his Plan to the Ground, conſults Nature in the Diſpoſition of his Trees, the Opening of his Proſpects, and the Management of his Water. Thus, becauſe an Author is good, you ſhould not therefore, although it were poſſible, compel yourſelf to take his Ply: The prudent Method is, to chuſe out for your Model one as nearly as you can conformable to your own Genius, although leſs excellent.

Where

Where you fall short in your Plan, you will abundantly compensate for it, by great Superiority in the Execution.

A THIRD Caution is, "Beware of imitate-"ing even such, too closely," or in the Poet's Words,

Ne desilias imitator in Arctum. HOR.

By so doing, you cramp your own Genius; you fetter it in such Manner, that you cannot exert your Talents: He, that labours to tread exactly in the Steps of one going before him, must move with Pain and Aukwardness: And by this Difference it is, that almost the best Copies may be distinguished from the Original; by an Air of Stiffness; the Pencil is not free.

BESIDES, the Merit of a Copy, suppose it in other Respects equal, falleth far short of the Merit of an Original. You ought therefore so to imitate, as to be like, not the same.

YOU cannot learn better to conduct yourself herein, than by observing, how the *Roman* Poet and Orator imitated the *Greek*. They are far from copying servilely: Whatever they take from the others, by mixing with it somewhat of their own, by giving the Whole a new Turn, or applying it in a new Way, they make their own. Oftentimes the Ground is the same, but the Figures are different, or disposed so differently, that the Whole seems new. They frequently indeed follow the others; yet often depart from their Track, and strike out unbeaten Paths, not less pleasing. They are for

for the most Part on the same Line with their Leaders, and from Imitators become Rivals. The *Roman*, in his [c] Panegyrick on *Cæsar*, and his Countryman, in the Episode of *Dido*, appear with as much Advantage, as in any other Part of their Works; yet in neither of these had they their Guides to point out the Way. He only can be an excellent Imitator, who may be a good Original.

THIS leads to a fourth Rule. "Be very "cautious how you confine yourself to the "Imitation of one." In that Case you can scarcely avoid too close a Resemblance.

AT the Revival of Letters in *Europe*, this was the reigning Mistake: All Writers of Reputation affected to imitate *Cicero*. No Period could be endured that had not the Cadence of his; no Thought could please, that was not in his Manner; nor Word be admitted, that wanted the Sanction of his Authority. *Erasmus* ridicules this superstitious Excess of Fondness with much Humour and good Sense, in a Dialogue intitled, *The Ciceronian*: But it is hard to keep the Mean; he ran into the other Extream, and is charged with a faulty Negligence in Language (*d*).

IN

[*c*] Oration for MARCELLUS.

[*d*] Our Countryman *Linacer*, his Cotemporary, though excelling in Stile, was also unreasonably prejudiced from the same Cause, against *Cicero*; for it is related of him, that he could not approve of *Cicero*'s Diction, nor hear him read without Weariness, *Ciceronis dictionem nunquam probare potuit, nec sine fastidio audire.*

Gardineri Epistol. ad Chek.

IN Truth, nothing is more likely to make one ridiculous, than ſuch a confined Imitation. In Dreſs and Behaviour it is prudent to follow the beſt-bred and moſt polite Perſon; but if you ſhould carry this ſo far as to affect every Motion and Geſture, to ſpeak in the ſame Tone, to ſmile and look in the ſame Way, with every minute Peculiarity which you obſerve in him, muſt you not expoſe yourſelf to Ridicule and Laughter? In outward Deportment there is a general Grace which becometh all, and every one ſhould aim at it; but there are innumerable ſmall Things, the Graces only of Individuals, which are fixed to them, and cannot be transferred, at leaſt not ſo as to pleaſe in another. Thus it is in Productions of the Mind: Bind yourſelf down to the Imitation of one, all will ſee and laugh at the aukward Reſemblance.

YOU ſhould therefore give yourſelf a larger Scope. As there are many good Writers, ſo far as your natural Talents will allow, chuſe out of all. By ſkilfully mixing and molding them together, you make ſomething that is new and your own: As in the burning of a rich *Grecian* City, the Confuſion of the various Metals which had been melted, and had run together, gave Riſe to a new and much valued one, named from the Place of its Origin, *Corinthian Braſs*.

MEN with learned Envy may toil to trace out your ſeveral Originals, as they have endeavoured to do by *Virgil* and *Horace*, but none regard

regard them. Such Imitation is ever Original: Like the Sun's Light, it is uniform and beautiful. A natural Philosopher may come with his Prism, and separate and decompound it into various-coloured Rays; but still it remaineth to every Eye one simple, equal, unmixed Splendor; or, to use the common but apt Allusion of the Poet,

Floriferis ut apes in saltibus omnia libant.

You should, like Bees, fly from Flower to Flower, extracting the Juices fittest to be turned into Honey. The severest Criticks allow such amiable Plundering.

IT is true, you may not equal the Merit of any of your Models; but you acquire a new, and become yourself an Original. Thus Criticks in Painting say, that *Annibal Carraccio* endeavoured to unite in himself the Merit of both *Roman* and *Venetian* Schools, to join the Grace and Accuracy of *Raphael* to the Colouring of *Titian*; by which Means, although equal to neither, he yet became himself an Original, and worthy of Imitation.

A FIFTH Rule is; "Have Regard to particular Circumstances of Time, Place and Occasion."

THE different Genius of Countries, but much more the Changes which have been made in Religion, Manners, and Customs, render it necessary in those who write or speak in Publick, to vary from the antient Patterns in many Things. Who doth not feel somewhat of Indignation,

dignation, at hearing a [*e*] Cardinal in a famous History, instead of mentioning the Providence of God, introduce the classical Pagan Expression of *Dii Immortales?* In the same Manner *Sannazarius*, in a [*f*] Poem upon the Birth of our Saviour, hath brought in Heathen Divinities as Actors; an Absurdity, which the Elegance of his Verse cannot atone for. And *Michael Angelo* hath erred in the same Way, representing *Charon* with his Ferryboat in the [*g*] most awful Transaction which the Christian Faith hath disclosed.

IMITATING the Antients, therefore, retain what is common in Eloquence; suit Particulars to your Occasion and Circumstances. He is not a *Demosthenes*, who can copy with the utmost Exactness any, even the most shining Passage in his Orations; but He is, who can speak or write as *Demosthenes* would have done in a parallel Conjuncture. A Christian, who is about to explain a Point of Religion or Morality, must express himself in a very different Manner from a Heathen Orator; neither can a Discourse delivered to a learned Audience, serve as an exact Model for one that is addressed wholly to the Vulgar and Illiterate: You cannot harangue in the *British* Parliament, as a Tribune did in the Assembly of the *Roman* People.

[*e*] *Bembus*, in his History of *Venice*.

[*f*] *De partu Virginis*; in which Poem, *Proteus* is introduced, in a prophetick Speech giving an Abstract of our Saviour's History.

[*g*] Picture of the Resurrection.

People. There is not any Thing of greater Moment than this Caution. The pureſt Stile, the fineſt Imagination, the beſt claſſical Imitation, is of little or no Value, unleſs employed in ſuch Manner as to ſuit the Occaſion. This Care is like Diſcretion in common Life, the Want of which renders the moſt ſhining Talents uſeleſs, or even hurtful.

LASTLY, "The moſt judicious Imitation is "not alone ſufficient." A meer Imitator is but a low Character. It was remarkable of a [h] well-known Actor in the Reign of Queen *Anne*, that he had ſuch Power of mimicking, as to counterfeit the Voice and Pronunciation of any, even the beſt Player, ſo perfectly, that no Hearer could diſtinguiſh the Copy from the Original; and yet this Man, ſo happy in his aſſumed Character, was in his real one but a Player of middle Rank. It is not enough, that you can imitate well the beſt Writer; you muſt likewiſe add ſomewhat of your own. Nothing is more rare than a perfectly-original good Genius; yet ſome Degree of Invention is not uncommon, and it is expected in every new Work.

IMITATION is indeed neceſſary and ſufficient, while you are a Learner, to inſtruct and put you into a right Method: If you would ſet up for yourſelf, you muſt have beſide ſome Stock of your own. Hitherto you have ſubſiſted by the Help and Bounty of others; you are now fledged, ſhould leave the Support and Track

[h] Eſtcourt. *See* Spectator.

Track of the Parent-Birds, if I may ſo ſpeak, truſt to your own Wings, and ſoar alone.

INDEED the Perfection of Imitation conſiſteth herein; not in borrowing the Deſigns and Words of the Antients, which, if done with Diſcretion, is not only allowable, but generally pleaſing; but in acquiring their Air and Manner, in a Reſemblance of their Purity, Life, and Elevation. Let the Materials be as much as you can your own; but endeavour to poſſeſs yourſelf of their Skill in putting them together, and in finiſhing; ſo that your Work may in Evenneſs, Solidity, and Luſtre, reſemble the Maſter-pieces which they have left behind them.

HE who takes the Whole, is rather a Plagiary than an Imitator: But he who, rich in a Fund of his own, adds to it by diſcreetly borrowing from the Antients, transferring into his Performance their Skill and Spirit, and makeing one regular uniform Work, is truly an Imitator, and may be allowed to have the Praiſe of an Original.

I have purpoſely avoided, in this Lecture, the Mention of imitating modern Writers. In the ſame Language it is ſcarcely to be ventured upon; and, indeed, is not to be attempted without very great Caution in any. The Writings of the Antients are conſidered, by common Conſent, as a kind of publick Magazine, to which Authors of all Nations may repair, and take from thence what Materials they want. If they have Skill enough to work them up well,

well, they are deemed the Property of the Workmen: But every Composition of a Modern is regarded as belonging to the Author alone, which no other can with Honour invade.

LECTURE

LECTURE the Eighth.

Concerning Eloquence, as it addresseth itself to REASON.

THE Order laid down in the Beginning requireth, that I should now proceed, to consider Eloquence, as it addresseth itself to REASON.

SOME wise and thinking Men, among whom I find Mr. *Lock*, have been of Opinion, that the Study of Eloquence ought to be discouraged, as being the Art of deceiving agreeably. In which Censure, they have manifestly mistaken for the Art, the Abuse of the Art. She furnisheth Arms for the Defence of Truth only; if any bred up in her Schools have employed these in the Service of Falshood, their's, not her's, is the Reproach; they are not her Sons, but Deserters from her. Eloquence, saith Lord *Bacon* [a], is inferior to Wisdom in Excellence, yet superior in common Use. Thus the wise Man saith, *The wise in Heart shall be called prudent; and the Sweetness of the Lips increaseth Learning* [b]; signifying, that Profoundness of Wisdom will help a Man to a Name or Admiration;

[a] In the Advancement of Learning.
[b] Prov. chap. 16.

ration; but that it is Eloquence, which prevaileth in active Life.

LET us then consider Eloquence in this Light, in her genuine State, as the Handmaid of Truth.

THE first great End which should be proposed by all Speakers, to which every other should be subordinate, is to *Convince*.

FROM whence it appears, that every Man, who seeketh to excell in Eloquence, should make it his earliest and principal Care, to strengthen and improve his reasoning Faculty. He must acquire *Sagacity* in discovering Arguments, and *Skill* in ranging them to the best Advantage.

THE former of these, *Sagacity*, is indeed the Gift of Nature: Yet we know from Experience, that it may be much bettered by Study and Exercise: Although we cannot bestow Sight to a Mind altogether destitute of it; yet Art can supply Helps to its Faculty of seeing, can strengthen it where weak, and quicken it where dim.

WITH Respect to this Operation it is, that the same [c] Lord *Bacon* observes, Rhetorick to be defective; that one Branch is almost wholely wanting, namely, the *Topical Part*: By which is meant, a Number of Observations on all common Heads, digested into convenient Order; which should be ever ready at Hand, that the Orator may have Recourse to them; and draw from them, as from a general Store, Materials

[c] Advancement of Learning.

Materials on all Occaſions. The Antients were ſenſible of the Uſefulneſs of ſuch Collections; and many among them laboured much in compleating this Part of Rhetorick, although little of that Kind is now extant: But the Deſign, we find recommended by the Approbation and Practice of the greateſt Perſons amongſt them. There remain many Precepts to this Purpoſe in the Works of *Cicero* and *Quintilian*: And *Demoſthenes* is ſaid to have prepared Forms, particularly of Exordiums, on all Occaſions; it being the moſt difficult Thing in an extemporary Speech to begin well, and the Part in which a Miſtake is the moſt dangerous.

ON the contrary, the Moderns have not only neglected, but deſpiſed this whole Matter; it ſeems not with good Cauſe. And the ill Effect of ſuch Contempt appeareth in unpremeditated Diſcourſes; where you often perceive the Speaker at a Loſs for Matter, beating about, and leading you round and round; when he has ſtarted any Thing, purſuing it on to irkſome Prolixity: Then, if I may ſo ſpeak, again at a Fault; filling up the Interval of Argument with tedious Expletives, or unmeaning Digreſſions. One good Way of avoiding which Inconveniency, it ſeems, would be, the Imitation of the Prudence and Induſtry of the antient Orators in this Article, who had theſe Topicks always at Hand; Fountains as it were, continually full, from which they drew the Streams of Eloquence, with Eaſe and Quickneſs.

FROM

FROM the Principle laid down, That the great End of Eloquence is to convince; it follows also, That the Orator should be early initiated and carefully instructed in those Sciences, which strengthen and direct Reason, by Rules and Exercise. Such professedly is *Logick*.

[d] *ARISTOTLE* informeth us, that the Arguments used by the Logician are chiefly, Syllogism and Induction; and that those of the Orator answering to them, are Enthymem and Example: The Relation between which, their Difference, the Force and proper Use of each, he deduceth at large, with much Subtilty and Solidity.

WITHOUT entering into this nice detail, it is easy to see, why these latter are more fit than the others, for the Orator. The Form of Syllogism continually recurring, would be dry and disgusting. Besides, two Propositions give the Sense of the Whole, the Mind of the Hearer always supplying the other, which therefore it is better for the Speaker to suppress. Again, Induction or an Enumeration of Particulars tireth out both Attention and Memory: Example hath the Evidence of Experience and Charm of Novelty to recommend it; at once proves and entertains.

NOTWITHSTANDING, in the Use of both, Caution is needful. A continued Chain of Enthymems hath an ill Effect, and is by no Means suited to a popular Audience.

IT

[d] Rhetorick, Book 1st.

IT keepeth the Attention on a perpetual Stretch: It becometh too ſubtle and thorny, from whence hard and obſcure: And by its abrupt Conciſeneſs, breaketh the ſmooth Current and Flow of Diſcourſe.

AGAIN, as Examples, ſtrictly ſpeaking, are rather Illuſtrations and Preſumptions, than Proofs; a Frequency of them enfeebleth your Reaſoning, cauſeth a Suſpicion of Fallacy, draweth out into immoderate Length: Inſtead of proving, at firſt they entertain; next tire; at laſt neither prove nor entertain.

WHICH Conſideration furniſheth theſe Rules;

" THAT Examples ſhould be always perti-
" nent.

" THEY ought to be ſhort.

" As little trite as poſſible.

" YET drawn from known Perſons or Things."

FARTHER. Your Diſcourſe however ſtrictly Argumentative, ſhould be at proper Intervals unfolded and opened out from the Cloſeneſs of Enthymem, into more eaſy and ample Proportions, that the Mind may have ſome Place of pauſing, where it ſhould reſt and unbend itſelf. A very rapid Stream, in order to pleaſe in Proſpect, ſhould have certain ample Spaces, into which it diffuſeth itſelf with gentler Motion, that the Eye may have whereon to repoſe itſelf agreeably.

THUS it appeareth without Controverſy, that Logick is a neceſſary Preparative to Eloquence. It may furniſh Helps in the Invention of Argu-

ments,

ments, and is certainly useful in the second Article, in the *Arrangement* of them. But the Science which seems most conducive to instruct an Orator in the Art of Reasoning, is *Geometry*.

It proceedeth usually from the most simple Elements to those which are less known, and so leadeth by the Hand to the remotest Truths: Or equally regular in descending, beginneth with what is general, and conducteth you from thence to particular Truths; both which correspond with the natural Progress of the Mind, either in discovering Truth, or in the communicating it when found, to others; and are therefore useful and agreeable; this latter especially, as more suited to the End proposed by the Orator,—Instruction.

Having ascertained one Truth, Geometry proceedeth to build upon it another, on which it raiseth the subsequent, so that the whole Pile becomes firm and unmoveable. It is more especially beneficial to the Orator, as it demandeth and introduceth an Habit of Attention in each Step, shutting out every Thing foreign from the Purpose with inexorable Severity; by which Means it preserveth from all needless Digression, from wandering and multiplying superfluous Words, Faults exceedingly frequent, and with Difficulty avoided.

For these Reasons, the Study of this excellent Science never can be too earnestly recommended to all young Persons, who would attain to a rational manly Eloquence.

LOGICK may give Acuteneſs and Subtilty; but from Geometry it is, that you are to ſeek for Clearneſs, Strength, and Preciſion.

IT is however material to be obſerved, that this is indeed the beſt Foundation, not the Whole of Eloquence; the Method of the Orator differeth in many Articles from that of the Geometrician. He muſt not, like this latter, require Demonſtration in every Step, becauſe his Subject rarely can admit of it. He muſt not extend his Chain of Reaſoning to a very great Number of Links, leſt the Hearer ſhould not be able to bear in Mind, or recollect them. He muſt not confine himſelf to the direct Line of cloſe Argument, but take in greater Scope; he muſt gather in Circumſtances, collect Probabilities; and from the Union and Combination of theſe, form an aggregated Argument. Other Differences there are, ſuch as the Neceſſity of repeating, of enlarging upon what hath been ſaid, and of preſenting it in different Lights, in order to impreſs it on the Mind; that alſo of illuſtrating, varying, and adorning, forbidden by the Auſterity of Science; of which we ſhall have Occaſion to treat more fully hereafter:— The Foundation is principally to be inſiſted on, — "You can ſcarcely raiſe Eloquence on any " firm Baſis, except that of Geometrical Know- " ledge."

EXPERIENCE it is true appeareth ſometimes to contradict this Poſition. Ye can name to me perhaps Perſons, who excel in ſolid Eloquence, yet are deſtitute of all Geometrical Science.

Science. I dispute not the Fact. But these Persons will be found to have from Nature, what is here recommended as the Effect of Art. Every Kind of Science was meant for the Assistance of Nature; where this latter hath been exceedingly bountiful, the Assistance is needless: But such Instances are rare, and disprove not the general Usefulness of Science.

Nay, I am perswaded, that if we examine into such Instances of this Kind as we are acquainted with, we shall find the foregoing Remark confirmed by them: They are natural Geometers. The Truth is, Nature where excellent, may be still improved by the Help of this Science; and where defective, may be supplied with what is wanting, and perfected.

Upon the Whole, I think it may be laid down as an universal Rule in the Point, That in laying the Plan of what you are to say, and in selecting your Materials, you should arrange all at first in a Geometrical Method; by which Means you will see the just Value, the Force and Connexion of each Argument: Afterwards, if you think it expedient, in order to win the Attention of the Hearers, to add any Ornament, you may be at least certain, that the Foundation is right: You have chalked out a well-known and sure Path; and, if, for the Sake of pleasing Prospects, you should now and then lead your Hearer to some Distance from it, yet you may be certain of recovering it at Will, and of conducting him safely to his Journey's End.

It

IT might ſeem ſcarcely needful to add, that it is a neceſſary Caution for all, to make themſelves thoroughly acquainted beforehand with the Subject they are to treat of, if one did not ſee frequent Inſtances of Careleſſneſs in this Reſpect; if one did not daily hear Perſons even in premeditated Diſcourſes, ſpeaking ſo confuſedly and ſuperficially concerning Points they undertake to explain, that it is evident, they had a very imperfect Knowledge of the Things they talked about.

WHEREFORE,——" Revolve a Subject long " in your Mind, explore it on all Sides, behold " it in all Lights." Many Advantages ariſe from this Habit. You will be enabled thereby to talk pertinently and properly. You will avoid Repetitions, which are ſo common and tireſome. You will become qualified to go to the Bottom, and exhauſt the Whole. You will abridge what you have to ſay, and by ſo doing acquire Strength and Solidity.

BESIDE all which, knowing thus before-hand the Quantity and Quality of your Materials, you will learn to give to each Part its due Proportion, not dilating and extending one beyond its proper Length; which is the Caſe of many Speakers, who are thereby compelled to ſhorten and cramp another Part, it may be of much more Importance, thus reſembling imprudent Managers, who, ignorant of the State of their own Affairs, and not forecaſting their Expence, ſpend in the Beginning profuſely, and are after-

wards

wards obliged to employ an ill-judged and untimely Parsimony.

FROM hence it happens, that you may have observed one Head to swallow up almost a whole Discourse: And after having squandered away Abundance of Words on Trifles or Matters little related to his Purpose, a Speaker comes with an ill Grace to slur over the main Part, in an Apology, because of the Shortness of Time, or his Unwillingness to trespass on the Patience of his Audience: A Method of proceeding not unlike the common OEconomy of Time in the World; Men throw away Years in Idleness and Folly; yet with Regard to the main Business of Life, the Attainment of Virtue and Happiness, are for ever complaining, and excusing themselves on Account of the Shortness of their Lives.

A FARTHER Advantage of this mature Consideration of a Subject, and little attended to, is this: From the View of your whole Scheme, you will be able to fix upon that Method which suiteth best with your particular Design; whereupon in a great Measure will depend the Force and Success of your Discourse. For, although in Mathematical Reasoning, where the Points considered are abstract Quantities, and strict Demonstration is demanded at every Step, all Methods may be reduced to two [e]; yet greater Latitude is admitted, nay must be taken in the usual Topicks of Eloquence, in Points of

[e] ANALYTICK and SYNTHETICK.

of Morals or Juſtice, in Facts and the common Buſineſs of Life.

FOR the Evidence here, reſulting only from a Combination of Probabilities, much Skill is requiſite in collecting and ranging Circumſtances, ſo as beſt to ſtrengthen each other, and when laid together to make the firmeſt Body, that can be compacted from ſuch: Which Method you may eaſily conceive to be capable of almoſt endleſs Variety; eſpecially, if you add hereto, that the Time, Occaſion, the Temper and Diſpoſition of your Audience ought alſo to be conſidered, and ſhould have great Weight in determining the Courſe you take. I ſhall endeavour to explain my Meaning by a remarkable Inſtance of this Skill.

CTESIPHON had propoſed a Decree, that *Demoſthenes* ſhould be honoured with a Crown of Gold, and that the Herald ſhould publiſh in the Theatre, that this Honour was conferred upon him, on Account of his Probity and Love of his Country. *Eſchines* accuſeth *Cteſiphon* of having violated the Laws by this Decree, in three Points. In crowning one who had been a Magiſtrate, and had not as yet according to expreſs Injunction of the Law, laid before the People an Account of his Adminiſtration: In crowning him in the Theatre before the *Greeks*, whereas this Ceremony was confined to the Aſſembly of Citizens; And laſtly, for falſly repreſenting in his Decree *Demoſthenes* as a good and zealous Citizen of *Athens*,

Athens, who was according to him, a wicked Man, and a Traitor to his Country.

IT was natural for *Demosthenes*, who appeared as Advocate for *Ctesiphon*, to have answered these Articles in the same Order; but observe how artfully he varies it. He beginneth by removing the ill Impression his Adversary's Accusation might have made on the Minds of his Judges; giving a full History of his own Life and Actions, proving his Innocence, and displaying at large the Services he had done to his Country, as Orator, Magistrate, and Embassador. Next, the two Articles relating to his Magistracy, and to the Place of publickly conferring the Crown, which were of least Consequence, and in which he was weakest, (for the Letter of the Law seems to have been rather against him,) he crowds into the Middle; where they were least likely to be observed; and returneth to his own Character and Actions, contrasting with them the Behaviour of his Accuser, whose Treasons and Crimes he describeth with such a Torrent of rapid and vehement Eloquence, as seemed likely to hurry away with it his Judges; and did in Fact obtain for him a glorious Victory.

BESIDE this previous Knowledge, this mature Consideration of the Subject prescribed, it is expedient also, to consult the Opinions of other Men, to add the Assistance of Books to your own Meditation. From them, you may furnish yourself with necessary Materials. They also present the best Examples to follow; and may

may encourage to a happy Emulation. Beside which, it often happens, that after you have long thought to little Purpose, a particular Passage in a good Author shall open a new Track in the Mind, and waken a Set of Ideas lying hitherto dormant therein; one of which when put in Motion, draws after it the whole Number with surprizing Quickness and Ease; a single Hint kindles, as it were, this long Train of Thoughts, and the Mind before cold and dark, becomes at once all Light and Flame.

THIS is no infrequent good Effect of Reading, and is not liable to any Exception. The former, that of employing old Materials, although exposed sometimes to Objection and Danger, the severest Critick cannot wholely disapprove of, especially in serious Argument. In Productions of Fancy, what is new and original is more justly demanded; for here the unbounded Spaces of Fiction lye open, in which Invention may expatiate unconfined, and display all her native unassisted Fertility.

BUT in serious Argument the Scene is narrow; Reason is uniform in her Motions, the Road she pointeth out is nearly the same to all, whence it cannot but happen, that many Times different Persons should light each on the other, should travel in the same Path, sometimes follow, and often seem to follow those who went before them. In such Kinds of Writing the Ground-work is nearly the same in all, the Manner usually maketh the Difference. In Works of Fancy, through Novelty we seek for Pleasure;

Pleaſure; but in Works of Reaſon, through Argument we ſeek for Truth.

ALLOWING this Diſtinction, ſtill it ſhould be your Care, in ſerious Argumentation, whatever Materials you derive from others, to mix ſkilfully and incorporate with what you furniſh from your own Fund of Reaſon; to melt down, and caſt as it were all anew: So that the whole Compoſition ſhall appear one Maſs, equal, uniform, and ſolid. This will obtain, and deſerveth the Praiſe of an Original. If this Conduct be in a moderate Degree indulged in Works purely of Imagination; how much more muſt it have Place in ſerious Compoſitions, in Diſcourſes of Reaſon and Truth; wherein it ſeems hardly poſſible at this Time, to deſerve in any other Way, the Praiſe of an Original,

LECTURE the Ninth.

Continuation of the Foregoing.

CONCERNING the Arrangement of Arguments, which was mentioned as the second Article to be considered in Reasoning, there is a Question proposed by [a] *Quintilian* as of some Nicety, and variously answered: In what Manner shall an Orator dispose his Arguments, so as to give them the greatest possible Advantage? Shall he place in the first Rank those which are strongest, and so proceed to the weaker?

BUT, herein there appeareth manifest Inconvenience: We know that what is said last, usually maketh the deepest Impression; from whence it is to be apprehended, that a weak Argument following shall enfeeble the stronger, which went before.

How then? Shall he take a contrary Course? Shall he set out with the weaker, and rise gradually from thence, concluding with the most weighty? Is not this liable to Objection? Is it not likely, that the Beginning may raise unfavourable Prejudices in the Hearer; and offer-

ing

[a] Lib. 5. Cap. 12.

ing to his View at first Sight only Trifles or Reasons of little Force, may excite his Scorn, or at least indispose him to attend?

Or lastly, shall he marshal his Arguments according to the Disposition of *Nestor*'s Army in the *Iliad* [b]; throw the feeblest Reasons into the Middle, as that Leader stationed the worst Troops in the Centre, while the bravest and most experienced formed his Van and Rear? This seems to be a prudent Disposition when the Case permitteth; when there is sufficient Variety and Choice of Arguments: But these, you are not without Necessity to multiply, rather than break through a fixed Method; which, if this Disposition were laid down as the best, you might be tempted to do.

The Truth is; as each of these Methods hath its Inconveniency, so are there Occasions, in which each may be the most fitting; and the Case cannot be reduced to one general Rule. But which of these Ways soever you chuse, Cautions necessary to be observed, are these.

Use no Argument that is false or frivolous.

Lay upon each no more Stress, than you are assured, that it can really bear.

Where there are Proofs sufficient to satisfy a reasonable Person, do not multiply needless Arguments.

As much as may be, avoid those which are subtle; few can understand such; all suspect them.

QUIN-

[b] *Iliad* Lib. 4. V. 297.

QUINTILIAN's Anſwer to the Queſtion is this; They may be diſpoſed in any of theſe Ways according to the Nature of the Cauſe, with one Exception, that the Diſcourſe ſhould not ſink from thoſe which are ſtrong, to the light and feeble.

IF I might attempt to give a more particular Anſwer, it ſhould be the following.

ALWAYS begin with ſome Argument at leaſt pertinent; and end with one weighty, and likely to have Effect. If the Cauſe require, that you ſhould propoſe the weightieſt firſt, (which you muſt do if there be but one that is of much Weight,) and you judge it needful afterwards to add others more feeble, for ſuch ſeparately inconſiderable, collected may have Force; in this Caſe, I think it adviſeable, at the Cloſe to reſume, and dwell a little upon that which was firſt propoſed, that you may leave with the Hearer the moſt powerful and convincing. In which Way of Proceeding, you muſt take Care, not to exhauſt the Argument at firſt, but to ſhew ſo much of it only, as may be ſufficient to raiſe Attention and good Expectation; otherwiſe, little more being left than meer Repetition at the End, inſtead of convincing it is likely to diſguſt and tire.

FARTHER. The *Kind*, as well as the Order of Arguments demands Attention. Thoſe drawn from *Authority* are often uſed. Concerning which you are to remark, That although conſidered with the Severity of a Philoſopher, they are not ſtrictly concluſive; yet ſuch

ſuch is the Veneration ever paid to the Names of eminent Perſons, that they have always great Influence in popular Speeches.

But this Caution ſhould be obſerved; That the Citations themſelves, and the Occaſions on which they are brought, ſhould be worthy of thoſe Names. In ſuch alſo, Moderation ſhould be preſerved: Numbers of Quotations are diſagreeable, and illuſtrious Names heaped on each other at length tire: There is more in it: There is a Pride in Man which makes him unwilling to be governed by any Thing, but his own Reaſon; he diſdains to bow his Neck to the Yoke of Authority. Wherefore it is prudent, to uſe Arguments of this Sort ſparingly, and for the moſt Part, rather as a Confirmation of Points already made probable, than as ſufficient Proofs.

Arguments alſo drawn from the Experience of others, or from Hiſtory, contribute not a little to perſwade; and are the moſt entertaining of any, relieving the Mind, which Attention quickly fatigues, by a pleaſing Variety. They are to a Hearer, as to one who hath long journeyed in a cloſe and ſhady Road, are certain large Spaces and Openings, which without leading out of the Way, pleaſe and amuſe, by letting in upon the Eye wider Proſpects, and new Light and Images. But herein particularly, Shortneſs is neceſſary, as Paſſages taken from Hiſtory carry often into great Length.

Proofs frequently ariſe from, are often interwoven with, *Narration*; which alſo demands

mands much Care in the Orator, it being no very common Quality to relate well.

NARRATION ſhould be clear, lively, and conciſe. Clear in order to inform; lively to ſtrike and affect; conciſe, that it may not tire, and that it may be remembered. Clearneſs is obtained by Purity of Stile and Accuracy of Method. Livelineſs ſprings from Imagination; and Conciſeneſs from a judicious Choice of Circumſtances, and from Cloſeneſs of Diction. In one Word, all may be ſummed up in *Simplicity*, the Perfection of Narration; which conſiſts in true natural Thoughts, expreſſed without Affectation, without Superfluity; and well connected, without Chaſm, Abruptneſs, or forced Tranſition.

ONE Miſtake there is relating to this Point, very general and hurtful; That the Narration of an Orator ſhould be always much more raiſed, more adorned, and wrought up with higher Figures, than that which is allowed to an Hiſtorian.

[*c*] I MENTION this as a Miſtake; becauſe it doth not appear to me, that there is any Foundation in Reaſon for making this Diſtinction; the Ends of both Orator and Hiſtorian being in Narration exactly the ſame, to give a clear Repreſentation of a Fact. Nay, I am certain, that actually this Diſtinction doth not prevail, is not kept up.

I DO

[*c*] Narrationes credibiles (*ſint*), propè quotidiano ſermone explicatæ dilucidè. CIC. de Orat.

I DO not think that there can be found in any Orator, Pieces of Narration more animated, enlivened with more ſtrong and glowing Colours, than the Account of the Plague of *Athens* given by *Thucydides*; than the Relations of the Sacking of *Alba*, and the Journey of *Hannibal* over the *Alps*, by *Livy*; that of the Mutiny in the *Roman* Armies upon the *Rhine* and in *Hungary*, by *Tacitus*; together with the Murder of *Agrippina*, *Nero*'s Mother, by the ſame Hiſtorian. Compare with theſe, if you pleaſe, that admired Narration of *Demoſthenes* which begins with, "It was Evening [*d*]": That of the Death of *Clodius* in *Cicero* [*e*]; or any others the moſt applauded; and I am perſwaded, you will acknowledge, that the Hiſtorians do not fall ſhort of the Orators in Fire, or Force, in Strength and Boldneſs of Expreſſion.

THIS Opinion therefore is in my Apprehenſion ill-grounded: And it ſhould be the more carefully guarded againſt, becauſe in Narrations, Occaſions of which very often occur, through a falſe Notion of Oratory, it betrays the Speaker into ſwelling and florid Bombaſt; Inſtances whereof I could produce in Plenty, and from Perſons of Talents not contemptible; eſpecially from the Panegyricks of our Neighbours upon the Continent, who, although in many Reſpects commendable, have fallen into this Miſtake more generally I think, than our own Writers:

[*d*] In the Oration for the Crown.
[*e*] Pro Milone.

Writers [*f*]: And it is in this Spirit of Criticism, that I have heard the Funeral-Sermons preserved among those of *Tillotson*, severely censured as cold and languid, because that excellent Person hath drawn the Characters of his deceased Friends, by a Relation of their Life and Actions, delivered with an unaffected, and as I think, truly moving Simplicity.

BESIDES, this Mistake hath received the Sanction of a [*g*] much-esteemed Critick in the seventeenth Century, who hath accordingly given Examples of Narratives in both Kinds, conformably to this Idea, less happily as I conceive, than is usual with that Writer.

IF however, it be an Opinion persisted in, that we ought to distinguish between these two Kinds of Narration, I should place the Difference not as usually is done in the Stile, but in the Manner, and should determine it thus.

THE Narration of the Historian is continued; That of the Orator ought not to be pursued to much Length, requiring the agreeable Variety of Interruption from Reflexions and Arguments. The Historian delivereth only the great and striking Circumstances: The Orator descendeth properly into the minutest Detail. The Historian giveth a fair, general, impartial Account: The Orator aimeth at a particular Point,

[*f*] The Funeral Orations of BOSSUET, much the best of any, abound with noble and sublime Passages; yet with a great Allay of declamatory Embellishment.

[*g*] STRADA in the Dialogue entitled MURETUS.

Point, and selecteth, and dwelleth chiefly on the Circumstances conducive to his End.

BESIDE direct Proofs of your Point hitherto mentioned, it is often necessary, to refute your Adversary; and answer Objections made to your Proofs.

IN the former of these, in refuting your Adversary, the most material Cautions are,---" To " deal ingenuously. To cite from him fairly. " To answer those Objections which have most " Force, not to chuse out as often is done, on-" ly the least weighty. Not to wrest his Words " from their natural and intended Sense. Not " to catch greedily at an Advantage from an " unguarded Expression. Not to charge him " with Consequences, which you skilfully draw " from his Positions, but he disavows. And " carefully to avoid all Acrimony."

I HAVE mentioned Proof and Refutation in this Order, because it seems a more natural Method to begin with establishing Truth: And afterwards the more fully confirm it, to proceed in removing any Difficulties, which may occasion Doubt. This in general: At the same Time I acknowlege, that this Method may be varied from, nay successfully inverted. You may begin by removing Prejudices, and afterwards establish Truth. But this hath Place, only where Prejudices have been entertained, such as are likely to shut up the Attention and Understanding against you.

UPON this Occasion of refuting it is, that Orators are frequently tempted to step out of the Province of Reaſon, into one altogether different, yet ſometimes of great Advantage to their Cauſe, that of Raillery and Ridicule. And ſo uſeful have theſe been judged, that the greateſt [*b*] Maſters of Rhetorick have taken the Pains of delivering Rules concerning the Art of excelling in them, and have with much Gravity attempted to teach Men how they might ſet others a laughing.

BUT whether Rules can at all avail towards acquiring or improving a Talent, which ſeems to depend entirely upon Nature, appeareth at leaſt very doubtful. My Judgment is, that conſidering the ſtrong Propenſity of Mankind to Sallies of this Sort, the beſt Uſe of Rules would be, to reſtrain and ſet Bounds to it, to preſcribe Caution and the utmoſt Delicacy in the Management of a Weapon, often more hurtful to the Perſon who wieldeth it, than to him againſt whom it is directed. The *Ridiculum Acri* is a true, but hazardous Maxim. Pleaſantry hath ſometimes the happieſt Effect; but it is ſo very pernicious when it fails, and it may fail from ſo many Cauſes, that we ſhould tremble in touching a Weapon thus keen and unmanageable. Where the Talent is natural, it is but too apt to become exceſſive: Where it is not, Rules cannot beſtow it.

ONE Thing we may lay down as certain, that it is an erroneous Opinion to ſuppoſe Ridicule to be the Teſt of Truth: And the Orator, who attempts

[*b*] Vid. CICERO de Oratore, Lib, ii.
QUINT. Lib. vi, Cap. 3.

attempts to form himself upon this Maxim, is as likely to become a bad Speaker, as the Moralist, to be a vain and superficial Philosopher.

AND we may remark by the Way, that the celebrated [i] Assertor of this Doctrine hath in no Part of his Work failed so remarkably, as in Attempts of this Kind; this Master of refined Criticism and polite Stile, being, if I mistake not, awkward in his Mirth, and forced and insipid in his Ridicule.

IN answering Objections, which was the second Article mentioned, you either answer those which have been, or anticipate those which you foresee shall be, made. In the former of these, a fair Field is open. Such Answers, if clear and full, are ever heard with Attention and Pleasure. Because, they are Proofs of Quickness and a good Capacity in the Answerer, appearing, however they may have been before considered, unpremeditated: And because, we behold with Pleasure Truth drawn forth to View, and Falshood stripped of the Ornaments Sophistry had thrown round her. Add, that we all naturally delight in Comparison and Contention.

BUT in the other, in anticipating or framing to yourself imagined Objections, much Care and Circumspection are necessary. By multiplying Objections you fatigue the Hearer; you break his Attention, splitting it on so many Objects, that it loseth Sight of the main one. Some enumerate frivolous Objections. Some

revive

[i] Lord SHAFTSBURY.

revive ſuch as are exploded. Some raiſe up others, ſo very nice and ſubtile, as it is likely would never otherwiſe have been thought of. But principally, beware of their Miſtake, who propoſe Objections, which themſelves cannot clearly anſwer: Even if they ſhould, the Practice is attended with this Evil, that the Scruple remaineth when the Anſwer is forgotten.

THE moſt prudent Way is, to confine yourſelf to Objections which have been urged, and are known: Or, if you think fit to raiſe up any to yourſelf, let them be ſuch only, as ſpring almoſt neceſſarily from the Subject; ſuch as you imagine will in all Probability occur, if not mentioned, to the Minds of the Hearers; ſuch as you think they would wiſh, as yourſelf if a Hearer would wiſh, to have cleared up: And let your Reaſoning in ſuch Caſes be as clear and ſhort, as the Nature of the Thing will allow.

A FARTHER Remark is, That as in Works of Fancy, one is apt to run into Florid and Bombaſt; ſo in Reaſoning, you are ever in Danger of going into Nicety and Subtlety. Diſtinctions may be neceſſary to expoſe the Fallacy of a Sophiſm, to clear up a Point, and give a preciſe Notion of it: But the Uſe of many ſuch confounds the Judgment, oppreſſeth the Memory, and is highly unpleaſing. Some who affect the Character of Reaſoners, are fond of refining on every Subject, and run up the plaineſt into all the Myſtery of Metaphyſicks. Others, whatſoever be the Topick, ſet out with a huge Apparatus of Lemmas and Propoſitions premiſed,

premiſed, and trail behind an immenſe Train of Corollaries and Conſectaries: We have ſeen Morality taught to ſpeak the Language of Geometry; and Pleaſures and Pains, Virtues and Vices confronted in all the impoſing Pomp of Algebraical Symbols [k].

ALL which prepoſterous Science flows from Miſtake or Oſtentation. "Suit your Arguments to your Subjects: Seek not laboriouſly to demonſtrate that which is plain: Nor dreſs up in the Garb of Science Truths of common Senſe:" For nothing that is unnatural can long pleaſe.

LASTLY. There are two Ways in which a Diſcourſe of Argument may be fitly concluded. One is by a Recapitulation of the ſeveral Arguments employed; the Uſe of which is obvious; as it collects and ſhews at one View, what was more copiouſly proved before.

THIS Part muſt be ſhort; otherwiſe the Repetition diſguſts: It ſhould therefore mention only the principal Matters. The Art is, to touch upon ſuch, as ſhall beſt recall the others to Mind.

A

[k] This Cenſure is not deſigned to include two learned and virtuous Perſons, who may be ſuppoſed to be here glanced at, Mr. WOLLASTON and Mr. HUTCHESON: But the Fault was very general about the Beginning of this Century, and remained long; occaſioned, as I ſuppoſe, partly by a Paſſage of LOCKE miſunderſtood; partly by the high Honour approaching to Enthuſiaſm, into which the aſtoniſhing Genius of NEWTON had brought Mathematical Learning.

A SECOND Way of concluding is, by turning from the Underſtanding to the Heart, by ſeeking to intereſt the Paſſions on the Side of Truth. But as this openeth a diſtinct Source of Perſwaſion, it deſerves to be conſidered more at large in another Lecture.

LECTURE

LECTURE the Tenth.

Concerning the PASSIONS.

ORDER requires that I ſhould in the next Place conſider Eloquence as addreſſed to the Paſſions. But as there is much Obſcurity and Confuſion in the Notions commonly received concerning theſe, give me Leave to premiſe ſome ſhort Obſervations upon the Nature, Uſe, and Qualities of the Paſſions; from whence the Duty of an Orator in this Point may be more clearly determined.

THE Manner in which both Moraliſts and Rhetoricians have treated of the Operations of the Mind, hath given Occaſion to a great Miſtake concerning them. Examine cloſely into the Opinions uſually entertained about them, you will find that they are looked upon as ſeveral independent Principles, diſtinct Beings, grafted as it were into the Mind, and acting by their own Force. How elſe, ſhall a common Reader think of *Conſcience*, when he meets with it ſupporting various Characters: Now it is a Judge, then an Accuſer; at one Time an Advocate, at another a Witneſs; it hath a Bar, a Tribunal, is armed with Laſhes and Scorpions? What other Idea ſhall he form of of *Taste*, as it is described by Criticks, the chief Author and sole Judge of Order, Beauty, Perfection in the fine Arts. In a like Manner do Metaphysicians speak of Understanding, and Will, and Liberty, describe their Power, settle their Privileges, and limit their Jurisdiction: An Occasion of frequent Misapprehension in the Writers themselves, I believe; undoubtedly in the generality of Readers, who follow the Author's Expression without taking the Pains of becoming acquainted with the Constitution of their own Nature.

A VERY little Application to this Study would teach them, that it is the whole Soul which acts in every Case, that judges, imagines, reremembers; that every Mode of Apprehension from simple Sensation up to the most abstract Reasoning, many of which we distinguish by the Names of several Faculties, are only Actions of the same Faculty of the Understanding; or more properly of the Soul exercising this Faculty, and differ solely by means of the Objects, or of their Circumstances. Conscience is the Understanding, judging of Actions compared with the Moral Law. Taste, judging of Works according to the Laws prescribed to such Works by natural Discernment, improved by Knowledge and Care: And so it is in all the others.

IN pursuing this Train of Thought, it is not difficult to obtain a sufficient Knowledge of our own inward Constitution. The Mind apprehendeth and judgeth. These are essential

to

to it. It ceaseth not at least in our waking Hours, from performing these Acts.

BESIDE which it hath, as inseparable from it as the Consciousness of it's own Being, a Desire of Well-being, or Happiness. This we feel every Moment of our Lives whensoever we reflect; it's Influence is perpetual, though not attended to; and for that Reason it is likely, not attended to; what is constant and uniform being, as if it were, not at all. Whatsoever the Mind judgeth to contribute hereto, it liketh and wisheth to obtain; every Thing which thwarts this, it disliketh, and seeketh to avoid or remove; naming that Good, this Evil: Which varying infinitely in Kind, Degrees, Occasion, Circumstances, Duration, cause a vast Variety in these Affections, in this Desire and Aversion, that springing from them follow their Nature and Proportion.

IF the Good be absent and probable, we are affected by Hope; if Evil by Fear. If the Good be present by Joy; if Evil by Grief. Good lost, raiseth Sorrow, Regret; obtained, Joy. If it be pursued by others together with us, Emulation; if obtained by another, oftentimes it excites Envy: If by the Unworthy, Indignation. If we have sustained Evil, we feel Resentment; which continuing becomes Revenge. If Praise be the Good ardently pursued, the Passion is named Vanity; when mingled with a Contempt of others, Pride. If Riches, Avarice. If Honours, Ambition. Evils falling upon another move Compassion.

WITH-

WITHOUT entring into a more minute Detail, thus much we infer from what hath been said, that the Passions, however the Catalogue may be swelled by a Multitude of Names, are in Truth no other than the two original Emotions of the Mind before mentioned, *Desire* and *Aversion*, or as they are commonly stiled, Love and Hatred; Love of Happiness and Hatred of Misery. The rest are no more than different Modifications of these two, determined by the different Circumstances, in which the Mind is placed with Respect to the Objects it is conversant about. Yet concerning all these, because differing in Names, Men are apt to argue as if they were Actions totally in Kind and Nature distinct, a Source of much Confusion and Mistake.

TRACE Things back to their Original, you will, I believe, find in this Matter a farther Mistake.

WRITERS agree in mentioning two Faculties of the Mind, of undoubted Reality, and altogether different, The *Understanding* and *Will.* Next after which they place as different Springs of Action, the *Passions*; in this last it seems, mistaken: For look into your own Breasts:---- Is not the Case thus?

YOU apprehend a certain Object to be good; you instantly desire to obtain it; if it be of much Importance, vehemently.---What then is Will, what Passion? Are they not the same Operation, differing but in Degree? For observe; The general Act of desiring, we name *Willing*; add

add hereto Heat, Ardour,---it is *Passion*. Passion then is the *Will* acting with Vehemence.

What then shall we say of that Philosophy, which condemned all Passion, as contrary to Virtue? For all Virtue being necessarily an Act of the Will, and Passion being such likewise, it certainly cannot be contrary thereto in it's own Nature: It may be, and often is faulty through Excess or Choice of wrong Objects; but this is an Abuse, not it's own original Guilt.

Nay it is past Doubt, that the Passions are useful. Without their Assistance we should sink into Sloth, and Mankind languish in total Inaction. For say, that Reason were your only Director, and it informs you that some certain Object is good and fit: You approve of; but will you meerly from this Approbation be induced to pursue it, especially, if you foresee that Difficulties shall occur in the Pursuit? No, undoubtedly: You would in most Cases sit down, wrap yourself up in Ease, and have no more Concern about it. This we see is really the Conduct of those who have from Nature weak Passions, they lie buried in Indolence: It is indeed the Conduct of all in Cases, where Passion interfereth not; the Love of Ease prevaileth.

The Conclusion is evident; Passion is highly useful, or rather necessary to Man, by prompting him to act, being a Spur within the Mind incessantly rouzing it from Sloth, and urging it to pursue or avoid with Earnestness. Without it, Life would lie as a dull dead Lake, stagnate-

ing

ing in muddy Tranquillity: This supplies the Gales which agitate, keep it moving and pure.

THE next Question is, " Are these Passions " under the Government of the Mind? If they " be Acts of the Will, as it was said, it should " seem not; for we must will the greatest " Good."

THE Answer is; In some Measure they are; In some they are not. It is allowed, that the Will must tend to Good; it's first Determination or Tendency cannot be prevented; which first is sometimes very violent: Whence I grant that the Passions may be kindled necessarily; we cannot hinder, we must feel the first Emotion:---But here the governing Power of the Mind beginneth: We can stop it at this Point, and hinder it's Progress.

CONSIDERABLE Differences it is true, must arise in this Power, from the various Constitutions of Men; from Temper; more especially from Habit the great Nurse of Passion; as well as from the Strength of Reason and the Care with which it has been cultivated: Notwithstanding, we may lay down as certain, that the Will however in it's first Motions not governable, is in the subsequent. We can restrain Passion. This is a prime Article of human Liberty, and principal Source of human Virtue.

" BUT how may this Account be true? According to it, the Passions being excited by " Views of Happiness or Misery, must be all " referred to ourselves. Yet what is more " known, than their interfering with extreme

" Violence

" Violence where we are not at all concerned?
" We ſhed Tears for the Queen of *Carthage* or
" of *Troy*, who have died many Ages before
" our Birth,

" *What's* Hecuba *to us, or we to* Hecuba [*a*]?"

IT is true: Yet herein is no real Contradiction; the ſeeming one ariſes from not adverting to the very great Celerity of the Mind: for this is the Caſe.

THINGS which we look upon as productive to us of Happineſs or Miſery we love or hate, pronounce Good or Evil; this Tendency fixeth their Nature. We form the ſame Judgment of their Effects with Regard to other Men, who have the ſame Affections as ourſelves.

HENCE whereſoever they fall, although their Influence ſhould not reach to us, we ſtill account them Good or Evil; we are in ſome Degree affected alike; becauſe the Mind upon their firſt Appearance inſtantly maketh the Application to itſelf, and eſtimates them from thence. This Act is habitual, immediate, perpetual, and thus by its Quickneſs and Familiarity paſſeth unperceived: And this is the Cauſe of that Pleaſure and Pain ſo commonly experienced in reading a Piece of Hiſtory or well-wrought Fiction. The Events relate not to us; but we feel their Effects by this ſecret, conſtant, and involuntary Application.

FARTHER; that the Paſſions may accompliſh their End, in rouzing to Action, there is by Nature

[*a*] SHAKESPEAR in HAMLET.

Nature annexed to their Operation, Pleaſure, independent utterly of the Succeſs or Event; for we cannot but obſerve numberleſs Inſtances wherein we are fond of having Paſſions excited, and are pleaſed with the Exertion of them. We like to admire, to love, to pity: As Perſons in good Health are impatient of long ſitting ſtill, and receive Pleaſure from the Employment of their Limbs, from mere Motion and Exerciſe; in like Manner doth the Employment of our Paſſions pleaſe by the very Agitation, whilſt Indolence fatigues.

WHICH however, is to be underſtood of Paſſions not in their own Nature or Degree, diſpleaſing. Thus, a certain Suſpence of Mind, hoping with ſome Mixture of Fear, is agreeable; encreaſe very much this Fear, it will have an oppoſite Effect. In playing for ſmall Sums of Money the Anxiety about the Event employeth agreeably; make the Sum exceedingly large, this Anxiety becometh painful, ſometimes beyond the Power of Diſſimulation to conceal.

THIS Remark openeth an Anſwer to a Queſtion of Moment in the Point before us. "Why do Objects which diſguſt when real, "pleaſe in Repreſentation? Paſſions torment-"ing, delight when excited by Art?" Let the Skill of an Orator or Poet raiſe Terror, Grief, Hatred, painful Affections, they ſhall then beſtow great Pleaſure: For as a judicious Poet ſays,

Nature's

[a] *Nature's worst Forms, that living shock the Sight*
Exprest by mimick Art, afford Delight,
The Pencil's animating Pow'r conveys
Beauty at Will, and makes ev'n Monsters please:
The Muse thus charms us, when in tragick Scenes
With Wounds fresh-bleeding OEdipus *complains,*
When mad Orestes *raves our Eyes o'erflow*
With soft Distress, and Pleasure springs from Woe.
In whatsoe'er you write let Passion's Heat
Go search the Heart, there touch, warm, penetrate;
The Secret is at first to please and move;
Find Springs that may attatch in Hate and Love.

THE Observation just made points out the Answer. In general, The Exercise of our Passions administers Pleasure: But where these spring from Misery suffered, or threatened to ourselves, Pain becomes the predominant Sentiment, and is alone perceived. Accordingly, remove

[a] " Il ne point de serpent, ni de monstre odieux,
" Qui par l'art imitè ne puisse plaire aux yeux,
" D'un pinceau delicat l'artifice agreable.
" D'un objet tout affreux fait un objet aimable:
" Ainsi pour nous charmer la tragedie en pleurs
" D'*OEdipe* tout sanglant fit parler les douleurs,
" D'*Oreste* parricide exprima les alarmes,
" Et pour nous divertir nous aracha des larmes.
" Que dans tous vos discours la passion emue
" Aille chercher le cœur, l'echauffe, et le remue.
" Le secret est d'abord de plaire et de toucher:
" Inventez des ressorts qui puissent attacher."

remove this Misery, this Apprehension for ourselves, the natural Effect follows, the Passion becometh pleasing.

HENCE in Fiction, the Distress of a captive Prince, a despairing Lover, a disgraced Favourite, the Tortures of a jealous Man, and Fury of one angry, excite Anxiety, Grief, Terror; but because the whole Spectacle is accompanied with a perpetual Consciousness of our own Security; it inspireth Pleasure only, that before mentioned, which by the Bounty of Nature is annexed to the Exercise of Passion.-----Bring these Evils near; shew them ready to involve our selves, the agreeable Scene vanisheth, we feel Pain, Misery.

PLACE upon the Stage a City besieged, with the Calamities usually attending such a State, let it appear even in Flames, we look on with Pleasure; but suppose these to have caught any Part of the House, the Reality terrifies beyond Expression where the Image delighted.

BESIDES, the Image of grievous Distress pleaseth, because it presents to us, in the most lively Colours, a View of our own Happiness, in being exempted from such Distress. A comparison with Misery alleviates Misfortunes, with Misfortunes gives a sweeter Relish of Prosperity.

WHICH Reasoning is confirmed by observing farther, that all Representations affect us more or less according as they bear Relation to our selves in Nearness or Similitude: Thus we are more affected by Things animate than the inanimate, by Beasts more than Insects, by human

man Creatures more than Beafts; among Men by thofe of our own Country more than by Foreigners, ftill more by thofe who are in like Circumftances of Age, Fortune, Rank, Relation. The Origin whereof can be no other but this fecret Reference, which we always, however unperceived, make to our felves, confidering thefe Events as more or lefs probable to become one Day our own Concernments.

THIS Power of working upon us by engageing our Paffions is that which conftitutes the whole Charm of the imitative Arts; and it is yet more ftrong in Eloquence than in any other: My Reafon for thinking fo is this.

DISTRESSES reprefented in Poefy and Painting are the Sufferings of Perfons, who never had Being, or long ago ceafed to have. Now although in contemplating thefe, the Mind perceiveth Satisfaction, namely, that which Nature hath annexed to the Excrcife of the Paffions, yet hath it intimately prefent with it a Confcioufnefs of their being unreal, feigned, or paft. It is true, it endeavoureth to fupprefs the actual View hereof, and gives itfelf up induftrioufly to the pleafing Delufion prefented before it. Notwithftanding, this it cannot fo entirely fupprefs, but that a Senfe thereof ftill accompanies the Mind through all it's Motions; it perceiveth it's own Safety, and beholdeth the Danger from a Point beyond it's Reach; or at moft, the Deception is momentary, in fome great Crifis, and vanifhing inftantly enhances the returning Pleafure of reflecting on one's own Security.

THE Case is different in Eloquence. It's End being to persuade, to exhort or deter Men by presenting a View of real Advantages or Evils involving themselves, it is altogether free from Delusion. The Passions it excites being grounded in Truth, must be more forcible: Yet they have not the Disadvantage of Reality in giving Pain, because it's Aim being to redress or prevent Evils, it always mixeth Hope, and softens the Impression: If it terrify by exhibiting the ill or threatning State of Affairs, it tells you at the same Time how to remove or avoid the Evil; it joins the Pleasure of Fiction to the Force of Truth. To which we may add, That in the other Arts there is some Mixture of Weakness in giving Way to the *Pathetick*; and although we willingly resign ourselves to a Deceit thus agreeable, yet we are conscious, that herein we indulge to the Imperfection of our Nature. In Eloquence, there is not this Diminution. The Passions raised here are according to our natural Frame, they spring from Reality, and are the Ministers of Justice: The Pleasure is pure without Allay, the Passions are exercised, and for a worthy End. From whence my Inference, that Eloquence hath a Power over the Passions superior to that of Poesy, Painting, or any of the imitative Arts.

" BUT why should there be this Application
" to the Passions? May it not be an Abuse?
" Would it not be much better to appeal to the
" Understanding only?"

THE

The Anſwer is not difficult.

As the End of Eloquence is Perſuaſion, and ſtrictly ſpeaking, all Perſuaſion ought to be founded in Conviction alone, it muſt be acknowleged, that all Addreſs to the Paſſions is grounded in the Imperfection of Mankind; it is faulty if not neceſſary. If our Hearers were always ſerious, attentive, knowing and unprejudiced, we ſhould have nothing to do but to lay Truth before them in it's own genuine Shape: But as Men actually are, we find it neceſſary, not only to ſhew them what is right, but to make Uſe of all the Skill we have, to induce them ſtedfaſtly to behold it. In every publick Aſſembly ſome are ignorant, many wandering in their Thoughts, or otherwiſe intent, not few biaſſed, and all indolent and quickly fatigued, Impediments which every Speaker muſt ſtudy to remove, or the Goodneſs of his Cauſe will but little avail: Truth hath Enemies within, who would bar up every Avenue againſt her; you muſt raiſe up Friends there, if you ſeek to have Admiſſion granted to her.

Now this being not the Frailty of particular Perſons, but the State and Frame of human Nature, the Orator who would attempt to perſuade upon Principles of ſevere Reaſon, muſt be for the moſt Part unſucceſsful. His Fate would be much the ſame with that of the Politician; who ſhould deal with Men as if they were perfectly juſt, and ground all his Schemes upon a Suppoſition of univerſal Probity.

THE

THE Philoſophy of the Stoicks was built on a Foundation of this Kind, requiring conſummate unmixed Virtue, and ſhutting out all Paſſion as weak and faulty: What was the Conſequence? As their Philoſophy was falſe, their Writings were dry and diſguſting; neither of them could obtain it's true End, That could not reform, nor theſe perſuade.

ADDRESS to the Paſſions being thus neceſſary, the firſt Queſtion fit to be conſidered is,---- " How may we beſt ſucceed in this Deſign?"

THE great Maſter in his Rhetorick anſwers; Make yourſelf thoroughly well acquainted with the Nature of theſe Paſſions. For which Purpoſe, he delivers a very accurate Account of them, ſo far as they fall within the Purpoſe of an Orator: And this Part of his Work cannot be too carefully ſtudied by all who ſeek to arrive at this Knowlege: And it is remarkable, that all the Induſtry of modern Ages hath added little that is conſiderable to his Diſcoveries on this Head.

BUT the Knowlege which may be acquired by Precepts, however right and judicious, cannot alone ſuffice to anſwer the Intentions of an Orator. You muſt add your own Obſervation. Look within. What is it that raiſeth your Love, or Hatred, Indignation or Pity, that toucheth, warmeth, tranſporteth? Compare with it the Effects which you ſee produced in others. From hence you ſhall learn by Degrees to know the true Sources of each Paſſion, to make Allow-

ance

ance for the Variety of Tempers and Circumſtances, and thus you ſhall hit upon the right Path which opens to you the human Heart.

UPON looking back on what hath been advanced in this Lecture, the Novelty of Part may I fear, want an Apology: Permit me to add a few Words to that Purpoſe.

THE Knowlege of our own Frame, of the human Mind, would undoubtedly be very uſeful, if it could be obtained; and the Search into it is therefore right. But Difficulties that ſeem to be inſuperable quickly ſtop our Progreſs, and appear to diſcourage all ſuch Attempts. Concerning which however, we ought to remark, that theſe interrupt not the Search in Points ſo far as we can judge, really uſeful: It is a Spirit of meer Speculation and Curioſity, that puſh Enquiries into abſtruſe Queſtions.

CAST your Eyes on the Performance of *Ariſtotle* in the Point before us. He though by no Means an Enemy to Subtilty, yet confineth his Reſearches to the Object, Qualities, and outward Circumſtances of the Paſſions; and from thence layeth down Rules for the Orator, as eaſy as they are ſure. Modern Metaphyſicians endeavouring to go beyond theſe Bounds, have intangled themſelves in endleſs Perplexity.

AWARE of this, yet willing to gratify a Curioſity in ſome Meaſure juſtified by Cuſtom, I have attempted to find a Clue which might guide our Steps through this Labyrinth: And however

however probable I may think my own Notions, yet I do not expect a general Assent to them. Where Men wander in Twilight without certain Road, each may well be allowed to chuse his own Path. The following Reflection however, before you condemn, let me intreat you to make.

ASK yourselves; In the many Treatises on this Subject, in Discourse where it hath been mentioned, what have we read or heard? How are the Passions described or defined? As Modifications of the Mind, Emotions, Agitations, Instincts;---Words either vague or metaphorical, conveying none, or no clear Meaning.

TAKE them now in this Point of View.---- We easily conceive two Powers or Actions of the Mind, *Understanding* and *Will*. Under the first are ranged all the Modes of Thought; Perception, Imagination, Reasoning: Under the second, all practical Determination framed thereon, from the first simple Motion of Assent, or Preference to the most rapid *Impetus* of Desire or Aversion; comprehending all the Affections and Passions, often so voluminously and obscurely described. Here is Order, Plainness, Simplicity; from whence it seems agreeable to Nature, simple in Causes, however abundant and various in Effects.

BUT whether or how far this Speculation is true, and solid, I leave to your Judgments; adding this only; that however that be, the main Point is not greatly affected thereby: The Passions

Passions with respect to the Influence Oratory hath over them, may be sufficiently known, by considering them as the great Master hath done; and the Rules herein remain the same. The first of which we have mentioned;-----
" Observe, which, of what Kind and Turn are
" the Passages, that most affect your selves and
" others; from thence take your Direction."

LECTURE

LECTURE the Eleventh.

A Continuation of the Foregoing.

WE ſhall lay down as a ſecond Rule, the Precept, moſt generally recommended and inſiſted upon, without which nothing ſhould be attempted, nothing of Moment can be accompliſhed in this Way, thus expreſſed by the Poet,

Si vis me flere, dolendum
Primum ipſi tibi.

" BE yourſelf poſſeſſed with the Paſſion, you " would excite."

How would you receive a Perſon ſpeaking upon a Subject of the utmoſt Importance with Coldneſs and Phlegm; or bemoaning a grievous Calamity with an Air and Tone of the calmeſt Unconcern? Would you not turn away from him as a Deceiver; or at leaſt deſpiſe him as a Trifler unworthy of Attention?

PLUTARCH relates a Paſſage of *Demoſthenes* very apt to this Purpoſe. A Citizen of *Athens* came to this Orator, beſeeching him to plead his Cauſe againſt one, by whom he had been treated with great Cruelty. As the Perſon

ſon made his Complaint with an Air and Stile of perfect Coldneſs and Indifference, " This " Affair cannot be as you repreſent it, ſaid the " Orator; you have not ſuffered hard Uſage." " How," anſwers the other, raiſing his Voice, and with the utmoſt Emotion, " I not harſhly " uſed! I not ill-treated!"—Nay, now ſaid *Demoſthenes*, " I begin to believe you,—That is " the Form, that the Language of an injured " Man.—I acknowledge the Juſtice of your " Cauſe, and will be your Advocate."

NATURE hath ſo framed us, that all ſtrong Paſſions ſtamp themſelves upon the outward Form. They are viſible in the Air of the Countenance, in every Geſture and Motion. The Uſe or final End of which Conſtitution is very evident; that our Paſſions may be communicated. Theſe form a Kind of natural Eloquence, which, without the Help of any other, is moſt powerful in winning over the Spectator, ſpreading as if by Contagion. Hence, in Perſons altogether illiterate, Grief and Anger burſt out in Exclamations more affecting, than the moſt conſummate Power of Speaking unaſſiſted by that inward Impulſe can furniſh, becauſe flowing freſh from the Heart, the Voice of Truth and Nature.

FROM hence we may account for the remarkable Difference between the Effects, produced by extemporary, and by premeditated Diſcourſes. A Diſcourſe prepared before-hand, although regular in its Method, juſt in the Sentiments, pure in the Stile, ſhall yet move and pleaſe

please less, than one spoken off-hand, which is defective in all these; because this latter, inspired by the Occasion, proceedeth directly from the Heart, from a Mind agitated by the same Passions which the Speaker would raise in his Audience. This Effect is most observable in Replies, where the Matter being unexpected, the Answerer is rouzed and warmed with such Heat as enlivens his Discourse, animates his Form and Action, and carries the Flames which glow in his Breast into those of his Hearers. The former may be compared to a fine Statue wrought by vast Labour and Skill into the truest Symmetry, yet hath it not Half the Graces of this other, those inimitable Graces, which Life giveth to a Body less perfectly proportioned.

THE same Principles shew likewise the Truth of a Rule often repeated; "That an Orator "ought to be esteemed a good Man." You cannot be much affected by what he says, if you do not look upon him to be a Man of Probity, who is in earnest, and doth himself believe what he endeavoureth to make out as credible to you.

Is it not from hence, that there have been Times, in which the Words publick Spirit, Good of the Community, Love of one's Country occurring often in a Discourse, however used, have yet been treated with some Degree of Scorn or Ridicule? Why? Because these Terms naturally representing very noble Ideas and sublime Springs of Action had been sullied, contaminated, as it were profaned by Tongues, where

where the Heart was governed by corrupt, base, and mercenary Principles.

A VERY material Question relating to the Subject before us, is this; "Upon what Occasions may an Orator most properly employ this Branch of his Art; address himself to the Passions?"

IN Answer to which observe, first, Where a Person is called upon to speak on a Point of Importance before one or few chosen Judges of acknowledged Skill and Integrity, he ought to be very sparing in the Use of the Pathetick: Because here the Discovery of Truth being the only End in View, and Reason being the only certain Guide leading to that End, every Deviation from it, every Appeal to Passion will be looked upon by such Men as an Attempt to deceive, will therefore offend, cannot fail of raising some Prejudice against the Speaker, and it is likely against the Cause which he pleadeth.

THIS Fault becomes unpardonable, if the Cause be good. It is then like to the Painting over a fair Face, destroying real Beauty by artificial Embellishment. In such Circumstances a natural, clear, well methodized Explanation of the Case is the only just perswasive Eloquence.

A VERY different Conduct is required in those who speak before a large Audience, as in a popular Assembly. Here Address to the Passions is not only allowable, but necessary. For the first Thing to be compassed is to gain their Attention. And this you cannot so well effect in any Way, as by insinuating yourself into their Affection.

Affection. The Multitude is wonderfully quick, I might ſay raſh, in forming Judgment. They have not Patience to mark the Series, and wait for the End of an Argument. There muſt be ſomewhat agreeable to allure them on; dry Truth quickly diſguſts them. To make them liſten you muſt affect them.

AGAIN, Suppoſe this firſt Point accompliſhed, that they are attentive. Yet the greater Number cannot comprehend a Chain of cloſe Argument. They cannot retain in their Memory the ſeveral Steps, and before you come to draw your Concluſion, the whole Series of Proofs is vaniſhed. Lay your Thoughts in the juſteſt Order, expreſs them with all poſſible Clearneſs, yet if there be many Arguments, or of various Kinds, they cannot apprehend them; Attention becomes painful; they cannot underſtand, and will not liſten.

SOME Difference in this Rule muſt however be ſuppoſed, where the Genius of the People before whom you ſpeak, is very different. The leſs improved and poliſhed an Audience is, the more needful is the Pathetick. Criticks attribute to this Difference, in a great Meaſure, the Unlikeneſs between *Demoſthenes* and *Cicero*: The *Athenians*, by Nature the moſt acute of all the *Greeks*, by a long and careful Cultivation of Arts, had become in general attentive, curious, and judicious: Whereas the *Romans* engaged from the Birth of their State in perpetual Wars, had not until very late applied themſelves to Arts and Sciences, and were of Conſequence far

far less polite and discerning; which made it requisite for an Orator here to direct himself more to the Passions, than was needful at *Athens*, more perhaps than would have pleased there. Not that the *Greek* is really less pathetick, but he concealeth it more, and interweaveth more and closer Arguments.

THIS Kind, the Pathetick, seems more especially requisite, where the Design of the Speaker is to vindicate and recommend the Cause of Religion and Virtue. Instruction is indeed the first Thing necessary, to which Purpose the Pathetick is useless, nay improper. But that Part is usually not difficult.

THE natural Notions of Mankind lead them so strongly to distinguish what is good, that short Directions, few Proofs are sufficient: The Hardship is, to engage them heartily in the Pursuit of that which they know and acknowledge to be right. Here it is, the Orator is to open the whole Sails of his Eloquence, to wake, to rouze, to shake the Soul; to hold out Rewards and Punishments, Promises and Threatnings, alternately to encourage and terrify, to raise Joy, Sorrow, Fear, Shame, Hope, Anguish, Remorse. To search the deepest Recesses of the Heart. To enter as it were into the Soul, and like the sacred Orator [*a*], to make a Governor amid all the Pomp and Power of his Office, hardened besides, and grown old in Sin,—to make him tremble [*b*]. For the Passions standing for the most Part in Opposition

[*a*] St. PAUL. [*b*] FELIX TREMBLED.

tion to Virtue, you muſt find a Counterpoize to them in—Paſſions: Without theſe, Reaſon is a weak Sovereign without Forces: In gaining her you gain only a Name, a Shew of Authority; Power and Activity are on the oppoſite Side.

WHAT hath been ſaid ſeems to prove unanſwerably the Truth of a Point beforementioned, the Uſefulneſs and Neceſſity of ſpeaking to the Paſſions; a Point which I now return to, becauſe there are many who aſſert that an Orator ſhould ſeek to prove only, not to move; a Miſtake the more dangerous, as it ſets out upon a worthy Principle, the Love of Truth, and can recommend itſelf by the Sanction of great Names. But ſurely the Patrons of this Opinion forget that Paſſion belongeth as truly to the Nature of Man as Reaſon, and however abuſed, and by that Abuſe rendered pernicious, was given for uſeful Purpoſes, and is capable of anſwering them. What then, ſhall we totally reject it;—or rather ſhould we not apply ourſelves to regulate? There is beſides a View in which this Matter hath not, as I remember, been conſidered, and yet I think it may help in throwing in Light upon it.

MEN have generally looked upon Reaſon as wholely diſtinct from, indeed for the moſt Part as oppoſite to Paſſion: Becauſe the Conſequence of ſuch Oppoſition is exceedingly bad when it doth happen, they regard them only in that Light of Oppoſition. Wherein there is Miſtake. For undoubtedly very often, I might ſay

for

for the most Part, there is an intimate Connexion between them; so that you cannot make any strong Impression upon one, without affecting the other. An Instance may best explain my Meaning.

DEMOSTHENES undertakes to stir up the *Athenians* to make Head against *Philip*, at that Time preparing to invade them. Suppose the Orator to have delivered his Sentiments on this Occasion in the plainest, most unadorned Manner, must not the bare Enumeration of *Philip*'s former Actions, of his Fraud, Dissimulation, of his having corrupted their Allies, their own Magistrates and Orators, much more the Relation of his many dark Designs and Plots to rob them of their Glory, their Territory, their Liberties, have raised violent Indignation in their Breasts? Was it possible to produce the several Arguments offered by the Conjuncture, so as just to render them intelligible, without working this Effect?

LET us now say, that you on the other Hand aim at striking the Passions only: If you do this with Skill, you must without designing it, convince. Here also the same Orator furnisheth an Example.

INTENDING to inflame the Minds of his Hearers with Hatred against *Eschines*, his Adversary, he describes the Character of this Man; his Youth infamous, his Manhood factious, mean, flagitious; adds Venality, Calumnies, Treachery, complicated Treasons; he paints, amplifies, inveighs:—Now do not these Charges by kindling Indignation, Aversion, Horror against his Accuser, tend directly to acquit himself? Could you feel any of these Passions without an Inclination to believe the Innocence of the accused? And doubtless, they had an actual Influence in the Event.

I MIGHT easily point out the Source of this Mistake, by recurring to the Reasoning in my last Lecture, the evil Habit there mentioned, of considering the Understanding, and Will, and Passions, not only as distinct Actions of the same Agent the Mind, but as distinct Agents; whence that imaginary Independence, Rivalship, Enmity, so much and confusedly talked of: But I shall not now return to metaphysical Disquisition, in which I fear I may have been thought to have then dwelt too long. This Inference is clear and sufficient to my Purpose. "We "should not seek imprudently to separate what "Nature hath framed inseparable. The Art "of Perswasion preferring Reason, cannot yet "reject Passion, because very often the closest "Reason necessarily affecteth Passion; the "deepest Pathetick convinceth Reason."

IT remains to finish my Design, that I should point out some Cautions, very useful to be observed in Attempts to move the Passions.

First, "CONSIDER well whether the Point "you are to discourse upon requires or may "admit of the Pathetick." It is obvious, that there are many Subjects which do not; the Value of one, its Circumstances, Nature may render that Treatment improper. For certainly, nothing

nothing can be more disgusting to an Audience than to observe a Speaker torturing himself and them, in order to affect them mightily on a Subject of small Importance. As again, it must be an unpleasing Disappointment to be paid with Exclamations and Vehemence of Sound, where they expect solid Argument. The Rule is, reflect thus within yourself before you begin;

" IF another were to speak on this Point, " how would I wish him to treat of it?" " Should I desire to be instructed or moved, " pleased or convinced? Act thou accordingly."

ANOTHER material Observation not always adverted to is, that " The principal Regard " should ever be paid to Reason. To per- " swade you should convince." Conviction indeed need not, nay cannot always be brought about by a Chain of strict Argument, which few can perfectly comprehend, and yet fewer are disposed to listen to: But in all Cases the Groundwork must be, Reason. This should be the Basis; upon which you may raise whatsoever you think conducive to your Purpose, of Ornament or Pathetick; but this it is, which must give Strength and Consistence to your Discourse. Without this, the most enlivened and most magnificent Oration is but like those Fabricks which appear sometimes in the Clouds, that the first Blast of Wind disperseth into shapeless Air.

THE Ground of this Remark is in human Nature. We are conscious that Reason is the governing Principle of our Nature, that we ought to be directed by it alone. It is true, we often prefer Passion, we often follow it in Contradiction to Reason: Yet we well know, that in so doing we err. Hence we look upon it as a Kind of Indignity, that others should appeal directly to our Passions; we regard them as Persons who seek to take Advantage of our Weakness; who despise, or mean to deceive us.

HENCE follows a third Rule. "Let your "Address to the Passions be as short as it con-"veniently may, for two Reasons," both upon the last mentioned Account, that you may bestow more Time and Care upon the rational Part: And likewise, because, Nothing more quickly tires and disgusts than Addresses of this Sort. The Passions as we have seen, were given to rouze us from Indolence, to make us active and enterprizing. Hence they are quick, lively, powerful, but soon subside. And this was graciously ordained, that having answered their End, they might become weak, and easily manageable by Reason. Wherefore, "follow "Nature. Seek not to keep long in Motion a "Spring formed for quick, but short Action."

ACCORDINGLY we find in the best Writers, that the Passages which affect us most are not long and laboured, but short sudden Strokes, like Flashes of Lightning that just shine and vanish. It would be easy to bring Instances hereof from both the *Greek* and *Roman* Orators: But for the Sake of Conciseness, I shall mention only

only ſome few from a Poet, who excelleth all others in theſe ſhort and delicate Touches.

SPEAKING of the Weakneſs of *Orpheus* in looking back on *Eurydice*, he hath this very affecting Turn,

[c] *Cum ſubito incautum dementia cepit amantem,*
Ignoſcenda quidem, SCIRENT SI IGNOSCERE MANES.

THE following in *Eurydice*'s Speech is not inferior,

[d] *Invalidaſque tibi tendens,* heu non tua! *palmas.*

MUCH of the ſame Kind is that beautiful Repetition concerning *Caſſandra* taken Captive,

[e] *Ad cœlum tendens ardentia lumina fruſtra,*
LUMINA, *nam teneras arcebant vincula palmas.*

WHAT a fine Image of Melancholy do theſe two Lines preſent,

[f] TE *dulcis conjux,* TE *ſolo in littore ſecum,*
TE *veniente die,* TE *decedente canebat.*

SUCH

[c] When ſudden Madneſs ſeiz'd th' uncautious Lover,
Madneſs, to be forgiv'n,—could *Hell forgive.*

[d] Stretching to thee her feeble Arms, alas!
No longer thine!

[e] Raiſing in vain to Heav'n her ſparkling Eyes,
Her Eyes, for Fetters bound her tender Hands.

[f] THEE deareſt Conſort, on the lonely Shore
He ſung; with riſing Morn, with ſinking Day,
Thee, ſolitary ſung.

SUCH alſo is that of the young *Greek*, who having followed *Evander* from *Argos* was killed in *Italy*,

[g] *Et dulces moriens reminiſcitur Argos.*

IN the Deſcription of the Murrain, what a moving Circumſtance is the following,

[h] *It triſtis arator*
Mærentem abjungens fraternâ morte juvencum,
Atq; opere in medio defixa relinquit aratra.

AND this of *Dædalus*, which I know not whether it can be parallelled in any Poet,

[i] *Tu quoque magnam*
Partem opere in tanto ſineret dolor, Icare haberes;
Bis conatus erat caſus effingere in auro,
Bis patriæ cecidere manus.———

OF this Kind is the Queſtion of King *Lear* to *Edgar* diſguiſed as a Lunatick;

"What, have his Daughters brought him to this Paſs?
"Could'ſt thou ſave Nothing? Didſt thou give them all?"

AND

[g] And his lov'd *Argos* recollects in Death.

[h] Sorrowful
Departs the Hind, disjoining from the Yoke
The Steer that mourns his Brother's Death, and fix'd
In the unfiniſh'd Furrow leaves his Plow.

[i] Thou too, O *Icarus*, did Grief permit,
A Place in this illuſtrious Toil hadſt found;
Twice he eſſay'd to frame in living Gold
Thy Fall untimely, twice the Fathers Hands
Sunk down.———

AND this of *Macduff*,

" He has no Children."

PITY indeed is the most difficult of our Passions to be long kept up: It is easily raised and ceaseth instantly. For which Reason we may observe, that such Tragedies as turn chiefly upon Terror, please more than those which are calculated to move Compassion: The Impression is stronger and more lasting. Thus we prefer the *OEdipus* of *Sophocles* before his *Electra*, and yet more before his *Philoctètes*: As indeed this seems to give that Writer the Advantage over *Euripides*, who excels in the tender Passions.

FOR this Reason *Shakespear* is not only the first of our Tragick Poets, but I am inclined to think him, with all his Faults and Irregularities, the noblest Genius in that Form of Poesy which ever appeared. I doubt, whether human Invention can devise a Scene of more striking astonishing Horror, than that which is wrought up from the Death of *Banquo*,—*The* TABLE'S FULL."

A FORMER Observation leads to a fourth Rule; " In speaking to the Passions, as " much as possible conceal your doing so." It should be perceived only by the Effects, otherwise it appears like a Design to deceive, and puts your Hearer on his Guard. To this Purpose a *Greek* Critick [*k*] recommends the Use of the Sublime, as hiding the other in its superior Brightness. BUT

[*k*] LONGINUS.

BUT there is nothing more carefully to be avoided, more destructive of the End proposed in speaking to the Affections, than Elegancies and Prettinesses, fine turned Periods and glittering Conceits.

IN the Midst of the deepest Affliction or most violent Anger, we meet with Persons in the Tragedies of *Seneca*, declaiming for several Lines together, in all the sententious Wisdom of a Stoick: And our own Poets do not scruple to introduce an Heroe expiring with a florid Similè in his Mouth [*l*]. The Writings of *Seneca* the Philosopher, the younger *Pliny*, and the Declaimers of the lower Empire, together with Crowds of Moderns, have been before taken Notice of, as abounding with Beauties of this Sort. But as in Life, so in Writings, Excellence consists in following Nature; and without Doubt strong Passions express themselves in the most unstudied and the least artificial Manner.

THIS is so true, that not only Gaiety and Gawdiness, false Decorations of Stile, but even the true Ornaments are little suited to the Pathetick. The Sentiments should be such as flow naturally from the Passion, and the Words such as the Hearer may be likely to pass by unnoticed, that is, easy and simple.

HEREIN it is, that the *Greek* Poet hath far excelled all his Followers. He, that is so elevated in his Sentiments, so lofty in his Stile, that describeth a Battle or Storm in Numbers as sounding

[*l*] See Death of *Montezuma* in the *Indian Emperor*, &c.

ſounding and rapid as the Images which he preſenteth, is here humble, and plain, and unadorned. If you would form a right Notion of his Excellence herein, compare the Complaints of *Eurialus*'s Mother, or thoſe of *Evander*, occaſioned by the Death of their Sons, with the Lamentations of *Hecuba*, or with that which is ſuperior to every Thing of the Sort, the Lamentation of *Andromachè* when *Hector* was killed; you will ſee how far the ſtrongeſt Efforts of the moſt curious and beautiful Art fall ſhort of Nature.

AND in this Reſpect: *Laſtly*, There is one Fault very common, againſt which we can never be too well prepared; that is, "The perſiſting in a pathetick Strain before "an Audience entirely unmoved." In which Caſe a Speaker not only diſguſts and tires, but never fails to become ridiculous. If one ſpeak off-hand, or from Memory, he may eaſily perceive how the Audience is affected by viſible Marks in their Countenance and Behaviour: If he find them liſtleſs and unconcerned, he may lower his Tone, he may ſhift his Sails, and change his Courſe: But where you rely on a ſtudied Diſcourſe, this is impracticable; you have engaged in a Career which you muſt finiſh, however diſgraceful. For this Reaſon an [m] eminent Writer of our own hath laid it down as a Kind of general Rule, not to attempt moving the Paſſions in a premeditated Diſcourſe, becauſe the odds are that you fail.

BUT

[m] Dr. SWIFT, Vol. 1ſt.

BUT he seemeth to have carried this Matter too far. This Effect indeed his Argument ought to have, to make Men exceedingly careful what they offer to the View of the Publick: If you never attempt to move the Passions, you can be at best but a tolerable Speaker: If you persist in unsuccessful Attempts, you become ridiculous. But between these two, there are various Degrees of Excellency, to which we may and should aspire.

THE best Advice which occurs to me in the Point is this; "Engage in no Cause but such "as you approve of: Study it thoroughly. Be "sincere. Possess yourself with the Passion "you would raise. Never sit down to write, "nor stand up to speak but under this Impres-"sion." By these Means, you may hope to unite the Justness and Correctness of Study to the Force and Fire of extemporary Elocution. You shall at the same Time please and convince, instruct and affect, become Master both of the Understanding and Passions of your Hearers.

LECTURE

LECTURE the Twelfth.

Of ELOCUTION, *or* STILE.

ELOQUENCE, as it addresseth itself to the Senses, cometh next to be considered,—in this View, comprehending chiefly Elocution, or Stile. Pronunciation, the other Part, I shall take an Occasion to treat of hereafter [*a*].

HERE, as in other Matters, the surest Way of determining what is right and what is faulty, is to have always in View the End and Design. Now the great End of Language, being to communicate our Sentiments for the Instruction or Perswasion of other Men, it is manifest, that the first and most necessary Property is *Clearness*: Whatever renders it very difficult or dark, so far contradicteth its original Intention.

HENCE it appears, that we ought to employ such Words as common Use hath made known and familiar.

FOR the same Reason, our Language ought to be *pure*. Because, whatsoever departs from the true Standard of a Tongue is so far dark. It is besides, offensive on another Account, betraying

[*a*] Lect. 22d.

traying either Want of Knowledge, or a low and bad Education.

THE ſame Principle leads to a third Rule. " As far as the Genius of the Language admits, " range Words in their natural Order." For harſh and bold Tranſpoſitions always occaſion Perplexity in the Hearer. To this Fault the Writers of the *Roman* Language ſeem peculiarly liable.

ANOTHER Fault oppoſite to Clearneſs, which modern Tongues more than the antient, our own perhaps more than the others, eaſily fall into, is " Equivocal Expreſſion ;" when mentioning different Perſons or Things, it is not always plain which you mean, but the ſame Action or Attribute may be aſcribed equally to either. This Fault ſhould be carefully avoided.

FROM theſe Principles it followeth, that we ought to ſhun all obſolete Words ; new Phraſes which Caprice is for ever introducing ; all low Expreſſions ; conceited, far-fetched, and affected Manners of Speech.

IT might appear ſuperfluous to recommend *Clearneſs*, which is the firſt and moſt obvious Quality requiſite in Speaking or Writing, if Obſcurity were not a very common Fault : Nay, and great Perſons among the Antients, who beſtowed incredible Pains upon this Article of Stile, are juſtly charged with it. But we ſhall ceaſe to wonder hereat, if we reflect, that there are other Cauſes of Obſcurity, beſide thoſe mentioned. Such as regard the Thought alone I ſhall not inſiſt upon, as being foreign to the preſent

present Design. Within our own Subject there is a principal one,—" The Ambition difficult " to be suppressed by the best Genius, of throw- " ing what one has to say out of the common " Form, of raising it above the Level of fami- " liar Dialect, and of drawing the Notice and " Attention of the Hearers."

NOT seldom, the Harmony and Sound of Periods are the Speaker's Object. The Thought becomes darkened by a Multitude of Words: An Exuberance of Leaves concealeth the Fruit: This among the *Greeks* was named the *Asiatick* Stile; to which was opposed the *Attick*, being pure, terse, and properly concise.

BUT the principal Cause of Obscurity in Persons of good Talents, is that mentioned by *Horace*,

[*b*] " I aim at Shortness, and become obscure."

They labour to compact their Sense so closely, and wrap it up in so few Words, that it is difficult to unfold it. Their Writings resemble an Army, whose Ranks are so close, that they cannot wield their Arms. They contain valuable Treasures which you cannot well get at; like one who is possessed of great Wealth, but consisting wholely in Jewels; very rich, but not for common Use. This is in some Degree the Character of *Thucydides* and *Tacitus*. A Fault, which although springing from an excellent Cause, such as indeed is not to be often apprehended,

[*b*] ——— *Brevis esse laboro,*
Obscurus fio. De Arte Poet.

hended, yet ſtill it were better that we ſhould avoid.

THERE is likewiſe another Kind of Brevity, which renders Writings obſcure, more dangerous, becauſe more frequent, not through ſuperabundance of Senſe and Parſimony of Words, but through an Affectation of Elegance. Here, the Speaker affects to give to every Sentiment a quick, briſk Turn; and contracts his Expreſſion, to make it lively and pointed. Theſe Perſons lead you on from Prettineſs to Prettineſs, through a Courſe of Antitheſes, a friendly Strife of Words, through a String of Riddles, which have juſt Myſtery enough to afford you Pleaſure in finding them out; like the Sheperdeſs in one of our Poets,

[*c*] "But feigns a Laugh to ſee me ſearch around,
"And by that Laugh the willing Fair is found."

This is *Pliny*, *Seneca*, and *Florus*.

WE may compare the Diſcourſe of the great Speakers of Antiquity to a River, ſometimes flowing in a ſtraight Line, again winding, here ſwift, there ſlow, as the Ground directs; but always clear, majeſtic, and full to the green Verge: On the contrary, the Speech of theſe others is a Torrent rolling over Pebbles, broken among Rocks, tumbling down Caſcades, here and there pretty enough, but rattling, ſhallow, and muddy by its own Agitation.

THUS

[*c*] POPE's Paſtorals.

THUS Discourse must be clear——That, however, is not enough. It sufficeth, indeed, for Instruction: But an Orator must aim at more; in Truth he hath no other Way of certainly arriving at that, but by aiming at more: For what avails it to be clear, unless I can make you think it worth your while to attend? However intelligible I be, importeth not; for you will not understand unless you listen, and you will rarely listen if I be no more than intelligible. The Orator must therefore *please* and *move*. He must, to Perspicuity, add Ornament. This openeth to us a very large Field. It would be impossible to comprehend all Particulars: I shall speak briefly of those which seem to be of most Importance, or have been less copiously treated of.

BUT the remaining Part of this Discourse I shall confine to one Particular, introductory to the rest, and very useful to be considered; because it may preserve, from a Fault, the more dangerous, as deceiving under the Appearance of Beauty, and by that Means very incident to young Persons, who are readily caught by Show and Splendor.

IT is an Observation of *Aristotle*, which I have formerly mentioned, that the first Kind of Writing, the most antiently used, was Poesy. Hence, they who first began to compose Discourses in Prose, which in *Greece* happened about the Time of the Persian *Cyrus*, finding Poesy in Possession of the publick Esteem, in Compliance therewith, retained the Expressi-

on

on of Poesy, although they had departed from from its Numbers; which Manner continued long; and according to him, was that of *Gorgias*, who was Co-temporary with *Socrates*: And this Fact is confirmed by some little Fragments of that Sophist remaining at this Day, which are pompous and poetical. Now this, he observeth was an Error. The tragick Poets, themselves found it necessary to lower the majestick and grand Elocution which the Muse had hitherto made use of; and in order to render their Dialogue natural, invented Iambicks, a Measure approaching to Prose; a convincing Argument, that Orators should avoid the Stile peculiar to Poets.

IT must be confessed, however, that this Fault, if I may venture in all Cases to name it such, remained always among Writers, both good and bad; although from different Causes. The former having their Imagination filled with the Grandeur of their Subject, and being exceedingly desirous to impress due Conceptions of it upon the Reader's Mind, ventured beyond the Bounds of their Art, and rose into Expressions too high and ardent: Instances whereof may be observed in *Plato* and *Longinus*, in *Livy* and *Tacitus*.

THE others, finding admired, and admiring the Elevation of Poesy, endeavoured to copy out in Prose, her Ornaments; not considering, that They are Beauties of different Kinds, and the Embellishments of the one deform the other. This was the Case of Writers in the

Decline

Decline of the *Roman* Empire, and is that of Multitudes among the Moderns.

BESIDES, they found it much easier to scatter over a Discourse Flowers here and there, than to give it throughout, its due Spirit, Strength, and Connexion.

IF you should ask, as some have done, "What is the Ground of this Distinction? "Why should not that which pleaseth in one "Kind of Writing, please in another?" The Answer is easy: The Ends are entirely different, of Course the Means.

[*d*] THE chief *End* of Poesy is to please: Instruction indeed contributes, is often necessary to this End; Instruction then is only a subordinate End,—that is, the *Means*.

WHEREAS in Eloquence the Reverse hereof obtains: Its chief End is to instruct; and Pleasure being often a necessary Mean to Instruction, becomes here a subordinate End. The Truth of this Distinction appears from hence; that Poesy, although it should be instructive, yet if it do not please, is never in Esteem as a poetick Work; so that Pleasure is its chief End. On the other Hand, let a Piece of Eloquence please: If it convey no Instruction, it cannot be held in Esteem; a Proof, that Instruction is its principal End. The Ends of each being thus fixed, point out the Means, and

[*d*] Totumq; illud studiorum genus ad ostentationem est comparatum; præter id quod *voluptatem* SOLAM *petit*, &c. QUINT. lib. x. chap. 1. (de Poetis loquitur.)

and demonſtrate that they ought not to be confounded.

THE Stile of Poets is that of certain Numbers returning, in the ſame Cadence, at ſtated Intervals. This Harmony having both Variety and Rule, is agreeable to the Ear, fitted to an Art, the Deſign of which is to pleaſe. But in ſerious Speech, ſuch Harmony would be offenſive. For where the View is to inſtruct, it muſt appear too much ſtudied, an Indication of ſome Lightneſs or trifling Diſpoſition in the Speaker. Hence we are offended at the Cadence of Verſe in a Proſe-work, becauſe it is not expected, and thus diſappoints the Ear.

WE find no leſs Difference between theſe two Kinds of Writing in many other Reſpects, ſome of which, chiefly with Regard to the Point in View, *Stile*, I ſhall briefly enumerate.

THE Method uſed by an Orator ſhould be natural; all Parts ſhould be diſpoſed as much as may be in the juſteſt Order, both Sentiments and Words: This Regularity tends to perſwade, hath the Simplicity and ingenuous Air of Truth. Now Poets are by no Means tied down to this Exactneſs; nay it is fit, that they ſhould depart from it, preferring that Diſpoſition which may ſtrike the Fancy and Ear moſt agreeably.

THE Poet generally makes Choice of the moſt ſounding Words, the moſt pompous Expreſſions, as moſt conducive to Harmony: The Orator is required rather to avoid ſuch, as approaching to Affectation. The Poet is allowed

to

to frame new Words, to revive old, that he may pleafe by Novelty or a venerable Air of Antiquity: Such Licences are forbidden to the Orator, becaufe not readily underftood and uncouth.

AGAIN. The Poet is obliged to raife his Stile above that of Converfation, and make it in Contexture and Colour altogether different: The Orator is for the moft Part to come near to, never to feem induftrioufly to avoid it. The Poet is allowed to tranfgrefs the Bounds of ftrict Truth; to raife his Images beyond Nature; to heap Ornaments upon Ornaments; to crowd and vary his Figures, ufing the ftrongeft and moft bold; to fport in Allegories; to wander in Digreffions; entertain with Comparifons; enliven with Allufions: His Tranfitions may be quick; Metaphors may fhine in every Line; he may extend Defcriptions, introduce as many Perfons fpeaking as he pleafeth, create Perfons who never had Being; in fhort, he may employ every Art, that can give Life, and Spirit, and Fire to his Work; Fable, Sentiment, Figure, Painting, Harmony, fonorous, copious, glowing Expreffion.

IN all which Particulars, the Orator is reftrained to much narrower Limits. He muft confine himfelf to Truth, at leaft to the ftricteft Probability; muft be exceedingly fparing in Digreffions; his Tranfitions fhould be ufually nice, and almoft imperceptible; his Comparifons tend only to illuftrate; he fhould rarely venture into Allegory; his Metaphors fhould not be frequent, seldom bold; Hyperboles are very dangerous to him; Descriptions should be short, and introduced only where they seem necessary; his whole Stile should be pure, clear, modest in its Ornaments, removed if possible from all Appearance of Art, and seeming to flow naturally from the Occasion.

As a Kind of Illustration of what hath been said, a little Specimen of this Difference, observe the following Passage that I have somewhere met with, in which the whole Sense is taken exactly from the *Roman* Poet, and the Expression so varied, as to convey the Image contained in his Verses with somewhat of their Spirit, in the Language of Prose.

Sicut in vastâ qualis est hæc nostra, civitate, si forte accendantur, ut sunt mobiles, plebis animi, it primo murmur incertum, dein atrox clamor; hinc currunt ad arma, vis vi repellitur: Sin assurgat vir sapientiâ et virtute præclarus, extemplo siletur; Ille compescit iras, docilesq; animos flectit fingitque.

THE Original, which most of you probably recollect, stands thus:

[e] *Ac veluti magno in populo cum sæpe coorta est*
Seditio, sævitq; animis ignobile vulgus,
Jamq;

[e] As oft when Strife divides a num'rous State,
And the fierce Rabble catch the factious Heat,
Stones

Jamq; faces & saxa volant; furor arma minis-
trat:
At pietate gravem et meritis si forte virum quem
Conspexêre, silent, arrectisq; auribus astant:
Ille regit dictis animos, et temperat iras.

I SHALL not detain you with a Comparison of each particular Expression in these two Passages, which I think it better to leave to your own Observation. Instead of this minute Detail, it occurred to me as much better, to lay before you an Instance more at large, and in our own Language: With which View, I have prepared the same historical Event, related in the Manner first of an Orator, then of a Poet. Although the Strokes be less bold, and the Colouring much fainter, than in corresponding Passages, which might be gathered out of the Works of the Orators and Poets of Antiquity; yet, if the Proportions be kept and the Characters rightly marked, this, however rude Workmanship, may answer the End proposed, and shew the Difference between the two Manners described. The Usefulness whereof, the Advantages ariseing to Eloquence from the Study and judicious Imitation of the Poets, I shall take Occasion to shew at large hereafter [f].

THE Fact I have chosen to relate in these two Ways might appear incredible, if a parallel Event

Stones fly and Torches;—Fury Arms supplies;
But if they see an honour'd Sage arise,
In Act to speak; they turn and listning gaze;
He rules their Spirit, and their Rage allays.

[f] Lect. 16 and 17.

Event had not happened before, in one of our own Colonies, at *Port-royal* in *Jamaica* [g]. And a Person then preserved in the same wonderful Manner, returned to these Islands, and lived here many Years, well known, and an Object of great and just Curiosity. But I proceed to the Relation itself, which runs thus in the Stile of an Orator.

THE Plains, in which *Lima* the capital City of *Peru* is placed, are the most beautiful in the World. They are of vast Extent, reaching from the Foot of the *Andes* or Cordelier-mountains, to the Sea; and are covered with Groves of Olive-trees, of Oranges, and Citrons; watered by many Streams; one of the principal among which, washing the Walls of *Lima*, falls into the Ocean at *Callao*; in which latter Place is laid the Scene of the ensuing History.

TO this City, Don *Juan de Mendoza* had come over with his Father from old *Spain*, yet an Infant. The Father, having born many noble Employments in *Peru*, died much esteemed and honoured rather than rich. This young Gentleman had in early Youth conceived a very strong Passion for Donna *Cornelia di Perez*, Daughter to a very wealthy Merchant, who dwelt in the City of *Callao*, at that Time the best Port in the whole Western World.

BUT although the young Lady, who was reputed the most accomplished Person in the Indies, returned his Affection; yet he met with an insuperable Difficulty in the Avarice and inflexible

[g] See Philosoph. Transactions, No. 209.

flexible Temper of the Father; who, preferring Wealth to every other Consideration, absolutely refused his Consent. At length, the unfortunate Lover saw himself under a Necessity of returning to his native Country, the most miserable of all Mankind, torn away for ever from all that he held most dear.

He was now on board, in the Port of *Callao*. The Ship ready to sail for *Spain*. The Wind fair. The Crew all employed; the Passengers rejoicing in the Expectation of seeing again the Place of their Nativity. Amid the Shouts and Acclamations with which the whole Bay resounded, *Mendoza* sate upon Deck alone, overwhelmed with Sorrow, beholding those Towers, in which he had left the only Person who could have made him happy, whom he was never more to behold: A Thousand tender, a Thousand melancholly Thoughts possessed his Mind.

In the mean Time, the Serenity of the Sky is disturbed; sudden Flashes of Lightning dart across, which encreasing fill the whole Air with Flame. A Noise is heard from the Bowels of the Earth, at first low and rumbling, but growing louder, and soon exceeding the roaring of the most violent Thunder. This was instantly followed by a trembling of the Earth: The first Shocks were of short Continuance; but in few Moments they became quicker, and of longer Duration. The Sea seemed to be thrown up into the Sky, the Arch of Heaven to bend downwards. The Cordeliers, the highest Mountains of the Earth, ſhook, and roared with unutterable Noiſes, ſending forth from their burſting Sides Rivers of Flame, and throwing up immenſe Rocks. The Houſes, Arſenal, and Churches of *Callao* tottered from Side to Side, at laſt tumbled upon the Heads of the wretched Inhabitants.

THOSE who had not periſhed in this Manner, you might ſee of every Age and Sex, ruſhing into the Streets and publick Roads, to eſcape from the like Ruins. But even there, was no Safety: The whole Earth was in Motion; nor was Ocean leſs diſturbed: The Ships in the Harbour, were ſome of them torn from their Anchors, ſome of them ſwallowed up in the Waves, ſome daſhed on Rocks, many thrown ſeveral Miles up into the Land. The whole Town of *Callao* late ſo flouriſhing, filled with Half the Wealth of the Indies, diſappeared, being partly ingulfed, partly carried away in Exploſion by Minerals burſting from the Entrails of the Earth. Vaſt Quantities of rich Spoils, of Furniture, and precious Goods, were afterwards taken up floating ſome Leagues off at Sea.

IN the Midſt of this aſtoniſhing Confuſion, *Mendoza* was perhaps the ſole human Creature unconcerned for himſelf. He beheld the whole tremendous Scene from the Ship's Deck, frighted only for the Deſtruction falling on his beloved CORNELIA. He ſaw, and mourned her Fate as unavoidable, little rejoicing at his own Safety, ſince Life was now become a Burthen.

FOR,

For, after the Space of an Hour this terrible Hurricane ended; Earth regained her Stability, the Sky its Calmneſs. He then beholdeth cloſe by the Stern of his Ship, floating upon an Olive Tree; to a Bough of which ſhe clung, one in the Dreſs of a Female. He was touched with Compaſſion, he ran to her Relief: He findeth her yet breathing, and raiſing her up, how unſpeakable was his Aſtoniſhment, when he beheld in his Arms, his beloved, his lamented *Cornelia!* The Manner of whoſe miraculous Deliverance is thus recorded.

In this univerſal Wreck as it were of Nature, in which the Elements of Earth and Water had changed their Places, Fiſhes were born up into the Mid-land, Trees and Houſes, and Men into the Deep; it happened, that this Fair one was hurried into the Sea, together with the Tree, to which in the beginning of the Commotion ſhe had clung, and was thrown up by the Side of that Veſſel, wherein her faithful *Mendoza* was, which was one of the few that rode out the amazing Tempeſt. I cannot paint to you the Emotions of his Mind, the Joy, the Amazement, the Gratitude, the Tenderneſs:—Words cannot expreſs them.

Happy Pair! The Interpoſition of Providence in your Favour was too viſible, for any Man to diſpute your being at laſt united for ever. And O thrice happy *Mendoza*, how wonderfully was thy Conſtancy crowned, thy Merit rewarded.—Lo, the Wind is fair! Haſte, bear with thee to thy native *Spain* this ineſtimable Prize. Re-

turn

turn, no less justly triumphant, than did formerly the illustrious *Cortez*, loaded with the Spoils of *Montezuma*, the Treasures of a newly-discovered World.

HERE follows the same Piece of History in a poetical Dress, in which, the Manner of *Spenser* is aimed at, with some Variation in the Form of the Stanza:

Inscription; To *Doctor* EDWARD MAURICE [*h*].

O THOU who imp'd with Praise the Muse's
  Wing,
 Yet feeble, still behold with gracious Eyes
What from the Critick's Chair she dares to sing,
 Unequal far I ween to such emprize.
Yet should'st thou OSSORY, propitious smile,
 Fearless tho' weak, she'd urge the bold Design,
Maugre foul Envy and Detraction vile;
 For ev'ry Form of Eloquence is thine,
Whether high Truths thou teach in nervous
  Prose,
Or Fancy's glitt'ring Wealth in tuneful Strain
  disclose.
SUCH mitred [*i*] *Bembus* on th' *Ausonian* Coast,
 To *Latian* Notes join'd native *Tuscan* Rhime,
At once the Poet's and Historian's Boast;
 Such *Vida*, [*k*] Critick sage, and Bard sublime.
Yet

[*h*] Late Bishop of *Ossory*; an excellent Preacher and Poet. Among many Performances in both Kinds, he hath left in the Hands of this Lecturer a Translation of the *Iliad* into *English* Verse, in the Manner of *Milton*: Which it is hoped the Publick will see and approve of.

[*i*] [*k*] Two excellent Writers in the 16th Century; both Bishops in *Italy*.

Yet what avails, if Action's current ſtray,
The Poet's Song, or Preacher's Eloquence?
Thy Life is ſtill more perfect than thy Lay,
And Manners add new Energy to Senſe.
Here Sons of ALMA look, here emulate;
For Genius few, but all may Virtues imitate.

I.

" YE Plains adorn'd in Nature's laviſh Pride,
" Where Spring and Autumn ever-ſmiling dwell,
" Thou Stream, whoſe Waters faſt by *Lima* glide
" Imperial City, take my laſt Farewel:
" Oft ſtraying on thy Banks thro' Citron Groves,
" The fair CORNELIA heard my tender Pain,
" With Smiles and Bluſhes heard: (Ill-fated Loves
" Which Parents ſtern forbid and Avarice mean!)
" Pity a Wretch from ev'ry Comfort torn,
" And driv'n to native Soil in Baniſhment forlorn.

II.

" AND ye rich Tow'rs of *Callao*, that incloſe
" The faireſt Maid e'er ſeen by mortal Eyes,
" Late Scene of Joy now chang'd to bitter Woes,
" Receive my laſt Adieu, theſe parting Sighs.
" Thou Sun, this World's long worſhip'd God ſupreme,
" Outcaſt of thy bleſt Land, ſad Imp of Woe,
" Why linger I beneath thy unfelt Beam,
" Bereft of Life, of Her?---Ah, there beſtow
" Thy

" Thy choicest Gifts, Health, Joy; if such there be
" Last grant her Love a Youth, more fond, more true than me."

III.

THUS from the Ships tall Deck MENDOZA mourn'd,
His Eyes on *Callao* fix'd: Beneath resound
The busy Crew; for ev'ry Bosom burn'd
To reach *Iberian* Shores, sweet natal Ground:
As Bees that to provide new Seats prepare,
With hoarse mix'd Hum and rustling Pinions, crowd,
The Straw-built Dome resounds; they mount in Air,
Eager for flight, and hang a living Cloud.
Kind Zephyrs breath, Sails open, Streamers fly,
The Shores, the Ports, the Streets rebound the Sailor's Cry,

IV.

WHEN sudden shifts the Scene.—Dire Sights astound
All Hearts: From op'ning Skies red Lightnings gleam,
Still bursting quicker; 'till Heav'n'sConvex round
Envelop'd, seems one Canopy of Flame.
Deep hollow Rumblings roll thro' Earth's dark Womb,
Like Billows breaking on a distant Shore;
Low-murmuring first, but louder soon become
Than volly'd Thunder, or *Bellona*'s Roar.

The

The *Cordelliers* their Entrails, molten Stone
And Metals, hurl on high; the burning Caverns groan.

V.

THEN *Callao*'s Domes and *Lima*'s princely Tow'rs
All glitt'ring with *Potosi*'s precious Ore,
Quake on the waving Ground, like slender Flow'rs
That tremble at the Blast of *Eurus frore*;
This Way and that they bend, 'till loosen'd quite
The massy Fabricks tumble down; beneath
In pond'rous Ruins whelming many a Wight,
That wanted Care, or Speed, to shun such Skaith:
Ah slain unweeting! some retir'd from Day
In silent Slumber; some o'er Ev'ning Banquet gay.

VI.

THEN might you see the Crowds distracted roam,
Thronging thro' Streets to Fields and open Air,
For Safety flying from their treach'rous Home.
Here Mothers at the Breast their Infants bear:
Round the sad Husband's Neck with vain Embrace.
There cling new-marry'd Dames, whilst up and down
Virgins and hoary Sires with frantick Pace
Totter: Beneath their Footsteps rocks the Town.
Their last Relief in Pray'r, to Heav'n they call
With late Devotion; one huge Ruin swallows all.

VII.

VII.

NIGHT wraps all Nature in her pitchy Robe;
Fame ſays, the yawning Graves gave up their Dead.
Forth iſſue Spectres o'er th' aſtoniſh'd Globe,
Indians, who by *Spain*'s cruel Av'rice bled,
Theſe with dire Goblins in the wild Uproar
Combin'd, the craſhing Elements confound,
Shake the curs'd Land yet red with guiltleſs Gore,
And mix loud Yellings with the Whirlwind's ſound;
Dreadful Avengers! And with fell Delight
Their proud Oppreſſors whelm in Gulphs of endleſs Night.

VIII.

EARTH by contending Min'rals inly torn
Yawns wide; Part ſink into her Bowels drear
Ingulft; Part upwards by Exploſion born
Are hurl'd aloft through the tormented Air,
Then Piece-meal fall. Old Chaos ſeems again
Returning, Earth and Ocean lie confus'd;
Rich Works of Art float on the diſtant Main,
And ſcatter'd Ships on Mid-land Rocks are bruis'd.
Their Cloud-top'd Brows th' eternal *Andes* bend
To boiling Ocean's Brim; and Seas to Heav'n aſcend.

IX.

THE Tumult ceas'd; the Sky became ſerene:
Earth long convulsd' to firm Repoſe return'd.
Mendoza view'd unhurt the dreadful Scene,
And only for his lov'd *Cornelia* mourn'd:

Now

" Now art thou loſt indeed unhappy Fair,
 " For ever loſt, Ah periſh'd in thy Bloom!
" Yet I ſurvive.—Ye Pow'rs why did ye ſpare
 " A hated Life? Your cruel Gift reſume.
" Earth gape once more, O ſnatch me, ſwal-
 " low, rend,
" And with her mangled Reliques mine, ſad
 Solace, blend!"

X.

THUS wail'd he ſtooping o'er the Veſſel's Side:
 When floating on the Surge that fretful ſwell'd
A Female dight in gay Attire he ſpy'd,
 Born on an Olive Tree, ſhe claſping held.
Compaſſion fill'd his Breaſt; he flew, he ſeiz'd,
 And from the Wave the languid Burthen
 rear'd
Yet breathing: Eager on her Face he gaz'd,
 That lovely in the Midſt of Death appear'd.
O Extaſy! O Tranſport! heav'nly Face!
Cornelia panting ſtill, and warm, thine Arms
 embrace.

XI.

RECALL'D by his Embrace, Life creeps anew
 Thro' the chill Veins, and ſhoots a feeble Ray,
With gradual Progreſs lights each kindling Hue;
 Laſt op'ning her bright Eyes confirms its Sway.
As one condemn'd to die, who kneeling low
 Awaits th' uplifted Steel, ſhould Mercy come
With ſudden Pardon and arreſt the Blow,
 Yet pants and trembles, in Amazement dumb;
Like Paſſions in thy Breaſt *Mendoza*, roll;
 Doubt, Wonder, conq'ring Joys at length
 poſſeſs thy Soul.

XII.

XII.

" And doſt thou live? Myſterious Heav'n! I
" bow
" In Adoration of thy high Beheſt;
" Juſt are thy Ways: Forlorn and loſt but now
" How haſt thou made me beyond Utt'rance
" bleſt?
" O let me claſp thee ever thus, my Bride,
" Since Parents now no more our Loves con-
" fine,
" In ſafer Realms let the dear Knot be ty'd,
" Heav'n by preſerving thus, decrees thee
" mine.
" Yet raiſe thoſe Eyes, yet liſten, fix my Fate:—
" She hears; that Smile conſents:—Enough;
" my Joy's complete.

XIII.

" Yet happy, thus poſſeſs'd of Life and you,
" Pardon this Drop;--'Tis Duty's, Pity's tear;
" This Tribute's to a fallen Country due:
" This to thy Parent honour'd tho' ſevere.
" And thou dear Relique of a World deſtroy'd,
" Welcome to Life, to Health, to Bliſs. Still
" glide
" Thy Hours thus Heav'n-preſerv'd, in Love
" employ'd;
" And ye, whom worldly Views too oft miſ-
" guide,
" Read in this Day's Event Heav'ns Will made
" known,
" Parents, join Hearts, not Wealth; to Merit
" Gold poſtpone."

XIV.

XIV.

THRICE happy Pair! Recorded in this Lay
Your Tale, (if to these Lays such Pow'r be giv'n,)
Shall to late Times this Lesson sage convey,
"*Virtue and Truth are ay the Care of Heav'n.*"
And thou blest Youth, while smooth the Skies and Main
Haste with thy charming Prize to native Soil.
Not so triumphant to Imperial *Spain*
Return'd *Columbus* from *Herculean* Toil,
With Sails o'er wond'ring Ocean first unfurl'd,
Less wealthy in the Spoils of a new-conquer'd World.

LECTURE the Thirteenth.

Concerning ORNAMENT.

TO what was ſaid in my laſt Lecture concerning Clearneſs, this Remark ſhould be added; that however neceſſary, yet it may be ſtudied too much. One of our greateſt Philoſophers, in order to be very Intelligible, hath incurred the Cenſure of Prolixity [*a*]. This Care, for the ſame Reaſon that Brevity gives Strength, enfeebles Diſcourſe, renders flat and languid. In purſuing it beyond a certain Point you ſacrifice to it all the Graces of Writing; and beſide make an ill Compliment to your Hearer; of whoſe Sagacity this Exactneſs, Superſtition let me call it of Clearneſs, implieth Diſtruſt: We wiſh that ſomewhat ſhould be left to our own Underſtanding to ſupply; enough to employ, yet not to puzzle.

AN Orator therefore will aim at ſomething farther; will, as I ſaid before, to Purity and Perſpicuity add ORNAMENT; in which is placed, if not the Uſefulneſs, at leaſt the chief Splendour of Eloquence. This it is, which gives to Diſcourſe Magnificence, Sweetneſs, Beauty;

[*a*] Mr. LOCK.

Beauty; that engageth the Attention, that captivateth the Hearts, and extorteth the Applauses of an Audience; that distinguisheth the Orator from the Philosopher and Man of Business, that raiseth his Language above the Simplicity of common Prose, that tempereth the Austerity of his Arguments, improveth the Keenness of his Wit, and enliveneth the brisk Sallies of his Fancy, rendering him a Person honoured and admired. This it is, which properly speaking, maketh Rhetorick an *Art*: All other Parts whereof may be attained by meer Felicity of Nature, but without Discipline, without much Study and Experience you cannot arrive at the Perfection of *Ornament*.

SENSIBLE hereof, Rhetoricians have bestowed infinite Labour upon this Branch, and have entered into innumerable Details concerning it; through which intricate Labyrinth I shall not attempt to follow them, as it would lead me out into Length far exceeding the Limits prescribed to Discourses of this Kind.

BESIDES, that in my Opinion, the vast Number of Precepts delivered defeateth their End, perplexing what they would clear up, and bewildering those whom they undertake to direct.

HOWEVER, all should not be past over. Two Branches there are, *Composition* and *Figures*, from which chiefly all true Ornament ariseth; these it seemeth right to make some Remarks upon, such as are most necessary, or have been less fully explained. But some general Obſervations there are, which it appeareth fit to premiſe, as they may clear the Way to others, and afford a more diſtinct Knowledge of this whole Affair: They ſhall employ the preſent Lecture.

WITH Reſpect to the Point before us, Ornament, many are of Opinion, that it ought to be principally, if not ſolely regarded. What is entirely plain appears to them inſipid: For what is it that ſets the Orator above an ordinary Speaker? What elevates Diſcourſe above common Converſation? What, but Life and Spirit, in other Words, Ornament?

NOW this is a wrong Judgment. For undoubtedly there is a beautiful Simplicity, a Plainneſs where the Expreſſion is no more than an Inſtrument to convey the Thoughts, unnoticed it ſelf it exhibits them: Like a pure tranſparent Stream, whoſe Waters the Eye paſſeth through unobſerved, and beholdeth the Sand and Pebbles of the Bottom.

AND not ſeldom is this the beſt Manner, as being moſt ſuitable to the Occaſion or Character of the Speaker. Thus in Narratives of Importance: In Exigencies, in Haſte, whereſoever the Speaker is of high Rank or venerable for Wiſdom, a plain ſhort Stile is to be preferred. Such is the Relation of the Funeral in *Terence*,

Effertur, imus.

Such is the Line of *Virgil*, expreſſing Hurry and Precipitation,

Ferte

[b] *Ferte citi flammas, date tela, ſcandite muros.*

And the beautiful Exclamation of *Niſus*

[c] *Me, Me, adſum qui feci, in me convertite ferrum*
O Rutuli; mea fraus omnis, nihil ille nec auſus,
Nec potuit, cælum hoc & conſcia ſidera teſtor;
Tantum infelicem nimium dilexit amicum.

Such is the Eloquence attributed by *Tacitus* to a *Roman* Emperor;

Profluens, et qualis decebat Principem, Oratio.

THIS is the Manner in which the Commentaries of *Cæſar* are written, and for the moſt Part the Speeches in *Homer*; and is that, which peculiarly diſtinguiſheth *Xenophon*; who through the whole Courſe of his Writings, whether he relates great Tranſactions, deſcribes Sieges and Battles, draws up Armies, harangues in the Perſon of Generals, recounts private Converſations, or explains the Doctrine of *Socrates* in philoſophical Reaſoning, preſerveth every where the ſame Character, this eaſy natural Tone, and without any View of pleaſing is always amiable; ſo that one may aptly apply to

[b] Bring Flames; be ſwift; give Weapons; mount the Walls.

[c] Me, me, behold the Criminal, on me
Pour all your Darts, mine all the Guilt; but he
Nought did nor dar'd; this Heav'n theſe Stars can tell;
He only lov'd his wretched Friend too well.

to him the Words of the *Elegiack* Poet of his Miſtreſs;

[*d*] *Where'er ſhe goes, a nameleſs Grace preſides,*
Follows unſeen, and ev'ry Motion guides.

Such kind of Simplicity giveth at once an Air of Truth and Grandeur: We think a Perſon ſincere, who ſhews ſo little of Care and Study; and we entertain a high Opinion of one whom we find ſo pleaſing without ſeeking to pleaſe: It is the Caſe of true Beauty in Undreſs, leſs ſhining, but more touching. Beſides, that a Care about Words ſeemeth unworthy of a great Character.

THESE Obſervations lead into an oppoſite Opinion, which hath alſo had many Defenders. This whole Affair according to them is grounded on Miſtake; "The End, the only "one worthy of a wiſe Man in ſpeaking, is "to *prove:* We deſire only to be rightly in-"formed, and to be aſſured that we are ſo. "To which Purpoſe, what elſe is neceſſary, "but to offer your Arguments clearly and me-"thodically? And the more plainly and ſhortly "this is done, the better. What then is it "which you call Ornament? Superfluous, and "ſhould be rejected; or deluſive, and ſhould "be abhorred. The Affectation thereof it is, "which hath perverted Eloquence, and from "a Servant of Truth made her a Patroneſs of "Falſehood."

IT

[*d*] ——— Quoquo veſtigia movit,
Componit furtim, ſubſequiturque decor. TIBULLU

IT is obvious that this Opinion ſtrikes at the Foundation of what we would eſtabliſh, and is inconſiſtent with the Courſe of our Reaſonings hitherto: Let us however, examine into it more particularly; the Article we treat of will receive from thence new Light.

AND Firſt, We acknowlege the Ground it proceeds upon to be right. Inſtruction and Conviction are the only Ends of Eloquence. What then? Doth the above-mentioned Inference follow? Are there not ſtrong Prejudices in Mankind which reſiſt, and muſt be overcome? How will you raiſe, how fix their Attention? How conquer their Indolence, and Averſion from ſerious Thought? By exciteing their Curioſity, gaining their good Will: And can this be performed without Ornament? "Men love Truth naturally," I allow it: But are they not often biaſſed by Affection, Habit, Rumor; ſunk in Sloth, governed by Traditions and Faſhion, and drawn aſide by every Trifle? And how may all theſe Hinderances be removed? "By plain artleſs Truth:" Certainly not; It muſt be ſet off and beautified.

THUS we may conclude, that they refine too much, who would reduce all to the ſevere Standard of ſtrict Truth. Some Criticks carry this Auſterity ſo far, as to diſapprove the direct Speeches, with which the Works of the beſt antient Hiſtorians abound; becauſe they think it incredible, that theſe very Words ſhould have been pronounced by the Perſons to to whom they are aſcribed; they are fictitious therefore, and unworthy of Hiſtory.

BUT are we certain, that Speeches of the very ſame Import (for about mere Words we contend not,) were not then and there delivered, as related by theſe Hiſtorians? The Cuſtom of thoſe Times had eſtabliſhed Harangues, made them oftentimes neceſſary; and why may not we ſuppoſe, that theſe preſerved to us were the ſame in Subſtance at leaſt, with thoſe made at the Time? I grant that modern Hiſtorians have erred herein by injudicious Imitation, not conſidering the Difference of Times; For ſet Speeches would be abſurd now, on Occaſions wherein they would have been neceſſary at *Athens* or *Rome*.

BUT if we ſhould allow thoſe Harangues to be fictitious, they hurt not the Truth of Hiſtory: They impoſe upon none. We regard them only as a full State of both Sides of the Queſtion; rendered more lovely and affecting, by being put into the Mouths of celebrated Perſons, who were real Actors on the Occaſions. And how have modern Hiſtorians avoided this ſuppoſed Fault? They give an Abſtract or Skeleton as it were of the Arguments on each Side in the indirect Way; or what is yet worſe, deliver their Opinion in their own Perſons; during which Time the Action ſtandeth ſtill, you are called home from this illuſtrious Theatre to converſe with the Hiſtorian; whereas in the other Way, the Action is continued; you never once loſe Sight of the Actors; it

is

is *Cæsar* and *Cato* and *Scipio*, not *Sallust* or *Livy*, with whom you discourse; you remain without Interruption engaged and interested, by Means of this innocent and beautiful Fiction.

But if you condemn these, what will you say of Parable and Fable, where Truth, in order to insinuate herself into the Mind, borroweth the Dress even of Fiction? Yet the wisest of Men have used Fables and Parables: Nay, and one far greater than any of them; "*Behold, a greater than* Solomon *is here.*"

The right Way of determining this Point, is to consider the Nature of Man. Is Reason the sole Principle therein? If it be, that only are we to regard. But we have already seen, that there is another of mighty Influence; Passion. We know also, that there is a third, to which Regard must be had, namely, Sense. And before we go so far, we shall find out another, a Kind of intermediate Faculty, or rather Act of the Soul, partaking of Reason and Sense, which is of great and peculiar Moment in the Point before us.

When external Objects are presented to the Mind, there are formed therein certain Images of them, which it contemplates, and from the Survey of them frameth its Judgments. Those Objects being removed, the Images disappear, but usually are not lost; for at the Distance perhaps of Years they return, and offer themselves to View, sometimes without apparent Cause: And the Mind, we know, hath a Power of reviving them at Will, comparing them

them anew, and dismissing, as Occasions require. This Power, which we name Memory or Recollection, is the Foundation of all Learning and Knowledge, and varieth much in different Persons; being in some wonderfully tenacious; in others it exerteth its Action with great Readiness and Facility, and gives that useful Quality to Speakers, which we name Quickness and Presence of Mind.

THE Mind, thus endued with a Faculty of recalling Images before received, stops not there; is not obliged to confine itself to the Order of real Existence, but can range them, when thus recalled, according to its Pleasure; and, by joining or separating anew, can form Collections of Images which never did exist, This Act of the Mind we name *Imagination*, by which it can multiply without Bounds the Number of its Ideas; deriving, indeed, the Materials from Nature, it works them up into new Forms and Modes of Being, framing within itself a World altogether its own. Memory we may name the Storehouse of the Soul, from whence the Understanding furnisheth itself with Notions, which it makes the Source of real Knowledge; the Imagination moldeth these into agreeable Scenes, pursuing Pleasure, not Truth.

ON the Vigour wherewith this latter Operation is exerted, dependeth chiefly Excellence in the imitative Arts. The Painter can draw Figures more finely proportioned, can throw greater Variety into his Landskips, make his

Trees

Trees more ſhady, and enrich his Flowers with brighter Colours, than the Hand of Nature hath beſtowed. The Poet may fill his Battles with more Horror, may add more Fury to his Tempeſts, inſpire his Heroes with nobler Sentiments, and embelliſh his Narration with Circumſtances more diverſe and more affecting, than are to be found in real Exiſtence, or hiſtorical Record: And in Proportion as they perform theſe Things with greater Energy, they are deemed more excellent in their Art, obtaining, by Means of this Power, a ſovereign Empire over the Imaginations of thoſe to whom their Works are addreſſed.

Now to apply theſe Obſervations to the Point before us: We have here diſcovered to us an Operation of the Mind, which muſt needs have mighty Influence in Oratory. A rich and ſtrong Imagination is not leſs powerful here, than in the other Arts above-mentioned. Rich, it charms by preſenting a Variety of Images, beautiful and new: Strong, it preſents them lively and glowing, ſo as to convey and impreſs deeply on the Hearer's Mind the ſame Images.

Now this is a neceſſary Source of Ornament, which an Orator cannot, without greatly weakening his own Power, neglect. If to ſatisfy the Underſtanding he muſt follow Nature and Truth, he muſt ſet off and embelliſh theſe, to win the Imagination. If Reaſon makes Diſcourſe convincing, Paſſion vehement, a fine Imagination,

Imagination, renders it beautiful and charming.

FROM whence it happens, that they who ſpeak to it chiefly, are very apt to be miſled: The flowery Roads through which it guides are ſo amuſing, that one goeth far aſtray before he is aware. Such are they, who indulge themſelves in pleaſing Deſcriptions, gay Alluſions, ingenious Allegories, lively Compariſons, who play in Metaphors, glitter in Oppoſitions, ſwell in Hyperboles; which ſeldom promote the main End of ſpeaking, as leading from the Purpoſe; and are beſides, on Account of their Gaudineſs, very diſpleaſing to a Man of Senſe. It ſhould be our Buſineſs to aim at a judicious Uſe of Imagination, which undoubtedly bringeth much Advantage to Diſcourſe, ſoftening the Severity of Reaſon, winning Attention and Goodwill: Which judicious Uſe we may define to conſiſt chiefly herein; "Never to employ it "except in the lighter Parts; ſo as to illuſtrate "the more ſerious, not to obſcure."

ONE Thing remark; "Imagination is more "contrary to Paſſion, than it is to Reaſon." For in the cloſeſt Argument, ſome of its livelieſt Strokes may find Place; but it is utterly inconſiſtent with the pathetick: Wherever you would affect much, beware of mingling Sallies of Fancy; be ſimple, be plain, be natural. Inſtances of Failures in this Article you may ſee in *Ovid*, *Lucan*, and *Seneca*; innumerable in modern Tragedies, where you may obſerve Rage venting its Fury in harmonious Simile,

and

and Sorrow pouring out its Tears through all the Brilliancy of quaint Antithesis.

I DO not acquit *Shakespear* of this Fault: But it appeareth from a Passage in his Works, that however unacquainted he is supposed to have been with the Rules of Criticism, yet he knew this, even in committing it, to be a Fault: The Passage is remarkable; *Ross* is introduced, relating the miserable Estate of *Scotland* under the Usurpation of *Macbeth*, in these Words:

"Alas, poor Country!
Almost afraid to know itself; it cannot
Be call'd our Mother, but our Grave; where nothing,
But who knows nothing, is once seen to smile.
Where Sighs, and Groans, and Shrieks that rend the Air
Are made, not mark'd: Where violent Sorrow seems
A modern Ecstasy. The dead Man's Knell
Is there scarce ask'd for whom; and good Men's Lives
Expire before the Flowers in their Caps,
Dying or e'er they sicken."

IN Reply to which, *Macduff* observes very justly;

O Relation
Too nice, and yet too true!

AND the Ground of this Remark is not difficult to find; for all strong Passion is serious; it must employ the whole Soul. Points and

Turns

Turns abſolutely deſtroy it. And you are to remark, that Paſſion being in the Order of Nature before Imagination, you are to give it the firſt Place: He is more an Orator who affects, than he who entertains.

THE fourth Faculty of our Nature is *Senſe:* In order chiefly to pleaſe which, a Care of Style becomes neceſſary, that it ſhould be muſical and agreeable to the Ear; a Care, to which the Antients applied themſelves with incredible Labour. It ſeemeth ſtrange, at firſt Sight, to obſerve a Perſon of *Ariſtotle*'s deep Knowledge and ſolid Judgment, ſo exceedingly accurate as we find him to be, in a Point thus apparently ſlight, delivering, as he doth, Precepts concerning the ranging of Words according to the Quantity of Syllables in certain Feet, ſo that each Period ſhould have a numerous Cadence, and each Member flow in due Time and Meaſure.

WE can account for this only from the Neceſſity which the Speaker then lay under of employing this minute Care. The Ears of the *Athenians* were ſo delicate, as to be offended with the leaſt Violation of this Cadence. At the ſame Time it muſt be owned, that this is a Degree of Nicety, of which, in Fact, we have but a faint Notion. Nay, we find in antient Criticks, Paſſages celebrated for Exactneſs of this Sort, the Beauty of which abſolutely eſcapeth us. It may be doubted, whether we ſhould eaſily diſtinguiſh between what is ſo highly

highly extolled, and that which perhaps would not have been endured.

By the Way, this Remark ſhews, in a ſtrong Light, an Article before treated of, the Vanity of labouring to compoſe, or of admiring exceedingly when compoſed, rhetorical or poetical Performances at this Time, in the *Greek* or *Roman* Languages: In which, we underſtand but faintly perfect Purity and Force: But of this important Article now mentioned, Numbers and Harmony, we have no diſtinct Conception at all. In our own Language, happily, this ſcrupulous Accuracy is not required; yet even here, we are by no Means exempted from all Care of this Kind, free to neglect the Judgment of Senſe: There are Rules here alſo, built upon the ſame Foundation, but varying from the different Genius of the Tongue; which I ſhall ſpeak of more at large in my next Lecture.

In the mean Time, that I may give you in one View my whole Senſe of this Article, Ornament, I ſhall conclude with laying before you an Idea of a Speaker perfect herein.

He conſiders well before-hand the Subject he is about to enter upon; whether it requires to be explained only, or demands Proof likewiſe; or whether needing both theſe, it doth beſides intereſt the Paſſions of the Hearers. To judge rightly hereof, he ſubſtitutes himſelf in the Place of his Hearers: If one ſhould ariſe before me to ſpeak upon this Point, ſaith he, what would I expect? Explanation, Arguments, Pathetic,

Pathetic, Imagination. He proceedeth accordingly.

IF his Subject be a complex one, he weighs the ſeveral Parts of it diſtinctly; here he expounds, there argues, again affects; in another Place, ſoftens the Rigour of Reaſon and Tumult of Paſſion with the gayer Colours of Fancy. He is always pure, clear, and harmonious in his Style; and is more eſpecially attentive to ſuit it to the Occaſion: It ſeems to ſpring from his Subject, and the Words wait ready, without his Induſtry, to cloath his Thoughts, as faſt as they riſe in his Mind. He is plain and modeſt in propoſing; diſtinct and accurate in unfolding; weighty and preſſing in confirming; in the Application touching, warming, penetrating. He is cloſe, connected, full of Dignity and Energy in Reaſoning; clear and diſtinct in explaining; lively and ſhort in relating; exact, though conciſe, in deſcribing; quick, rapid, animated in Paſſion.

HE mingles the Fire of a Poet with the Simplicity of a Philoſopher, and the grave Majeſty of the Hiſtorian; is ſparing of Digreſſions, eaſy in Tranſitions, accurate in Compariſons, weighty in Reflexions. Never more artful than in concealing Art. Seeming moſt natural, where moſt ſkilful; moſt eaſy, where he had laboured moſt; correct with Spirit; entertaining with Solidity; with ſeeming Liberty obſerving always ſtrict Method; never appearing to wander, but in order to make his Return more effectual; nor ſeeking to pleaſe, but with

a Veiw

a View to persuade. Still gratifying your Curiosity with somewhat new, yet still keeping it up by a Prospect of more; ever rewarding your Attention, at the same Time redoubling it. At every Step, as in the ascending a high Hill, he presents to you a new Prospect, with a Glimpse of more, opening behind. Thus still satisfied, still unsatisfied, you are led on from Expectation to Expectation, and remain in Suspence, until you arrive at the Summit, the Close and winding up of all; from whence you see the Scheme compleat, one just, well-conducted Whole; and the Mind entirely acquiesceth in it.

LECTURE the Fourteenth.

Of COMPOSITION.

THE ſeveral Parts of Rhetorick are ſo cloſely connected, that it is ſcarcely poſſible to treat of one Branch, without anticipating, in ſome Meaſure, what is to be explained afterwards, or repeating what hath been ſaid before. The ſame Objects recur, although in different Points of View. I take Notice of this, becauſe in ſpeaking of Ornament in general, I was obliged to mention ſome Articles, which I proceed now to diſcourſe of more fully: And I am willing to hope, that ſuch former imperfect Mention will not cauſe to appear ſuperfluous, or to prove tireſome, what I now propoſe to conſider more at large. Some Figures are grouped, of which you get a partial Glympſe; but this preventeth not your beholding the ſame afterwards with Pleaſure, when drawn out ſingle and at full Length.

THERE are many Ways of expreſſing the ſame Thought; ariſing from hence, that different Words convey the ſame Notions, and the Manner of diſpoſing theſe Words may be various. Yet among theſe, generally ſpeaking, there

there is but one perfect, one that renders the Thought with all possible Compleatness: As in viewing a Picture, there is one Point, in which the Whole appears exact in every Lineament, from whence the Light and Shade are seen justly distributed; beyond, or short of which, there is always somewhat of Confusion.

FROM hence it is manifest, that to chuse the best Expression is a Work of Skill, even in a short Course of Thought; but where the Chain is long, as in a considerable Performance, in a whole Discourse, the Variety being greatly increased, renders it a Work of mighty Difficulty. This Reflexion leadeth to the Consideration of that Branch of Eloquence, which we name COMPOSITION; by which is meant, "The due Arrangement of Words with Regard to Signification and Sound."

WITH respect to the former, Signification, they are to be placed in such Manner, that their Sense may appear distinct and clear; concerning which Part, I have nothing material to add to what hath been already said. The latter, the Arrangement of Words with respect to Sound, I shall now proceed to enlarge upon.

I SUPPOSE that you have chosen the most proper Words for expressing your Thoughts, which requireth a perfect Knowledge of the Language you write in; and that I assume as granted, in the present Case to be your native one, holding it not possible to be compleatly Master, so as to vary Expression at Will and always properly, of a dead Language.

YOUR next Care muſt be, to place theſe Words in ſuch Order, that they may in no Caſe offend, ſhould, in general, pleaſe the Ear. I make this Diſtinction, becauſe in Matters of meer Argument or Inſtruction, it is enough not to offend; in other Caſes, it is requiſite that Language ſhould have the Grace of Harmony, and pleaſe in order to perſuade.

THE *Greeks* very early applied themſelves to cultivate this Art, and attained to a Degree of Perfection in it which no other People, not all the Induſtry of the *Romans*, who from Imitators became Rivals, could equal. *Dionyſius* of *Halicarnaſſus* hath left a Treatiſe [*a*], which ſhews with what wonderful Attention they ſtudied, and to what Nicety, ſcarcely conceivable, they carried their Cenſures in this Point. The Wrok itſelf, as being of moderate Length, and containing many curious Remarks, I ſhall not attempt to abridge; but recommend it to your Peruſal.

INDEED the Study of the *Greek* Originals is uſeful to us, not only in the Article we now treat of, as they afford the beſt Models in this Way, in the Art of Compoſition; but alſo, becauſe their Language bears a peculiar Reſemblance to our own. Whoſoever hath attempted to render a *Greek* Claſſick into *Engliſh*, muſt have obſerved a Similitude between the Idioms of the two Tongues, and that the one floweth oftentimes naturally into the other. And in comparing ſome *Latin* Interpretations with thoſe in our own Tongue, I think, that I have perceived

[*a*] Of the Compoſition of Words.

perceived the Turn of the Original to be much better preserved in the latter.

THERE is not any Thing, about which Commentators have been more divided, than the precise Meaning of those Precepts, delivered by the Antients, concerning the Observation of certain Numbers and Feet in Prose. That this was esteemed not an indifferent or light Matter, is evident from the curious Detail into which the most famous Criticks [b] have entered concerning it, and the great Stress they always lay upon it. The Truth is, Doubts and Disputes herein should not be wondered at. The Subject seems to me one of those, which it is impossible for us distinctly to comprehend: For the Whole is grounded in the Manner of Pronunciation peculiar to that People, includeing the Tones and Inflexions of the Voice, upon which the Length or Shortness of the Syllables, and therefore these Feet, must in a great Measure depend. Now of these we cannot, at this Distance of Time, form any clear Conception.

EVEN in Verse, where the Measure as regularly returning, is exactly known, we are yet ignorant of the right Pronunciation; nor do we, in our Manner of Reading, make any Distinction between long and short Vowels in many, I might say in most Cases [c]; which, we cannot doubt, were accurately distinguished in

[b] ARISTOTLE, CICERO, DIONYSIUS of *Halicarnassus*, QUINTILIAN, LONGINUS.

[c] As in the first, and often in the last Syllables.

in their Speech: Much more ignorant muſt we be in the Feet of Proſe, which depend upon the Ear alone, not being ſubjected to any fixed Rule, nor returning at known Intervals.

THERE cannot be a ſtronger Argument of the Truth of what I have now been ſaying, than the Caſe of Accents, which were an Invention of modern *Greeks*, to preſerve the ſeveral Tones uſed by the Antients in ſpeaking: And of what Utility have they been? They have occaſioned endleſs Diſputes about their true Uſe: They gave Riſe to a moſt unreaſonable Error, which prevailed widely, and is not yet rooted out, that of giving up Quantity to Accent, the pronouncing the ſame Words in Verſe and in Proſe altogether differently. And they have rendered it an extremely difficult Work to print *Greek* correctly; without bringing, ſo far as I can underſtand, any, at leaſt any conſiderable Advantage. In Truth, the Intention could not be anſwered; Tones in Speech being innumerable, cannot be preſerved by Marks, at leaſt of this Kind.

This Nicety, therefore, of rythmical or meaſured Proſe, at beſt, we can only gueſs at; and it ſeems the moſt prudent Way to give it up rather as Matter of uncertain Speculation, than to lay out upon it unprofitable Study; much leſs ſhould we make it the Ground of Debate and Controverſy. Strong Marks, I confeſs, of this Skill one may diſcover in the Writings of the Antients; but in a Point ſo uncertain, a great deal of Imagination, Prejudice, even Enthuſiaſm,

thusiasm may enter; and it seemeth not safe to indulge very much to such Curiosity, never useful, often visionary.

PASSIONATE Admirers of antient Eloquence have fancied, that they might improve our own, by transferring these Rules of rythmitical Composition, and fitting them to the *English* Language. Soon after the Revival of Letters, the same Project was attempted with regard to Poesy. We have at this Day in *Italian* and *French*, as well as in our own Tongue, many Essays of this Kind remaining, of Hexameters, Alcaicks, and Sapphicks, some by celebrated Writers [*d*]. And whoever will be at the Pains of reading these, cannot wonder that the Project was dropped, I suppose for ever; nothing being more forced, more lame, and unpleasing, than such Performances.

IF this Attempt proved thus unsuccessful in the *Italian* Language, which so nearly resembles the *Latin*, it must be despaired of in both the others, abounding as they do in Monosyllables, and of Consequence falling less easily into Feet. I cannot help considering this other Attempt of fitting our Prose to the Rules of the antient Rythmus or Measure as an Enterprize of the same Kind; or rather still more chimerical, as it is more difficult to resolve Prose into Feet than Verse, for the Reason before-mentioned; in Verse they are distinctly marked; the Ear alone judges in the other. From all which I would conclude it

[*d*] TRISSINO. RONSARD. Sir PHILIP SYDNEY.

it to be a fruitless Attempt, wherein we should find thrown away much Labour, that might be otherwise usefully employed.

In rejecting this Nicety, I would not however be thought to mean, that none, or little Care should be taken in the placing of Words. Sound hath great Influence, and whatsoever offends the Ear, will not easily gain Admission into the Mind; it is presented with Disadvantage; whence the Necessity of arranging the Words skilfully. But herein, the Turn, the Contexture, what is usually named the Genius of the Tongue, must be consulted; for the Care which is successful in one, may be superfluous or hurtful in another. I shall go on to mention such Observations as have occurred to me, with relation to this Matter, in our own.

WE have already taken Notice of it, as the first Thing to be considered after the Choice of proper Words, "to place them so as that the "Sense may be *clear*." All Transposition, whether used for the Sake of Emphasis or Harmony, if it do materially hurt Perspicuity, is to be condemned, as destroying the main End of Language; for who speaks or writes without designing to be understood? Herein the *Roman* Writers have been charged with being faulty.

NEXT, it is required, "that this Order should "never be such as to shock the Ear with jar-"ring Sounds:" For Instance, by the Concourse

course of long and open Vowels. [e] A *French* Poet is said to have been so exact in this Article, that no such *Hiatus* is to be found in his Works. And some late Writers of that Nation contend to have the Rule extended to Prose: A Degree of Strictness, which must be very burthensome; and may, as I think, have an ill Effect, by rendering the Stile languid and enervate [f].

THE *Romans* avoided this clashing of Vowels in Verse by Elisions, which became under the Management of their best Poets a Source of Beauty, for Elisions so far as we can judge, are an Ornament to *Virgil*'s Versification. Something of this Kind *Milton* attempted, although sparingly, to introduce among us, wherein however he hath not been followed.

THE *Greeks* we find admitted this Meeting of Vowels without Elision; in this as in many other Particulars, approaching more nearly to the Form of our own Language.

BUT some Cautions are necessary to be observed. "Not to permit this Conrcourse of "Vowels frequently." "Never in very quick "Succession. "Especially not in pleasing "Subjects, which demand Smoothness, and "if I may be allowed to use the Word, Amenity of Stile." Which points out another Rule, "Such clashing may be happily em- "ployed

[e] MALHERBE.

[f] Habet enim ille tanquam hiatus concursu vocalium molle quiddam, & quod indicet non ingratam negligentiam, de re hominis magis quam de verbis laborantis. Cicer. de Orat.

" ployed on Occaſions that ſuit with a Stile
" ſlow, rough and difficult."

A SECOND Rule is, " Be on your Guard
" againſt Monoſyllables; too frequent in our
" Language." You may find twenty of theſe
together even in our good Writers, which render
the Speech harſh, heavy, embaraſſed. It
ſhould be your Care to avoid this Fault: Crowd
not ſuch together; but, if it be poſſible, interpoſe
at proper Diſtances Words of Length to
ſmooth and ſupport theſe broken disjointed
Tones, by ſome Modulation and Continuity of
Sound.

THIRDLY. " The Length of Periods de-
" ſerves Attention." When the Language began
to be poliſhed, our early Writers extended
their Periods to a Length oftentimes exceſſive:
They ran one Sentiment into another in
a continued Chain without Interruption, ſometimes
for Pages together; in which Practice
there are three Evils; " This Length cauſes
" ſome Degree of Obſcurity. It overburthens
" the Memory. And is alſo diſpleaſing to the
" Ear." For Nature hath in this reſpect preſcribed
certain Limits, beyond which every
Thing diſpleaſeth. Theſe Limits are in general
determined by our own Frame; as in particular
Caſes by the Power of the Speaker:
Whatſoever you can ſpeak diſtinctly, without
being obliged to pauſe improperly for Breath,
or to precipitate your laſt Words, may be comprized
in a Period. Lengthen it beyond this
Bound, the Speaker ſuffers, and with him the
Hearer.

Hearer. Instances of this Fault we find in an excellent Writer, Lord *Clarendon*; neither are *Hooker* and *Rawleigh*, scarcely indeed any of that Age, free from it.

MODERNS observing the Inconvenience of this Manner, have been very careful to avoid it; but frequently by running into a contrary, and perhaps more faulty Extream, dividing their Sense, breaking as it were and splitting it into very short Sentences; so that they present you with a new Period almost in every Line.

THIS Practice hath some ill Effects in common with the other; it causeth Obscurity by cramping the Expression, and by affected Conciseness; it burthens the Memory by presenting to it many minute Objects: And it hath this peculiar Fault besides, that it is destructive of Harmony. Long Periods may give Majesty and Pomp to Discourse, these curtail it of its due Proportion; if those sometimes overload the Ear, these always defraud and disappoint it: A Prospect of the Sea bounded by no fixed object doth indeed soon tire; but it is much worse to be hemmed in on all Sides, to have your View stopped at every second Step you make.

ONE Cause of this shortened Stile hath been assigned above, namely a Sollicitude to avoid the opposite Fault: Another less obvious hath occurred to me, which I shall mention, and leave to your Judgment.

POESY as it began before, so hath it in every Country much influenced Prose, polishing this as itself improved, and in its own Decline corrupting. In Queen *Elizabeth*'s Time, the Kind of Versification which prevailed most was the Stanza; which tho' an harmonious and majestick Measure, as we see in the Muse of *Spencer*, was liable to one Fault; being very long, it tempted the Poet to lengthen out his Thought to its own Extent; thus weakening both Sense and Stile. To the same March, the Prose of those Times conformed its Gait, being full, sounding, and flowing in Luxuriancy of Expression, in extended and redundant Periods.

AFTERWARDS Couplets, improved by *Waller* and perfected by *Dryden*, became the reigning poetick Stile; in which the constant Return of Rhime cramped the Sense, usually to a Distick: The Infection whereof quickly as I imagine, reached Prose, which about the same Time began to march in short and broken Steps; like one accustomed to Fetters, who when set free shall yet by Force of Habit move in contracted Steps. Accordingly we find that among the *French*, where the same kind of heroick Verse prevailed, it went attended by Prose of the like narrow Gait.

WHICH Reasoning seems farther confirmed by observing what passed beyond the *Alps*. The Poesy of *Italy* in its most flourishing Days was in [*g*] Stanza: The Stile of Prose was then long

[*g*] Named, Rime Octave, as consisting of eight Lines, this is the Measure used by ARIOSTO and TASSO.

long as you may ſee in *Guicciardino*, Father *Paul*, and *Davila*, much more than it was in *Boccace* long before, or in *Bentivoglio* who flouriſhed after them.

THE Precepts I would deduce from the whole are theſe. " Obſerve a reaſonable Li-" mit in Periods, never exceeding the uſual " Power of the Breath to utter with Eaſe ; " which may be about the Length of ſix of " our heroick Verſes [*b*]."

" SELDOM let two, never three of this Ex-" tent ſucceed each other."

" AVOID no leſs the contrary Extreme of " ſhort Sentences, which are unmuſical, harſh, " abrupt. Eſpecially ſtring not together many " ſuch." The beſt Method is, " To mingle " thoſe of each Kind ;" ſo may the long de-rive Vigour and Vivacity from the ſhort, theſe, Numbers and Harmony from the long.

FOURTHLY. As Periods conſiſt uſually of ſeveral Members, " you ſhould take the ſame " Care in each, as of the whole." If there be four or ſix Members, which laſt Number a Period ſhould very rarely if ever exceed, they ſhould bear a juſt Proportion to each other, either nearly equal, or what is better, unequal in ſuch Manner, that they ſhould go on

[*b*] SPENCER's Stanza conſiſts of nine Lines ;—the laſt an Alexandrine.

CICERO preſcribes the Length of four Hexameter Lines as uſually the utmoſt for a Period :---Equatuor, quaſi hexametrorum inſtar verſuum quod ſit, conſtat *fere* plena comprehenſio. Cic. de Orat.

on lengthening, and the longest close; for the Ear is in that Case filled, and acquiesceth in the Sound as compleat. If there be but two Members, this latter Condition should be observed; only one Caution is to be used; suffer not many Periods of two Members to follow; because this giveth Stiffness and disagreeable Monotony to Discourse: At least the Members should be different, equal in some, in others unequal.

NEXT in the uniting of Periods, "Much "Attention is required, to make the Joints "smooth and close, both for Clearness of Sense, "and Gracefulness of Stile." Observe that nothing be loose, clumsy, imperfect; for one of the most common Faults in Writing, is Ignorance or Negligence with regard to the connecting Particles.

"BE careful that weaker Expressions do "not follow stronger; [*i*] Let them rise in Energy, closing with the Strongest."

"Be sparing in the Use of Epithets and Synonomous Terms, which clog the Discourse "with idle Sounds."

"THE principal Care of Harmony respects "the Close," for that being the last Sound left upon the Ear, dwells there, and remains with

[*i*] As in this Line,
She moves a Goddess, and—*she looks a Queen.*
POPE's Hom. Book 3.
And in the latter of these two Lines,
High Heav'n with trembling the dread Signal took,
And all * *Olympus* to the Center shook. POP. Hom. B. 1.

* *The Mountain Olympus.*

with the Hearer: the Voice likewise naturally falling there, is frequently lost, and suppresseth the last Syllable: For this Reason, it were best, that the concluding Word should be one of Length, or ending with long Syllables, that the Voice dwelling upon it might prevent or lessen this Inconvenience; so that we should if possible avoid ending with a Monosyllable, especially a short one, which it is very difficult to pronounce distinctly and properly in that Situation.

THESE are general Rules, which should be observed, where-ever th Language permits without Prejudice to the Sense, for the Sense is ever to be preferred: In which Respect, I am sensible that a superstitious Adherence to these or any other Rules relating to Harmony, must be hurtful: Herein both *Greeks* and *Romans* had greatly the Advantage; the former from the natural Sweetness and Copiousness of their Tongue abounding with harmonious Words; the other from the Liberty they took of transposing the Verb or any Word of most Importance to the End; a Liberty indeed as we remarked before, turned into Licence; in which Practice even *Cicero* was charged by his Cotemporaries with Affectation, on Account of his frequently concluding Periods, with an *Esse videatur*.

I SHALL not enter into several minute Remarks, which however might have their Use, but the Time and my Design allow not of them. Such are these, "Avoid putting together many
" Words

" Words of the ſame Sound. Let not Mem-
" bers of Periods end with like Sounds, which
" often occur. Shun frequent Hiſſings of
" Plural Nouns, and of Verbs ending in the
" Letter *S*. Shun likewiſe Tenſes of Verbs,
" which thruſt together by Eliſion rough Con-
" ſonants, as *judg'd*, *diſturb'd*, *alledg'd*; which
" you may avoid, by reſtoring the ſuppreſſed
" Vowel, or by uſing the Expletives or rather
" Signs of the Tenſes, *did* or *hath*. Set not
" out in the Opening of a Paragraph with
" harſh Sounds; for the firſt Words are al-
" ways remarked. Avoid the Meaſure of
" Verſe, and Uniformity of Cloſe." But leave-
ing theſe and ſuch like to each Perſon's own
Obſervation; I ſhall add one Remark, which
appears to be of Conſequence.

" THE Sound ſhould be conformable to the
" Senſe.,' Every Paſſion hath it's peculiar
Stile: Grief ſpeaketh in broken disjointed
Accents: Anger burſteth out impetuouſly in a
Torrent of Words, ready, quick, rapid, redundant: Joy expreſſeth itſelf in Numbers
light and flowing, full of Chearfulneſs and Vivacity. The attributing to one Paſſion the
Language proper to another, is an Offence
againſt Nature and Reaſon: It is the ſame Im-
propriety, as it would be in a Muſician, to ſet
joyful Scenes to melancholy Meaſures, or to
give Hope and Deſpair the ſame Movement.

WE may extend this farther. " A good
" Speaker even in Deſcriptions and Alluſions
" would

"would suit his Stile to the Subject." A Discourse that representeth Images of Horror, should flow in a different Measure from one, that conveyeth pleasing Ideas: And herein Nature favoureth, inclining Men in the Formation of Names to preserve a Correspondence between the Sound and Object, at least in remarkable Cases; and this Conformity we actually find in all Languages; shocking Things have harsh Names; the pleasing, usually soft and melodious Appellations.

EVERY one hath observed Marks of the Care now prescribed, in Poets. Every Book of Criticism abounds with Instances of it from *Homer* and *Virgil*; and not fewer, I believe, nor less beautiful, might be drawn from our own *Milton*: Some of which give me Leave to mention; you may be led thereby to remark many others.

[*k*] "Immediately the Mountains *huge* appear
Emergent, and their *broad bare Backs upheave*
Into the Skies.

[*l*] "Nature from her Seat
Sighing,——gave Signs of Woe."

[*m*] "Thee another Flood
Of Tears and Sorrow,—*a Flood* thee also drown'd."

[*n*] Plumb down he drops
Ten thousand Fathom deep."

[*k*] Parad. Lost, Book vii. [*l*] Book ix. [*m*] Book x. [*n*] Book xii.

[*o*] " Awake, arise, or be for ever fallen."

[*p*] " O'er Bog, o'er Steep, thro' strait, rough,
" dense or rare,
" He swims, or sinks, or wades, or creeps, or
" flies."

The Opposition between the two following Descriptions is remarkably beautiful:

[*q*] " On a sudden open fly,
With impetuous Recoil and jarring Sound,
Th' infernal Doors, and on their Hinges grate
Harsh Thunder."

[*r*] " Heav'n open'd wide
Her ever-during Gates, harmonious Sound,
On golden Hinges turning."

[*s*] Learned Criticks have remarked the same Care, and brought Instances of it from Prose Writers, especially among the *Greeks.* But I acknowledge, that in this latter Case, the Observations do not at first Sight appear to be as just, nor the Instances so strong and certain, as in the Poets. The Reason of which I take to be this:

ORATORS, whose Business it is to persuade, not daring openly to depart from the common Manner of Speech, for that would prejudice their Hearers against them, which Poets professing

[*q*] Parad. Lost, Book i. [*p*] Book ii. [*q*] Book ii. [*r*] Book vi.

[*s*] *Longinus* hath from *Demosthenes*; and more especially *Dionysius* from that Orator, in the above-mentioned Treatise of the Composition of Words.

fessing chiefly to please, are free to do, find it necessary to use Art, and to conceal their Art: The good Effect may be, in some Degree, felt by all; but the Address used in procuring it is discoverable only to sharp and watchful Eyes. This is the Heart of Man; we love to be agreeably deceived, but we rise up in Indignation against a declared Intent of deceiving us; too fond of Pleasure to love strict Truth, too proud to seem fond of ought but Truth.

WHICH Remark points out a very useful Limitation to the Rule laid down.

"IN this conforming Sound to Sense, keep within certain Limits." In describing uncouth Objects, and in harsh Passions, your Stile should be industriously roughened, but not so as to offend the Ear: Neither in opposite Cases, should it be softened into Weakness and Effeminacy. Poets, by carrying the Rule into Excess, offend often in both Ways. Of the first Sort seems to be the Translation of the beautiful Lines in the Iliad [*t*].

First march the heavy Mules, securely slow,
O'er Hills, o'er Dales, o'er Crags, o'er Rocks, they go;
Jumping high o'er the Shrubs of the rough Ground,
Rattle the clatt'ring Cars, and the shock'd Axles bound.

IN

[*t*] Book xxiii. POPE's Homer.

[*t*] πρὸ δ' ἄρ οὔρῆες κίον ἄυτῶν;
Πολλὰ δ' ἄναντα, κάταντα, παραντα, τὲ δοχμια τ' ἔλ[illegible]

IN the following Line, how naturally do the Trees fall in the Original, in a sudden and broken Cadence,

ταὶ δὲ μεγάλα κτυπέουσαι
πίπτον.

Which, in the Translation, seems to me quite over-laboured.

——deep-ecchoing groan the Thickets brown,
Then rustling, crackling, crashing, thunder down.

WHAT is this but a fine Genius, who, striveing to keep Pace with a great one, overshooteth himself? His Muse within certain Bounds enchantingly melodious, seeking to equal the Sound of the *Greek* Trumpet, raiseth her Voice until it well nigh cracks. It is *Strada*'s Nightingale, that labouring to match the Variety and Tones of the Lyre, swelleth, straineth, tortureth her whole Frame; at length falls breathless on the victorious Harp.

INSTANCES faulty in the other, the soft and florid Way, abound in our Poets; some might, I think, be drawn from the same Work: Such is the Speech of *Paris* to *Helen*, in the third Book; and some Passages in the Episode, of *Juno* laying *Jupiter* asleep on Mount *Ida*, in the fourteenth.

I HAVE been sometimes tempted to imagine this Line of *Virgil* less exact in the Language, than is usual with that most accurate Writer:

" *Et*

[u] " *Et ſola in ſiccâ ſecum ſpatiatur arenâ.*"

Three ſucceſſive Spondees, ſo many Words beginning with S, a Letter of difficult Pronunciation, and ending with ā, a long and open Vowel, expreſs admirably ſlow and ſolitary Walking: But are not the Terms *ſola* and *ſecum* the very ſame in Senſe, and one ſuperfluous?

So difficult is it to keep the due Mean: Paſs but the Limit, the greateſt Beauties become Faults: And I am apt to think, that the Refinement of an eminent Muſician, mentioned by Pope in this Line,

[w] "And *Jove*'s own Thunders follow *Mars*'s
" Drums,"

who employed Cannon to fill up his Chorus in a rejoicing Anthem, was a Tranſgreſſion of the Kind now mentioned, an outrageous Imitation of Nature.

BUT to return to Orators. If it be fit that Poets, the Votaries of Fiction, ſhould keep within due Bounds, in this Article of Ornament; it is much more neceſſary that theſe others ſhould, becauſe the Dreſs of Truth, whom they ſerve, is more ſevere. The general Idea of Beauty is the ſame to both; but theſe muſt be diſcreet and chaſte: To theſe, Beauties border on Faults, a Step beyond Excellence is Defect, nay Meaneſs. Which leads to

[u] And wanders *by himſelf* on the dry Strand *Alone.*

[w] *Dunciad*, Book iv. line 68.

to a general Reflection that ſhall cloſe this Lecture.

THERE is always Hazard to an Orator in endeavouring to excel. Whence every one who means to ſpeak in publick ſhould aſk himſelf;

" SHALL I content myſelf with being meerly plain and reaſonable, thus be a Speaker blameleſs, and it is likely not unuſeful? Or ſhall I aim at Excellence, thus riſk Diſgrace?" Weigh well your own Abilities, and act accordingly.

LECTURE

LECTURE the Fifteenth.

Of FIGURES, *or* TROPES.

CLEARNESS, Propriety, and Harmony, are not sufficient to answer the Ends of Oratory, which require beside these, that Discourse should be lively and animated: To this Purpose the Use of Figures is necessary; concerning which I now proceed to make some Observations.

IT is a Question which hath received various Answers, and occasioned no small Debate, whence it cometh to pass, that Figures render Discourse more pleasing: What is there in the Mind of Man, which disposeth it to entertain with more Delight, Notions conveyed to it in this Disguise, than in their own natural Form?

THE Variety of Opinions concerning this Point seemeth to have sprung from hence, that different Men fixing upon different Causes, have persisted in reducing the Effect, each to the Cause assigned by himself, excluding all others; to the Production of which Effect several, perhaps many do concur. I will explain myself.

FIRST. It hath been observed long ago, indeed Instances occur every Day in Proof of it, that

that the Mind is pleaſed with Things uncommon and new: Now Figurative Speech hath this Charm of Novelty to recommend it, for leaving the uſual Track, it taketh you thro' Paths untrodden and unexpected: You ſee a certain Point laid down to be proved; you have a general Notion of the Arguments likely to be made uſe of to this Purpoſe; but inſtead of having theſe placed before you in the common Form, you find them in one very different, and the Knowlege you ſought for communicated in Expreſſions altogether foreign, yet theſe conducted by ſuch happy Skill, that they lead you as rightly and ſhortly to the End in View, as the plaineſt and moſt literal: Thus you are entertained in your Journey without being retarded.

ANOTHER Cauſe that recommendeth Figures, thoſe eſpecially diſtinguiſhed by the Name of *Tropes*, to our liking, is the Pleaſure which the Mind naturally feels in *Compariſon*. When a Word which in its original Senſe conveyeth a a certain Idea to the Mind, is uſed in ſuch Manner, as together with this to convey another, connected to the firſt by a natural Reſemblance; yet ſo that this latter acceſſory Idea becomes now the Principal; here the Mind hath the Pleaſure of contemplating at once two Images, yet without Confuſion: Nay with this Advantage, that by Means of ſuch Compariſon the principal Image becomes more bright and ſtriking: As in theſe Examples,

" [*a*] Now laugh the Fields."—

" [*b*] Admires

" [*a*] Nunc rident agri. VIRG.

" [b] Admires new Leaves and Apples not
" it's own."

" [c] With Floods and Whirlwinds of tem-
" pestuous Fire."

THE Pleasure received from the imitative Arts hath it's Ground in this Love of Comparison. Thus we are delighted with the Likeness between the Forms and Colours of Nature, and those taken from her by the Pencil: Nay we are often pleased with seeing Nature imitate as it were herself, Reflecting to our Sight the Landskips of Wood, and Hills, and Skyes, portrayed on the glassy Surface of untroubled Water: Something whereof I think there certainly is in the present Case, in the Use of *Metaphors* or *Translations*.

To which you should add, that these Comparisons are frequently drawn from Objects in themselves beautiful, which being of Course pleasing, diffuse new Charms as well as Light over a whole Discourse.

OTHER Causes of less Influence might be assigned, but I hasten to the Chief and most Universal.

THE truest Representations of Nature please most: And it is for this Reason, that Figures are agreeable, being the Voice of Nature; when rightly used, the Way wherein she expresseth herself on all such Occasions. " Yet how may " this be? Are not Figures artificial Speech, and " considered as such? In what Sense then do I " stile

" [b] Miraturque novas frondes et non sua poma. VIRG.
" [c] *Milton's* Paradise Lost. Book 1.

"ſtile them the Voice and Language of Nature?"
This will need ſome Explanation.

DETERMINE firſt, what are the Occaſions, upon which Figures are properly employed. Are they not chiefly thoſe, in which the Mind is ſeized, warmed, tranſported by a ſudden or ſtrong Paſſion, as Admiration, Aſtoniſhment, Love, Rage? Now conſult the great Book of Nature, the Original and Model of all true Art:—How do all, young and old, learned and illiterate, Men and Women, expreſs themſelves in ſuch Conjunctures? Is their Diſcourſe clear, direct, and flowing? Or rather is it not diſturbed, broken, disjointed? The Mind overcharged by Paſſion, labouring yet unable to pour it all forth, maketh every Effort, ſtruggles in vain for Words anſwerable to it's Ideas, ſtarteth from Hint to Hint, heapeth Images upon Images, and painteth it's own Diſorder in the Irregularity and Confuſion of it's Language. What doth Indignation? Invoke Heaven and Earth, and ſeek to intereſt all Nature in it's Quarrel. Thus *Dido*—

"[*d*] Be Arms oppos'd to Arms, be Shore to
"Shore,
"May ev'n our Seas with adverſe Billows roar,
"And ye my Sons, purſue thro' ev'ry Age
"His Offſpring with hereditary Rage."—

What ſaith Revenge,

"[*e*] Abſent

[*d*] Littora littoribus contraria, fluctibus undes,
Imprecor, arma armis; pugnent ipſique nepotes.
VIRG. Æneid 4.

" [e] Absent I'll torture thee--a vengeful Shade
" Pursue; Wretch! dearly shall thy Crimes be
" paid."

—— [f] No, let us rather chuse
Arm'd with Hell-flames and Fury, all at once
O'er Heav'ns high Tow'rs to force resistless Way,
Turning our Tortures into horrid Arms
Against the Torturer."

What is the Language of Grief?

" O Woods, O Fountains, Hillocks, Dales, and Bow'rs,
With other Eccho late I taught your Shades
To answer, and resound far other Song!"

Of Remorse and Shame?

—— " [g] Cover me ye Pines,
Ye Cedars with innumerable Boughs
Hide me."

FROM these Considerations it appears, that Figurative Speech is so far from being as it hath been oftentimes represented, meerly artificial, and a Departure from Nature, that it is a faithful Image of Nature. Inward Emotion displayeth itself as readily in the Language as in the Features; and he, who from the Circumstances he describeth, or Subject of which he treateth, ought to be, or appear to be possest with a strong Passion, yet speaketh in a calm, untroubled Easiness of Stile, acteth as much against Nature, as

[e] —— Sequar atris ignibus absens,
Omnibus umbra locis adero, dabis improce pænas.
VIRG. Æneid.

[f] MILTON, Book ii.
[g] —— Book x.

as doth the Man who would expreſs great inward Agitation of Mind by a ſmooth unaltered Serenity of Countenance.

FIGURES are the Language of Paſſion; Univerſal Experience demonſtrates this to be the Caſe, as all of every Rank and Capacity who are under the Influence of ſuch Paſſion, ſpeak Figuratively: Now it is acknowledged, that the Orator in almoſt all Cauſes of Moment findeth it requiſite to excite ſome Paſſion in his Hearer, which he cannot otherwiſe accompliſh than by feeling, or ſeeming himſelf to feel the ſame: And how ſhall he aſſume this Appearance? How? But by making Uſe of the Language, which Nature hath rendered inſeparable from the Paſſions. If you are enflamed with Anger or ſoftened with Pity, ſpeak to me as Men are wont to do, while they are under the Power of ſuch Emotions: Otherwiſe you talk in vain; I ſhall either not regard you at all, or ſhall turn away from you as an Impoſtor. Nature hath rendered Paſſions whereſoever ſtrongly marked, catching; but where theſe Marks are wanting, how ſhall they catch?

WHAT I have been ſaying is however to be underſtood with ſome Degree of Caution. Ye have doubtleſs heard it obſerved, that Figurative Speech is not friendly to the Pathetick, as carrying the Air of much Study and Artifice, the Work therefore of a Mind vacant and at eaſe.

WHICH Obſervation, how contradictory ſo ever it may appear, yet a little Attention will reconcile, to what hath been advanced above. To

this

this Purpose, you should distinguish Figures into two Kinds: One Sort consists in Words, as *Repetitions*, *Likeness of Sounds*, and *Cadence*, and *Oppositions*; to which we may add as being useful in embellishing Stile, certain Kinds of *Metaphors*, *Transpositions*, *Reduplications*. Now these being calculated to please the Ear or Imagination, being conducive to Prettiness and Elegance only, are Enemies to the Pathetick; are too insignificant and idle for Occasions of such Importance, and from all such ought to be excluded.

BUT there are Figures of a second Kind, whose Power affects the Sense principally, which bestow Force and Spirit; such as the Rhetoricians name *Apostrophes*, *Hyperboles*, [*h*] *feigning of Persons*; to these it is, that what hath been said is applicable; these are so far from hurting the Pathetick or being inconsistent with it, that they are the natural Language of Passion. Agitated by Passion, the Peasant breaketh out into such, no less than the Orator; the only Difference is, that in the latter, the Rudeness of uninstructed Nature is polished, it's Extravagances corrected, the Air and Resemblance are preserved, but softened and adorned. We may pronounce of Eloquence in this Respect, as the Poet doth of Comedy, it is not the less just Representation of Life for rising sometimes into a higher Stile:—

" If *Chremes* in the Drama chide his Heir
" Profuse and wild, in Eloquence severe,
" Doth

[*h*] Or Prosopopœia.

"Doth not the World's great Stage like
Scenes display,
"And Fathers rage as loudly ev'ry Day?" [i]

HAVING thus assigned the Causes why Figures please, it might be expected, that I should go on to give a Detail of the several Figures, with Examples of each; but this I shall decline, as they may be found in the Writings of every Rhetorician, deduced indeed usually with tiresome Exactness, so that it is not altogether without Reason that the wittiest of our Poets saith,

"For all the Rhetoricians Rules
"Teach nothing but to name his Tools."

HUD.

VOSSIUS as I remember having recounted an Hundred and defined them, excuseth himself from proceeding to others; that is, having oppressed his Reader with such a Multitude, he maketh an Apology for not overwhelming him. The Truth is, those Writers have multiplyed them without Cause. Many which they mention are so trivial and common, that they do not deserve Notice; not few are real Faults in Sense or Language, of which having gathered up some Instances in Authors of Reputation, they immediately erect them into Beauties, and consecrate them under the Appellation of Figures.

NOTWITHSTANDING, in thus disapproving an Excess of Attention to these Minutenesses, I would

[i] Interdum tumido Chremes delitigat ore:
——— Numquid Pomponius istis
Audiret leviora, pater si viveret? HOR.

would not be underſtood to recommend entire Neglect of them. Some Acquaintance with them will help us in diſcerning where an Orator leaves the beaten Track of Expreſſion, and for what Purpoſe; a kind of Knowlege uſeful in forming and perfecting the Judgment.

I mention this as the only true Uſe of the mechanical Part of Rhetorick which hath been explained with ſo much ſuperfluous Labour, becauſe the Streſs laid upon it may have, and I believe hath cauſed Miſtakes, inducing Men to believe it of great Value. "A celebrated Writer of Antiquity hath uſed ſuch and ſuch Figures in Diſcourſe, for which Reaſon I ſhall ſit down to write with a Reſolution of employing the ſame, eſteeming my Work the more perfect as it abounds more with ſuch Ornaments."

Thus we often Reaſon; whereas it is neither the Kind nor Number of Figures, but the right Application which renders them commendable.

I have read, or met with in Diſcourſe, an Obſervation which I think judicious and new: An Actor, who would excel, ſhould appear to be poſſeſſed with the ſtrong Paſſion his Part expreſſeth, and ſeem the Man he repreſents; but he ſhould not feel that Paſſion, ſhould not be that Man. Why? Becauſe the Strength of the Paſſion would diſable him from expreſſing it: Violent Rage, Grief, or Deſpair, would choak up his Words; Nature would ſwallow up Art, and Imitation be loſt in Reality.

This

THIS Remark may help to explain ſome Things before ſaid and unavoidably repeated concerning Points in which we often miſtake. A good Speaker muſt ſeem to feel the Paſſion he would excite, he muſt have it's Air, it's Language, the Figures moſt expreſſive of it's actual Influence; but I now add, that he muſt not be under that actual Influence: However outwardly in Tranſport, he muſt retain a Fund of Coolneſs within, Reaſon muſt rule there, "Calm "and ſerene ride in the Whirlwind, and di-"rect the Storm:" Otherwiſe loſing Command of himſelf, he muſt ſtray from all the Rules of Eloquence.

[k] THE Perfection of Art ſaith a good Judge, *is to become*; with which, ſtrong Paſſion cannot will conſiſt. Accordingly, the greateſt Speakers when they have given Way to ſuch, have erred. Is not the perſonal Invective againſt *Eſchines* in the admirable Oration of the *Crown*, to ſay no worſe, unjuſtifiably bitter? In the ſecond Philippic, Divine as [l] one ſtiles it, are not the Circumſtances of Abuſe againſt *Antony* heightened with Paintings deſervedly offenſive? Can one read them without wondering, that an excellent Perſon ſhould deliver ſuch in full Senate, if it be true that this Oration was delivered.

FROM hence it appears, that Figures being the proper Stile of Paſſion, they ſhould not only be juſt and natural, but conducted with much Care

[k] Caput artis eſt decere. *Cicero de Orat.* lib. I.
[l] Quam te conſpicuæ divina Philippica famæ,
Volveris a primâ quæ proxima. JUV. SAT. X.

Care and Diſcretion: Which Remark leads to point out ſome Abuſes neceſſary to be avoided in the Uſe of them. I ſhall ſpeak of theſe under three Heads; 1, the Number; 2, the Kinds; 3. the Application of Figures.

FIRST, As to the Number of Figures.

EXCESS herein is a very common Fault: It is in Writings as in Life, whatever is commended in a certain Degree, we are apt to carry beyond the Bound, and then it becometh wrong. Becauſe Figures aptly uſed have a good Effect, they are multiplyed without Meaſure, introduced every where, and heaped up with Profuſion, which produceth the worſt Conſequences.

FIRST, *Nothing ſo quickly tireth.* The natural Food of the Underſtanding is Truth; We are indeed ſo framed, that this Truth muſt be rendered by Art agreeable to the Taſte; what do theſe Men? Abuſing that Frame, they give us the Sauces only without the Food. We demand ſomething plain and ſolid,—find all Flouriſh and Shew. In this Caſe, the Hearer diſappointed turns away with Diſdain.

SECONDLY, This Exceſs taketh away *Credibility from the Speaker*. Truth hath not that Air of Study and Labour: To pleaſe ſhe needs but to be ſeen: We look not for Her amidſt a Crowd of Ornaments. Sincerity is moſt powerful to perſuade; Figures are ſtrong Inſtruments of Perſuaſion, becauſe ſtrong Proofs of Sincerity: But poured forth in Exceſs, are held Marks of Inſincerity, Means of ſetting off a bad Cauſe, and of extorting or ſurprizing undeſerved Aſſent: Hence the Hearer becometh diffident, ſuſpicious, guardeth himſelf againſt the Appearance of dangerous Art, and receives with Prejudice whatſoever is dreſſed up in theſe elaborate Embelliſhments.

Thirdly, THIS Exceſs rendereth Diſcourſe *obſcure*. The expreſſing of Things under borrowed Images muſt preſent them to the Mind with leſs Clearneſs, than if offered in their own: And much Skill is requiſite in making ſuch Choice, that while they add Force to the Thought, they may not diminiſh Perſpicuity. We ſee Objects through Figures as in a Mirror: Some are by this Means ſeen more diſtinctly; ſome we cannot view well directly; ſome we behold thus with more Delight; but if we attempt to ſhew all in this Way, the Truth of Things vaniſheth; we confound the Original with borrowed Forms, and the whole Scene becomes faint and confuſed.

THIS is the Caſe of *Perſius*, although otherwiſe in many Reſpects commendable; of *Lycophron* among the *Greeks*; and it ſeemeth of their Lyrick Poets ſometimes, as you may prove particularly in the Choruſes of the beſt Dramatick Writers, where the Senſe is frequently ſo wrapped up in a Cloud of Figures, that it cannot without much Difficulty be developed.

A SECOND Miſtake mentioned is in the *Kind* of Figures. We ſhould, generally ſpeaking, avoid all ſuch as turn meerly upon Sound; Prettineſſes much ſought after in former Times, ſuch as

"O

[*m*] "O fortunatam natam *me consule Romam.*"

[*n*] " *Beseeching* or *besieging.*"
" And at one *Bound* high overleapt all *Bound.*"

At the Sight of Sin and Death, in the Midst of a sublime Passage, saith our great Poet, " The " Planets were *Planet-struck.*" But these at present seem deservedly exploded.

REPETITIONS of the same Word are also sometimes graceful. One of the most beautiful of which Sort is the Passage of *Virgil*, thus imitated by one of our Poets,

[*o*] Yet ev'n in Death *Euridice* he sung,
Euridice still trembled on his Tongue;
Euridice the Woods,
Euridice the Floods,
Euridice the Rocks and hollow Mountains rung [*p*]."

But Beauties of this Kind are generally speaking easily attained in a Degree of Mediocrity; and therefore should be used sparingly.

THERE is a Point of more Nicety, the using many Words nearly synonimous, of which you may find numerous Instances in the *Roman*

S 2 Orator.

[*m*] 'Till I her *Consul sole consol'd* her Doom.
DRYD. Juv.

[*n*] Parad. lost, Book 10.

[*o*] ——— *Euridicen vox ipsa et frigida lingua,*
Ah miseram Euridicen, animâ fugiente, vocabat;
Euridicen toto referebant flumine ripæ. VIRG. Georg. 4.

[*p*] POPE, Ode on St. CÆCILIA.

Orator. *He hath departed, fled, escaped, broke away* [q]. These often weaken the Sense, and tire the Hearer by a Heap of unmeaning Sounds; yet are sometimes useful by giving Strength and Energy. Although each Word do not convey a distinct Idea, yet taken together they make the whole collected Idea much larger and more grand. I should not therefore altogether condemn such; but recommend the utmost Caution in employing them. They should be rare, and introduced on well-chosen Occasions.

THERE are other Figures affecting the Sense, which are likewise to be used with Caution. Such as very bold Metaphors, and those the Rhetoricians name *Catachreses* or *Abuses*; which, although allowed in Verse, Speakers should never venture upon, but where the Poverty of the Language may have rendered them necessary, and Custom hath established them.

Hyperbolès also are dangerous Figures. The Poet mentioning two Persons of extraordinary Size, describes them thus,

[r] " Youths equal to the Pines
" And Mountains of their Country."—

COWLEY seeking to improve upon this Image in applying it to *Goliah*, hath made it altogether extravagant:

" The

[q] Abiit, excessit, evasit, erupit. In Catali. Orat. 1.
[r] Abietibus juvenes patriis et montibus æquos. Eneid. 9.

" The Valley now this Monster seem'd to fill;
" And we methoughts look'd up to' him from our Hill [s].

HOMER says very sublimely of an allegorical Person, *Discord*,

" Her Head she rais'd to Heav'n and trod on Earth:

Which *Virgil* hath applied with great Propriety to another allegorical Person, *Fame*. But is it not with much less Exactness imitated of *Satan*, described before indeed as of gigantick Size [t], yet far different from this,

" His Stature reach'd the Sky."

Poets are indulged in Liberties of this Kind, which they have for the most Part abused, the Moderns especially; but the same Licences are not to be suffered among those, who would perswade, who profess the speaking of Truth.

Opposition is a Figure, which also should be used discreetly. If meerly in Words, once a fashionable Kind of Wit, it is manifest trifling; if in Sentiment, it is of a delicate Nature. It sometimes giveth Life and Energy to the Thought, as in this of the [u] Historian, concerning a great Person one of much Pride, " He resorted sometimes to Court, because " there only, was a greater Man than him- " self;

[s] COWLEY Davideis, Book 3.
[t] Lay floating many a Rood. Book 1.
[u] Lord CLAREND. Book 1.

" ſelf; and went thither the ſeldomer, becauſe " there was a greater Man than himſelf," which ſeems to be imitated from a parallel Paſſage of *Cicero* concerning *Roſcius* [w].

HOWEVER, theſe are dangerous Beauties: I know not of any Writers who have uſed them much, without abuſing. Even *Cicero* in his nobleſt Oration, ſeems through Love of them to have departed for a Moment from the Character of manly Eloquence. " This new Form " of Judgment, ſaith he, ſtrikes Terror; we " are ſurrounded by Arms, placed indeed for " our Security; but we cannot *be* [x] *freed* " *from Fear, without fearing.*" Is not this too pretty? And chiefly in the Beginning of his Oration, where Simplicity is moſt requiſite?

SOME few Specks of the ſame Kind may be ſpyed elſewhere even in his Writings; but ſucceeding Orators carried this Fault to the higheſt Exceſs. In modern Times it reigned long in *Italy*; from whence it infected *French* Elegance; nor did the plainer and more manly Genius of *Britain* eſcape the Contagion.

UPON the Whole, I dare not venture to condemn the Uſe of *Antitheſes*. But I am perſwaded, that it is the better Way to follow herein the Example of the *Greeks*, who are exceedingly ſparing in Ornaments of this Kind, I think

[w] *Etenim cùm Artifex eſt ejuſmodi, ut ſolus dignus videatur eſſe qui ſcenam introeat; tum vir ejuſmodi, ut ſolus videatur dignus, qui eo non accedat.*

CICERO pro Quinto ROSCIO.

[x] *Ne non timere quidem, ſine aliquo timore poſſimus.*

Pro Milone.

I think rather did ſtudiouſly avoid them. By rejecting them, you will gain in Strength and Clearneſs, more than you loſe in Glitter and Show.

THERE is not any Figure more commonly uſed by Orators than Gradation or Climax; which ſetting every Article of the Speaker's Senſe diſtinctly before the Hearer's Mind, gives the Whole an Appearance of Grandeur. Yet herein alſo Frequency is faulty; it ſavoureth of Affectation, is too artificial, and groweth tireſome: But the moſt common Errror ariſeth from an ill ordering of the Parts. It is a known Rule that the Gradation ſhould grow ſtronger, the following Member riſing ſtill upon the foregoing; the contrary whereof is not ſeldom the Caſe. When the Poet calls a fine Piece of Architecture

The World's juſt Wonder—and ev'n thine O
Rome, [y]

Doth this latter Idea comprehend more than the firſt? Doth not the Image rather ſink? Mr. *Addiſon* hath commended a Paſſage of *Milton*;

And had Earth been then,
All Earth had to her Center ſhook.

Yet it ſeems that it may be doubted, whether the Poet after repreſenting all Heaven reſounding with the Tumult of the Angels engaged in Battle, hath not gone out of his Way, to add an Image that weakens the foregoing.

THE

[y] Eſſay on Criticiſm.

THE third Miſtake was ſaid to conſiſt in the *Application* of Figures: Thoſe in themſelves good are miſapplied: Which Error ariſeth from Want of Attention to the Subject and to the Occaſion; what would be proper and pleaſing on one, being offenſive and abſurd on another.

THE fineſt Embelliſhments Rhetorick can furniſh, introduced in a Cauſe which demandeth only Diſtinctneſs and Perſpicuity, deform inſtead of beautifying. Who can bear the Laws of the lower Empire and Writings of Civilians about that Time, compoſed in the long florid Stile of Declamation; And ſome of the earlier modern Phyſicians, who forgetting or deſpiſing the proper diſtinct Simplicity of *Hippocrates*, and Purity of *Celſus*, load all, one might almoſt ſay even to their Preſcriptions, with Flouriſh? How long did the moſt auguſt Aſſemblies and national Councils reſound with the Pomp of verboſe Amplification; and Pulpits lull patient Congregations with the fantaſtical Mixture of the Thorns of ſcholaſtick Theology, and the Flowers of claſſical Elegancy? If where I ſeek to be taught, you attempt to put me off with Amuſement, I cannot but turn from you in juſt Diſdain of ſuch Puerility.

FARTHER, One of the greateſt Sources of Beauty in figurative Writing is Metaphor; attending which you may obſerve two Dangers. One is, The purſuing it too far. A Train of Metaphors carried on formeth an *Allegory*; which Figure, or rather Chain of Figures, if every Part be apt, well connected, and agreeing with

with the original Idea, is justly pleasing; but pursued too far errs in one of these two Ways. Either the Truth shadowed under it lies too open, and then it becometh flat and tedious; the Case sometimes of *Spenser*'s Allegories, which even the rich Imagination and beautiful Poetry of the Author cannot always fully support: Or else the Resemblance is too remote; in which Case the Allegory degenerates into a Riddle, and offendeth because it puzzles. Thus you see the Nicety requisite in the Use of this Figure: You must form a Veil so transparent that it shall disclose all one wisheth to see, yet thick enough to cover what should be concealed; obvious it satiates quickly, dark perplexeth. Let the Mind seem to discover somewhat itself, but make not that Discovery a laborious Work. The Episode of Sin and Death [z] considered as an Allegory, not Part of an heroick Poem, seems one of the most perfect. The Moral is important, the Circumstances affecting, true in their allegorical, just in their literal Sense, the Imagination noble, the Stile grand, sublime.

A SECOND Danger attending the Use of Metaphors is, the mixing different and inconsistent. Criticks have taxed even *Cicero* with a Slip of this Kind; [a] "I observe, says he, my Discourse "to be *coloured* by their *Harmony*." Nor has the most correct of Poets escaped the same Censure; as for this Line,

"And

[z] Parad. Lost.

[a] *Sentio orationem meam illorum quasi* Cantu colorari. *De Orato.*

[*b*] "And to the Anvil ill-turn'd Verses bring
Anew."

In which Case the Censure is perhaps undeserved:—But is the Conclusion of a fine Ode altogether free,

"Into what *Whirlpool* art thou *plung'd*
"O Youth, O worthy of a better *Flame*."

We may observe the same of these Lines, otherwise beautiful,

"The Man by his own Brightness *burns*, that *weighs*
Inferior Artists down; yet *quench'd his Blaze*,
All love, and crown him with impartial Praise."

Need I add that much Vigilance is required in guarding against a Fault, the Infection of which seems to have reached in some Degree even these Heroes?

THE last Figure I shall mention as frequently ill-conducted is *Irony*, where the Speaker means differently from what his Words literally understood, import. This Figure is useful not only in Comedy and Satire, its most usual Province; but hath Place also in the Pathetick and Sublime: As in this spirited Irony of *Dido*,

Go

[*b*] *Et male* tornatos incudi *reddere versus.* HOR.
Ah quantâ laboras in charybdi
Digne puer meliore flammâ.
Urit enim fulgore *suo qui* prægravat *artes*
Infra se positas: extinctus *amabitur idem.*

[a] Go follow *Italy* thro' Tempests, haste,
Seek flying Kingdoms o'er the watry Waste."

And this of *Satan*,

" Or have ye chos'n this Place,
" After the Toil of Battle to repose
" Your weary Virtue, for the Ease you find
" To slumber here, as in the Vales of Heav'n?"

The Dangers attending this Figure are these three; one is ever apt to break in upon it. Your real Sense is ready to burst out, and mingle itself with the ironical, which makes an odd incoherent Mixture. This Fault in long continued Irony seemeth scarcely avoidable, since it is laid to the Charge of *Lucian*, *Cervantes*, and *Swift*, the three great Masters of this Figure.

ANOTHER Danger is, Ironies are often intermixed with serious Truths, which is abrupt and hard: As in the latter of the two following Lines, speaking of Dr. *Swift*,

[b] Or thy griev'd Country's Copper Chains unbind,
Or *praise the Court* or *dignify Mankind.*

All before and after the latter of these Lines, are understood in their literal Sense.

OR lastly, Ironies are made to turn upon Subjects foreign, and are improperly bitter; as in this of the Orator to *Antony*,

" In

[a] *I sequere Italiam ventis, pete regna per undas.* Eneid 4.

[b] POPE's Dunciad. Book 1st.

" In one Place alſo you aimed at Pleaſantry;
" Good Gods how little did it become you! In
" which you are faulty; for you might have
" derived ſome Wit *from your Wife, an Actreſs.*"

To conclude, concerning the Subject before us it may be obſerved in general; that Exceſs and Defect are both Faults: Exceſs is indeed the more dangerous: For ſpeaking without Figures you will appear dry, inſipid, unaffecting, but ſtill may be inſtructive, for which End the Curious will liſten: But if you uſe too many, you muſt offend, incurring juſtly the Cenſure of Affectation, Vanity, and Obſcurity.

NOTWITHSTANDING which, this Fault, Exceſs, is more eaſily corrected than its oppoſite, Defect: For it is eaſier to bring down an over-warm Imagination to the Level of plain Senſe, than to elevate the low and creeping to the Height of adorned Eloquence. For this Reaſon, as the Poets abound moſt in Figures, it might be fit, that all who mean to excel in Eloquence ſhould at leaſt in their Youth, be converſant in their Writings. But this Subject, as being in my Opinion of Importance, deſerveth to be opened more at large in a future Lecture.

Etiam quodam loco facetus eſſe voluiſti; quam id dii boni non te decebat! in quo eſt tua culpa nonnulla; aliquid enim ſalis ab uxore mimâ trahere potuiſti.

LECTURE

LECTURE the Sixteenth.

Of the USEFULNESS *of reading the* POETS *to an* ORATOR.

IN the Conclusion of the foregoing Lecture, I took Occasion to mention the Expediency of reading the Poets to all, who would excel in Eloquence, on the Account of one Article of mighty Moment, *Figures*. And I am persuaded, that, upon a nearer View, others, not less material, will appear to concur in recommending it; for the Discovery of which, the present Disquisition is intended. But in a Point variously thought of, for this hath its Opposers, and is in its Nature delicate, I do not mean that you should rely on my Judgment; instead of which, I shall lay before you the Sentiments of one well versed in this, as in most other Parts of Learning: Sentiments, which may add to Reason the Weight of Authority. My Purpose is, to deliver the Substance of a Conversation upon this Subject, held by *Eubulus*, a Person of known Eminence both in the Senate and at the Bar, with his Friend *Philemon*; which latter was pleased, at my Request, to furnish me with an Account of it.

THE

THE unusual Manner, that of Dialogues, in Compositions of this Sort, will be compensated by the Character of the principal Speaker; and it is hoped, that Indulgence of borrowing will be granted, where one's own Stock affordeth nothing equal. You readily excuse an Host in carrying you Abroad, if it be into better Company, and to better Entertainment, than his Home could have afforded. The Occasion which gave Rise to the Conversation above-mentioned, was this:

Philemon happened to make a Visit to *Eubulus*, then, during the Summer Vacation, in his Country Retirement; and finding, at his Arrival, that his Friend had walked Abroad, he went, with the Freedom of an Intimate, to amuse himself in the Library of *Eubulus* till his Return; which happening in no long Time after, *Eubulus*, the first Salutations being over, expressed the Pleasure he had in seeing his Friend, and, at the same Time, his Fear, that *Philemon* had felt some Uneasiness in waiting for him so long.

Phile. BE under no Concern, *Eubulus*, for I could have passed much more Time here, without thinking it long. Nothing can be more pleasing than the Prospect from these Windows. What can be more beautiful than that vast Bay, which expands itself with such wide Circuit before us, presenting to the View so many Objects: Those Ships particularly of different Sizes; some fixed at Anchor, some in Motion, with all their Sails spread, and steer-

ing

ing with the ſame Wind Courſes almoſt contrary. Beyond, we ſee the oppoſite Coaſt, covered with Houſes, reflecting the Rays of the Sun, ſet off with the darker Shade of Gardens and Groves; and at ſtill greater Diſtance, behold thoſe Mountains which ſeem to vaniſh into the Clouds, and terminate the Scene with a rude and noble Magnificence! It ſeems to me, that a View of ſo much Beauty and Variety could never tire.

Eub. THE Proſpect is indeed charming; I have heard Travellers ſay, that ſcarcely any Country in *Europe* affords a more beautiful of the like Kind. However, it is certain, that ſuch Beauties appear more ſtriking to a Viſitant than to the Owner; Familiarity renders him indifferent; or, if it did not, I doubt whether ſuch Situations be proper for Study, as the Multitude of foreign Objects diſtract the Attention.

Phile. SAY rather, that it affords an eaſy and uſeful Relaxation. But it ſeems to me that you have prudently ſuited your Kind of Reading to your Situation, at leaſt I cannot otherwiſe account for it.

Eub. IN what Reſpect?

Phile. CURIOSITY led me to take the Liberty of opening ſome of the Books, which lie in Heaps upon this Table; and the Truth is, the View ſurpriſed me. I found them to be all of the poetical Kind; Authors which I ſuppoſed that you might have converſed with in your early Youth, but imagined, that you had

had long dismissed all such frivolous Acquaintances.

Eub. SOFTLY, good *Philemon*; beware of using such harsh Epithets to a Set of Gentlemen, who have been honoured in all Ages; whose Names are consecrated to Immortality; who have always laid Claim to peculiar Inspiration; whose Genius and Language have been esteemed somewhat divine.

Phile. I KNOW they have not been sparing in their Praises of their own Art: But without amusing ourselves with their Enthusiasm, or rather Presumption, answer me seriously; Have these Books been thrown here by Accident, or have you really, as it should seem by their Situation, been trying to entertain yourself with reading such?

Eub. The latter is true; I have been trying, and what is more, do pass much of my Leisure in such Entertainment, as you call it; but, in my Stile, *Employment*, and useful Employment.

Phile. YOU amaze me. Is it then true, that *Eubulus*, engaged as he is in the Study of serious Eloquence, and universally allowed to excel therein, consumeth his Time in the Perusal of Writers, not useless only, but exceedingly hurtful to his Purpose?

Eub. WHY useless? Why hurtful? Why do you think them so? There remains yet some Time until Dinner, and the Heat of the Weather prevents us from any Amusement without Doors, What say you? Shall we spend this Interval in discussing that Matter? It may be be no unuseful Speculation. Let us then sit down together in this Bow-Window, from whence you have a full Command of your admired Prospect.—Very well.—Now, if you please, explain upon what Grounds do you build this Opinion?

Phile. You take me ill prepared for such a Disquisition; I have never yet thought maturely on the Point, much less have I in Readiness Arguments to produce ranged in Form and Method. Yet I look upon it as one of those Truths in themselves so clear, that Arguments for the Proof of them can never be wanting.

Eub. Be so good then as to propose them: I request it not through Love of disputing, but from a better Principle; I would gladly justify myself to you; beside, I have some Hope of doing you real Service, by reconciling you to an Acquaintance, which we usually commence early in Life, but break off too soon, to reap the Pleasure and Advantage it would afford to our riper Years; at which Time, Disuse, Business, and mistaken Notions, prevent the Renewal of it.

Phile. I hope that I shall be always open to Conviction; and since you will have it so, I will mention Things briefly, and without Order, as they occur to me. My Charge is, that Poets are Enemies to true Oratory; the Reasons I ground it upon are these: Answer me, *Eubulus*, Are not the Ends of Eloquence to inform and to convince?

Eub. THEY are.

Phil. FOR this Purpose, must not the Understanding be enlightened?

Eub. IT must.

Phil. BUT Poets address themselves to the Imagination and Passions; therefore turn away their Admirers from the true Ends of Oratory.

Eub. SHALL I stop you now? Or were it not better, that you should propose all your Objections, which we will afterwards consider distinctly?

Phil. WITH all my Heart; it is the shorter Way. Well, then, you have heard my first Objection.

NEXT, Poets deal entirely in Fiction; they subsist by it; thus infuse an Indisposition to, a Dislike of Truth.

THEY confound Times, Persons, Circumstances, and Characters; and throw their Thoughts together (such as they are) with the utmost Confusion; nay, they condemn Regularity as insipid, and formal, and inconsistent with their imaginary Beauty.

THEY abhor Argument, the only Instrument of Knowledge and rational Persuasion; and, to compleat the Whole, are swelling, florid, and unnatural in their Stile. I need not delay you by giving Instances of each Particular, which are well known to you; for their Works abound with them.

Eub. THIS indeed, *Philemon*, is a summary Way of Proceeding. If these Things be so, the Poets are not only guilty of your Charge, of of being hurtful to Eloquence, but are Enemies to Reaſon and common Senſe. But let us examine theſe Articles in Detail. Before I go into Particulars, give me Leave to propoſe a Queſtion or two, the Anſwers to which may clear up ſome Prejudices that lye againſt your whole Argument. Ought not Facts, where they can be had, to hold the firſt Place among Arguments, as being obvious, not liable to Miſtake, indeed carrying with them Conviction at firſt Sight?

Phil. THEY ought.

Eub. Now, *Philemon*, what do Facts ſay? Do they agree with your Reaſoning?

Phil. THAT Queſtion cannot be anſwered on the ſudden.

Eub. IT may be ſo: I will therefore aſſiſt you in the Anſwer: If I miſtake, ſet me right.

Phil. I ſhall not fail.

Eub. IT ſeems then, that the greateſt Orators have ſtudied, nay, and have copied from the Poets. This is ſo manifeſt in the Caſe of *Demoſthenes*, the firſt of all Orators, that *Lucian* has written a Dialogue upon this Subject alone, his Imitation of *Homer*. *Longinus* affirms the ſame Thing of *Plato*; adding, that he was not the Imitator only, but the Rival of *Homer*. Another *Greek* Critick carrieth this very far: The Proſe of *Demoſthenes*, ſaith he, is pleaſing, becauſe it reſembles the Verſe of *Homer*: And the Verſes of *Homer* charm us, on Account of their Similitude to the Proſe of *Demoſthenes* [a].

[a] DIONYSIUS HALICARNASSENSIS.

Open *Livy*; you will find him in many Places ſcarcely leſs poetical than *Virgil* himſelf: And Criticks have charged *Tacitus* with Exceſs in this Way. You diſcover the Fancy and Expreſſion of a Poet in many ſpirited Deſcriptions of the elder *Pliny*. *Tully* himſelf, although no good Poet in Verſe, is yet in Proſe oftentimes an excellent one. Now doth not this inconteſtable Fact overthrow all your Arguments? If the moſt admirable Orators have ſtudied, and manifeſtly copied from Poets, can the Reading of Poets be hurtful to Oratory?

Phil. IT may be in general dangerous, although it proved not hurtful to them. The Skilful only can extract Medicines from Poiſons.

Eub. WELL, but do theſe very Perſons think ſo? Conſult them: Hear *Cicero*. "The Poet "is allied to the Orator; more confined in "Numbers, but enjoying more Freedom in "the Uſe of Words: In every Kind of Or-"nament a Partaker, and almoſt equal. The "Poets are to be read. In an Orator is re-"quired nearly the Expreſſion of a Poet [*b*].

QUINTILIAN is very expreſs to the ſame Purpoſe. [*c*] *Theophraſtus* ſaith, he, affirms, "That an Orator may derive much Advan-"tage from reading Poets, and many agree "with him,—not undeſervedly: For Energy "in Senſe, and Sublimity in Expreſſion, and "Skill in moving the Paſſions, and what is "becoming in Character, are derived from "them." The Paſſage is remarkable, and goes

[*b*] Lib. I. de Oratore. [*c*] Lib. x. cap. I.

goes on farther; I will turn to it in his Book, if you please; it is worthy of your Perusal.

Phil. I DOUBT it not; but I looked for Arguments drawn from Reason, not Authority.

Eub. I DO not mean to convince you meerly by Authority: Its Use, and I intend no more, I take to be this; before an Opinion is proved, the Authority of eminent Persons removeth Prejudices which may lie against it, shewing it to be at least not absurd: If it hath been proved, strengthens and confirms it, and may help to make the Mind acquiesce in it more easily.

BUT not to insist longer on what you seem to lay small Stress upon, I proceed to follow you in your own Way; to Facts and Authority I shall add Reason.

YOU say, first, That Poets address themselves to the Imagination and Passions. Granted: But must not the Orator also?

Phil. WHY is it necessary to him?

Eub. Is not his End to persuade? In order to obtain which, must he not please?

Phil. It is sufficient if he address himself to Reason, the highest and ruling Faculty.

Eub. THE highest, I grant, in the Order of Nature, but never the only, and often not the ruling one. This Sovereign is accessible only through her Officers, the Fancy and Affections. Now it follows, from your own Argument, that the Poets can best instruct in this Art; they who make it their principal Aim to sooth and flatter these Favourites. Tell me, *Philemon*, do you think that a Chain of Geometrical Propositions

positions would have any Effect either in teaching or persuading a common Audience?

Phil. IT could not.

Eub. JUST such a Chain is every Discourse consisting of pure, strong, closely-connected Reasoning, such as you recommend; Demonstration to the intelligent Listener, it will not be listened to, nor can it be comprehended, by the Many.

Phil. WELL, but if this were the Case, if it were needful to work upon Fancy and Passion, the Poets are pernicious Teachers. Their Art subsists by Fiction, is wild and extravagant in its Images, confounds all Truth and Nature. What more opposite to every Idea of Eloquence?

Eub. THIS is the heaviest Article in your Charge, and deserves to be well weighed. Answer me then; Do you mean, that Poesy is an Enemy to all Kinds of Truth, and always? or is she a Friend to Truth in general, and departs from it only on certain Occasions, and in certain Circumstances?

Phil. POESY is an Enemy to Truth in general; not at all, or scarcely ever befriending it, and then by Accident, not Design.

Eub. HOW may that be? Certainly all Poets profess the contrary. Say the Ground of their Work be a Fable, the Circumstances fictitious, yet there is a Moral usually intended, which is some important Truth. Could a Tragedy please, if there were not Justice in the Sentiments, Consistence in the Design, Truth in the

the Characters? It is the same in every other Branch of this Art: Nature and Probability must be preserved; and what are they but Truth? And the Poets who neglect these, do not understand, but abuse their Art.

Phil. BUT Probability is only the Appearance of Truth, not Truth.

Eub. Right, but it differs not in Effect from Truth, where the avowed End is not to deceive. Otherwise you might infer, that every Figure of Rhetorick is Falshood, and so destroy all Eloquence, I might say all Discourse, which cannot be kept up without some Mixture of Figures. But I will try to put this Matter in another Light. Consider, in every Art there is somewhat peculiar to it self; yet may it not have many Things in common with other Arts; some of which it can supply better than those others, and which it may be prudent to borrow from it?

Phil. I BELIEVE that may be the Case.

Eub. NAY, this is the Case in different Branches of the same Art. I will explain my Meaning by an Instance. A Maker of Portraits hath a very distinct Business from that of an History-painter; he is tied down closely to a fixed Model, to the Features, the Air, the Mien of the Person whose Picture he draws: In all which, the other, provided that he do not violate the Truth of History, is at Liberty to follow his own Invention: Yet this hinders not, but that a Maker of Portraits may derive much Advantage from the Study of historical Painting,

ing, may labour with much Improvement to attain the Expression of a *Raphael*, or the Colouring of a *Titian*.

Now to apply this to the Subject before us. The Orator you may call a Maker of Portraits, he is confined to one Cause, to it's Circumstances, and to Truth: The Poet like the History-Painter hath indeed his Rules of Truth and Nature, which he may not transgress, but is yet left much at large, and may give great Scope to Invention. Notwithstanding which, the former may study this latter with much Advantage, and draw from him many Graces and valuable Embellishments. For the Manner in which Fiction is treated may set off Truth; and the being conversant with the Lofty, even extravagant Images, which the unbounded Regions of Fable present to the Fancy, may warm and elevate a judicious well-governed Imagination. Your venerable *Juno* of the Orators may borrow the *Cestus*, the Dress of the Smiles and Graces, from the Laughter-loving Goddess, the *Venus* of the Poets, provided these new Charms be put on for a good Purpose, to make a lawful Conquest.

Phil. IT is not clear to me, that a Lover of Truth may venture safely into this your unbounded Region of Fable; he may catch some Part of the Infection, which is but too general. Or granting for the present what you advance, how ridiculous a Figure must he make in his Return from thence, with his borrowed

Orna-

Ornaments, in his poetick Dreſs; delivering what he would have paſs for ſerious Truths, in the ſwelling Bombaſt of poetick Language.

Eub. You come now to another Article of your Charge; but here likewiſe I am prepared for you. Tell me *Philemon*, would a Perſon of Senſe who has learned to ſing perfectly, for that Reaſon ſpeak or read publickly, in the Tone or Cadence of ſinging?

Phil. No, certainly.

Eub. DEMOSTHENES is ſaid to have learned Pronunciation from an Actor. *Cicero* conſulted *Roſcius* in his Art. Now, do you think, that either of theſe great Men brought into the Senate-houſe of *Athens* or *Rome*, all the ſcenical Poſtures and Geſticulations, all the Violence and comick Mimickry, neceſſarily employed by thoſe Actors? Or did they retain only ſo much of the Art of thoſe others, as might be applied with Grace and Propriety to their own.

Phil. THE latter undoubtedly.

Eub. AGAIN, do you ſuppoſe that any Man of good Underſtanding, ſay even a Poet by Profeſſion, if he were to talk with you, or to write a Letter about ſerious Buſineſs, would ſpeak or write in Verſe?

Phil. I think not.

Eub. In my Opinion theſe Inſtances fully reach your Objection. Exerciſe and Skill in Muſick and Acting, may improve the Voice and Pronunciation in grave Diſcourſe; yet you would not in ſuch, either ſing or act. In like Manner,

Manner, the more ſpirited Stile of Poets may raiſe and enliven Proſe; yet you would not play the Poet in Proſe. A Poet will not uſe the Meaſure of Verſe, where he knows that he ought to employ Proſe: Why? Becauſe they are different Arts, and the Diſtinction is ſtrongly marked: And as he will not uſe the Meaſure, ſo neither will he uſe the Language peculiar to Verſe, which is almoſt as ſtrongly marked: Such as long Compariſons, daring Metaphors, crowded Figures, lively and florid Deſcriptions, unuſual Expreſſions; which belonging, or indulged to his own Art, cannot be transferred from thence into Proſe; or, if that ſhould be attempted, would offend the Underſtanding, as much as the Cadence of Verſe often intermingled, does the Ear. Notwithſtanding which, nothing hinders, but that the bold Painting of Poets, their animated Phraſe, their ſtrong and conciſe Sentences, their lively and glowing Colouring may be ſtudied with Profit, may with Care and Diſcretion be advantageouſly and happily copied in Proſe-writings. It is as the Poet ſays very aptly,

They move eaſieſt who have learn'd to dance [*b*].

The Movement of Dancing would be ridiculous in ordinary Walking, yet it is confeſſed, that Skill in Dancing beſtows Gracefulneſs in our common Motion.

Phil. But the Difficulty of keeping within theſe

[*b*] Eſſay on Criticiſm.

these Limits is great, the Danger of transgressing mighty, the Effect very absurd.

Eub. I grant it. But Excellency in every Art, is exposed to Danger and Difficulties. If you aim only at plain Sense with the Probability of being dry and insipid, it is well, study Logick and Geometry, or confine yourself to your Statutes and Reports: But, if you aspire to somewhat nobler, to add the Pleasing, the Sublime, the Pathetick, you must have Recourse, to those who exercise Power over the Fancy and Passions. After all, *Philemon*, you seem in the whole Turn of your Argument to shut out good Sense and all Regard to Truth from Poesy, in which you deal unjustly by it: These are necessary as well as to Poets as Orators.

Phil. THAT is a Point which I believe would puzzle you to make out.

Eub. NOT according to my Manner of conceiving Things. The Difference between the Arts I take to be this.

IT is my Intention to furnish out for Mankind a polite Entertainment, or say, that I wish to instruct and make them better, which if it seldom is, yet should be one View of a Poet in writing: I am to be read in their Closets; for to this, even theatrical Performances must come in the End: In either Case, you see that I must endeavour to please; it is a capital Point; for otherwise Men not being under any Necessity free from every urgent Motive, will not sit down to read my Work. This is the Poet's Case.

Case.—Pleasing therefore becomes to him a main Point; he can do nothing without it.

BUT again; I am to instruct them in somewhat of immediate necessary Utility, in the Decision of Property, in a weighty Point of Morality, or in the enacting of a good Law; here the visible great Use disposes them to hear; nevertheless such is the Nature of Mankind, that if my Subject carries me out into any Length, Men will not listen, unless I can contrive to make my Discourse agreeable. Pleasure is then, even in this Case a most beneficial Help, or rather necessary Means. And how shall you enable yourself to employ these Means, this powerful Instrument? How, but by consulting and learning from those to whom it is indispensibly necessary, to whom it becomes for that Reason the main *End* of their Art. You therefore borrow Ornaments from Poesy to dress up and make Truth beautiful; but it must be your Care to borrow such as really beautify, not hurt or deform her.

Phil. I fear that he must be not only very Sharp-sighted in discerning, but singularly discreet in the Choice of Ornaments, who can stop precisely within these Limits. But what will you reply to my other Objection? I think you will allow, that Method is necessary to a Speaker; and that the Poets are professed Enemies to Method. It hath a Formality to them intolerable; they are persuaded that it would render their Works dry and insipid; and cast Fetters on their Imagination, which is never

so

ſo well pleaſed as when fully indulged, and left free to rove in all the Luxuriancy of wild uncontrolled Irregularity.

Eub. I do not know how this Opinion hath obtained Admiſſion, and become prevailing, deſtitute as it ſeems to me of all Foundation. On the contrary, I am perſuaded that Method is eſſential to every good Compoſition. But it is of different Kinds; from not attending to which it is likely, the Miſtake ariſeth. There is one Kind of Method uſeful in the finding out of Truth, and another ſaid to be moſt proper for teaching it when found: In one you begin with the ſimpleſt and moſt known Truths from thence proceeding to the more complex and obſcure; in the other, beginning with what is complex you deſcend to the Simple; you reſolve Cauſes into their Effects, or trace back Effects to their Cauſes.

Again, there is a declared Method, which leading you from Step to Step, points out each, as it proceeds: And there is a concealed one, as regular, but leſs diſtinct in the ſeveral Parts of its Progreſs, which hath likewiſe its peculiar Uſes. There is farther an hiſtorical Method, which follows the Order of Time; and a Poetical, which breaks that Order, but in a certain Way, and for a certain End. Every Man of Senſe on all Subjects rangeth his own Thoughts in the moſt natural Order; but it doth not follow; that he would, or ought to chuſe the ſame Order in unfolding them to others.

Phil.

Phil. WHY ſo? You order your Thoughts, that you may conceive clearly; and clear Conception produceth clear Expreſſion.

Eub. TRUE: But it is manifeſt from what we ſaid before, that Clearneſs is not enough; you muſt amuſe, entertain, attract; how elſe will you obtain Audience from Men uſually nice, faſtidious Judges, always indolent? Hence it is, that Orators however regularly they conceive Things, do yet find it neceſſary on many Occaſions, quitting the natural Method, to imitate that of Poets, who chuſe ſuch as by raiſeing Curioſity keepeth the Reader attentive. They diſpoſe all their Thoughts and Incidents ſo, as that each may give Luſtre to the other, and the whole by that Means appear agreeable as well as intelligible. An obſerving Perſon tho' little ſkilled in Drawing, can mark down ſeveral Objects occurring in a fine Proſpect, ſuch as this now before you; all in their natural Form and Situation; here a declining Ground, there Sea or a River, beyond Houſes or Trees, at a great Diſtance Rocks and Sky: You underſtand all perfectly: But put this Taſk into the Hands of a Painter, he will chuſe out the moſt ſtriking Objects, he will diſpoſe them according to the Rules of Perſpective, he will throw ſome back in Shades, bring others forward, and give you not only a true Image of the Landſkip, but ſhew it to you in the beſt Manner, in all its Beauty and fair Proportion.

NAY, I will venture to ſay, that an Orator muſt ſacrifice Clearneſs to a certain Degree, to Beauty;

Beauty: It is what every good Speaker hath done from the Beginning: And what is more, it is what even the best Mathematicians have done, for the Sake of Conciseness and Elegance in their Demonstrations. The Nicety and Perfection of Art is to hit the true Bound; for Neatness ends if carried into Obscurity.

I AM perswaded moreover, that a Poet should observe as exact Method as the Orator is bound to, who must rarely employ more than he can conceal; for the Custom of dissecting his Discourse before his Hearer, into it's constituent Parts, and the distinct Enumeration of each Member, as it is brought up and as it is closed, must needs give to it an Air of disgusting Formality. And this Perswasion of mine is confirmed by Fact: For the Harangues in the *Greek* Dramatick Poets, which are very frequent and usually highly poetical, are often not less methodical or close than those even of the *Greek* Orator. I cannot think the Epistles of *Horace* less regular than the Treatises of *Cicero*, notwithstanding the Judgment of a celebrated Poet concerning them,

" *Horace* charms by graceful Negligence,
" And without Method talks us into Sense [*c*].",

But I consider this as spoken from a first slight View, and in Contradistinction to formal logical Method. Take any one, suppose the Epistle to *Augustus*, I am much mistaken, if I could not shew, that one Scheme is carried on thro' the

[*c*] Essay on Criticism.

the whole with good Method, that there is preſerved throughout Order but with Eaſe; Regularity, but with Gracefulneſs.—But ſee we are ſummoned to go in.

Phil. I ATTEND you; but with Condition, that after Dinner we ſhall return hither to finiſh this Subject; for my Scruples are not yet removed, nor what is more, my Curioſity ſatisfied.

LECTURE

LECTURE the Seventeenth.

Continuation of the Foregoing.

Phil. I AM glad that we have been released from our Company so early: We shall have Time to finish our Conversation, before the Evening oblige me to return Home. If I remember rightly, one Part of my Objection remains yet unanswered: It was to this Purpose; Argument is absolutely necessary to a publick Speaker, which the Poets avowedly abhor; must not the Study of them be hurtful to an Orator?

Eub. IT seems that it would, if the Case really were as you put it: But that may well be doubted. I allow that Poesy does not endure the Course of a long Chain of Reasoning running on Link after Link; at the same Time it is also true that it employs Reasoning, oftentimes close and very urgent; but requires, that it should be intermingled with Illustrations, and enlivened with Images; and the Perfection of its Art consists in so disposing these, as to add Grace without diminishing Strength. And ought not this to be the very Plan of the Orator? He is by no Means to string Syllogisms together, nor proceed by Lemmas, Propositions, and Corollaries. He who would be a popular Speaker, must follow the Example of the Poet, in tempering the Austerity of strict Argument, and while he seeks to convince the Understanding, endeavour to allure the Attention.

Phil. I WILL not say, *Eubulus*, that your Reasons have made me an entire Convert to the Poets; but I acknowledge, that they have removed some

Prejudices. However, in the mean Time, granting you to have proved one Point, that the Study of Poets is not hurtful to a Speaker; yet how will you make out your second, that it is useful; which I look upon to be of Importance in the present Question?

Eub. IN my Opinion, that follows easily from the Observations already made: But for your farther Satisfaction, I will enter into some Detail. I only premise once for all; that there is a wide Difference to be made between useful and necessary; a fine Imagination may excel without any Assistance from Poesy, indeed, from Art at all: I only mean, that, notwithstanding, such Assistance is in general advantageous.

Phil. I AGREE to, and shall bear in Mind your Limitation.

Eub. TELL me then, *Philemon*, is not Shortness, such as doth not prejudice Clearness, a Perfection in Speaking?

Phil. Granted; but this makes against you. For the Poets abound in Paraphrase; they never lead you directly to any Point, but seek for amuseing and round-about Ways.

Eub. LET us consider.—Is that Discourse always to be esteemed the shortest, which is pronounced in the smallest Space of Time?

Phil. How can that be doubted?

Eub. How? Suppose a Man to speak but a few Minutes, yet little to the Purpose; another many, but so closely and pertinently, that every Period tends to the Illustration of his Subject; I ask, which of these two, considering Shortness in the Light we now do, as a Degree of Perfection, do you account the shorter Speaker?

Phil.

Phil. I must own, the Man who speaks only what is necessary.

Eub. VERY well. You see then, that Brevity is two-fold. One is computed only by the Number of Words uttered, or by the Minutes that flow during the Pronunciation, which affects not the present Question. The other is that Number of Words or Minutes, compared with the Propriety of what is said: Which latter it is that principally determines Brevity, as it is a Perfection; the Quality, not the Quantity of Discourse. So that he, who speaks for half an Hour, may be in reality a shorter Speaker, than him, whose Declamation exceeds not one fourth Part of that Time.

Phil. I cannot deny it.

Eub. Now apply this Distinction to the Poets. I acknowledge that whatever Subject they treat of, they usually are, it is requisite that they should be, circumstantial: They are minute in Descriptions, distinct in Painting, enter into great Detail; insist and amplify, so that the whole Work may be of considerable Extent; but does it follow from thence that they are prolix?

Phil. IF the Sense and Substance of what they say can be comprized within narrower Limits, why not?

Eub. TELL me, do you think the Oration for the *Crown proli* ?

Phil. IT contains nothing superfluous.

Eub. TRUE; yet the Work itself is of some Length. Will you say that the Defence of *Milo* is more tedious than one of the Declamations ascribed to *Quintilian*, which might have been delivered in half of the Time required by the other?

Phil. MUCH otherwise.

Eub. LUCIUS FLORUS relates the Conſpiracy of *Cataline*, in a ſingle Page, which employs I believe an Hundred ſuch in the Hiſtory of *Saluſt*; will you infer that this latter is prolix, or that the other is a better Hiſtorian?

Phil. WELL, ſuppoſing me to anſwer as you would have me, which doubtleſs I muſt do, what is the Tendency of all theſe Queſtions?

Eub. THAT Poets, altho' they do make uſe of many Words, are not prolix; becauſe they ſelect only ſuch Circumſtances as are of Importance, either inſtructive or pleaſing, and they treat of each in ſuch Manner, as conſtantly to keep up, even while they are gratifying, your Curioſity: And herein principally conſiſteth their great Art; however bulky their whole Work may be, they never ſay too much, each Part appears to be laboured with the moſt judicious Care. In this very Particular it is, that I ſay the Orator may imitate them with much Profit. He ſhould chuſe the moſt material Circumſtances, ſhould handle each in ſuch Way as never to ſatiate the Hearer, but to keep up his Attention through every Article, perpetually teaching or entertaining. In my Opinion, the Man who does this, whatever be the abſolute Duration of his Diſcourſe, ſpeaks ſhortly.

LET me give an Inſtance of what I am ſaying. [a] A *French* Author of not mean Talents, but a Critick of over-much, allow me to ſay conceited Delicacy, accuſeth *Homer*, among many other pretended Faults, of intolerable Prolixity; acknowledging, at the ſame Time, that the *Iliad* contains many noble Paſſages, and deſerves to be made known

[a] La Moth Houdart.

known to his Countrymen; which he undertakes to do. And how doth he proceed? He attempts to render that Poem into *French* Verſe, purged of all Superfluity; in which Way he contracts it into leſs than a third Part of the Original; and is— I ſhould not ſay more, but is truly prolix.

Phil. BECAUSE his Work, compared with the Original, is flat and languid.

Eub. TRUE: But this ingenious Perſon ſeems to have judged of Brevity meerly from the Number of Lines. You look as if you thought that I have been maintaining a Paradox; but if you examine it, I am perſuaded that you will find it to be ſtrictly true.

Phil. I MEAN at preſent to learn, not to diſpute: But I own, I find much Difficulty in admitting your Doctrine, that the Poets are Teachers of *Brevity*.

Eub. YET their Works abound with Inſtances hereof: What think you of this Paſſage, when *Æneas*, after his Addreſs to the Ghoſt of *Hector*, ſays,

" [b] He nothing, nor to Queſtions vain replies:
" Haſte from theſe Flames, fly Goddeſs-born.
" (he cries)
" *Greece* hath our Walls; *Troy* tumbles from her
" Height."——

SHEW me in any Proſe-writer more Senſe in the ſame Number of Words, than is contained in this Line,

[c] " Matchleſs in Manners, Beauty, Prudence,
" Arts."

BUT indeed Inſtances may be produced without Number.

Phil.

[b] Ille nihil, nec me quærentem vana moratur.
Heu fuge nate Deâ, teque his ait eripe flammis;
Hoſtis habet muros; ruit alto a culmine Troja. *Æneid* 2.

[c] ὐ δέμας, ὐδὲ φύην, ὔτ' ἂρ φρένας, ὖδέ τι ἔργα. ILIAD lib. 1.

Phil. WELL—if you pleaſe let us paſs on from this Point.——

INFORM me, are there any other Articles beſide this of Shortneſs, in which Poets may be uſeful?

Eub. I think there are; and ſome conſiderable.

THAT admirable Quality which diſtinguiſhed *Demoſthenes* above all other Orators, for which our Language hath not a Name, but we may call [*d*] Vehemence, is greatly promoted by ſtudying their Writings. I take this Vehemence to conſiſt chiefly in lofty Sentiments, bold Figures, and Expreſſions full of Energy.

CONCERNING the firſt of theſe, *lofty Sentiments*, there is no Difficulty in ſhewing that the Poets excel peculiarly in them.

AN unanſwerable Proof of which is, that they who have written upon Sublimity of Sentiment have drawn the Examples they cite, chiefly from Poets; And this it is plain muſt be the Caſe, both from the Nature of the Thing, and from Fact. By a lofty Sentiment is meant, as I ſuppoſe, whatever conveys to the Mind an Idea of ſomewhat noble and grand, whether it ſtrike more immediately the Underſtanding, or, as ſome love to ſpeak, the moral Taſte or Senſe; or whether it ſtrike the Imagination. Of the former Kind are moral Sentiments, ſuch as beſpeak Greatneſs of Soul, a ſublime diſintereſted Virtue; or undaunted Courage, unbounded Ambition. Of the other Sort, are ſuitable Deſcriptions of magnificent Objects. Of the firſt is the Anſwer of *Hector* to *Polydamas*——

His Sword the brave Man draws,
And aſks no Omen, but his Country's Cauſe.
POPE.

[*d*] δεινότης. [*e*] Iliad, Book 12.

THAT of *Ajax* in his Prayer to *Jupiter*;

Grant me to see, and in the Light destroy.

SUCH likewise is that of Satan, so well suited to the Speaker,

Better to reign in Hell, than serve in Heav'n.

THIS also of *Coriolanus*, when Sentence of Banishment had been just pronounced against him by the Tribunes,

——*I banish you.*

AND that which follows after, indeed truly magnanimous,

Thus I turn my Back,
There is a World elsewhere.

NOT less nobly *Cæsar* in the Storm,

——*You carry Cæsar.*

SUCH is the Insult of *Macbeth* over his Enemy slain,

Thou wer't born of Woman.

SUCH is this of *Corneille*,—*Medea*'s Answer to her Attendant, who says,

Thy Lord betrays thee, [h] *Athens* hates,—all fly;
In this Distress what is remaining?——*I.*

AND this admired Passage in the *Horace* of the same.—Old *Horatius* says to *Julia*,

[i] Deplore our Race now stain'd with Infamy:
(Jul.) What should he do when three oppose him?—*(Hor.) Die.*

OF the latter Kind, sublime Sentiments that strike the Imagination; there are Instances innumerable

[f] Paradise Lost, Book [g] *Shakespear.*

[h] Votre païs vous hait, votre epoux est sans foy:
Dans un si grand revers que vous restet il?— MOY.

[i] *(Hor.)* Pleurez le deshonneur de toute notre race.
Jul. Que vôuliez vous qu'il fit contre trois?——*(Hor.)* Qu'il mourût.

merable in the Iliad and Paradiſe Loſt. That of *Neptune* is juſtly celebrated. I cannot help mentioning the two laſt Lines of Mr. *Pope*'s Tranſlation, which deviates from the plain Magnificence of the Greek into Ovidian Elegance.

[*k*] The parting Waves before his Courſers fly.
The *wond'ring Waters* leave the Axle dry.—

Phil. You bring to my Mind a Note of his more extraordinary, I mean the Judgment he paſſes on *La Moth*'s Imitation of the Ceſtus, which he calls *wonderfully beautiful* [*l*]; the Paſſage ends with this Epigram, ſurely very much miſplaced here.

[*m*] *Venus* preſented, *Juno* took the Zone,
And prov'd its Pow'r, from handſome charming grown.
The Smiles and Graces, at the Change amaz'd,
Which was the real *Venus*, doubting gaz'd:
Ev'n Love miſtakes, preferring *Juno*'s Charms,
And flies with erring Fondneſs to her Arms.

BUT I aſk Pardon for this Interruption:—— Proceed.——

Eub. THE eighth Book of the Iliad concludes with a glorious Compariſon in this Kind, which I will repeat to you in the Tranſlation of a Friend, whom we both deſervedly eſteem.

As

[*k*] Il. lib. 13.——

[*l*] *Pop.* Hom. Note on the 14th Book—218th Line.

[*m*] En prenant ce tiſſu, que Venus lui preſente,
Junon n'etoit que belle, elle devient charmante;
Les Graces & les Ris, les plaiſirs et les jeux
Surpriſes cherchent Venus, doutent qui l'eſt des deux:
L'amour même trompè trouve Junon plus belle,
Et ſon arc à la main, deja vole apres elle.

As when the Moon with her attendant Train
Of living Saphirs mounts the Cloudless Sky,
Snatching from Nature's Face the Veil of Night;
Sudden the Valleys wind, the Rocks ascend,
And Mountains in rude Majesty; from Heav'n
Bursts wide Effulgence, whilst unnumber'd Stars
Gild the blue Vault: The Swains enraptur'd
gaze. [n]

Of this Sort also in Paradise Lost are the Passage of Satan thro' Chaos, the whole Episode of Sin and Death, the Battle of the Angels, and particularly the Description of the Messiah, his Victory and Return; to which I might add, if Need were, a Multitude of others equal, or little inferior.

Now I ask; can a Man capable of understanding and of relishing these Writers, be much and intimately conversant with them, without acquiring some Spark of their noble Fire, which shall break out sometimes, which shall shine out thro' the Gravity of Argument, and spread Warmth and Lustre even thro' the Dryness and Coldness of Business and Questions of Law?

The second Article mentioned as constituting Vehemence, was, Figures; of which I need not say much, as they are in a Manner peculiar to Poesy; it is built upon, and subsists by them. And it will not surely be denied, that they mightily

[n] Mr. *Pope*'s Imitation is extremely beautiful; but the two last Lines seem to lengthen out and weaken the Thought;

γεγήθε δὲ τὲ φρένα ποιμήν. ——

The conscious Swains rejoicing in the Sight
Eye the blue Vault, and bless the useful Light.

mightily enliven whatever they are brought to adorn. Where ſo well as from the Poets ſhall we learn to break out into a ſpirited *Apoſtrophe*:

[*o*] O thou that with ſurpaſſing Glory crown'd,
Lookſt from thy ſole Dominion, like the God
Of this new World.——

WHERE ſhall we learn to ſuſpend, or change beautifully the begun Senſe—

[*p*] Quanquam O,—ſed motos præſtat componere fluctus.

I will have ſuch Revenges on you both
That all the World ſhall,——I will do ſuch Things,——
What they are yet I know not;——but they ſhall be
The Terrors of the Earth. *Shak. Lear.*

WHERE ſhall we learn to feign happily Allegorick Perſons,

[*q*] *Confuſion* heard his Voice.

AND this very fine one

[*q*] *Silence* was pleaſed.

THIS ſublime one,—on his Creſt

[*q*] Sat Horror plum'd.——

WITH this other of the ſame Kind,——

[*q*] Expectation ſtood in Horror.

WHO ſo abundant in Tranſlations as the Poets, ſo rich in Compariſons, ſo full of pathetick Repetitions; above all, who ſo well qualified to inſtruct us in an Art, upon which the Succeſs of

[*o*] Paradiſe Loſt, Book iii.

[*p*] Although,———Yet let me rather ſtill the Waves. VIRG. ÆNEID.

[*q*] Paradiſe Loſt.

of Speeches, Pleadings, Sermons, in a great Meaſure depends, that of repreſenting Things in ſuch Manner as to place them before the Eyes of the Hearer?

WHEN you read the following Line,

> "[r] Sounded the Bow, String twang'd,
> "and Arrow flew."

WHO does not hear the Sound of the Bow-ſtring, and ſee the Flight of the Arrow? Such in *Milton* is the Deſcription of Satan and Death meeting; you ſee the Joy of the latter in this noble Picture,

> "Grinn'd horrible a ghaſtly Smile."—

I BELIEVE it may be affirmed, that whoever is Maſter of this Art, altho' he ſhould not excel in cloſe Reaſoning, tho' he ſhould not be conciſe, nor very correct, yet will never fail to pleaſe, rarely to perſuade; at leaſt in a popular Aſſembly. It was rightly obſerved, [ſ], that whatever we hear affecteth us more faintly than what we ſee: Now Things told ſimply, altho' with Elegance, we only hear, what is told in this ſpirited Manner we ſee; and thus it is that Poets tell.

NEITHER can we reaſonably doubt concerning the laſt-mentioned Article. *Expreſſion* hath ever been the peculiar Study of the Poets; it is that which diſtinguiſhes them from all other Writers at firſt Glance, which is eſſential to the Excel-

[r] λὶγξε βίος νευρη δὲ μὲγ ἴαχεν, ἆλτο δὀιςος. *Hom.* Il. lib. 4.

[ſ] Segnius irritant animos demiſſa per aures,
Quam quæ ſunt oculis ſubjecta fidelibus.----
Hor. de Arte Poeticâ.

Excellence of their Art, which adds Life and Grace and Beauty inexpressible to every Subject it is used to adorn, and if it be not the noblest, is one of the most pleasing Productions of Genius. This I freely acknowledge is raised in Poesy by Art into a Kind of Language foreign from common Use, too bold, too glowing, too harmonious, to be adopted exactly by any Speaker. Nevertheless, I am firmly assured, that a perfect Acquaintance with this Language conduceth much to the Improvement of Eloquence. The Richness of its Phrases, the inexhaustible Variety of its Turns, its Licences, its Boldness, its Luxuriancies, its very Restraints and Difficulties from Measure, Melody, and Rhime, all contribute to furnish one conversant in it with much greater Plenty of Words, with more Change and Newness, and not seldom with a more happy Boldness of Expression, than the unpoetical Speaker ever can attain to.

Phil. BUT you take no Notice of the mighty Dangers which attend these Advantages.

Eub. THAT Objection I thought obviated before. " I have small Hope, saith a good " Judge [*a*], of a young Orator, who is per- " fectly correct: Give me one, who hath much " youthful Redundancy; Instruction and Ex- " perience will bring him down to the true " Standard." So we may say here: Give me the Man, who warmed with the Flames of poetick Genius, ventures beyond the Limits usually prescribed to Prose; Time and growing Discretion

[*a*] QUINTILIAN.

Discretion will keep that Flame within due Bounds. He who sets out low and cold, will grow by Time mean and frigid. You may cool, but how shall you kindle?

Phil. BUT, if the Poets be really thus useful, tell me *Eubulus*, are all to be read with Advantage; or some only? If some, which? I ask for the Direction of my own Choice, that I need not wander idly through a Multitude, nor yet neglect the few who may be read with Profit.

Eub. PERHAPS none are to be altogether excluded; but it is necessary to make a Distinction. In general, Poets of the lighter Kind, as Writers of Pastorals and Elegies, are rather for elegant Amusement, than of much Advantage. We may pronounce nearly the same Sentence on Lyrick Writers.

SOME others have a Tendency rather hurtful, such as the Epigrammatists, who from their lively Manner are but too likely to please, and often recommend to the Imitation of their Admirers their sharp pointed Turn of Wit, ever a dangerous Enemy to Eloquence. The *Greeks* indeed, and among the *Romans*, *Catullus*, are pretty free from these Conceits, which, in after-times, became the fashionable Way of Writing, spreading from these Trifles their Infection to the most serious Works. And I cannot help thinking it a very hurtful Mistake in modern Education, to bring up, as I am informed is industriously done, young Persons in making Epigrams after the Model of *Martial*, the great

Hero

Hero of this falſe Taſte: By which Exerciſe they are likely to get a wrong Turn, and retain it through their whole Lives.

TAKE one Inſtance of this Manner. There is not I believe in all Antiquity a more natural, even ſublime Sentiment than that of *Arria*, when having, in order to encourage her Huſband to dye bravely, ſtabbed herſelf, ſhe delivered to him the Sword with theſe Words; Pœtus, *it is not painful* [*b*]: How has *Martial* hurt this noble Thought by falſe Refinement; and yet I look upon it to be one of his beſt Epigrams, and I doubt not, there are very many who prefer it to the hiſtorical Narration?

[*c*] When *Arria* from her Boſom drew the Sword,
And gave it yet freſh-reeking to her Lord;
This hurts not, *Pætus*, that alone ſhe cries,
That Wound ſhall hurt, by which my *Pætus* dies.

SOMETIMES, as I ſaid, among the *Greeks*, we meet with little Pieces of this Sort where both Thought and Expreſſion are natural and pathetick; and now and then in *Latin*, as in this modern one,

I dy'd

[*b*] PÆTE, *non dolet.*

[*c*] *Caſta ſuo gladium cum traderet Arria Pæto,*
Quem de viſceribus traxerat ipſa ſuis;
Si qua fides fides verbis, hoc vulnus non dolet, inquit,
Ad quod tu facies hŏc mihi Pæte, dolet.

[d] I dy'd untimely; happier Doom be thine,
Live out thy Years beſt Huſband, live out mine.

HOWEVER, it may well be doubted whether the Danger of converſing much with Perſons of Wit, ſuch as theſe are, who abound with agreeable Faults, is compenſated by any Advantages they may afford.

BUT not to dwell longer on ſuch Minuteneſſes; we may affirm in general, that the Study of good Epic Writers is highly beneficial to an Orator. They are grand, lofty, pathetick, excel in Narration, are rich, copious in Expreſſion, with Variety and Dignity, harmonious. They open and enlarge the Mind; they give a Maſtery over the Paſſions; they inflame the Imagination, they inſpire a Love for, an Emulation of heroic Virtue.

BUT it ſeems to me, that the moſt uſeful of all are the Writers of Tragedy, eſpecially thoſe of antient *Greece*; my Reaſons for thinking ſo are theſe.

Firſt, THE Stile they write in, approaches more than that of the others, to Proſe: The Nature of their Work required that it ſhould be ſuch; it being entirely Dialogue, in which many Things muſt be ſaid recurring often in ordinary Converſation, and the Whole ought to have a natural Air. Again, the Kind of Verſe they employ is admirably ſuited to this Purpoſe, differing little, except in the Regularity of the Meaſure,

[d] *Immatura peri: ſed tu fælicior annos*
Vive tuos Conjux optime, vive meos.

Meaſure, from harmonious Proſe: Thus with the Simplicity of almoſt common Converſation, it is capable of being elevated to all the Loftineſs of Poeſy. In which laſt Particular we, as well as the *Italians*, by the Uſe of blank Verſe, have a great Advantage over the *French*, who are forced to uſe the ſame Meaſure for their Tragick, as their Epick Performances.

BESIDE this general Advantage, theſe Writers of the Drama may be of much Uſe to an Orator, as they excel in thoſe particular Things in which he ſhould endeavour to excel, becauſe frequently occurring; ſuch is for Inſtance *Narration*.

THE Poets in order to preſerve the Unities of Place and Time were obliged to make frequent Uſe hereof; and to prevent the Audience from being tired or growing inattentive, of which in ſuch Caſes there is perpetual Danger, they wrought up theſe Paſſages with their utmoſt Skill. If you read the Hiſtory of the Death of [*e*] *Polyxena*; of [*f*] *Oedipus* blinding himſelf; of [*g*] the Death of the ſame *Oedipus*, and of [*h*] *Hæmon* and *Antigone*; [*i*] the Relation of the Rage of *Hercules* when poiſoned, and the beautiful one of [*k*] *Ajax* killing himſelf; I am perſwaded that you will be delighted with them, and acknowledge them to be Models of perfect Narration. What Choice of Circumſtances!

[*e*] In the Hecuba of EURIPIDES. [*f*] OEDIPUS Tyrannus. [*g*] OEDIPUS Coloneus, [*h*] In the Antigone, [*i*] The Trachiniæ. [*k*] AJAX of SOPHOCLES.

ſtances! What Order, Clearneſs, and Brevity in relating! What Strength and Beauty of Expreſſion! And above all, what natural, affecting, bold Painting! This Art of the Antients ſeemeth indeed to make the whole Tragedy uniform; you appear to be a Spectator no leſs of what is related, than of what is repreſented. Some Moderns, although rarely, do alſo afford Examples of this Skill; ſuch is the Relation of *Sampſon*'s Death [*l*]; and that of *Polyphontes* in the *Meropè* of *Scipio Maffei*; of which latter, as the Piece is not common among us, nor the Language ſo much ſtudied as it deſerves, I will here preſent you with a Tranſlation, as a Kind of Proof of what I have advanced: Here it is; you may read it.

Phil. And now began the ſolemn Rites: The Prieſt
Had newly ſever'd from the Victim's Brow
The ſacred Lock, and thrown into the Flames.
Here was the Tyrant plac'd; there *Meropè*,
As one reſolv'd to die. The Crowd around
Intent in Expectation, ſilent gaz'd,
And motionleſs. I plac'd by Chance on high
Beheld *Cresfontes* open thro' the Preſs
His Way with Labour won, in Viſage chang'd,
And all inflam'd. At length he fix'd him ſf
Faſt by the Altar, at the Tyrant's Side;
There ſtood a while, gloomy, and darting round
Fell Looks aſkance. How ſhall I ſpeak the reſt?
Since

[*l*] SAMPSON AGONISTES of MILTON.

Since on the ſacred Ax which lay prepar'd
For Sacrifice, with both his Hands to ſeize,
To rear, to brandiſh, and impetuous cleave
The Neck of the Uſurper, was the Work
Of but one Moment: The ſame Inſtant ſhew'd
The Steel uplifted glitter thro' the Air,
And the unhappy Prince fall prone to Earth:
Sudden the ſpouting Blood the Prieſt's white
Robe
With Crimſon ſprinkled. Shouts reſound. The
Youth
Pierc'd with new Wounds him fallen. To his
Aid
Advanc'd *Adraſtus*, whom the Conq'ror's Hand
Arreſting ſwifter, plung'd into his Breaſt
The reeking Weapon.--But the [*m*] Mother, who
Can paint? Fierce as a Tygreſs rouz'd to Rage,
Whom of her Young the Hunters would bereave,
Forward ſhe ſprung, and ſtood before her Son,
To ev'ry Jav'lin pointed at his Breaſt
Her own oppoſing; whilſt aloud ſhe cry'd
In broken Words, "He is my Son,—he is
"*Cresfontes*,—is your King."—The Tumult
drown'd
Her Voice. One ſeeks to fly, one to advance;
Thus forward, backward, preſs'd, repell'd, the
Crowd
Like heavy Harveſts bending to the Winds,
Alternate wav'd; not knowing why, confus'd,
They ruſh, retire, aſk, juſtle, murmur, grieve.
Shouts, Shriekings, Terror, Children trampled
down,

Women

[*m*] *Meropè*, Mother of *Cresfontes*.

Women o'erturn'd, O Scene of dire Dismay!
Spread wild Disorder round. Mean while the Bull
Raging at Will, now free, augments the Fright,
And bounds and bellows; the vast Dome resounds.
These struggle to get forth, hasten, and choak
The Passage, by their Speed delay'd: In vain
The Guards which at the Temple-gates were plac'd,
Attempt to enter, by the Torrent's Force
O'erpower'd and born away. A Band of Friends
Mean Time around us gather. In the Midst
Cresfontes eager for the Fight, his Eyes
Sparkling with Courage, labours to break through
Environ'd. I who disengag'd beheld
At Distance, to the dark and secret Gate
Which open'd to the Palace safe Access
My Steps directed, fearful, looking round:
When in mid' Way, Sight horrible and foul!
Lo! *Polyphontes* mangled, and deform'd,
Struck my scar'd View: Amid a Lake of Blood
Prostrate he lay, cloven his Head, his Side
Riven with gaping Wounds. *Adrastus* near
Wallow'd yet half-alive, and in the Pangs
Of Death still writhing. Me blank Horror thrill'd
To mark him as he lay, with Face convuls'd,
Open in sighing deeply his glaz'd Eyes.
The Altar lay o'erturn'd, dispers'd and broke
Vases and Tripods, Canisters and Knives.—

But wherefore do we loiter? Arm your Slaves,
Haste, guard the Gates, all Means of strong Defence
Provide, for fierce and sudden comes the Foe.

Eub. THIS Relation, even under the Disadvantage you see it, that of Translation, does I think give no mean Idea of the Original, and may serve as a Confirmation of what I have been saying, that the Tragick Poets afford excellent Models of distinct spirited *Narration*.

THE same Poets introduce into their Tragedies very often set Speeches, a Custom which strictly speaking, they carry to Excess; but this they did to comply with the Liking of the *Athenian* People, who were exceedingly fond of Harangues. Thus *Hecuba* and *Polymnestor* plead their Cause before *Agamemnon* as in a Court before a Judge [n]: *Oedipus* and *Creon* before *Theseus* [o].

INDEED there is scarcely one of the *Greek* Tragedies, that doth not afford Instances hereof. And you will find upon Examination, that these Harangues are compleat, regular Pieces of Eloquence, very close in the Reasoning, Part short, nervous, and pathetick, containing usually in small Compass, Matter enough to furnish out a Declaimer with a long Oration. Which shews the Truth of a Remark formerly made, that the Poets in Argument and Moral Observation especially, afford Patterns of the most comprehensive Brevity.

IN

[n] In the Hecuba.
[o] In the *Oedipus Coloneus*.

In this Way of Harangues, *Corneille* who hath imitated the Antients much in this Article, has ventured to introduce an extraordinary Scene; that wherein he gives a Detail of the Reasonings for and against *Augustus Cæsar*'s resigning the *Imperial* Power, put into the Mouths of *Maximus* and *Cinna*. [*p*] Without Doubt, a long Debate such as this, meerly Political, must have proved very tedious and disgusting to the Audience, if it had not been enlivened and supported by singular Force of Argument and Expression. And the same Tragedy affords a Piece of noble and sublime Eloquence, in the Scene which passeth between *Augustus* and *Cinna*, where the former convicts, upbraids, and at length pardons this Conspirator.

I should upon this Occasion mention Comedy also, which is recommended particularly by [*q*] *Quintilian* as useful to an Orator: But of this Kind one Writer [*r*] only remains from antient *Greece*, and he, on several Accounts the least proper. *Rome* furnisheth two, [*s*] who should not be omitted. I purposely avoid saying much of our own Countrymen, however excellent in their Way, as less beneficial in our View. The Taste for Wit and Humour which they principally follow, carries them another Course. Besides, their Confinement of themselves to Prose, whatever other Advantages it may have, cuts off this of serious Eloquence.

Perhaps

p] In his Tragedy of *Cinna*.

[*q*] Lib 10. chap. i.

[*r*] Aristophanes.

[*s*] *Plautus* and *Terence*.

PERHAPS the Poets on the new Settlement of the Stage after the Reſtoration, miſtook in the Manner they eſtabliſhed, and might with better Judgment, even Succeſs, have retained that of *Beaumont* and *Fletcher* ſo far as relates to Stile. Comedies in eaſy well compoſed Meaſures might it ſeems, admit Familiarity without Meaneſs; and Seriouſneſs, and, on fit Occaſions, even Sublimity, without Dryneſs or Bombaſt. This was the antient Model; and is ſtill followed by the beſt Writers among our Neighbours.

THIS Obſervation however I ſhall not inſiſt upon; but go on juſt to mention one other Particular very uſeful to an Orator, in which the ſame Tragick Poets remarkably excel, that is, a Courſe of Debate carryed on in ſhort Anſwers and Replies, where uſually one, at moſt two Lines contain an Argument, retorted on the Adverſary with the utmoſt Brevity and Acuteneſs. Such is the Controverſy between [t] *Teucer* and *Menelaus*: Between [u] *Tireſias* and *Oedipus*: [w] *Electra* and *Clytemneſtra*; and is more eſpecially frequent in *Euripides*. A Talent manifeſtly of the greateſt Efficacy in Debates, where it is required that one ſhould reply; and even in continued Diſcourſes by no Means uſeleſs.

THESE among others are the Reaſons *Philemon*, which induce me to lay out ſome Time and Care in reading the Poets, not only as afford-ing

[t] In the Ajax of SOPHOCLES.
[u] *Oedipus Tyrannus.*
[w] In the Electra of the ſame.

ing an agreeable Amusement; but highly beneficial in my chief Scheme of Study; as most likely to set off the Knowlege required in my Profession by the Addition of copious and powerful Elocution. I will not say that I have found good Effects from this Kind of Application, for we are too apt to Flatter ourselves; yet to a Friend I may venture to own, that I do imagine, I have. Thus much at least I am sure of, that I have perceived ill Effects from the Want of it in others; in Advocates, who defeat in a great Measure the good Consequence of many valuable Endowments, of Sagacity, Learning, Acuteness, by the dry, insipid, unaffecting Coldness of their Manner, the Inelegance, and often offensive Meaness of their Language.

For which Reason, as you are yet young and have before you much Time, I recommend to join with your more serious and toilsome Studies a Knowledge of the good Poets, both antient and modern. Among the latter, those chiefly of our own Country, for the Sake of Stile and Language: Among the former, I would advise by no Means to neglect the *Greeks* as the Custom is, who besides that they are at least equal to those of *Rome* in Strength and Elevation, have much more of Simplicity and natural Beauty; an Excellence I believe in Poesy; certainly a great and valuable one in Eloquence.

Phil. I am much obliged to you for your Advice, and shall not fail to observe it; what

may

may be wanting in your Arguments to convince me, being abundantly made up in your Authority.

Eub. I WISH that I could Merit this Deference. In return, I will entrust you with what I fear, even you will esteem a Weakness in me: So thoroughly am I satisfied of this Advantage arising from the Study of the Poets, that I often employ myself in putting into Prose such Passages of them as please me most, imagining that by this Practice I shall gradually transfuse some Part of their Spirit into my own Speech and Writing. This I have lately done by the Speeches of the fallen Spirits in the second Book of Paradise Lost; Pieces of Eloquence in my Opinion no Ways inferior to those of the most consummate Orators or Historians.

NAY, I have carryed this Matter much farther; I have sometimes taken the Trouble of turning into Verse, Passages from Orators or Historians, hoping by these Means, not indeed to produce any Thing in the poetical Way worthy of being preserved, but to elevate my Fancy and Stile, and borrow some Sparks of poetick Fire.

YOU smile *Philemon* at this Instance of Enthusiasm:—Yet allow me to add, that I think this Trouble not altogether thrown away. If I have, as you are pleased to say, at the Bar, and especially in Parliament, transported as it were by Zeal for my Client or Country, soared at some Times to an unusual Height, and perswaded or born down by a Torrent of Elocution even unwilling Hearers; behold the Cause! I open

to

to you here the Fountains from whence I draw this Practice; which I think you ſtill continue to condemn.

Phil. I SHALL not eaſily condemn what you pronounce, eſpecially from Experience, to be uſeful; the good Effects whereof I have likewiſe ſeen often and admired. But whatever I may think of your Arguments on this Head, this laſt Inſtance of laborious Induſtry convinces me that you are ſincere in them. I muſt add farther, that I ſhould be mightily pleaſed with ſeeing one of your little Works of this Sort. I have my Eye at this Inſtant, on ſome Papers lying looſe upon the Table, which greatly raiſe my Curioſity; by the even Length of the Lines I conjecture that they contain Verſes, which are probably of the Sort you mention.

Eub. VERY true. And as you expreſs Curioſity about them I ſhall not diſappoint it. Trifles of this Kind may End more agreeably a Converſation, which has been perhaps too ſerious and dry. Here are two Performances. This ſhorter is a Dialogue taken from *Lucian*'s Proſe; here is the Original marked down, with which you may compare it. This other is a Fact related by an Eccleſiaſtical Hiſtorian [x]; which I have endeavoured to tell in Verſe, with ſuch Variation of Circumſtances as I judged proper. You may amuſe yourſelf, if you can, with reading them, until your Coach be got ready. In the mean While, I will ſtep into the Garden,

[x] *Nicephorus.*

Garden, to give some Orders, which I perceive from hence to be much wanted.

Phil. I thank you; and am sure, that I shall not think the Time of my Stay here tedious.

A DIALOGUE.

VENUS and *CUPID*.

Venus. O'ER Heav'n and Earth my Son, thy Pow'r extends,
And *Jove* himself beneath thy Empire bends,
In vain his Thunders roll, his Lightnings fly,
Thine Arrows pierce the Monarch of the Sky.
But say, why *Pallas* in her blooming Age
A stubborn Virgin, triumphs o'er thy Rage?
Henceforth renounce thy Pow'r, resign thy Dart,
Thus impotent to wound a Female Heart.

CUPID.

STRUCK with just Terror I revere, O Queen,
Her Form majestick and her warlike Mien.
Whene'er I would approach, I shrink thro' Fear,
Aw'd by her nodding Helm and beamy Spear,
Eager to wound, but without Force I stand;
And the Bow drops unstrung from my slack Hand.

VENUS.

THE Iron God of War thy Pow'r obeys;
And shrinks thy Soul if female Armour blaze?

CUPID.

CUPID.

THE God of War himself demands the Stroke,
Tempts me to conquer, and invites the Yoke;
Softens in Smiles the Rigour of his Face,
And runs with open Arms to my Embrace,
Pleas'd from the Toils of Battle to remove,
And taste the Sweets of Luxury and Love:
But She, attentive still when I draw nigh,
Beholds me with a fierce suspicious Eye:
In Opposition stern as I advance
The Gorgon's Head uprais'd and pointed Lance
Forbid approach; in vain I bend the Bow,
Fear chills my Blood, and disappoints the Blow.

VENUS.

POORLY evaded: What? Shall Arms affright
That Courage, which can *Jove*'s own Thunder slight?—
Yet grant thy Plea were just; let *Cupid* fly,
And *Pallas* bright in Arms thy Shafts defy;.
Whence is it that the Muse's tuneful Train
Fair, lovely, mild, unconquer'd still remain?
Is their Form dreadful? Do they also wield
The threat'ning Spear, and poize the Gorgon-Shield?

CUPID.

A BAND of Virtues throngs to their Defence,
Sweet Modesty, and bashful Innocence;
Pure Decency, fair Truth, Discretion sage,
White Chastity, and Wisdom's rev'rend Age.
Besides, when joining in harmonious Quire
They raise the Song, and tune the sacred Lyre,
Ev'n

Ev'n I, attentive to the heav'nly Sound,
Catch the ſoft Rapture, and forget to wound.

V E N U S.

By Harmony and Wiſdom guarded ſo,
Grant that the Muſes may defy thy Bow:
Yet ſhall *Diana* range each Vale and Grove,
Love's cloſe Receſſes, and not yield to Love?

C U P I D.

DIANA's Boſom can I hope to ſhare,
Poſſeſt already by a diff'rent Care;
With the ſhrill Horn to wake the early Dawn,
And in full Chace ſkim o'er the dewy Lawn?

For once let *Cupid* teach, and liſt'ning Youth
Thro' Fiction's Veil diſcern this moral Truth;
" By Courage and by Wiſdom Love's ſub-
" du'd;
" Bus'neſs and other Cares his Fires exclude."

E M I L I A.

EMILIA.

AN

HISTORICAL POEM.

FROM *Scythian* Realms, where Winter rears
her Throne,
White with eternal Snows, a Race unknown,
Rude, hardy, fierce, their Limits bursting, run
To happier Climates, and a Southern Sun:
Fierce TOTILA leads on th' unnumber'd Swarm:
Rome's Genius sinks beneath his thund'ring Arm;
A Prey the World's Imperial Mistress falls
To *Gothick* Fury. Through her gaping Walls
They rush victorious. 'Twas still Midnight's
Hour,
When from her smoaking Ramparts down they
pour,
Intent on Plunder: Rage and Av'rice dire
Range her broad Streets, and wrap her Walls
in Fire;
Campanian Skies reflect the horrid Blaze,
Nor less the Sword beneath wide-wasting slays;
Bathes the warm Pavement in a crimson Flood,
And swells the *Tiber* with Patrician Blood.
The mighty Manes, *Greek* and *Punick* Dead,
Heroes, that by *Rome*'s wild Ambition bled,
Behold

Behold, and smile aveng'd. Mean while, the worst
Offspring of War, lewd Violence accurst,
With the Sword's Havock joins more impious Force;
Loud Shrieks and Screams attend the Monster's Course:
Thro' Temples, Palaces, he bursts his Way,
And from the Altar drags his trembling Prey.
Chaste Maids and Matrons, ah how late ador'd!
Your Love now bleeding by the hostile Sword
Leaves you forlorn, defenceless; vain your Cries,
Heav'n only can relieve, and Heav'n denies.

BUT loudest rose the Storm, where with the first
The Monarch fights in Blood and Slaughter nurst,
Excites their Fury, rules the wild Uproar,
And bids th' impurpled Conduits foam with Gore.
Less dreadful *Mars*, when adverse Hosts engage,
In groaning *Thrace* inspires, and guides their Rage
In the grim Front of War; with Blood and Slain
He dyes the River, and he heaps the Plain;
Fear, Grief, Dismay, his Train, around destroy;
Earth trembles, Heav'n resounds, Hell smiles with Joy.

THERE stood a Palace in an open Space,
The Mansion of the fam'd *Emilian* Race:

This

This Dome with Carnage and with Gore he
fills,
On the ſtain'd Marble *Rome*'s beſt Blood diſtills.
Here flying from the Tumult, he deſcry'd
The young *Emilia*; *Rome* in all her Pride
Ne'er vaunted Daughter deck'd with Gifts ſo
rare,
A Soul ſo noble, and a Form ſo fair.
Amazement ſtruck the Prince; he ſaw, he gaz'd
Aſtonied, motionleſs; new Paſſion ſeiz'd
His ruthleſs Heart, and Love, a Stranger-Gueſt,
Furious at once inflam'd his ſavage Breaſt:
As Heaps of nitrous Grain, for warlike Deed
Prepar'd, if touch'd by Spark or kindling Reed,
Catch the contagious Fire; with rapid Glare
A ſudden Blaze illumines the ſcorch'd Air.
He ſtretch'd his Arms to ſeize: Can Words
impart
The Pain, the Terror, of her virtuous Heart?
Low on the Floor before the ſavage Man
She fell, and mingling Sighs with Words be-
gan:

O BY whatever Name is dear, if Love
E'er touch'd thy Breaſt, if Pity e'er could move,
By Friendſhip, Virtue, thoſe whom all revere
Gods of thy Country; I beſeech thee ſpare!
O let not Violence theſe Limbs profane,
Nor ſpot my Innocence with brutal Stain!
Alas! my Parents, Brethren are no more,
Yet reeks this Marble with their ſacred Gore;
O let me follow; pierce this Boſom here
While yet unſullied; Force, not Death, I fear.
Free

Free let me fall, not live a guilty Slave:
Strike, kill;—Why doubt'st thou?—Death's a
Boon I crave.

SHE said. He heard abash'd, and first knew
Shame;
Such Pow'r hath virtuous Beauty: But his
Flame
Reviving, quell'd Remorse: Again he prest
Onward to seize. She milder thus addrest:

CRUEL, since thou art deaf to Pity's Cry,
Yet hear; no more I Mercy beg, but buy.
I know thee, *Gothick* Prince, beheld afar
Oft from our Walls, the Thunderbolt of War,
Conquest thy prime Delight, thy Goddess Fame:
Yet would'st thou gain in Arms a deathless
Name,
What *Hun* or *Vandal* hath atchiev'd excel,
I can the Means impart; a magick Spell
Possessing of strange Pow'r, that mid the Strife
Of Battle shall bestow immortal Life,
Preserve th' impassive Body free from Wound;
Swords shall strike harmless, and vain Spears
rebound;
This I disclose:---But by the Gods first swear
To give me Freedom, and my Honour spare.

HE listens, pausing; much the Offer mov'd
His Soul intent on Arms, yet much he lov'd.
Besides, tho' credulous of Magick, still
He fears a Stratagem, and doubts her Skill.

SHE mark'd; and in his Silence, Air and Eyes
The Doubts which combated within, descries.

NAY

NAY, doubt not, then rejoins; thyſelf ſhall try;
Suffer me juſt retiring, to apply
The Spell Heav'n-wrought; then ſtrike;---the mighty Charm
Shall guard my Life, and ſcorn thy baffled Arm.

Which ſhould he chuſe; ſecure from Wound to fight
Immortal; or indulge in Love's Delight?
Cruel yet ſweet Alternative; by Turns
He pants for Pleaſure, and for Glory burns.

AT length 'tis fix'd to learn the Charm; his Fires
Then quench by Force: He ſwears: The Maid retires:
Low-kneeling, to the Pow'r that rules the Pole
She thus in Pray'r lifts up her ſpotleſs Soul.

ALMIGHTY, thou beholdeſt in what Net
Thy Servant ſtruggles, with what Ills beſet;
Direct, confirm: And O! if what is thine,
This Life, thy Gift, too raſhly I reſign,
Father, forgive!---Yet wherefore doubt I? Death
Is now thy Gift;---Life was: Receive this Breath,
Accept this Sacrifice. At Virtue's Call,
Let me chaſte Victim on thy Altars fall.
When Age or Sickneſs kill, 'tis nam'd thy Deed,
Fall I leſs thine in Virtue's Cauſe who bleed,
E'er Chains or foul Diſhonour blot,---yet free?
Can I more nobly, *Rome*, I fall with thee?

I come, great Anceſtors, your Shades to join,
Yet pure, and worthy of your noble Line.

So pray'd ſhe, with firm Purpoſe fix'd: Then ſheds
A Cake of melting Wax, and forming ſpreads
Around her Neck: And this ſhe hopes, might well
Paſs with the rude Barbarian for the Spell
Feign'd to preſerve from Wound by Magick Lore,
A coarſe Device; the Time allow'd no more;
And, knowing Beauty helps Deluſion's Snare,
She adds new Ornaments to ſeem more fair.

As the bright Moon, if Clouds a while conceal
Her Beams, emerging from the duſky Veil
Adorns her Silver Orb with purer Light,
And pours new Glory on the vanquiſh'd Night:

THUS deck'd, and ſmiling gay, the Fair returns
Bright in augmented Charms. He ſees, he burns
With double Hope. Behold at length apply'd
The Spell I juſtly boaſted of, ſhe cry'd;
This Gift from a renown'd Enchantreſs came,
Whoſe potent Art controll'd all Nature's Frame.
Pale Mortals oft have ſeen at her Command
Night blot the Sun, dire Earthquakes rock the Land,
Seas undiſturb'd by Winds loud-roaring ſwell,
And ſummon'd Spectres riſe from yawning Hell.

This

This Spell to me, much-lov'd, ſhe dying, gave;
And thou but mindful of thy Oath, receive,
Unhurt, unſpotted to preſerve my Youth.---
Nor doubt; let ſtricteſt Proof confirm my Truth:
Here ſtrike; I ſhrink not; nay defy, O Prince,
Ev'n thy dread Arm: This Trial muſt convince.

She ſpoke, in Semblance dauntleſs; mean while Fear
Ran chill within, for Death look'd dreadful near;
But tow'ring Virtue feeble Thoughts diſdain'd,
Check'd ſtruggling Nature, and her Brow ſeren'd.

Nor long the Pauſe: For ſudden at the Word,
Full on her Neck deſcends th' impetuous Sword.
"Receive me Heav'n," ſhe cry'd, with fault'ring Tongue,
Heav'n thro' the lofty Dome re-ecchoing rung.
The Trunk yet panting on the Floor falls dead;
Far on the ſlippery Marble rolls the Head.
Ah late of Form divine! how chang'd it lyes!
Pale that bright Cheek, and quench'd thoſe ſtarry Eyes!

As ſome tall Poplar, Glory of the Woods
That grace thy Bank, broad Shannon, King of Floods,
Beneath whoſe Shade the Dryads lead their Quires,
And Nymphs and Shepherds breath their faithful Fires,

Uprooted by the Thunder's Stroke, around
Spreads its fair Ruins o'er the blasted Ground;
Torn from the Trunk the scatter'd Honours lye,
Yet green in vernal Pride, and with'ring dye.

UPON the headless Trunk aghast, amaz'd,
In Silence long the fierce Barbarian gaz'd;
Then first knew Pity, and his savage Soul
Wond'ring relented, Sighs unwilling stole:
His ravish'd Bliss awhile he sullen mourn'd;---
Thence to destroy with double Rage return'd.

GO, Monster, glut thy Fury: Yet shall Fate
Hunt thy fell Steps, 'till at *Ravenna*'s Gate
Thy Carcase amid Heaps unbury'd hurl'd,
Avenge the murder'd Fair, and pillag'd World.

HAIL, glorious Virgin! Be thy Praise and Deed
Rais'd from Oblivion's Darkness; bold to bleed
Honour's chaste Sacrifice in Beauty's Prime,
Preferring Wounds to Shame, and Death to Crime!
Worthy of *Rome*'s best Blood, that fill'd thy Veins,
Pride of thy Sex: O may these humble Strains
To late Posterity record thy Name,
And weeping Virgins emulate thy Fame!

LECTURE the Eighteenth.

Of STILE. *Of* PLATO.

STILE is, " An Aſſemblage of Words " conſidered with regard to Propriety of " Signification, and Arrangement in Sound." As the Methods of expreſſing Thoughts are various, and theſe Expreſſions may be differently ordered, there muſt be great Diverſities of Stile. The moſt antient Diviſion, that of *Homer*, is perhaps the beſt: It is threefold; the Conciſe and Nervous; the Copious and Sweet; the Vehement and Sublime; which ſeveral Kinds he hath exemplified in three of his Heroes; preſerving to each his diſtinctive Character of Eloquence through the whole Poem.

It is not however to be imagined, that a Work of Length ſhould be written wholely in any one of theſe Kinds; becauſe the different Parts of it, may each require a diſtinct Kind; ſo that every ſuch Work may and uſually doth contain Inſtances of all the three Sorts: Yet this hindereth not, but that one may be predominant; which we may extend from the Works to the Authors. For every Perſon hath from Nature a peculiar Genius,

and

and altho' he may employ, as best suits with his Argument, these various Forms of Speech, yet that which is most conformable to his own Disposition will prevail, and constitute what we call his Character. Thus *Thucydides*, *Tacitus*, and *Montesquieu*, write in the first Manner: *Plato*, *Cicero*, and *Tillotson* in the Second. *Homer*, *Demosthenes*, and *Milton* in the Third.

WITH respect to this last Kind, some modern Criticks have been at much Pains in distinguishing the *Sublime* from *sublime Stile*; a Distinction according to my Judgment imaginary. For this I take to be the Truth. If a Passage consist but of one grand Thought or Image, the more simple the Expression, the more Sublime; because it renders a grand Thought with Precision: As in this,

His dantem jura Catonem. VIRG.

If there be a Course of lofty Sentiments connected together, the Expression must be continued, must have Length, and be supported by suitable Harmony and Strength, as in these Lines of the Iliad;

Hell felt the Shock, and her astounded King
Leap'd yelling from his Throne, afraid lest Earth
Should yawn, by Neptune riven, and disclose
To Gods and Men his dreary Realms, in Smoke
And Stench involv'd, and dreadful ev'n to
Gods [a].

In

[a] Book 23

In both Cases, the Stile, tho' in Appearance different, is alike sublime, being in both, the most proper Expression of sublime Conception.

FROM these Observations may be drawn useful Consequences. Some of which I will briefly mention.

FIRST, Stile is truly a Part of Genius, and so far depends upon Nature. For being determined to Thought, and this Power of Thinking arising from the Frame of the Soul, Stile must in this Respect be the Product of a natural Talent; so that without this Foundation, this Talent, no Degree of Art or Care can bestow a fine one; the utmost which these can do, is to preserve from gross Errors; and thus advance to Mediocrity.

HENCE Secondly; The first Endeavour of all Teachers should be, by forming the Judgment to assist the Genius. A young Person who is capable of thinking well, may be trained up to think better, to know what is right, to chuse among his own Thoughts the best, and range them to Advantage: The Consequence whereof will be, that he shall of Course form to himself a good Stile, for Thoughts make Words and mould them to their own Size. Whereas the usual Method is opposite hereto; to lay out much Time and Pains upon Words, to overwhelm the Memory with Rules concerning Tropes, Figures, Periods, Harmony; with little Care to form the Understanding, to settle distinct Notions of what is right and

and wrong, true and falſe; which is to begin at the wrong End: Stile cannot beſtow Judgment; perfect the Judgment, it will create a Stile.

THIRDLY, We may from hence learn how to anſwer a Queſtion often aſked, and much diſputed about, "Is a good Stile valuable, and "why?"

As it is really a Part of Genius, inſeparable from, and not to be acquired without that, it is like every other Branch of Genius, valuable. But the Queſtion is, "In what Reſpect is it "ſuch Part, being ſo far only of Value?" I anſwer, *Entirely* as a proper Cloathing of Thought: For fine Words without ſuitable Conceptions are ridiculous Sound; and the Cloathing of good Conceptions in mean Language is diſguiſing and debaſing them: Of which latter the Hazard is much leſs, as it can happen from peculiar Circumſtances only: For,

FOURTHLY. In general; clear, ſtrong, lofty Ideas paint themſelves in conformable Words; but the following Conditions are ſuppoſed in the Speaker: That the Language he employs hath arrived at ſome tolerable Degree of Perfection, otherwiſe Inſtruments for Genius to work with are wanting: That the Speaker hath a good Knowledge of this Language: And that by Exerciſe he hath acquired a Facility of expreſſing himſelf therein. To which may be added, that he ſhould have regard to the Age, to Cuſtom, to the Mode of Pronun-

Pronunciation, so as not to use Terms obsolete or low, nor depart from the received Tone or Idiom: Minutenesses, however easy, by no Means to be disregarded: In these Particulars Stile dependeth not at all upon Genius, but on Conversation and Knowledge of the World; accordingly, the Observance of them merits not Praise, but the Ignorance or Neglect of them is unpardonable.

I SHOULD now pass on to the last Head proposed in the Plan of these Lectures, but am called back by the Recollection of an Omission which I have been guilty of: In my second Discourse, I just mentioned *Plato* as an Improver of Eloquence among the *Greeks*, and promised to give a fuller Account of him: This I now proceed to do, in as few Words as the Subject will admit.

PLATO is to be considered in two Lights, as a Teacher of Eloquence by Precept; and as an eloquent Writer. Many Strokes of the first Kind are found dispersed in his Works; but one intire Dialogue; the *Phædrus*, is in this Way; and contains much excellent Instruction. I will trace out a short Idea of it, that ye may see somewhat of his Manner, and be induced, I hope, to study it at Length in the Original.

PHÆDRUS a young noble *Athenian*, is represented as charmed with a Discourse of *Lysias*, a famous Orator, which he had just heard, and of which he had received a Copy. *Socrates* prevails upon him to read it: A hardy

Attempt

Attempt in our Author; it being probably an Oration composed by himself in Imitation of *Lysias*, then living in *Athens*, and much admired. The Judgment formed of this Piece by *Socrates* is very different from that of his young Friend. He agrees in the Praises given to the Stile, but perceiveth many Defects in the Work. *Lysias*, he says, hath given no distinct Explanation of his Subject: The Subject itself is faulty, singular, and affected: He wants Method, beginning with what should be the Conclusion, and confounding the intermediate Parts; which led him into another Fault, frequent Repetition of the same Thought in various Expression, as if thro' a juvenile Ostentation of Fancy and Copiousness of Language.

TO illustrate these Remarks, *Socrates* repeats an extemporary Discourse on the same Subject, which is altogether free from the Faults he had objected to in the other: And because the Error of the Subject still remained, he adds another upon a different one, which is indeed a Noble and a Sublime Oration.

PHÆDRUS filled with Admiration, beginneth to see his former Mistake, and desireth to know whether Rhetorick be an Art, and if any Rules for writing well can be delivered. *Socrates* thinks there may: And layeth it down as the first.

THAT the Orator should have a perfect Knowledge of his Subject, that he may speak not plausibly only, but solidly and usefully; For Rhetorick consists not merely as the Sophists

phists taught, in haranguing to a Multitude, but extends to all Subjects and Occasions, even to common Converſation.

A SECOND Rule is, that a Diſcourſe ſhould be regular and ſo diſpoſed in all its Parts, that each ſhould have its own Place, and its Uſe in contributing to the Strength of the Whole: For it ſhould be conſidered as an animal Body, made up of many Members, all different in Office and Situation, yet neceſſary to the Whole, and to each other.

A THIRD Rule is, Reduce your Subject to its moſt general Idea, which having defined, diſtinguiſh accurately the ſeveral Species contained under it, that ye may have a full View of that you treat upon, with its Connexions, and the Differences bordering on it.

THESE Rules *Phædrus* thinks to be juſt, "but they are rather Logical than Rhetorical." What then, anſwers *Socrates*, do you eſteem to be Rhetorical? Thoſe commonly laid down by our Rhetoricians? Such as relate to the Exordium, then following in order the Narration, Witneſſes, Confirmation, Refutation, and laſtly the Peroration, which repeats ſuccinctly the Sum of all: To theſe they add Commonplaces, Obſervations concerning Figures, Similitudes, Ornaments of Diction, Inſtructions how to excite Anger, or melt an Audience into Pity. Points in the Opinion of *Phædrus* of very great Efficacy in the Art of Perſwaſion; but *Socrates* thinks them not the only, nor the main Points, and as they were then delivered

delivered far from being at all useful; for Rhetoricians in laying down these Precepts did not instruct Men in the Manner of employing them: It is, saith he, as if a Man having learned some good Medicines should set up for a Physician, although utterly ignorant upon what Occasions, and how to apply them.—He then proceedeth to deliver his own Doctrine.

To form a good Orator, he says, that three Things are necessary. Natural *Genius*, *Knowledge*, and *Practice* [*b*]. Which three met in the best Speaker of our Days, *Pericles*; who born with a great Talent for Speaking, added Knowledge which he learned from *Anaxagoras*, Logick namely, and the Science of Nature; and also continual Exercise. Logic teaches the Art of Reasoning clearly. The Study of Nature leads into the Knowledge of the human Mind, the Basis of all true Oratory. For the Mind is the Origin of all the Variety of Tempers and Dispositions among Mankind: Which knowing, with the Influence that each Kind of Discourse hath upon each, you will of Course know how to direct yourself with Success to every Kind of Disposition: And herein consists the Ground of the whole Art of Perswasion, the End of all Eloquence.

HAVING now possessed yourself of this fundamental Knowledge, then it is, and not before, that you may make good Use of the abovementioned Precepts of Rhetoricians; then you shall distinguish, when you ought to be concise,

[*b*] No mention is made of *Taste*.

cise, when to amplify; when you should be simple, when adorned, as your Subject and the Nature of your Hearers require.

PHÆDRUS acknowledges this Doctrine to be reasonable; but he objects to it as very difficult. Let us see, replies *Socrates*, perhaps there is an easier Way. Do you like better that of the Sophists, who maintain that an Orator need not be at the Trouble of understanding perfectly the Point he speaketh upon? He is to perswade the Multitude; why should he regard Truth? It is enough if he useth probable Arguments, such as appear true to them. A dangerous and pernicious Doctrine, deceiving Men it may be, to the Destruction of themselves, and of the State.

BUT grant it right for a Moment. How can you understand the Doctrine of Likenesses, but by understanding that of Realities? Who discerns best what is like Truth, but he who knows Truth? If the Appearance of Truth perswades, must not Truth itself more effectually perswade?

BUT it is not so, *Phædrus*; this whole is a destructive Error. *Tisias*, and *Gorgias*, and *Prodicus* holding those Doctrines, corrupt Eloquence as well as Morality. On the contrary, the true Orator will consider himself as speaking not to Men alone, but to the Gods; to his Lords and Sovereigns, not to his Fellow-servants only; and will therefore speak truly and sincerely. Much more ought we to observe the same Rules in Writing, and employ therein in more Pains, as it is intended to remain a lasting Monument to Posterity; in the same Manner as Trees which are to be of Use and Ornament to our Descendents are planted with more Labour and Care.

THE Sum is; the composing or speaking of Discourses is not a Dishonour to the greatest Person; it is the composing or speaking ill alone, that is such. The true Orator knoweth fully his Subject: Defineth clearly: Traceth up his particular Point to its general Idea, then descending by skilful Divisions, fixeth plain and distinct Notions of it. He is perfectly acquainted with the human Mind, and the several Tempers and Dispositions arising from its Frame; and knowing what kind of Discourse suiteth best with each; maketh his own agree, and be in Unison, as it were, with the Hearts of his Hearers: Then employeth skilfully and justly the Discoveries of Sophists, in adorning his Speech by Figures, Pathos, and Elegance of Expression.

TELL these Observations which we have made, O *Phædrus*, to *Lysias*; I will not fail to repeat them to my young Friend *Isocrates*, whose Genius, superior in my Opinion to that of *Lysias*, and, more especially his mild and virtuous Manners, promise great Excellence.

" AND now, O *Pan*, and all ye Gods, Guar-
" dians of this Place, grant me inward Beauty,
" and such outward Things as may be friendly
" thereto: May I think the wise Man only
" rich

" rich; and possess just so much Wealth as is
" consistent with Virtue!"

WITH this Prayer the Dialogue concludes. And from this imperfect Sketch you may see, that it containeth the fundamental Precepts of Rhetorick; enlarged afterwards, and reduced into a regular System by *Aristotle*; to which succeeding Writers have added little new; even the Eloquence and Experience of *Tully* did not much more than adorn these.

IF we consider *Plato* in the second Light, as a *Writer*, we shall acknowledge that Eloquence owed yet more to his Example than Precept. It is true, the Form of Philosophy which he learned from *Socrates*, that of enquiring and still seeming to doubt, together with the Manner of Dialogue into which this naturally led, oblige him to conceal the Method he pursued. But whoever will have Patience to read his Dialogues throughout, and afterwards to reconsider attentively the Design and Contexture of the Whole, will perceive, that there is in each a regular Scheme carried on with infinite Art; that what you at first object against as Digression and altogether foreign, is yet conducive to his Purpose, and leads to the Conclusion aimed at: He seems to go far back; but it is that he may advance more swiftly, and finish his Career with more Force and Rapidity.

OBJECTIONS doubtless there are, and some too well grounded, to particular Parts: But setting these aside, it may be affirmed, that Antiquity hath transmitted to us nothing for Strength

Strength of Reaſon, for Delicacy and Juſtneſs of Thought, for Sublimity of Sentiment and Moral, enriched with all the Ornaments of a ſtrong and lively Imagination, ſuperior to the Writings of this Philoſopher. His Stile, with all the Embelliſhments of Art, hath the Eaſe of Nature. He deſcends to the common Phraſe of Converſation, and riſeth from thence, without Conſtraint or Abruptneſs, into the loftieſt Speculations of refined Metaphyſicks. He is ſweet and inſinuating; is alſo conciſe and vehement. He can be ſimple and artleſs; yet when his Subject requires it, he enlivens moral Argument with the Harmony and Elevation of Poeſy.

IN which latter Article he is accuſed of having taken exceſſive Licence; of having ſoared above the Limits of Proſe, both in Thought and Stile: Some Inſtances whereof may be found in the ſecond Speech of *Socrates*, in this very *Phædrus*.

THIS Error, if ſuch it muſt be called, follows very naturally from what is related of *Plato* in his Youth; at which Time he applied himſelf wholly to Poetry. He wrote a Tragedy or two; and is ſaid to have attempted an Epic Poem: But he afterwards quitted the Muſe for Philoſophy. Yet his firſt Habit, although checked, retained ſome Force: This original Talent appears in his Proſe; and amidſt the Depth of philoſophick Reaſoning, the Beams of poetick Genius by Fits burſt forth.

UPON this Part of his Hiſtory, together with

with the Plan of a celebrated Fable, *The Judgement of Hercules*, which *Xenophon* hath preserved to us, is grounded a little poetical Essay, which I take the Liberty of presenting to you, in Hope of your usual Indulgence.

To the RIGHT HONOURABLE the

EARL of CHESTERFIELD.

GRAC'D with the Talents of each Rank and Age,
Statesman, or Ruler, Patriot, Poet, Sage,
To thee, O *STANHOPE*, I address the Lay,
From Climes that felt, that still record thy Sway,
When dire Rebellion shook the neighb'ring Land,
Safe in thy Prudence and well-poiz'd Command [*a*],
[*b*] Which offer'd Troops declining, wisely bold,
Watch'd without Fear, and without Force controll'd.

[*a*] His Lordship was Lord Lieutenant of *Ireland* dureing the Time of the late Rebellion in *Scotland*, in 1745; and was removed from thence by his MAJESTY to be Secretary of State.

[*b*] An Offer was made of raising 4000 Men; but declined by his Lordship, as of unnecessary Expence to the Publick.

O early lost, thro' an illustrious Choice!
Prais'd, bless'd, lamented, by a Nation's Voice;
Who now, secure from the loud Storms of
State,
Enjoy'st thy Muses,—glorious in Retreat;
Incline the lawrel'd Head, and Audience deign
To the low Musick of a moral Strain,
Which ALMA's Youth would raise from Sound
to Sense,
And build on Wisdom manly ELOQUENCE.

THE

THE

JUDGMENT of *PLATO*.

IF Fancy, without Reaſon wildly gay,
At beſt ſweet Trifler, ſport in idle Play;
And rigid Reaſon without Fancy's Aid,
Wiſe to no End, unheard, unreliſh'd, plead,
How ſhall I hit the Mean? How juſtly ſteer,
Gay, yet not gaudy, ſolid not ſevere?
How Senſe with Beauty, Cloſeneſs join with Eaſe,
Adorn without Redundance, teach yet pleaſe?

AH! let not Youth, unſeaſonably wiſe,
The Muſe's tuneful Elegance deſpiſe:
Nor yet bewilder'd in her Maze too long,
To ſerious Age protract th' untimely Song.

IN Fancy ſee a Bloſſom of the Spring,
That ſpreads its Foliage to the Zephyr's Wing,
Fed by kind Suns and Show'rs fair-op'ning blooms,
And fills the gladden'd Air with ſoft Perfumes,
In vain; if Age, mild Autumn's ſober Beam
Mature not into Fruit its tender Frame,
Which elſe frail Flow'r, ſoon pierc'd by mortal Wound,
Pines on the Bough, or withers on the Ground:
So blooms young Fancy, unleſs Reaſon's Pow'r
Fix and mature, a gay, a ſhort-liv'd Flow'r.
As ev'ry Seaſon ſhould its Bleſſing bring,
Uſe crown the Autumn, Beauty deck the Spring,

Thus ſhould each Age obtain its Grace; if Youth
Sport in light Strain, let Man contemplate Truth.
Youth's poliſh'd Toys diſhonour rev'rend Age,
And grey-hair'd Dullneſs threats the beardleſs Sage;
Happy, where each reigns its allotted Hour,
And Wiſdom fairer ſprings from Fancy's Flow'r.

THIS Truth, ſince Truths in Morals dryly told
Tales can enliven, let a Tale unfold.

THE firſt of Sages, *PLATO*, juſtly nam'd,
No leſs the Poet's Lawrel might have claim'd,
If Fancy ſtarting firſt, her rapid Courſe
Had held, uncheck'd by following Reaſon's Force.
In Dawn of op'ning Youth he wing'd his Flight,
Born by ſtrong Fancy o'er *Parnaſſus'* Height;
Nor to one Muſe confin'd, with various Fire
Now trod the Buſkin, and now ſtrung the Lyre;
Yet bolder, woo'd imperial *Clio*'s Charms,
Nor fear'd the Epick Trump, and Din of Arms.
Greece heard, and hail'd the Bard with glad Preſage,
And hop'd an Iliad from his riper Age.

BUT as he roſe to Manhood, Love of Truth
Grew on his Mind, and check'd impetuous Youth:
Man he reflects was born to Views ſublime,
Not fram'd to fetter Words in tuneful Chime,

Fictions,

Fictions, however ſweet, delude; the Mind
In Truth alone can laſting Pleaſure find:
Such Thoughts diſturb his anxious Boſom, long
Unfix'd, and oft' ſuſpend th' unfiniſh'd Song.

Once in a Grove, 'tis ſaid, the Youth retir'd,
Where oft' he wander'd by the Muſe inſpir'd;
Where under thickeſt Shade *Iliſſus* ſtrays,
Meandring ſweet in many a Silver Maze;
Penſive he walk'd, for Thoughts of ſerious Kind
Conflicting riſe, and ſadden all his Mind:
Much he reflects which Study he ſhould chuſe,
Think with the Sage, or warble with the Muſe,
This Fancy urges, Reaſon that approves,
One he admires, yet ſtill the other loves:

So doubts the Youth, whom loud Alarms invite
From his lov'd Beauty to the Toils of Fight;
Hither his Country's Danger calls; and there
With ſtreaming Eyes intreats the clinging Fair;
His Breaſt is torn by oppoſite Deſires,
Now Fondneſs melts him, and now Glory fires;
Stern Honour bids *Depart*, Loves urges *Stay*;
He ſighs, oft bids adieu, and ſlowly moves away.

While thus he wander'd, anxious and diſtreſt,
Reaſon with Rapture warring in his Breaſt,
Sudden two Forms celeſtial ſtruck his Sight,
The Foreſt glitter'd with unuſual Light.
One, roſy Youth adorn'd with ev'ry Grace;
And Bloom immortal brighten'd in her Face;
Her

Her Hand ſuſtain'd a Lyre; a Lawrel Bough
Inwov'n with twining Ivy wreath'd her Brow:
The youthful Poet ſoon deſcry'd his Queen,
Her Eyes far-beaming, and her graceful Mien.

AND now alighted on the Green, each Fair
Approach'd; when haſt'ning with familiar Air
And conſcious Beauty; firſt the tuneful Maid
Began; celeſtial Muſick fills the Shade;
Attention holds admiring Nature ſtill,
Soft the Breeze whiſpers, and ſcarce purls the Rill.

WHAT mean theſe Doubts that in thy Boſom riſe,
Illuſtrious *Plato*, fav'rite of the Skies?
Know better thy own Worth; to thee are giv'n
Invention, Genius, Taſte, beſt Boon of Heav'n:
Yet doubt'ſt thou? Can'ſt thou ſuch high Talents ſcorn?
Canſt thou forſake the Muſe celeſtial born,
For HER of earthly Mold, obſcure to dwell
With Want and Meanneſs in the Sage's Cell?
O rather follow where I point the Road!
Come follow Nature, 'tis the Voice of God.
Why glows thy Boſom with poetick Flame?
From Heav'n, from Heav'n the early Impulſe came.
Canſt thou to Fame thus call'd, inglorious lye,
And creep on Earth, who ſhould aſcend the Sky?
Behold, I lead the Way! Come, wing thy Courſe
Rapt by ſtrong Genius, to *Caſtalia*'s Source,
Where

Where on the Margin of the ſacred Spring
The tuneful Nine immortal Numbers ſing:
Oft from his Sun-bright Car the God of Day
Deſcends, his Lyre attuning to the Lay,
Celeſtial Symphony! Bards Lawrel-crown'd
Enraptur'd liſten to the ſacred Sound;
Fame takes the Note, and with her Trumpet ſends
The deathleſs Song to Earth's remoteſt Ends.
Hither I guide: To theſe with happy Choice
Companion not unworthy, add thy Voice.
Such, *Orpheus* ſtruck the Lyre, and Heav'n-taught ſung;
Beaſts fawn'd, Trees follow'd, Torrents liſt'ning hung;
The Force of Muſick Hell relenting felt,
Stern *Pluto* weeps, and ſnake-crown'd Furies melt.
Such was *Amphion*, whoſe melodious Call
Rocks heard, obey'd, and rear'd the *Theban* Wall.

SEE the *Mæonian* Muſe exalted riſe,
With what a rapid Wing ſhe cleaves the Skies;
Nations purſue her Flight with loud Acclaim,
Age follows Age, and ſwells her growing Fame:
As the ſwift Flood, that foaming from the Source
Gathers a thouſand Torrents in his Courſe,
Enlarging as he rolls his Bed diſdains,
And pours a ſounding Ocean o'er the Plains.

SEE Hoſts diſmay'd! *Tyrtæus* calls to Arms,
Diſplays in tuneful Numbers Glory's Charms;
They hear tranſported, combat, conquer, bleed:.
They fled—the Poet ſings—and *Sparta*'s freed.

EV'N

[*e*] EV'N *Solon* thy great Sire, who rais'd to Fame
Athens erst grov'ling, felt and lov'd my Flame,
Polish'd by me gave Statutes wise and good;
Her Son, *her* DRACO *wrote his Laws in Blood.*

EQUAL in Worth, in Glory equal those,
Scorning dull Earth, and philosophick Prose.
In untun'd Prose let the harsh Sophist creep,
And argue ev'ry Reader into Sleep,
Obscurely useful, like the rugged Stone
Doom'd in the massy Pile to lye unknown;
While the fine Genius like the Di'mond bright,
Polish'd and set by Art attracts the Sight,
Destin'd on Crowns and royal Hands to glare,
Or flame on snowy Bosoms of the Fair:

SUCH are my Sons: Thou happier than the rest,
Be dear to Beauty, and by Pow'r carest;
Eyes that charm Worlds shall thro' thy Volumes rove,
Weep with thy Woe, and languish with thy Love.
Thy Form on breathing Canvas shall be shown,
Enrich the Gold, and animate the Stone;
Assembled *Greece* thy Merit shall proclaim,
And crowded Fabricks labour with thy Fame;
Thee next to *Phœbus* Mortals shall invoke,
And fragrant Incense on thy Altars smoke.
Hear lov'd of Heav'n, enjoy these Gifts divine,
And leave pale SCIENCE o'er her midnight Lamp to pine.

THE

[*e*] PLATO was descended from CODRUS the last King of *Athens*, and from SOLON.

THE Goddeſs ceas'd, yet left in *Plato*'s Ear
So ſweet her Voice that he ſtill ſeem'd to hear;
As one, his Thirſt allay'd who left the Rill,
Hears its ſweet Murmurs in his Fancy ſtill.

MEAN Time the other Form advanc'd: A Dame
Leſs winning ſoft, but of majeſtick Frame;
Mature ſhe ſeem'd in Life's meridian Prime,
Her Aſpect ſerious, and her Port ſublime,
With eaſy Grandeur: Eagle-like to view
Her Eye, and ſeem'd to look all Objects thro'.
E'er Accents flow'd, her Looks Attention draw,
Imprint Reſpect, and Love inſpire with Awe;
The Bough of *Pallas* trembles in her Hand;
And thus her Words the liſt'ning Soul command.

I come, PHILOSOPHY, no Stranger---Gueſt
To *Plato*, oft by thee in Pray'r addreſt.
Thy Mind perplex'd I ſaw; to fix deſcend,
And from this wily Sorcereſs defend.

WEIGH well my Son, what ſpecious Words expreſs,
Flatt'ry is Error's moſt pernicious Dreſs.
Ill boaſts the Muſe her late Returns of Praiſe;
A Life's long Labour ſhe rewards—with Bays;
But Folly's Garland cannot long adorn;
Seeks't thou for Glory?—'tis of Virtue born.

VICE ſwells *her* Voice, Vice trembles on *her* Strings;
The Cares of Love and Joys of Wine ſhe ſings;
Strows

Strows Flow'rs on Falſehood's Path, deters
from Truth;
And leads to Pleaſure's Altars giddy Youth:
At Youth too ſurely Pleaſure aims the Dart,
Wit adds the Wings that ſend it to the Heart.

EV'N her exalted *Homer* fills the Skyes
With Monſters, Luſt and Fury deifies,
His Chiefs revengeful fierce, Gods partial blind
Pervert the Thoughtleſs, ſhock the Reas'ning
Mind;
Yet hope not with *Mæonian* Wings to riſe,
Howe'er the Muſe may flatter; Heav'n denies;
Like Genius glows not in thy Breaſt; his Lay
Unrival'd, leaves thee but a ſecond Bay.

WHAT tho' poetick Spirit warms thy Breaſt,
Miſtake not Fancy's Warmth for Heavn's Beheſt.
Say you may ſhine in Verſe; in Science too
You may; and will you the leſs Good purſue?
As the redundant Moiſture which would ſhoot
In Leaves, by Culture is improv'd to Fruit,
The Fire which would itſelf in Viſions ſpend,
By Diſcipline is render'd Wiſdom's Friend,
Lends Reaſon Ornament, and places Senſe
In the ſtrong Lights of manly Eloquence.

THUS foil'd by Truth the Muſe to Fable runs,
Amphion, *Orpheus*, boldly calls her Sons;
Both Sages, Friends to Truth, and Virtue's
Cauſe,
Who founded Cities, Governments, and Laws,
Muſick's known Pow'r employing to aſſwage
Hearts yet unſoften'd in a barb'rous Age:
What

What was Necessity to praise she strains,
Virtue the End forgets, and Verse extolls the
Means.

TYRTÆUS sung,—and Cowards conquer'd; Whence?
Because Opinion sways the Crowd, not Sense:
No Poet, Courage, and no Augur, needs;
His Countries Voice demands,—the brave Man bleeds:
Inspir'd by me, such *Codrus* falling cry'd,
" *Athens* is sav'd; I thank ye Gods:"—and dy'd.
And shalt thou waste thy Life in idle Strains,
With Blood thus shed for *Athens* in thy Veins?
Rarely so well employ'd, her highest Aim
Is to commend with Skill,—I give, the Flame.

IN erring, *Draco* shew'd the Path to good;
SOLON was mild, because HE wrote in Blood:
Thus Heav'n hath doom'd, that Man should gradual rise
By slow long Toil, thro' Errors to be wise.
Unbending, *Solon* trifled with the Nine;
Theirs was a leisure Hour,—his Laws were mine.
[c] To the sooth'd Ear less pleasing Sounds impart
The Lute and Lyre, than Reason to the Heart:
Nor ever Poet feign'd, or Painter drew
A Form more lovely to the outward View,
Than to the Mind's purg'd Eye the Soul serene,
Where Passion spreads no Cloud, nor Vice a Stain.

Could

[c] PLATO in Menon.

[*d*] Could Virtue to the Sight unfold her Charms,
Mankind would rush enamour'd to her Arms,
Hang on her heav'nly Lips, her Nod obey,
And never, never from her Dictates stray.

WHAT Credit can the Muse's Words obtain,
Whose Study's to deceive, whose Praise to feign?
Her Fount, her Pindus, her Elysian Scenes:
Of Harmony, exist but in her Strains:
The Choir of Muses, and the God of Day,
The Fame whose Trumpet spreads the deathless Lay,
Are pompous Visions by her Art devis'd,
Figures of Speech, and Fancy realiz'd.

THEN hear my Voice, e'er yet in Error's Way
Thy Youth but half misled, for ever stray.
By me instructed, Good from Ill discern,
To know thyself, Man's highest Knowledge, learn.

I FIX your Notions, Actions regulate,
Unfold the Duties of each Age and State,
With Precepts strengthen Reason's tott'ring Sway,
Quell Appetite, teach Passion to obey,
Explain from whence is Man, for what design'd,
His End, his Nature, his immortal Mind,
Raise his short View to Heav'n, and fix it there,
On the first Excellent, first Good, and Fair,
Teach

[*d*] Quæ (*Virtus*) si conspici posset (ut ait PLATO) Mirabiles sui amores excitaret. CICERO.

Teach him to draw his Rules of Life from thence,
And graft on Piety Benevolence;
That Man like God at gen'ral Good should aim,
And Happiness and Virtue are the same:
That Virtue opens Heav'n to mortal Race,
Life but a Trial, Death a Change of Place:
And the pure Soul should claim its native Sky,
Bright Emanation of the Deity.

THESE Arts be thine: These render good and wise;
Fame is their meanest Gift, *her* vaunted Prize.
How worthless are the pompous Scenes she draws,
Her Statues, Portraits, Theatres, Applause.
Pow'r, Beauty, *Greece*, commending? More is giv'n
To my scorn'd *midnight Lamp*,—the Praise of Heav'n.
Leave Shadows, Numbers, Fable, Emptiness,
With me Sense, Knowledge, Virtue, Worth possess:
Be thou the first to light the moral Ray,
And pour on *Greece* the philosophick Day,
With mine for ever blended shall thy Name
Descend, and Truth and *Plato* be the same.

SHE ceas'd; and doubtful seem'd th' Event to wait:
The Muse secure advanc'd with Looks elate:

"THEE I prefer, thee Wisdom, *Plato* cry'd,
"Transported, come my Goddess, Guardian, "Guide;
"O take me, seize me, all my Heart engage,
"Light of my Youth, and Glory of my Age!"

As

As o'er Night's ſparkling Hoſt, with keener Beams
At Dawn's firſt Riſe, the Star of Morning flames;
But when the Sun his orient Light diſplays,
It fades, it ſickens in the conq'ring Blaze:
The Muſe thus vanquiſh'd blends with ſhapeleſs Air:
Pallas remains in Victory more fair.

WELL haſt thou choſen, thus the Queen reply'd,
My Pow'r ſhall guard you, and my Councils guide.
Thus far was right, and uſefully you ſtray'd;
Science beſt flouriſhes where Fancy play'd,
Whoſe wandring Beam within due Limits brought
Gives Life to Knowledge, and inſpirits Thought.

THE Muſe departs:—Yet grieve not; Lo! I ſend
To form thy growing Years, a nobler Friend,
A Siſter-nymph, to whom by kinder Heav'n
The Muſe's Charms without her Faults are giv'n;
In artleſs Beauty, unaffected Air.
Humble tho' lovely, tho' polite ſincere,
Quick without Raſhneſs, without Weakneſs ſweet,
Adorn'd yet natural, tho' gay diſcreet,
Her Speech harmonious as *Apollo*'s Lyre,
Yet full of Spirit, Energy, and Fire;
Her, ELOQUENCE, I ſend, a heav'nly Gueſt;
Receive her *Plato*, open all thy Breaſt,

Imbibe

Imbibe her purer Rays. Her ſkill Divine
Shall temper friendly, and ſhall perfect mine,
The Store by me ſupply'd, with pleaſing Art
Shall to Mankind a publick Good impart;
And whilſt I deck the Soul, her Voice ſhall win the Heart.

As touch'd by *Pegaſus* thy Muſe hath ſung
From her rent Cliff that burſting Waters ſprung,
Fountain of Poeſy; in After-time
Whence laurel'd Bards inhal'd their Rage ſublime;
Thus open'd by her Touch ſhall Wiſdom's Source
From thee o'erflowing, in its boundleſs Courſe,
To ev'ry Age convey the ſacred Lore,
And Realms yet barbarous my Pow'r adore.

THE Goddeſs ſpoke: When ſudden to the Skies
On ſounding Pinions born, he ſaw her riſe,
In a long Trail of Light; behind her ſhed
Ambroſial Odours heav'nly Fragrance ſpread;
The Youth enraptur'd gaz'd: Then homeward turn'd
His Steps; with Hopes ſublime his Boſom burn'd.

LECTURE

LECTURE the Nineteenth.

Concerning the Eloquence of the PULPIT.

WE have lately been employed about thoſe Articles of Oratory which regard the Surface chiefly, and are calculated in a great Meaſure for Shew and Ornament, as Stile, Compoſition, Figures: I have even ventured to conduct you through the flowery Paths of Poeſy; in which I fear that I have detained you too long, deceived by the Charms of the Place. I am now to open a more ſevere Scene, and I hope, that what may be wanting in Agreeableneſs herein, ſhall be made up in Utility. I have arrived at that Part of my Undertaking, in which I propoſed to conſider Eloquence as it relateth to Difference of Profeſſion, it's ultimate View; ſince the End of all Study ſhould be ſerious, to render us in our reſpective Ranks truly uſeful to Society.

Two Forms of Life, two Situations in which this Quality is highly neceſſary, I ſhall not particularly treat of; becauſe few of the preſent Audience in Compariſon with the reſt, are likely to have Occaſion of appearing in either of thoſe Lights. And beſides, I cannot without Preſumption

ſumption attempt to deliver any other than general Remarks, on Scenes of Buſineſs, which it hath been my Lot to behold only at a Diſtance. Directions more immediately reſpecting ſuch ſhould be taken from thoſe only, who are themſelves engaged in them, who join Experience to Obſervation.

I SHALL therefore in this and the following Lectures, confine myſelf to that Kind of Speaking, which treats of *ſacred* Subjects.

A MATTER in itſelf of the utmoſt Importance; and an Office, for which the greater Number of Perſons here educated are undoubtedly deſigned.

IT is not however my Intention, to give a regular full Account of the Eloquence of the Pulpit, an Undertaking which would demand a large Treatiſe: Agreeably to the Nature of theſe Diſcourſes, I ſhall limit myſelf to a much narrower Compaſs, making ſuch Remarks, and delivering ſuch Precepts as appear to be moſt wanted; and ſuch at the ſame Time, the Knowlege of which ſeems moſt proper to unfold other Particulars, and diſcover to you the moſt important Conſiderations: Such, as the Obſervation of what is right, what wrong in others, added to the Examples of thoſe in paſt Times, who have left behind them Monuments of this Kind, together with the Experience of my own Miſtakes, have furniſhed me with. In which I ſhall endeavour ſo far as may conſiſt with Clearneſs, to avoid repeating Things before laid down, and ſhall dwell only upon ſuch Rules of

Eloquence as are peculiar to this Kind: For we cannot, ſtrictly ſpeaking, propoſe to ourſelves any of the antient Orators as Models in this Way; where the Subject, wholely of a different Sort, requires a Manner very different, and ſuited to itſelf alone. General Precepts before delivered extend their Uſefulneſs hither; what is peculiar remains now to be added: And I proceed without farther Preface to the Point itſelf.

WHOEVER intends to undertake an Office of this Sort, ought, First, to Reflect on the *Qualities* neceſſary to be poſſeſt by a Preacher, that he may previouſly acquire, or if he hath them not, deſiſt from the Attempt.

THE firſt of theſe is VIRTUE.

THE antient Writers lay it down as a Maxim, that an Orator ſhould be a good Man. If this be required in publick Pleadings and Conſultations, how much more neceſſary is it, where the ſole Deſign of the Speaker is to make Men wiſe and good? Truth it is confeſſed, ought to convince from any Mouth; yet ſuch are the Prejudices of Mankind, that we never can entirely ſeparate what is ſaid from the Character of the Perſon who ſayeth it. We feel juſt Indignation at hearing ſacred Truths uttered, we may ſtile it profaned, by a wicked Man; and through Averſion from him, it is but too eaſy, however wrong, to contract an Indifference to, it may be an Averſion from them.

BESIDES nothing contributes more to Perſwaſion, than a Belief of Sincerity in the Speaker. Here is a Man who profeſſeth to have well

con-

considered a Point, and from that Preparation to treat concerning it; his Authority as well as Arguments will have Weight with the Bulk of Mankind; it addeth Weight to those Arguments. But if his known Practice contradict his Discourse, that Influence ceaseth; nay, becometh opposite; he is a Dissembler and Hypocrite, we shut our Ears and Hearts against him. To which ye may add; That all are Judges of Actions, not of Reasoning.

MORE especially, the Preacher should join a Love of Religion and Piety to moral Virtue. If a noted Unbeliever or Despiser of Religion, discourse concerning the holy Mysteries of Religion, such Discourses however skilfully framed, are not only rendered useless by his Character, but raise Horror in every good Mind; and tend to confirm the Infidel and Scoffer in their evil Dispositions. It is true, we argue solidly against the Injustice of charging upon Religion the ill Lives and bad Principles of it's Ministers; but notwithstanding, such is the Nature of Men, that they will be led more by Sense than Speculation; and be tempted to doubt of the Truth of Religion from a Perswasion of Unbelief in it's Teachers, rather than be influenced by their Reasonings to believe.

BESIDES, a Person who hath no Reverence to, or firm Belief of Religion, although of good Capacity and Learning, never can recommend it with the same natural, ingenuous, efficacious Eloquence, as doth the Man, who is heartily convinced of the Truth of what he advanceth:

There is in all that ſuch an one ſayeth, I know not what, of forced and artificial, which appears thro' the Diſguiſe, diſguſteth and offendeth. Few, none but prudent conſiderate Men, believe or even attend much to Arguments, which they are perſwaded, that the Speaker who employs them, doth not himſelf believe.

A SECOND Quality is KNOWLEGE. It is obvious, that he whoſe Duty it is to teach others, ſhould himſelf know; otherwiſe he ſhall miſtake and miſlead; at beſt can talk but ſuperficially, convey empty imperfect Notions. In the preſent Caſe, every one ſees, that a Knowlege of the ſacred Writings is neceſſary. The more extenſive and exact this is, the better: And although a perfect Acquaintance with the Original of the Old Teſtament cannot be expected from all, yet ſome Progreſs in the Knowlege of it is highly uſeful, that they who inſtruct others ſhould not themſelves be obliged in all Points relative hereto, to depend upon the Authority of others; eſpecially, as the Connexion between the Sacred Writings of the *Jews*, and thoſe upon which our holy Faith is grounded, is ſo cloſe and intimate, and they throw much Light on each other.

I MIGHT, if this were a proper Place, lament the Abuſe which hath ariſen from a good Cauſe, the Study of this Original Hebrew, of late much cultivated among our Neighbours. For an Humour hath prevailed of finding out therein, and deducing from thence, Syſtems of natural Cauſes, and a new Philoſophy; as well

as

as the moſt profound Myſteries of the Chriſtian Religion, revealed to Mankind, not until many Ages after, by the divine Author: To this End, theſe Perſons indulge themſelves in ſtrange, and as it ſeemeth, very dangerous Licences, in altering the received Orthography of the Language, and inventing odd and unheard of Explications; the Conſequences of which Proceeding may be very hurtful. Yet, while we ſhun the Error of theſe Men, let us imitate their laudable Induſtry, in applying ourſelves to the Study of the Hebrew Tongue. If we join to this Induſtry other ſolid Learning and good Senſe, we ſhall be in no Danger of falling into their Error; ſuch Miſtakes being obſerved to meet with beſt Reception, either among thoſe who underſtand the Language but ſuperficially, or underſtand the Language only.

It ſeems ſcarcely needful to add, that a critical Skill in the Language of the New Teſtament is requiſite; both, as it contains our whole Faith, which whoſoever teaches, ought ſurely by no Means to take upon Truſt: And alſo, as the *Greek* Tongue, in which it is written, is a very uſeful, if not neceſſary, Introduction to Eloquence, indeed to every Branch of polite Literature.

Some Acquaintance with the Fathers of the Church, if not perfect Knowlege, ſhould be recommended to the Preacher. Thoſe, who lived neareſt to the Times of the Apoſtles, ought to be ſtudyed on two Accounts: Their Authority is deſervedly great, as they derived their Doctrines from Perſons who were Diſciples of, and

con-

conversed immediately with the Apostles. And secondly, their Manner of Writing, altho' unartful and unpolished, hath that Simplicity, that genuine Air of Truth, which is most becoming of a Preacher of the Gospel, and is difficult to attain and preserve, in these Days of Refinement and Curiosity.

MANY of the Successors to these good Men, are valuable for Eloquence as well as Piety. Among whom, in the first Rank are St. *Chrysostom*, and St. *Augustin*: One the Light of the Greek, as the other was of the Latin Church: The one easy, copious, flowing, pathetick; the other learned, close, subtle, even sublime. Whom I also particularly mention, because both of them have in some Degree treated of the Subject now before us, with much good Sense and Observation: *Chrysostom*, altho' not expressly, yet hath intermixed many Remarks to this Purpose in his excellent Work concerning the *Priestly Office*: The other more fully and directly in the fourth Book concerning the *City of God*: The careful Perusal of which Treatises I earnestly recommend to you, as my Design permits me to employ but a very small Part of the same Materials, to transplant but few Articles, as it were some detached Shrubs from their noble and lofty Groves. Besides, that after all the Industry and Skill we late Comers, whether Commentators, Criticks, or Imitators, can use, to diversify, enlarge, adorn, I know not how, there is still more of Pleasure, and I believe of Use, in drawing directly from the Fountain Head.

THE

THE ſeveral Branches of human Learning do not appear to relate immediately to the Office of a Preacher, yet are they of undoubted Utility. The Writings of Philoſophers and Moraliſts are eminently ſo, furniſhing many excellent Arguments and Obſervations concerning Manners; at the ſame Time, laying before him the beſt Models of Compoſition in that Kind.

ERUDITION likewiſe of a more abſtruſe Sort, and ſeemingly foreign from his Purpoſe, that which is converſant about Numbers and Quantity, appeareth from what we have formerly obſerved, to be very beneficial to him; ſharpening the Apprehenſion; enlarging the Capacity, and teaching the Art of ſtrict and cloſe Reaſoning.

AFTER this, it ſeemeth hardly neceſſary to add, that he ought to be verſed in the whole Circle of polite Literature; this being the Source, from whence is derived every Thing which tends to Perfection of Stile, all juſt Grace and Ornament.

To theſe ſhould be added likewiſe a competent Knowlege of the World. The Man, whoſe Duty and Profeſſion lead him to preſerve from Vice, or to reform the Vicious, ought to be well acquainted with the Nature, Manners, and Behaviour of Mankind. For Diſcourſe from meer Speculation is likely to be not ſeldom wrong, at beſt vague and general; if it ſhould be reaſonable, yet rarely touching the Heart. To tell Men, with any good Effect, how they ought to live, we ſhould know firſt how they

do

do live; what are their Faults, their Passions, their Delusions, the various Sophisms of Self-love by which they deceive themselves. We must lay open to them their own Hearts; and how can we, if we know not even their Actions?

A Person with this Knowlege, will not be in Danger of falling into loose general Declamation. His Observations drawn from Nature and Truth will not be scattered at Random among the Crowd, but will strike, will be felt. Each Individual will find his Sentiments, his own Heart painted in them; and imagine that the Preacher speaks to himself.—Thus shall the Discourse be as a well drawn Portrait; Spectators behold it from different Parts of the Chamber; and it appears to each as having it's Eyes fixed upon himself.

AND after all, this Work of Reformation is not to be executed bluntly and abruptly; but with much Address, according to the Manners, and with some Compliance to the Prejudices of the World; which Precautions judiciously taken will open an easier Reception for Advice, and are almost always necessary to make Reproof effectual.

EVEN the Prophets inspired and sent immediately by God himself have given us Examples herein, worthy of Imitation. When *Nathan* was sent to admonish *David*, and lay before him the Heinousness of his Crime, with Regard to *Uriah*, he doth not immediately upbraid him with the horrid Blackness of his complicated Guilt, nor

nor thunder in his Ears with the Authority of a Divine Meſſenger; but he addreſſeth himſelf to himi n a Piece of plain familiar Hiſtory, deſcribeeth to him his own Crime, couched under the Action of another, reſembling in general Circumſtances, but far leſs ſinful; and having raiſed his Abhorrence of it in this feigned Repreſentation, and his expreſs Denunciation as King, that the guilty *Perſon ſhould die*, he then applyeth it directly to himſelf, *Thou art the Man*:— The Stroke was irreſiſtable; it proved, convinced, aſtoniſhed:—The King confeſſeth and humbleth himſelf in ſincere Repentance.

To the Knowlege of other Men, the Preacher ſhould join that of himſelf. What is it of which you are capable? What may you ſafely undertake? What ſhould you avoid? What Imperfections ought you to amend? In which Manner are you moſt likely to excel? It is fit that you ſhould weigh all theſe maturely, and as far as you may without Prejudice; otherwiſe ſetting out wrong, you never ſhall arrive to the Worth you are capable of; and may beſide go on to the laſt in a wrong Way.

When we ſpoke of Acquaintance with the learned Languages, it was by no Means intended, that a Preacher ſhould neglect the Study of his own: On the contrary, this is an Article in which he ſhould omit no Pains to acquire a maſterly Skill. Certainly nothing can be more unreaſonable, more evidently wrong, than to diſregard the very Tongue in which one is to ſpeak; and yet we cannot doubt that the Caſe

is

is common. A Perſon well verſed in Latin ſhall offend by harſh, obſcure, even barbarous Stile in his native Dialect: The Foundations of which Evil are laid in the uſual Methods of Education; wherein great Pains are taken to inſtruct young Perſons in the Words, Form, and Structure of the Latin Tongue, ſo that they may be enabled to ſpeak it readily, and write in it with Eaſe, perhaps Purity, leaving them at the ſame Time to pick up ſuch imperfect Knowlege of their native Tongue, as Chance, Company, and the ordinary Occurrences of Life throw in their Way. The Conſequence whereof is very diſadvantageous, when they afterwards come into the World, where real Buſineſs is to be tranſacted, and they muſt converſe with *Engliſh*, not *Romans*, or *Athenians*.

FOR which Reaſon it ſhould be laid down as an invariable Rule, to bring up from Infancy young Perſons, in early Knowlege of what is proper and pure in their native Dialect, and exerciſe them in conſtant Habits of Speaking and Writing in it correctly: And Latin, which is now the firſt in Intention, ſhould hold but the ſecond Place, being cultivated chiefly with a View to the other, as it may contribute to render them accurate therein, furniſhing excellent Models, whoſe Graces they may transfuſe or expreſs in their own Speech.

MY Opinion of the other learned Tongue, the Greek, I have before declared; and the more I reflect upon it, am the more confirmed

in

in a Perswasion of the great Usefulness of an early Application to it. For our present Manner of studying it, by the Help of literal Translations, seldom enabling us to go on far without such poor Assistance, hurteth rather than bringeth Benefit; such Translations seldom rendering the compleat Sense, never any Part of the Spirit and beautiful Simplicity of the Original; in which last most valuable Quality, the Writers of that Nation bear away the Prize from all their Followers.

WHAT I have been saying is a Proof, how much Care is requisite in the choice of Persons, who undertake this Office of Preachers; how much those Persons should study themselves; what Labour they should employ in obtaining, perfecting, and preserving the necessary Qualifications. And although, according to the Course of Things, it is not to be expected, that all who offer themselves for this Purpose should be accomplished in the Manner laid down; and consequently, that the venerable Order of Men with whom the Wisdom of the Society hath entrusted the Power of appointing them, should insist upon admitting only such; yet undoubtedly, it is the Duty of all who have taken upon them the Charge, to employ their utmost Care in fitting themselves as nearly as they can in the Manner described, for the due Execution of it.

As to Caution in electing *such*, it would ill become one of my Mediocrity in Rank and Talents to interpose his Opinion; I shall therefore refer you in the Point to one of approved

proved Authority, to *Erasmus*, who hath written a Treatise on this *Art of Preaching*; in which, although published in Haste, and never rightly finished, whence sometimes prolix, there is much good Observation and solid Learning; and the whole Work well deserves your careful Perusal. I except some Reflexions dipped in Gall, not to be approved of, much less imitated by us; which the Times and Manners then very corrupt, may excuse perhaps, if not justify in him; we have fallen on better.

ANOTHER Thing which should be well weighed by every one who is, or proposeth to be employed in this sacred Office, is the *End*, which he should intend and aim at in the Discharge of it, namely the Advancement of Piety and Virtue, by laying before Men their Duty, and engaging them to the Practice thereof. This Reflexion duly repeated and insisted on, cannot fail of impressing upon the Mind a deep Sense of the Excellence of the Work which it hath undertaken; will support it under the Difficulties that attend the Preparation for it; will not fail to inspire that Seriousness and Earnestness so necessary and becoming in the Performance of it; and will be a constant Preservative against Faults too frequently observable, which are incident to the best Capacities, those which spring from Vanity and Ostentation: Such as an Affectation of deep and singular Learning; or an Ambition of displaying Wit and Invention; and in Consequence of these, the Use of obscure Subtilties, abstracted Erudition,

tion, pompous, glittering, and conceited Diction. For I am of Opinion, that some do indeed fail in executing this Office through Defect of Capacity; many more through Want of Care; yet most of all through wrong Motives and unfit Passions.

This Council of regarding the *End* is, I own, obvious, yet for its mighty Utility is worthy of being repeated, inculcated. It alone might stand instead of many Rules; at least would render easy the Observation of all. It would raise the Priesthood to the Degree of Usefulness it was intended to have, and would make it appear in the same advantageous Light to others. Complaints have been loud, and for some Time past, have, I believe, encreased, of the Contempt thrown upon this Order of Men; how unjustly thrown is not the Business of this Place to prove: But thus much one may affirm; that if the Conditions mentioned took Place, if Men of this Order were generally qualified in the Manner required, and especially, if they were actuated by an earnest Desire of answering the End of their Ministry, which is in the Power of all, these Complaints would quickly subside.

In Fact, what Sight could be so striking, as that of a Number of Men exempted from the Necessity of Labour and civil Industry, that they may explain to others the Nature, Excellence, and Benefits of Virtue; enforcing their Doctrines by Example; recommending them by Humanity, by Gentleness of Manners, by the Advantages of solid, and the Ornaments of polite

lite Learning? What could be a more beautiful Spectacle in a moral Light, even in a political what more useful? What Method so probable, of diffusing through a Society, Probity, Peace, and Regularity? This Perfection it is true, cannot as the World is now constituted, be hoped for; yet should we not despair of approaching to it; and it ought to be the Care, as it is the Duty of every one in this sacred Office, to have it constantly in View, and contribute his best Endeavours to the Accomplishment of it.

THIS End will farther point out the particular Means you should employ, namely to *Explain*, to *Prove*, to *Affect*. You are to explain, in order to instruct; you are to prove, in order to convince; you are to affect, in order to perswade. The mention of which Articles leads from these previous Remarks to somewhat more close and precise.

LECTURE the Twentieth.

Continuation of the Former.

LET us ſuppoſe now that you are thus rightly qualified, and ſit down to compoſe a Sermon: The firſt Thing you ſhould attend to is the *Choice of a Subject*; as from hence muſt flow, in a good Meaſure, the Uſefulneſs and Importance of what you are to ſay.

IN general, this ought to be either ſome Article of revealed Doctrine, ſome Point of Faith neceſſary to be firmly believed by your Hearers; or ſome Branch of Morality, ſomewhat fit to be done. Which different Subjects require a Diverſity in the Manner of handling them.

As our Church hath appointed certain Days for the Commemoration of great Events, which involve ſome principal Articles of our Faith, it is agreeable to the Deſign of ſuch Inſtitution, and may be reaſonably expected by the Audience, that every Preacher ſhould, on ſuch Days at leaſt, diſcourſe to them concerning theſe Articles; the not performing of which may be well judged an Omiſſion. For the right Execution hereof, ſome Precautions are neceſſary,

ſome

ſome Reflections there are, which it may be uſeful to obſerve.

PRINCIPALLY, on ſuch Occaſions, avoid entering into nice and ſubtle Queſtions. Abſtain from very difficult and abſtracted Reaſonings. In Times of Ignorance the Schoolmen introduced many of the firſt Kind, and the Sermons remaining from thoſe Ages are crowded with Diſtinctions for the moſt Part uſeleſs and unintelligible; ſome of which Controverſies do continue to be ſtill agitated among us, although the Manner of Writing admired in thoſe Days be now grown obſolete.

IN more modern Times, Metaphyſicks, long a faſhionable Study, brought in the latter Sort; and more particularly, the Neceſſity of purſuing Unbelievers through all the Subtilties and Refinements which their Art and Induſtry in attacking Religion had opened to them, engaged many pious and learned Men to go far into this Way, and confute Subtilty by Subtilty. But however right this may have been in thoſe who ſpoke from the Preſs, it is not to be imitated by the Men who ſpeak from the Pulpit; in which laſt Caſe, their Hearers cannot be ſuppoſed to underſtand, and conſequently will not attend to them. The Thread is too fine for vulgar Eyes. It muſt happen, that plain rational Men, after having taken ſome Pains to apprehend their Meaning, when they find it to no Purpoſe, ſhall give it up; and perceiving it a vain Attempt to keep Pace with them, ſhall ſtop

ſhort,

ſhort, and leave them to finiſh their Career alone.

FARTHER, It doth not ſeem prudent to urge nice Objections, many of which late Libertine Days have produced, before a plain Audience; nor ſeek to engage them in all the Intricacy of perplexed Controverſy. Much leſs doth it ſeem right, on ſuch ſacred Occaſions, to heap ſevere Remarks and bitter Invectives againſt Unbelievers; which I think is not very uncommon among good Men, of more Zeal than Prudence. The Minds of Men do not need to be ſharpened. Indignation, even in ſo juſt a Cauſe, ſhould be moderated, and, if it could be, ſuppreſſed. Defend the Truth; confute known and dangerous Errors; but ſpare the Perſons.

IN general; What you ſhould aim at in theſe Subjects, Articles of religious Belief, is, a plain, clear Explanation of the Doctrine, confined as nearly as may be to the Words of the Revelation, or deduced from them by eaſy unſtrained Interpretation, without entering into hazardous Conjectures, or attempting to gratify an unbounded, often preſumptuous Curioſity: Which Explanation you ſhould proceed to impreſs on the Minds of the Hearers, by laying before them the Uſes it ought naturally to have, in exciting their Devotion, or in regulating their Conduct.

POINTS of Controverſy among Chriſtians ſhould not be altogether ſhut out from the Pulpit, thoſe eſpecially which ſubſiſt between us and the Church of *Rome*, whoſe Doctrines are the most grosly erroneous; and besides, involve Danger to the State. But the Treatment of these is difficult. For you are to represent the Tenets of that Church impartially, not aggravating or altering; not following the Authority of particular Persons; nor hastily charging Consequences as Doctrines. Your Arguments should be simple, yet strong; drawn from Scripture, or plain Reason; not embarrassed with historical Deductions, or the Erudition of Quotations, or the Perplexity of numerous Objections proposed and solved; for you do not write to Readers, but speak to be understood. And what is perhaps the hardest Part, you are to preserve the due Mean: Convince, but do not irritate; shew the Heinousness of the Mistakes, without raising Abhorrence of the Mistaken; keep up your Hearers Zeal, without inclining to Persecution; and join the Moderation of a Christian with the Vehemence of an Orator.

As to the Articles in Dispute between us and our dissenting Brethren, these, if to be at all admitted; should be reserved for a masterly Hand. In Points of Difference which affect not Essentials, Prudence, as well as Religion, directeth to sweeten and reconcile Mens Spirits on both Sides; to win over, if it be possible, those who are divided from us, by the soft Methods of Gentleness and Affection: And most skilful and happy is the Preacher, who can open such Wounds with a Touch so delicate, as to aswage rather than enflame.

SUBJECTS

SUBJECTS of the ſecond Sort, Points of Morality, although of great Importance, require not the ſame Kind of Delicacy: They are not liable to the ſame Enquiries, have not been attacked with ſuch Violence, nor do they give like Offence to the Pride of impatient, and, in its own Conceit, all-ſufficient Reaſon. But you are to obſerve, that they have alſo their Inconveniencies.

THEY are the moſt *trite of all Subjects.* The Arguments they afford being drawn from common Senſe, are ſuch as muſt occur to many; may to all. Men in their own Minds anticipate what you are about to ſay; from whence they are apt to grow liſtleſs and fatigued. The only Remedy for ſuch Evils is, that you ſhould labour the more in giving Force, and Weight, and Power to all you utter; that you ſhould avoid Prolixity, common-place Repetitions, vague and general Reflexions.

FOR there is a wrong Method, very common, in treating of theſe Points, to which Perſons of Genius are liable; the Way of Eſſay-writeing: That is, a Courſe of general Obſervations, neatly expreſſed, put together with Eaſe and Freedom. In which Way, Mr. *Addiſon* furniſhes excellent Models. This, however, is not well-ſuited to the Pulpit; which demands a ſeverer Form. You may open your Deſign with ſome ſuch Reflexions; but theſe, we expect, ſhall quickly lead us into your Subject; to which you are to confine yourſelf ſtrictly; to purſue it through its whole Extent; fit it to the Lives, and preſs it cloſely upon the Conſciences of your Hearers. The great Art is, to be general, without wandering in lax, unſtriking Remarks; to go into Detail, without minuteneſs or trifling.

SPEAKERS of other Kinds, as in the Courts of Juſtice, and great Counſel of the Nation, have uſually Matters of leſs Dignity to diſcourſe upon; but their Arguments are often new. There are Laws, Facts, Evidences to be explained, ſtated, compared; which naturally raiſe Curioſity, and keep up Attention: Preachers have, as we obſerved, the Advantage of Subjects ſuperior in Weight, Beauty, and Excellence; but then all are beaten and exhauſted: And there is nothing within the Reach of human Art more difficult, than to beſtow upon what is common the Graces of Novelty. The wonderful Magnificence of Nature in its regular Courſe paſſeth unobſerved; every the leaſt Variation from this ſurprizeth and engageth. And it hath been well obſerved, that it is eaſier to riſe to Indifference in Preaching, than in Pleading; more difficult to arrive at Excellence.

WHEN you have thus fixed upon a Subject, your next Care ſhould be, to chuſe a proper *Text*. The Manner of chuſing a ſhort Paſſage of holy Scripture, and forming a Diſcourſe upon that, was introduced very late into the Church [*a*]; and is liable to much Inconvenience;

[*a*] Inſtances of it are found in ſome of the antient Fathers: but are very rare.

nience; it mightily cramps the Preacher, limiting him usually to a Part of a Subject, seen in a particular Light. It confines him often to a Method strained and unnatural: And frequently occasions Prolixity. But since we now find this Manner universally established, it should be our Business, instead of enlarging on its Evils, to guard against them, and improve on its Advantages, for some it may possibly have; one acknowledged; being useful to prevent a vague undetermined Way of Declamation; for which Purpose it was probably at first introduced.

It seemeth to be no uncommon Practice, after the Discourse hath been composed, then to search for a suitable Text; a Proceeding which cannot succeed well. For by this Means it cometh to pass, that the Text is little more than a Lemma or Motto, as it were, to the Discourse, bearing only a faint and distant Resemblance. The Preacher appeareth to have little Regard to it. After the first setting out, he quickly loseth Sight of it, and returneth to it no more; which is both improper and ungraceful. For the Discourse should be the Text unfolded, the Text should be the Discourse in Abstract: They should be as the Seed and Plant; which latter is the Seed drawn out by Nutriment, and organised in its just and full Dimensions.

From the Text whatsoever you observe should flow naturally, as from its Source; should tend to illustrate, to confirm, its Sense,

or

or ſhould recommend Conſequences deduced from it; for we ſhould firſt form right Notions, and then make them the Foundation of right Practice.

FARTHER, Experience teaches, that whenever your Text is pronounced, every attentive Hearer immediately formeth to himſelf ſome general confuſed Notion of that which you ſeem prepared to diſcourſe upon: Inſtead of proceeding in which, if you carry him a quite different Road, you diſappoint him, and therefore for the moſt Part diſpleaſe.

AGAIN. Some Perſons delight in chuſing a very ſingular Text, that they may ſhew their own Art in the Uſe made of it, in extracting much from what appears barren. Others again ſelect one the moſt diſtant, and exhibit, as they think, ſurpriſing Skill in bending it to their Purpoſe. Not ſeldom ye may obſerve others to pick out a difficult Paſſage, and make pompous Oſtentation of Learning in clearing all Doubts, and unfolding its true Senſe: Or what is leſs juſtifiable, they chuſe out a known Text, yet give it a new Interpretation, and make this imagined Diſcovery the Groundwork of their ſubſequent Remarks. Many other Singularities of a like Sort one might enumerate; but it may ſuffice to have mentioned theſe, and to obſerve, once for all, that every Thing of this Sort, every Deviation from the plain Road of Cuſtom and common Senſe in this Article, bordering on Affectation, and ſpringing from, or juſtly ſuſpected of Vanity, ought

ought to be avoided. The Scripture aboundeth in Doctrines and Precepts expressed with Clearness and Strength: Chuse out one the most apposite, full, and of moderate Length, so as not to puzzle the Attention, or burthen the Memory of the Hearer: From hence, as the Fountain, let your Discourse flow.

WHEN you have in this Manner determined on your Point, you should above all Things carefully consider it; revolve it often in your Mind, turn and return it, view it on every Side, in all Lights, in every Aspect and Position, in its several Connexions, Resemblances, Oppositions, Differences: Consult also those who have written well upon it, that you may have the fullest, most accurate Survey of it which is possible.

BUT in this last Article use some Caution: By reading you may furnish yourself with Materials; but the forming of these, the Workmanship, must be your own: Wherefore, beware of following any other too closely; an Inconvenience apt to spring from Study; your Thoughts, instead of opening to themselves a new Course, will flow in the Channel already opened. To prevent which, allow yourself, after the Perusal of good Writers, a proper Interval, before you attempt to write; that you may, in the mean while, have forgotten the Form and Order of what you have read; that now, finding the Materials dissolved and scattered, you may work them up according to your

your own Faculties, into a new Piece, of your own Composition and Contexture.

THUS you should gather your Materials from all Parts, and make your Collection as copious as may be, because out of these you are to select the best and fittest; and Superfluity is necessary, that you may be able and willing to reject.

Do we not hear every Day, Discourses flimsy, thin-spun, and Wire-drawn? The Cause of which is, that the Speakers set out upon scanty Materials, and not having Stuff enough to last out properly their Half-hour, are forced to make it up as they can, beating out into Surface what should have gone into Solidity.

GLIDE not over, as the Manner too often is, and lightly skim a Subject; but endeavour to go to the Bottom, touch only upon what may be useful, but exhaust that, and endeavour to leave your Hearers entirely satisfied. Some Persons labouring to grasp great Extent, embrace nothing but Surface: Let it be your Care to go deeper, and contract your Compass.

AFTER having collected your Materials; your next Care is to range them in good Order. Method is an Article principally to be regarded, because upon it chiefly depend the Clearness and Strength of what you deliver, of Consequence, its Influence and Usefulness: And [*a*] Foreigners

[*a*] *See* a very extraordinary Judgment in this Matter, attributed to Monsieur DAGUESSEAU, lately Chancellor of *France*, in the Preface of the 3d Tome of a Collection of

Foreigners who do Justice to the good Sense and Understanding of the *English*, charge them with Defect herein; they have Abundance, but in Confusion.

WHEN therefore you have selected out of the Mass abovementioned the Thoughts fittest for your Purpose, you are to dispose each in its proper Place, thus forming the Chain and Series of your Discourse. You may know when this is rightly accomplished by this Trial: Can you leave out any Part? Can you transpose any without injuring the Whole? For whilst this may be done, there is some Defect in the Disposition; and you must not quit the Work, until it stand the Proof of this Essay! This Task claims your first Care: Afterwards, you may apply yourself to polish and adorn.

HEREIN you may look upon yourself as following the Example of a Painter, suppose of History or Landskip: He first lays his Design, fixeth upon the Figures most suitable to his Purpose, disposeth them in the best Manner, sketches them out rudely, traceth the Outlines; which being done, he proceeds to work upon them, bestoweth Substance and Colour; and lastly, retouching all, addeth those lively Graces which compleat and animate the Whole.

BUT before you proceed thus far, there is one Thing relative to Design, worthy of particular

of Voyages, by Abbé PREVOST. His Words are these, *Voilà vos* Anglois *disoit il; avec de l'esprit & du savoir, qu'on ne leur conteste pas, ils n'ont jamais entendu la vraie forme d'un livre.*

cular Observation: That every Discourse should have *one principal Subject*; the Explanation, Proof, and Enforcement whereof should be the main Scope, to which all other Heads should be subordinate; or rather they should be only Branches or different Views of it, and all concur in the End to its Strength and Illustration.

THERE is no Work of Art, in which this Unity of Design is not essential to its Beauty and Perfection. Thus it is in Painting, where every Piece should represent one Subject, and contain one principal Figure. The Violation of which Rule is allowed to be a Defect in the Master-piece of the greatest Artist, the *Transfiguration*, which comprehends in one Piece, two distinct independent Actions; although it is at the same Time confest, that each of these singly considered, is admirable. The same Remark extends equally to Poesy; and the *Hecuba* of *Euripides* is in like Manner defective, containing two distinct Actions, faulty thus joined, separately very beautiful.

THE Rule is indeed founded in Nature. We can contemplate but one Object at once; this engageth our whole Attention; and although its several Appendages and Relations may please by adding an agreeable Variety, yet the Mind still seeketh to dwell on this one, and the chief Object must predominate, must govern, and reign through the Whole.

HENCE we see how unskilfully they act, who making Choice of a Text, containing a Recital of different Virtues or Vices, take their Divi-

sion

ſion from thence, and treat ſeparately of each. Thus they form, properly ſpeaking, not one Diſcourſe, but ſeveral tacked together, which bears a clumſy Appearance, and being confuſed, is burthenſome to the Memory. Beſides, multiplying Subjects, they talk ſuperficially of all.

THIS Error, where it is not the Effect of Lazineſs, ſprings from Barrenneſs of Invention; when one unable to write concerning one Point, ſo as to frame a Diſcourſe of proper or cuſtomary Length, tries to help this Poverty, by taking in a Multiplicity of Subjects.

INSTANCES hereof we ſee in the Comedies of *Terence*, who borrowing the Plots from *Menander*, hath formed each Play by crowding two of the *Greek* Poet, into one: And our modern Tragedies are uſually compoſed in the ſame Way; where the Poets wanting Genius, or Art, or Application, or partly perhaps in Compliance to the ill Judgment of a prejudiced Audience, inſtead of working up one important Fact into a compleat Drama, chooſe two or more independent Tranſactions; thus unſkilfully ſupplying in ill-joined Facts, Defect in Nature, Sentiment, and well-ſupported Character.

THE following may be a general Direction concerning Method in the Kind of Compoſitions now before us.

IF there be any Degree of Obſcurity in your Text, whether in the Expreſſion, or ariſing from its Connexion with other Parts, explain it.

DISTINGUISH the ſeveral Particulars which are contained in it, and which are to form the ſeveral Heads.

NEXT prove the Truth of each.

AFTER, remove, if you think it neceſſary, Objections.

Laſtly, DEDUCE important (practical) Conſequences.

CONCERNING each of which I ſhall proceed to make ſome ſhort Remarks.

BUT before theſe, I ſhould take Notice, that it is uſual to place an *Exordium*, or Introduction: Which ſeems to be a convenient and reaſonable Cuſtom, becauſe it leadeth the Hearer gently and by eaſy Degrees into the Subject, the Entrance into which would otherwiſe be harſh and abrupt. This was the Practice of the antient Orators, except in ſome very rare Caſes of high Paſſion, or in Affairs of unforeſeen Hurry and Precipitation: Or as *Milton* finely expreſſes it,

" As when of old ſome Orator renown'd
" In *Athens* or free *Rome*, where Eloquence
" Flouriſh'd, ſince mute, to ſome great Cauſe addreſs'd;
" Stood in himſelf collected.——
" Sometimes in Height began, as no Delay
" Of Preface brooking thro' his Zeal of Right:
" The Tempter all impaſſion'd thus begun."

Of this latter vehement Kind is the firſt Oration Againſt *Cataline*; and that of *Ajax* in *Ovid*.

BUT this, if to be ventured upon at all in the preſent Caſe, ſhould be very ſeldom. It hath been attempted by Perſons of good Talents, and

and their Succefs, I think, not encouraging [a]. If indeed you begin with ardent Paffion, how fhall you keep it up? There is great Danger of the Flame ending in Smoke [b]. It is therefore fit to premife fome few Words, that may befpeak Attention, may conciliate Favour, or excite Curiofity. But Care fhould be taken, that fuch Introduction be fhort; not far-fetched, nor pompous; not refined in Thought, nor affected in Diction; fomething different from, yet nearly connected with the Text; fuch as falleth without ftraining, into your Defign; fuch as feemeth not to have been looked for, but to have offered itfelf.

IT is of mighty Importance that this Part fhould be rightly executed, and it is that, in which there is moft Danger of failing. The beft Precept appears to be this: "When you "have formed your whole Plan, fearch among "your Inferences for the moft eafy and natural "one: This will furnifh a good Introduction: "But take Care that it do not afterwards ap-"pear; at leaft in the fame Light."

AFTER this Preface, you go on in the next Place, to propofe the feveral Articles, which you intend to make the Heads of your enfuing Difcourfe. Concerning which Cuftom, Opinions differ.

IN

[a] Of this Kind is the 22d Sermon of Dr. *Atterbury*— On thefe Words, *Bleffed is he who fhall not be offended in me*; which beginneth thus,—" And can any Man be offend-" ed in thee bleffed Jefu, who haft undertaken, and done, " and fuffered fo much? &c."

[b] Non fumum ex fulgore, fed ex fumo dare lucem. HOR.

IN Oppoſition to it, ſome have affirmed, "That it gives a diſguſting Air of Dryneſs and "Formality, by preſenting to the Hearer be- "forehand, a View of the Entertainment "which is deſigned for him; which Anticipa- "tion taketh away from it the Charm of No- "velty, and blunteth the Edge of his Curioſity: "Whereas it would be much better to lead "him on by Degrees, and let the Subject un- "fold itſelf. Then would all be preſerved "new: And beſides, he would have the Plea- "ſure of diſcovering himſelf that Method, "which theſe Diviſions too officiouſly point out "him. Accordingly it is in this Manner, that "the polite Antients have written; and if you "were to reduce a moral Treatiſe of *Tully* to "the faſhionable Form of diſtinct Heads, you "would greatly diminiſh it's Elegance and "Beauty."

THIS Reaſoning it is acknowledged, hath Force; and is in a great Meaſure juſt with Regard to Works, which are intended as were the Treatiſes of the Antients there cited, to be read in the Leiſure and Silence of the Cloſet: But doth it extend to thoſe which are pronounced only? A Reader may pauſe to conſider, may look back, may recollect, and if the Thread hath eſcaped, may uſe all Helps of Thought and Examination to recover it; none of which are in the Hearer's Power; but the Words once uttered if they be not imprinted on his Memory, or if they paſs too quick for his Apprehenſion, cannot be recalled. Such additional Helps there-

therefore as can be offered, to his Underſtanding and remembring what is ſaid, ought certainly to be ſupplyed.

IT ſeems for this Reaſon to be a wiſe and uſeful Cuſtom, to lay before your Audience a ſuccinct Account of the principal Points, which you mean to ſpeak upon. This general Survey will excite their Curioſity: Each new Head you paſs on to will be a kind of Breathing-place, and ſerve to renew their Attention: And when the Whole is finiſhed, they will by this Means have a more diſtinct Remembrance of what you paſt through. When you are to conduct one through a ſtrange Country; by ſhewing to him a ſmall Chart of it, or a ſhort Deſcription of the chief Towns or remarkable Objects, he is to meet with, you would contribute to render his Journey more agreeable; he would behold them afterwards with more Pleaſure becauſe of this imperfect Glimpſe; and would have alſo the Satisfaction of knowing frequently, what Part of his intended Courſe he was in.

THIS Part of dividing your Subject properly is of great Moment. And of ſo nice and difficult a Nature is it, that Criticks have obſerved among the many Diviſions in the Works of *Tully*, but one which they allow to be perfect, not liable to Objection [c]. This we may well account

[c] The Diviſion in the Oration for *Muræna:* "The "whole Accuſation, O Judges, may be reduced to three "Heads. One conſiſts in Objections againſt his Life; "the ſecond relates to the dignity of his Office: The "third includes the Corruption with which he is charged." This, ſaith *Eraſmus*, is perfectly clear; contains nothing

account Hypercriticiſm and Exceſs of Delicacy. What ſeems moſt material to obſerve is:

" THAT the Heads of your Diſcourſe ſhould
" ariſe eaſily from the Text. That they ſhould
" be few, I ſuppoſe hardly exceeding four or
" five at moſt. That each one ſhould be alto-
" gether diſtinct from the others. And if it
" may be, each ſpring from the foregoing."

IT would not be difficult to produce many Inſtances from our own Writers of good Diviſions; but Examples in theſe Caſes ſuit ill with the Brevity of my Deſign. One however of more than ordinary Exactneſs I ſhall juſt mention.

THE Text is this — *Judas, betrayeſt thou the Son of Man with a Kiſs?* The Preacher conſiders firſt the Fact; next makes ſome uſeful Obſervations upon it.—Upon the former Article, every Word in the Text ſaith he, tends to colour the Fact with a ſeveral Blackneſs. 1ſt. *Betrayeſt thou*, denoteth Malice. 2d. *Judas*, the Name prefixed pointing out the Betrayer, ſheweth Perfidiouſneſs. 3d. *Judas betrayeſt thou* THE SON OF MAN? implyeth Ingratitude. 4th. *Betrayeſt thou*, WITH A KISS? Charges him with Hypocriſy.—After which, he goes on to prove under the ſecond Head, that every voluntary Act of Sin in ſome Degree containeth all theſe. The Application concerneth every Man [*d*].

As

ſuperfluous; comprehends the whole Cauſe: And alſo is furniſhed by the Adverſary. (De arte concionandi, lib. 1.)

[*d*] See Sermons by Dr. *Young*, Vol. 1.

As to the concealed Method before contended for, that, in which the ſeveral conſtituent Articles are not ſpecifyed, it is to be obſerved, that altho' you do not make Uſe of it in the Whole of your Sermon, yet you may, and ought in the ſeveral Parts thereof. For, as every Head hath it's Method, ſo is it reſolvable into ſeveral Heads, which altho' you treat of in their exact Order, yet you are not to enumerate.

THUS may your Diſcourſe be ſaid to reſemble an Animal Body, in which the great Parts are at firſt Sight diſtinguiſhed; but the many leſſer Veſſels which ſupport and compoſe the greater, the Veins, Arteries, and Nerves, altho' equally diſtinct and eſſential to the Whole, are concealed from View, and appear only by Diſſection.

LECTURE the Twenty-first.

On the same Subject.

THE Proof or Reasoning Part, which is the next in Order, you are to regard as the most important of all, and accordingly take Care to be most exact herein. I shall not repeat the Observations [*a*] formerly made on this Head, all which are applicable here; but some not at all, or then slightly mentioned, as being peculiar to this Place, I shall now go on to lay before you.

IN this Part you never can be too clear; the only Caution is, in seeking Perspicuity not to become prolix. For Shortness is here of especial Use: It keeps up Attention by the quick Succession of Ideas; it renders Argument more easy to the Memory; and also gives Strength to it. For in lengthening the Chain, you weaken it. Mathematicians, the great Masters of Reason are sensible of this Truth; the most skilful among them study as much as they conveniently may, to abridge Demonstrations: And herein it is, that the Analytick Method in many Respects inferior, hath a considerable Advantage

[*a*] Lecture 8 and 9.

vantage over the Geometrical, being more concise.

A Fault before touched upon, and among Preachers even of Note, too common, is a Redundancy in this Article: The using of a Multitude of Arguments. Zeal for Truth is apt to mislead a Speaker into thinking, that no Proofs should be omitted; that he hath never said enough while any Thing remains unsaid, As an Instance of this Excess, I believe one may cite the Works of Doctor *Barrow*; who having a strong Faculty of Reason, together with a vast Compass of Learning, and a lively Imagination, abounds with excellent Arguments on every Subject: He exhausts whatever he treateth of; you can add nothing: But such Plenty often causeth Confusion. If somewhat were retrenched the rest would have more Vigour: You would see more distinctly, and comprehend more fully: For the Mind, like a Vessel once full, if you pour in more, runs over and loses: Or as the Poet well expresses it,

Omne supervacuum pleno de pectore manat.

BESIDES, in thus bringing together numerous Arguments, it is probable, that you will employ some that are weak, dubious, perhaps false; and Lord *Bacon* [*b*] justly observes, that one idle Reason weakeneth all the good which went before.

YOU should choose few, clear, and strong, and just; set these in the fairest Light from Order and Expression; drive them to a Point:

[*b*] Essays.

Thus ſhall their Force make ample Compenſation for the Want of Numbers. A ſkilful General preferreth few, well-diſciplined Troops to a raw unpractiſed Multitude, whoſe Number makes them unwieldy and unactive, a Crowd rather than an Army.

A Preacher after declaring that he hath demonſtrated a Point, yet goes on to new Proofs: But why? At any Rate, I ſhall not liſten; for if he hath performed what he ſays, what Need of more? What can be added to Demonſtration? If he hath not; how ſhall I believe him now? Or, already deceived, expect better?

A ſecond Fault, not leſs common nor leſs hurtful is this. Perſons who write in theſe Days complain, that they have come into the World too late; that there remain to them Gleanings only, to gather up, in the Harveſt of Letters: They have been prevented in all Subjects; and if they would not, as too often is the Caſe, teize with endleſs Repetition, they find themſelves compelled to leave the beaten Road. Hence their Ambition is, on all Occaſions, to ſay, not that which is juſt, but new; which, in Morals, muſt needs be oftentimes falſe.

To this Cauſe we may attribute the extraordinary Doctrines, of which modern Times have been ſo wonderfully and unhappily fruitful.

SUCH is the fancyed Conſpiracy between Divines and Atheiſts, with which the Imagination of a late Writer ſeems to have been as much haunted, as was that of *Don Quixot* by his Necromancers. Hence the chimerical Suppoſition, on, that because Reason in it's highest Degree of Perfection may discover a Man's whole Duty, therefore in all Cases and under all Disadvantages, it may. And the contrary Extreme to this; that all moral Knowlege undiscoverable otherwise, flows immediately from Revelation. Hence the Assertion, that the proper Trial of Truth is by Ridicule. And the Attempt to prove, that the Writings of *Moses* are divinely inspired, from this single Consideration, that he hath not made mention of a future State.

SOME of these are advanced with an ill Design; others by pious Men, and intended well: I take Notice of both Sorts, that we may be the more on our Guard; for all Errors, those flowing from the best Causes, may be dangerous: And it is by these Means, this Study of Novelty, that most of the Well-meaning at least, are betrayed into them.

BUT if, in all Cases they are hurtful, they are also most absurd in Sermons; which are designed for Practice, not Speculation; to make Men good Livers, not acute Disputants. I remember to have heard more than once from the Pulpit, the most subtle Conjectures concerning the Nature of the Soul, it's Subsistence and Actions in a separate State, explained, as the Preacher called it, to a drowzy, or astonished, assuredly fatigued Audience, I know not whether more unintelligibly, or presumptuously. I remember to have heard in the same Manner, Attempts to reconcile the Fore-knowlege of God with the Liberty of Man. The

most

most sacred Mysteries of the Christian Faith, the Motives and Councils of the Almighty, I have known likewise examined into with the same Temerity. Sometimes a plain reasonable Audience is entertained with new Discoveries in the Old Testament, deduced from a profound Skill in the Hebrew Tongue: Or, again, is edifyed with Attempts to revive the long dormant Notion of a Millennium.

I SPEAK not at present concerning the Truth of these Matters, nor concerning the Propriety or Expediency of discussing such in general: But certainly they ought not to be discussed on these Occasions; this is not their Place. On the contrary, retain you always in View the only End of preaching, the reforming the Lives of Men, the making them *wise unto Salvation:* You then cannot go wrong. Useful Points explained, recommended with Strength of Reason and Sincerity, make up the Whole; do this, and you need not apprehend that you shall not be listened to; good Arguments well handled are always sufficiently new.

INGENIOUS Men are liable to a third Error. From a Manner of reading and thinking deeply, they fix in themselves so strong an Habit, that on all, on the simplest Occasions, they are apt to run into this their accustomed Way. Are they to recommend a Branch of moral Duty, as Justice or Temperance? They raise upon it Speculations, which a plain Man cannot rightly understand: They are for ever running back to the Foundation, drawing Proofs from the eternal

nal Difference of Things, from the Love of Truth, universal Benevolence, or a supposed moral Taste: Which Principles, whether wrong or rightly fixed upon, is not now the Question; but undoubtedly, here they are altogether misplaced; and a Physician called upon for Advice, might as properly undertake to preserve or recover Health, by entertaining his Patient with a learned Dissertation of Anatomy, the animal Oeconomy, or Nature and Operation of Medicines.

FEW, if any there are, who seriously doubt, whether they ought to be temperate and just: But wherein consist these Duties; what Advantages they lead to; how we may be induced to practise them; what Motives there are to encourage, what Precepts to direct, what Temptations to avoid:—These are Articles intelligible and useful, not involved with Subtilties, and affecting all Mankind.

THE Writings of a very learned [c] Prelate seem liable to this Objection. In Discourses, wherein he professedly deduceth the Obligation to Virtue, from considering the Frame of human Nature, composed with strong and masterly Reasoning, yet as Sermons, in my Apprehension, not unexceptionable, allow to him, if you please, this Manner; at least, he hath excelled in them so much, that even in blaming, we cannot but admire. What I would remark is, that on other Subjects, where this Nicety of Disquisition is

[c] Dr. *Butler*, Bishop of *Durham*.

is not necessary, he, notwithstanding, useth the same.

DOTH he treat of Compassion? It's Nature, Origine, the Texture, as it were, of the Soul is here analyzed with refined Sagacity. If he is to warn you against Self-deceit, he leads you into the inmost Recesses of the Heart; with much good Sense; but who can follow? So it is in treating of Resentment; even in explaining the most obvious of all practical Duties, the Love of our Neighbour. It is indeed a reigning Character. And however valuable are the Works of this good and learned Man, for this I do with Pleasure acknowlege, yet considered, as delivered from the Pulpit, they are herein faulty. And I mention this Defect, the rather, as I have observed Men of Sense to have been led often astray by an Imitation of him; and in Truth such only can imitate him.

HENCE the Faults of eminent Writers, however unwilling we are to censure such, ought chiefly to be remarked in Lectures of this Kind, not only as the Merit of the censured makes the Example more Striking, but because their Faults are more likely to infect others, the Genius which excuseth their Errors, rendering them more dangerous: And, this I hope, will plead my Apology, if I sometimes blame where I most honour.

THE Sum is; We should in preaching on moral as well as religious Points, avoid whatever Things are nice, difficult, subtile: They puzzle without instructing, they confound without con-

convincing; and with regard to the Bulk of Mankind, in this Case most to be regarded, are altogether useless.

THIS leads to a farther Observation:—You should as much as possible, adapt yourself to the Capacities of your Audience. It may be a *learned* one; a *mixed*, or an *illiterate*.

BEFORE one of the first Kind, you are more at Liberty in the Point mentioned; but the Case occurs so rarely, that it is scarcely worth While to make an Exception for it.

BEFORE the second, you may be allowed to argue with Closeness; to a certain Degree of Length; perhaps not altogether without Subtilty; because you may suppose that very many of your Hearers shall comprehend you so far; and I will not say, but that in a *mixed* Audience, it may be reasonable to indulge somewhat to the pleasing of one Part, where due Care is taken of instructing the other.

BUT in the last Case, which is vastly the most frequent, every Thing of this Sort, all nice, curious, and complicated Reasonings should be laid aside; Arguments should be used, that are plain, consisting of few Steps, drawn from Authority, common Sense, and Experience.

AND of the three, this last, altho' least prized, is, I believe, the hardest to execute very well. To be perfectly clear, yet never tedious, unadorned, yet never insipid, close in Reasoning, yet never obscure, is no small Task: The true Value of which Simplicity is little understood or attended to by the Generality, who think that

any

any Thing, however carelessly written, may be sufficient for an unlearned Crowd; an Imagination as groundless, as it is presumptuous. For there is a Fund of natural Reason in the Breasts of the Illiterate, which enables them, so far as their Knowlege extends, to judge rightly. And it may be observed in Favour of such, that a fine Discourse which shall please a learned Hearer, and pleaseth usually the more, because it is addressed to him exclusively, is indeed lost as to these; yet a plain one suited to these, is, and deserves to be, approved by the most learned Hearer: Good Sense is for all Ranks and Understandings.

BUT here is a Difficulty which lies in the Way; "How can one be supposed to vary "the Form and Tenor of his Discourses ac-"cording to the Diversities of his Audience? "This is not possible."

FOR which Reason the following seems to be good Advice. Form them originally in such Manner, as to be capable of being adapted by small Changes to every Kind of Audience: The Way to accomplish which is, by bringing them as near as may be to the amiable Simplicity before-mentioned, which is suited to the Liking of all Ranks.

THIS I acknowlege is by no Means easy: Some happy Dispositions indeed there are, who fall into it naturally, but usually it is the Fruit of serious Reflexion and long Experience: It costs a Man of quick Parts and extensive Knowlege, much Pain and Self-denial to reject every Thing

Thing curious, and fine, and acute, which his Faculties and Erudition offer to him, and confine himself within the Limits of common Sense. But after all, the principal Difficulty herein is not from Nature, but our own Fault, from wrong Passions, Ambition, Interest, or Love of Praise. "Preach not for Preferment "or Fame, but for God and Virtue: If your "Genius admits it, you will then be concise, "nervous, and plain."

THIS Quality it is, which, in my Opinion, distinguisheth *Tillotson* as a Preacher. *Barrow* is more copious; *Clarke* more learned; *Atterbury* more neat; *Sherlock* more new, more concise, more ingenious: But it seems, that none have preserved together with such a Thread of just clear Reasoning, properly enlivened, so much pure unaffected Simplicity. His Language is that of Sincerity and good Understanding, so flowing and easy, that it is not until after examining and reflecting, that you discover it to be the Production of fine Genius: Which is perhaps the Cause, that his Works are now less read by the Laity, and, as I think, less imitated by the Clergy, than they formerly were.

BESIDES these Proofs, drawn from Reason, which we have hitherto treated of, others there are, taken from holy Scripture, which carrying with them the Weight of Divine Authority, are of the greatest Efficacy; upon which also there are some Remarks fit to be attended to.

INSTEAD

INSTEAD of crowding in a great Number, oftentimes the Caſe, you ſhould chooſe ſuch Paſſages as are expreſs to your Point.

CHOOSE ſuch, as in the original Intention of the ſacred Writer were meant in the Senſe wherein you apply them: For you may have obſerved, that Words are often cited as Authority, which yet compared with the Context have originally a very different Meaning.

NEITHER ought you to prove any Aſſertion by difficult and doubtful Paſſages, when you may do it by ſuch as are plain: Yet this is no uncommon Practice; and beſides other Inconveniences to which it is ſubject, hath alſo the Appearance of Oſtentation.

IT ſeems, that Doctor *Clarke* although undoubtedly not from this laſt mentioned Motive, hath exceeded herein. He goes out of his Way ſometimes for a Page or two together, in explaining difficult Parts of holy Scripture, altho' not neceſſary to the Proof of his Doctrine, and ſometimes ſcarcely, if at all connected with his Text.

" BUT his Reader is thereby uſefully in- " ſtructed." I do not deny it: And, if I were to conſult my own Liking, I will add, if you pleaſe Advantage, I would not have them fewer; but we ſpeak now of Propriety, of what is in itſelf fit, not what is recommended by extraordinary Talents; and that appears not to be the Place for ſuch *Inſtruction*. The Doctor acts here the Part of a very good Annotator, but not that of a Preacher. Why not write a Comment

ment for this Purpose? Why Sermons? It is true, his Genius as well as Reading led him this Way, as he was very learned, sagacious, and happy in such Interpretation; but here he should have resisted and confined his Genius. The Remark, at least, may be so far useful, in warning those not to follow his Manner, who want his Genius.

It is not unusual, beside Quotations, to interweave with your own, Expressions of holy Scripture, which gives to Stile an Air of Gravity and Dignity: Wherein however a Mean should be preserved. You should not appear to seek after such. Nor make the Mixture too frequent. Nor alter often the Contexture of the Scripture by breaking it and intermingling indiscriminately your own, which is not enough respectful: Neither use it on slight Occasions. Least of all, should you introduce these Passages, in Order to give them a new Application or Turn, containing Liveliness and Wit.

Heathen Antiquity likewise furnishes both Examples and Arguments of much Strength and Weight in the Cause of Virtue: But these should be at all Times used sparingly; before a popular Audience, scarcely ever: Because, they have an Air of Erudition, there misplaced: Because, on such Occasions our Thoughts are turned to a much higher History and Authority: And because, they are not necessary; Reason and Scripture want not such Aid.

To conclude this Head. It is fit for the most Part, in a Course of long Reasoning, and consist-

consisting of many Branches, at the End of each Head, or rather when the Whole is ended, to give a Summary or short Recapitulation of all; which, shewing at once the Substance of the whole Series of Argument, will both present a more distinct View of it, and will impress it more deeply on the Memory: And such Recapitulation may not improperly be used to close the Discourse.

BUT the more customary, and generally speaking, a much better Way of concluding, is that, we have before laid down; with an Application to your Hearers by Way of INFERENCES; for this is the last Article comprized under Method, which I undertook to speak upon.

IN the Choice of these, as in them chiefly consists the Utility and main End of the whole Discourse, great Care should be employed. The chief Cautions which occur to my Thoughts are the following.

First. CONFINE not yourself to very GENERAL Inferences. There is not any Text, from which you may not draw Inferences relative to our general Duty, or to almost any Branch of it, that you please; but this is unskilful and unpleasing.

CHUSE out such only, or principally, as are peculiar to your Text, and spring from it in the Light wherein you have considered it: They should follow and not be dragged after; should be such, as every Man when he hath heard them, imagines that he would himself have thought

thought of. Thus you ſhall preſerve Unity, and make your whole Work intire and of one Piece; which Union, beſide its agreeable Impreſſion on the Mind, will give Strength to every Part.

Farther. TAKE Care, that the ſame Inference do not appear in different Places; that the Beginning, or what was uſed in the reaſoning Part, or had occurred as an incidental Obſervation, be not here brought again into View; which offends by the Want of Method, and by Repetition: Or if ſometimes that be allowable, you muſt ſet it in a new Light, or ſhew it to be worthy of this ſecond Examination from its extraordinary Moment.

INFERENCES ſhould be ſo diſpoſed, that they may grow upon the Hearer; that each may be of more Weight than the preceding, and the moſt ſtriking be placed laſt. The ſame I would have underſtood of their Extent; the more general ſhould lead, the particular follow, ending with that which is cloſeſt, and comes home to each Man's own Breaſt.

THEIR Order likewiſe ſhould be ſuch, that each may bring in naturally the following; which will render them more clear to the Underſtanding, and eaſier to the Memory.

REMARK eſpecially, that although Reaſon hath Place in every Part, yet theſe Inferences are moſt properly the Seat of Paſſion. You have convinced and taught; here you are to incline, to perſwade.

AN

[a] AN eminent Person seems to have been defective in this Part. His Inferences right in Matter, just in Sense, clear in Reason, are yet cold: They leave the Hearers Mind indifferent, unenlivened.

YOUR Inferences grounded in Truth and good Sense, should, if possible, be highly moving; your Thoughts and Words should be Darts, as it were, of Flame, to pierce, to kindle, and remain fixed in the Hearts of your Hearers.

THIS last Consideration leads to a new Article in the Composition of a Sermon, very worthy of Consideration; the Address to the *Passions*. Concerning which Subject, before pretty largely treated of, there remain some Things untouched, and belonging more especially to this Kind of Writing, which I shall mention with all convenient Brevity.

IT is allowed, that a Preacher should be able to move the Passions: But the Attempt is delicate; if he miscarry, it is greatly prejudicial; he then becomes disgusting, not seldom ridiculous. "What therefore shall I do? Shall I "give up as desperate, the only Way whereby "one can greatly excel? Or shall I run so "great a Risk of Contempt?"

IN Answer, the best Advice I can think of is the following: Consider well, have you a Genius turned to this Pathetick? If not; by no Means attempt it; for you never can succeed well; Precept, Labour, Study, all are vain.

"BUT

[a] Dr. CLARKE.

" But how ſhall I know my own Genius?
" Nothing is more hard. Men misjudge there-
" in every Day."

It is true: And the following Rules may, I think, be of Uſe.

Recollect if you can, in the Eſſays of your younger Years, which is the Courſe you have taken: For at that Time Genius, leſs altered by Imitation or Art, diſplayeth its innate Bent, and Impulſe.

Observe afterwards. In thinking of any Subject, what is the Path into which your firſt Thoughts hurry you, before Reflection checks their Career? This ſpontaneous Wandering ſheweth the Direction of Nature.

Again, Which are the Studies you are moſt inclined to? Do you lean towards Mathematicks, or Metaphyſicks, or Works of Fancy; and in the mixed, which Part draws you moſt powerfully? In the Writings of others, what is it which pleaſeth you moſt at firſt View? This Inclination, this Preference ſpeaks the Voice of Genius.

Suppose that each of theſe Marks fail, that all taken together may; I believe you may ſtill judge ſecurely, if to them you add theſe others.

Reflect, wherein do you make the eaſieſt and quickeſt Progreſs. Every regular Diſcourſe conſiſteth of ſeveral Kinds; it would be abſurd to make one wholely up of Pathetick: Now, which of theſe ſeveral Kinds do you fall into moſt readily, and advance in moſt ſwiftly?

IF your Genius be truly pathetick, you will indeed take Care of the plain and argumentative Parts, because they are necessary to your Design, and to the Success of the Whole; but you will not find in them the same Facility, or Delight as in the others: You will go through them, like a Traveller in a rugged Road, with Discretion and Caution; whereas you come to the other as fair champain Ground, which you fly over with Pleasure and Rapidity.

AND lastly, to make this Characteristic compleat, take in the *Success* also.

EVERY Person may be sure of discovering this by the Help of reasonable Attention, without Imputation of Lightness or curious Anxiety; especially in the Point before us. Publick Miscarriage herein, affords too great Triumph to a revengeful or satirical Person, to be long past over in Silence. As you find the Event, regulate your Conduct.

FOR, if in all Cases, as we before observed, Men ought to be cautious of attempting the Pathetick, surely in this, we ought to be more especially so; because the more important the Subject, the more serious the Design and Argument, the plainer should be the Manner, the more remote from all Appearance of Skill, or Suspicion of Seduction.

So much for the general Attempt to address the Passions: Particular Observations are these.

OCCASIONS often occur in every Part of your Discourse, in the Explanatory, in the Argumentative, where the Pathetick may be proper: But

But in those Places, it ought to be meerly a Stroke, a Flash, rapid and instantly disappearing. Insist upon, lengthen such Passages: You soon offend, or fatigue.

THE Situation most fit for, I may say, peculiar to this Kind, is the *Application*. Here it is, that you are to unfurl all the Sails, or to raise the Metaphor, that you are to pour forth the whole Storm of your Eloquence; to move, to exhort, to comfort, to terrify, to inflame, to melt. Your Thoughts, your Language, your Voice, your whole Form should be animated. You cannot be too soft, too insinuating, too rapid, too various, too sublime. Among others, we see two Causes, why this (the Application) should be the peculiar Seat of the Pathetick.

ONE is, that before Conviction, every Avenue through which Passion might reach the Mind is shut up, or guarded, and nothing from that Quarter admitted without careful Examination. Convince your Hearer: — Suspicion ceaseth; you obtain Credit with him; he considereth you as a fair and safe Guide; thus openeth out his Passions to your Call; nay, conspireth with you, and industriously assisteth you in your Design of moving them. And because the Exertion of Passion is in the Act itself from our original Constitution, pleasing, he assisteth herein the more willingly, as he is now secure, that he may exert it safely. Before, you wrought against the Stream with much Labour and little Progress; here the Current sets with you, and you glide down easily and swiftly.

ANOTHER Cause is, that Impressions made on the Passions are the strongest, and most sensibly felt by all Men; whence it is prudent as in this Case, to leave them last in the Mind. A Man convinced by Argument believeth, acquiesceth; and often thinks no more of the Matter: Interest his Passions warmly, the Images remain, will be for a long Time at least, easily revived, and for ever returning. [d] *Did not our Hearts burn within us while he talked with us*, is the Character given of his Eloquence, who *spake as never Man spake.*

IT is true, wise States [e] prohibited by express Laws, Pleaders to direct their Discourse to the Passions of the Judges: But the Case of Preachers is very different. A Judge cannot interest himself in the Cause of the Parties without Injustice; to engage his Passions is therefore to seduce him: But in the Duty of a Christian, religious and moral, his most precious Interests are directly concerned; so that to judge of them rightly, his Passions must be, ought to be strongly engaged.

THE best Advice on this Head which we would do well constantly to follow, is this.— Raise your Imagination by a lively Portraiture of all the Circumstances, those in which you write, and those in which you shall pronounce what is written: The Dignity of the Subject, Excellence of the Design, Zeal becoming of your Office, Good that may be wrought, the Place,

[d] St. *Luke*, Chap. 24. ver. 33.
[e] *Egypt* and *Athens*.

Place, the Occasion, the Audience, the Stillness, the Attention, suppose all present at the Instant:—This will awaken every Spark of Genius within you; your Thoughts will be warmed, they will flow in Expressions, strong, lively, glowing; you will have Fire, Force, Dignity.

A Preacher should farther note on this Occasion, that the Effects of the Pathetick vary together with the Audience, and should take his Measures accordingly.

THE Passions are more easily excited in the young than in the old; in Women, as being of a Frame more delicate, than in Men; in the Poor and Distrest, than in the Rich and Fortunate, for Prosperity hardeneth the Heart: In the Illiterate, than in the Learned, because more prone to admire; and, for the same Reason, in those who have lived privately, than in Men of large Experience and much conversant with Affairs.

FARTHER. Fear is the most powerful of our Passions. It's Impressions are the most sudden, sink the deepest, remain the longest. This mighty Engine therefore you should not fail to employ in the Cause of Religion; notwithstanding the visionary Notions of Perfection and Disinterest, with which some have endeavoured to flatter Mankind, in Contradiction to universal common Experience. You should seek, not only to win Men to Virtue by Representations of it's amiable Nature, but deter them from Vice, by just Pictures of it's Deformity; and especial-

ly,

ly, of it's dreadful Consequences; and display before the Eyes of the Sinner, in as strong Colours the unspeakable Terrors, as the tender Mercies of the Almighty Judge: Which I the rather mention, because in this polished Age, I think, there are not wanting, Instances of that false and dangerous Delicacy, well described by the Poet,

To rest the Cushion and soft Dean invite,
Who never mentions Hell to Ears polite.

POPE.

INFERENCES we have said form the best Kind of Conclusion: But here one Thing should be adverted to, " The Time of concluding," Have you not observed many, in the Midst of an Argument or warm Exhortation, surprize their Audience at once with a sudden unexpected Ending?—But every Thing abrupt is ungraceful.

OTHERS there are, who fall into an opposite and worse Extream; who know not how to have done; who seem never to think that they have said enough: But when the Length of the Time, when their own Matter and Manner promise the End to be at Hand, when their Hearers expect it, add yet more, go round and round, and continue hovering about a Point, teizing by this Disappointment and fatiguing the Congregation. This ill Habit, whether proceeding from Zeal or wrong Judgment, omit no Pains to avoid, or correct.

LEARN to distinguish the precise Time of concluding; that is, " When you have executed

" ted the Scheme at firſt laid down; when, you
" have nothing new to ſay; nothing of more
" Weight and Force than what hath been ſaid;
" when you have brought your Argument to a
" Point; while the Impreſſion is ſtrong and
" ſtill warm in the Hearer's Mind."

For this Reaſon it ſeems not an adviſeable Cuſtom, to make ſeveral Sermons on the ſame Text. In which Way, each one loſeth of it's Beauty and Uſefulneſs. Of it's Beauty, becauſe there is no Point from whence you can have at once a View of the Whole, and ſo judge of the Proportions. Of it's Uſefulneſs, becauſe the former Parts leave the Inſtruction imperfect; the others bring it late, to a faint and now confuſed Memory.

Abundance of Matter is alledged as a Reaſon: A good one, where real; but you may for the moſt Part either take a narrower Compaſs; or abridge Words, and by condenſing, ſtrengthen Senſe. I dare not however condemn a Cuſtom juſtified by great Authorities: And ſhall only remark; " That it is much fitter for a Reader
" than Hearer. That it ſhould be uſed ſeldom:
" And not extended beyond two Diſcourſes."

Under the Heads of Proofs and Inferences, we have remarked what ſeems moſt material in the Preacher's Addreſs to Reaſon and Paſſion: It is farther uſeful, ſometimes neceſſary, to relieve and mitigate the Severity of Reaſon and Vehemence of Paſſion, by Strokes of Imagination: But, in Works of this very grave Caſt, theſe ſhould be uſed ſparingly and with Diſcretion.

tion. Such Licences are and may be indulged to young Perſons, in whom ſome Degree of Luxuriancy is to be wiſhed, for; that old Age may have ſomewhat to lop and prune away, without Injury to the Stock. But theſe ill agree with riper Years, and more ſerious Character. A good Rule ſeems to be this, borrowed from a Work ſerious in it's Kind.

IN Tragedy, ſay the Criticks, every Incident, every Speech, one may almoſt add, every Line ſhould have a Reſpect to the main Deſign, ſhould contribute to the Cataſtrophè. It is an Imperfection ever to let the Plot ſtand ſtill, to leave the Stage empty, much more to go out of the Way. In like Manner, having fixed exactly the Plan and Series of your Diſcourſe, examine every Period; doth it go on in the ſame Line? Doth it lead your Hearer nearer to the Concluſion? Do your Images throw in Light to direct, illuſtrate, prove? Or do they meerly entertain? If this latter be the Caſe, reject, cut them off as ſuperfluous. Admit nothing idle, howſoever pleaſing or pretty it may appear. Obſerving this Rule ſteddily, you ſhall not much tranſgreſs in the Uſe of Imagination; your Ornaments will be chaſt and manly.

LECTURE the Twenty-ſecond.

On the ſame Subject.

WE have now taken a particular View of the chief Qualifications requiſite in a Preacher. We have led him thro' the Compoſition of his Sermon; have choſen his Text; fixed on his Manner of collecting Materials; of ſetting out; of reſolving the whole into Heads. We have conſidered him as addreſſing himſelf to Reaſon in his Proofs; to Paſſion in the Inferences; or to Imagination by intermingling decent Ornament. Nothing now remaineth but to make ſome Reflexions on the outward Part, that which is directed to Senſe, on Stile and Pronunciation.

OF the Former I have little to add. If the Sentiments be ſuch as have been deſcribed, they will quickly form to themſelves a ſuitable Stile, clear, eaſy, and unaffected; preſerving throughout a certain Air of Serиouſneſs, and Sincerity, of Plaineſs and Probity.

WHAT hath been remarked as the principal Excellence of hiſtorical Stile, may be applied here

here with yet ſtricter Propriety: Which ſaith one, ſhould be like Oyle itſelf, deſtitute of Scent and Taſte, yet beſtowing an agreeable Flavour and reliſh to other Things. It ſhould appear to have no other Uſe, but to ſhew and communicate the Thought it preſents, itſelf in the mean Time unnoticed; like pure Cryſtal, which exhibiteth external Objects with ſuch perfect Tranſparency, that it eſcapeth the Eye, and nothing ſeems interpoſed.

HENCE on the one Side, the Florid and Swelling, ſet out with hard Words and pompous Phraſes, or encumbered with a Load of ſuperfluous Epithets, or rattling thro' the tedious Concatenation of ſonorous Parentheſes, or twining thro' the unmeaning Circuit of long, languid, polite Phraſeology, ought carefully to be avoided. On the other Hand, an aiming at the Familiar, the deſcending into minute Details, a Deſire of being particular and exact, the Painting of domeſtick Oeconomy, or private Life in their ſmalleſt Circumſtances, have betrayed many good well-meaning Men into Notions and Expreſſions, groſs and low, mean or unſeemly, have rendered offenſive or ridiculous.

FIGURES ſhould be uſed moderately. They are too artificial, and hurt Clearneſs. Hyperbolès and feigning of Perſons leaſt of all: They have the Air of, uſually approach too much, to Fiction. Apoſtrophe's break the Attention, if frequent, diſpleaſe, as turning away from, and for the Time forgetting as it were,

were, the Audience. All Study of Harmony alſo, Sentences ballanced in Oppoſitions, rounded Periods, meaſured Cadence: As again, broken rugged Conciſeneſs, frequent Interrogation, harſh Tranſpoſitions, obſolete or unuſual Conſtructions; all new Terms, whether Abuſes of the Vulgar, or coined in the fruitful Mint of Vanity and conceited innovating Mode, are Faults diligently to be guarded againſt; as deſtructive of that natural Simplicity, which is the Perfection of this Kind of Writing.

But, it is now Time, that I ſhould proceed to the laſt Article Pronunciation. Concerning which, the living Voice, the Council of a judicious Friend, or Inſtructions of a Teacher will be of much more Uſe, than Volumes of Precepts, written in a Cloſet. Theſe can no more lead to Perfection herein, than the ſtudying the moſt exact Theory of Muſick, can alone, enable a Reader to play well upon an Inſtrument, whereto long Application and Practice are requiſite. In like Manner, good Pronunciation muſt be the Effect of frequent Trials, of Diſcipline, and long Experience. Precepts may perfect the Judgment, but help little the performing Power; make Criticks, not Speakers. However, that nothing, ſo far as I can, may be wanting to my Subject, I will not altogether omit this important Article.

It comprehends two Parts, Pronunciation ſtrictly

ſtrictly ſo named, or Speaking; and Action, or Geſture. I will ſay ſomewhat of each.

IN the former, two Things are to be conſidered, the Voice, and the Management of it. The firſt, is the Gift of Nature; and is to be wiſhed for clear, full, and harmonious; and where it fails in theſe, ſuch Defects may to a certain Degree, be remedied, or helped by Care and Exerciſe.

THE Management of it, as being in our own Power, deſerves to be weighed more exactly. In which Point I go on to lay before you a Courſe of Obſervation, that I have often thought may be uſeful; may, at leaſt aſſiſt, a young Perſon to ſet out rightly, and put him in the Way of Improvement.

EVERY Art hath its Origine in Nature, is founded therein; and hath been gradually improved by an Imitation of it. A Collection of Obſervations, made by judicious and experienced Perſons on the Procedure and Operations of Nature, cleared from all Abuſes and Perverſions, form the Rules of each Art.

HENCE the right Method of knowing the true Point of Perfection in any Art, is by tracing it back to its firſt Element, that *Nature*, wherein it is grounded; from thence returning, by purſuing it upward to its higheſt Limit, you will ſee its Connexion with the Original, in every Step, until it arrive at its Height; by which Means, you will clearly diſtinguiſh what is genuine from all Corruptions, foreign Infuſions, and Mixtures of Conceit, Prejudice, or Ignorance.

Ignorance. Apply this for Example to the Point before us.

WOULD you determine what is the properest Manner of pronouncing a Sermon? Carry your Enquiry down to Nature in her simplest Form. See what Instructions she affordeth when beheld in this Light: Follow her from thence up to that Point of Art, whither you would arrive: You will by this Mean, find a Criterion whereby to fix your Judgment in the Article required.

THUS cast your Eye upon the simplest Form of Speech, upon two Persons conversing on a Point indifferent: Here every Thing is familiar, easy, and composed.

IMAGINE a Subject of Debate started: The Voice is instantly raised; the Words are uttered with more Emphasis, and follow each other with more Swiftness, encreasing herein as the Dispute grows warm; and the Dialogue loseth wholely its former tranquil Air.

SUPPOSE next the Scene enlarged. Let one of these Persons talk to a larger Number, as a Company, or whole Family, other Circumstances remaining the same: The Necessity of raising the Voice with the Increase of Number, will in this Case occasion some Change; the Accent will be stronger; the Emphasis every where more marked; the Words will flow with greater Rapidity.

OR, we may set this in a fuller Point of View. You have, it is likely, heard one Person relate to several, to a Dozen, or more, assembled,

ſembled, an Event, containing many Circumſtances; of ſome Length therefore and Variety; and farther of a Nature intereſting greatly the Hearers. Here you obſerve all the Diverſity before-mentioned, but more conſpicuous from the Circumſtances and Occaſion, from the greater Diverſity of Matter, and the ſtronger Effects upon the Audience, which, like Light reflected, act in their Turn by warming the Speaker. Nature herſelf dictates theſe unſtudied Tones, familiar, low, ſoft, quick, acute, loud, and vehement, as the Accidents related demand: To all which the Appearance of the Hearers, as by Sympathy, exactly correſponds.

ADVANCE but a few Steps farther, and you arrive at the Point now under Conſideration.

TRANSPORT in your Imagination, this Man into a Church. Employ him there, in laying before a large Aſſembly, Truths of the greateſt Moment; wherein he is to explain, prove, encourage, exhort, deter, holding forth Rewards and Puniſhments without End. Manifeſt it is, that here alſo, the Manner of Speaking will remain the ſame. As the Audience is now much enlarged, it is true the Voice muſt be raiſed in Proportion; all will be therefore ſomewhat augmented; more Strength, more Vehemence, more Paſſion, more Rapidity in Reaſoning, more Inflexions of the Voice, and more evident Variety; yet the whole Form of Pronunciation, the Tones, the Changes, the Emphaſis are the ſame. It is ſtill the ſame Nature

Nature that operates thro' all these Gradations; that reigns equally from the placid Sounds of familiar Dialogue, to the highest Strains of adorned Declamation.

Now it seems, that a due Attention to these Remarks would guard against the principal Errors, daily committed by publick Speakers; especially, from the Pulpit. One of the chief among which I have observed to be this.

A Person ascending the Pulpit imagines, that he is not to express himself from thence in any Sort, as he doth in private; but with this new Situation assumeth to himself a Character altogether new, a stately, solemn, pompous Gravity. His Language, his Utterance, his Cadences become all affected, and his Voice feigned; which Practice is undoubtedly wrong.

Observe the Foundation, the Progress of Nature; keep her Manner, her several Tones; only heightened so much as to be proportioned to the Place, and suited to the Subject. This is the sure, the sole Way to excel. Every Deviation from hence is wrong.

The several Sentiments of our Minds have each their own peculiar Form of Expression, in the outward Frame of the Body, especially, in the Complexion and Features of the Face. The Passions chiefly, display themselves by evident Signs; their Language is universal, extends to, and is understood by all.

Each of these Passions hath no less its peculiar Tone of Voice, by which it expresseth itself,

itſelf, even in Sounds inarticulate; an Exclamation, an Interjection, a ſimple Cry betray the Emotion, at that Inſtant predominant.

IN articulate Language, theſe Tones are ſtill more various; and the Ear is exquiſitely formed to catch every the minuteſt Difference, every Shade, if I may be allowed ſo to ſpeak, in this marvellous Variety, and report it faithfully to the Mind.

IF then you ſeek to change this eſtabliſhed Order of Nature, if departing from her, you endeavour to utter theſe Sentiments or Affections in a new Manner and Cadence, what do you but perplex and confound? No Ear will acknowledge you; every Heart will be ſhut againſt you; you offend, or at beſt talk to empty Air. Preachers ought maturely to conſider this; and not to ſuppoſe, as too often manifeſtly is the Caſe, that their Office doth immediately inveſt them with a new Perſon, and place them without the Limits of Nature and received Cuſtom.

AND yet, we may remark much of the ſame Miſtake prevailing in our Theatres alſo. Some who ſpeak plainly and well in Comedy, when they aſcend into tragick Parts, aſſume a new Voice; their Cadence, Emphaſis, Tones, are totally different; all become ſwoln, and high, and ranting. The Cauſe is, knowing in general, that there ought to be preſerved a Difference between the two Kinds, but not conceiving what ſhould remain common to both, they overſtretch this Difference to every Article;

Article; and thus become forced, and falſe, and offenſive.

It is worth while to trace this affected, howſoever we name it, Gravity or Solemnity, in Preachers, to its Source, that we may the better guard ourſelves againſt it. It may be in a great Meaſure accounted for thus.

They who have the Care of Children in their earlieſt Years, teach them to read in an unnatural Tone. Attend to the ſame Children talking and reading; their whole Voice is different. In this latter Caſe, they go on in a certain even, unchanging Uniformity, painful originally to themſelves, and inharmonious to the Hearer. And however Experience and Converſation may afterwards leſſen this Difference, yet they ſeldom entirely correct it; and very few read with the ſame Eaſe and genuine Variety of Pronunciation, with which they converſe. Now, as it is among us the univerſal Cuſtom to read our Sermons, the Influence of this early Habit ſheweth itſelf here: We fall into the ſame unnatural formal Pronunciation.

That this Account is true, we ſee farther confirmed by the Example of the Sectaries among us, who uſe extemporary Sermons: They have not any thing of this formal Stiffneſs and the Uniformity, of this, if I may ſo call it, Book-utterance.

This Remark openeth to us a conſiderable Advantage of that which was the antient Way, the preaching extempore. Herein the

 Preacher

Preacher delivering himſelf up, without Controul to his Genius, and uttering the Sentiments of his Heart, as in animated Converſation, expreſſeth himſelf in the ſame genuine, unaffected, always the moſt perſwaſive, Manner; thus transfuſing in all their Heat and Vigour, his own Sentiments, into the Breaſts of his Hearers.

BUT, in order to do Juſtice to this Point, we ſhould obſerve equally, that the Way of reading which we follow, hath alſo its Advantages. Sermons by the Help of Study are more correctly compoſed, with Reaſoning more juſt, Inſtructions more judicious, Points of Faith and Doctrine more fully and truly explained, and what is of mighty Importance, with more exact Regularity and Method: So that, upon the whole, it is not perhaps eaſy to decide, which of theſe deſerveth the Preference, the Advantages and Inconveniencies being ballanced on each Side.

NOR is it material to us; for being as we are by Cuſtom confined to one, we ſhould rather ſtudy to improve that, than admire or vainly regret the other. This much however we may learn from the Compariſon.

As that extemporary Diſcourſe, which approacheth moſt to a ſtudied one in Regularity of Compoſition and Purity of Stile, is the beſt; in like Manner, among ſtudied Diſcourſes that undoubtedly excelleth, which is compoſed with the eaſy Air, and pronounced with the unaffected

fected Warmth and Fluency of the Extemporary.

Of Courſe, the worſt of all, is the Method purſued in foreign Churches, that of ſpeaking elaborate Sermons without Book; which exposeth to all the Diſadvantages of Reading, diſturbing the Utterance by perpetual Fear of forgetting, and Hazard of miſplacing; with the additional Diſadvantage of miſpending much Time and Pains, in committing ſuch a Burthen of Words to the overloaded Memory.

Hence it follows, that the beſt, at leaſt in our Circumſtances the beſt, Method is, by frequent Peruſal, to render yourſelf ſo perfectly well acquainted with your Diſcourſe, that you can with very little Aſſiſtance from looking upon your Notes, repeat it throughout. This Care will enable you to join in a great Degree, the Exactneſs of elaborate Compoſition, with the Spirit of extemporary Elocution.

The Sum of theſe Remarks is, "That we "ſhould endeavour to acquire that Kind of "Pronunciation, which approacheth moſt to "the Tone uſed in Diſcourſe, by a wiſe and "grave Man, naturally eloquent, ſpeaking up"on a ſerious and intereſting Subject."

It is more eaſy to conceive than expreſs Things of this Sort: But, if I were to explain by deſcending to Particulars, wherein this Kind chiefly conſiſteth, I would reduce it to this capital Precept: *Study Variety*. This is the great Dictate of Nature. Obſerve her ſpeaking in the Young, the Unlearned, or where

 Paſſion

Paſſion throweth off all Reſtraint; ſhe is for ever changing in Accent, Tone, Emphaſis. But herein keep always in Mind one Caution, *Vary ſo, as ſtill to become.* Beware of running into Exceſs: For there are certain Limits, beyond which Variety diſpleaſeth; as you may have oftentimes obſerved in Converſation, where ſome are harſh or ſhrill, ſome too low, and ſink into Faintneſs and Languor.

IT is manifeſt from a thouſand Inſtances, that among us who read our Sermons, the moſt common Fault is *Monotony.* We go on for half an Hour, with ſcarcely any Change of Voice, except the neceſſary ſinking at the End of a Period to take Breath: And this Pauſe is alſo continually the ſame; which periodical Riſing and Falling conſtantly repeated, like the Whiſtling of Wind, or Fall of Water, ſpreads Indolence and Liſtleſsneſs, and tendeth uſually to lull the Audience into Sleep.

THE Fault oppoſite hereto, which hath not that I know, a diſtinct Name, is of Courſe among us very rare; but is general among the Enthuſiaſts of all Sects; who ruſh violently from one Extreme into the other, paſſing from the loweſt Key, at one Bound, unto the utmoſt Pitch of the Voice; in which Manner, they go on to the End, alternately Whiſpering and Bawling, without Regard to Senſe or Propriety, but meerly by theſe ſudden mighty Changes of Sound, to rouze, affect, and aſtoniſh the Audience; which Method, however to a judicious Hearer more abſurd and offenſive, hath better

better Effects upon the Multitude, than the other over-cool and equal Way; because this latter is altogether unnatural; whereas that, although a Perversion of, is yet grounded in Nature, the only Source of what is right and pleasing: And an Error in the Extream of what is right, may well pass with the Bulk of Mankind for right, and so please; but a Mistake in the contrary Extream cannot have the same Effect; nay, must offend in Proportion as the other pleased.

VARIETY therefore, however necessary, should not be carried into Irregularity. Ever change; it is the Life of Pronunciation: But change with Cause; not for the Sake of varying, but suitably to the Sense.

As in a publick Assembly, the Voice should be raised to a certain Pitch, otherwise not being audible to all, with respect to a Part the Advantage expected must be lost; so Care should be taken, that it be not advanced much beyond this Pitch; lest it be forced thereby and strained; which, always disagreeable in the Sound, is painful, and may be hurtful to the Speaker: and, is besides, liable to the ill Consequence before-mentioned, that of not being well heard; for the Voice, wherever it is compelled beyond the natural Compass, becomes indistinct and inarticulate.

A PERSON, who hath a tolerable Ear, cannot fail of discovering this Limit in himself, and of knowing where he should stop. The Return of the Sound, when it sufficiently fills the

the whole ſurrounding Space, hath ſomewhat peculiar, that a ſhort Experience will enable him to diſtinguiſh: Or, if there ſhould be any Doubt, he may form a pretty certain Judgment, from the Looks and Poſtures of his Hearers.

WHEN he hath hit upon this Key, it ſhould be his Care to remain within it, deſcending from, and returning ſkilfully to it, as his Matter requires. For it is an injudicious and hurtful Miſtake to ſuppoſe, that the more loudly one ſpeaks, he is heard the farther; the Sounds may indeed ſpread farther, conveying with them but few Words, ill articulated, much leſs the entire Senſe.

IF it were poſſible, he ſhould reſtrain himſelf to thoſe Limits, within which he can ſpeak without Pain; becauſe wherever one ſpeaks with Uneaſineſs, he is heard with the ſame. An Exception, and I know not another, to this Rule, may have Place in very young Perſons; who ſhould be encouraged, where it is ſafe, to ſpeak rather above the Extent of their Voice; becauſe at that Seaſon of Life, Exerciſe and Habit may ſtrengthen, and raiſe it to this Height.

UNIFORMITY of Pronunciation, before blamed, hath produced one Peculiarity; that going on thus evenly, ſinking at the Cloſe, and returning to its Height at the Beginning of each Period, by this regular Circulation of Cadence, it acquires an Air of *Singing*, not uncommon, and very diſagreeable.

AGAIN,

AGAIN, I have known ſome Preachers above the ordinary Rank of Underſtanding, deſcend induſtriouſly into the familiar Air of Converſation, nay, even of comic Dialogue: In which Kind, I will not ſay, but ſome what may be done with good Effect; but I think the Attempt very hazardous: While you ſeek for Eaſe, you may loſe all Dignity, and ſink into unbecoming Levity; on this Occaſion, one of the leaſt pardonable Faults.

BEFORE we quit this Subject, it may not be amiſs to add one Obſervation. Men are deſirous of accompliſhing every Thing by their own Skill, of ſupplying, by Art alone, whatſoever is furniſhed by Nature and Genius. This Ambition manifeſts itſelf on all Occaſions, in great and ſmall Enterprizes; from the celebrated *Deſcartes*, who undertook to frame a World by Laws of his own Contrivance; down to the ingenious Artiſt, who deviſed Tables for the making of Verſes, by pure Mechaniſm.

IN like Manner, ſome learned Perſons have imagined a Method of rendering juſt Pronunciation eaſy to all, in a Way which we may name mechanical; by marking the Tones, with which every Word in a Speech or Sermon, nay, every Syllable, is to be ſpoken, in the ſame Way, as Pieces of Muſick are written: By which Means, any Perſon, even without Knowledge of the Senſe, may learn to pronounce juſtly, in the ſame Manner as one may, by the Help of muſical Notes, ſing truly, a Song which he doth not at all underſtand. And it is farther

ther affirmed, that this valuable Art was known to, and commonly practised by the Antients [a]: Which, if it were true, would strongly concur with these Persons, and might recommend this Invention to present Study and Enquiry.

THE first Question upon the Point must therefore be; Is this Fact true? Was this Art practised in *Greece* or in *Rome? Cicero* and *Quintilian*, who speak very fully of these Matters, the last particularly, as is his Custom, descendeth to a very minute Detail, do not once hint at this Art; a strong Presumption against its Existence. And the Authorities cited in Proof of its Reality, are at best very obscure and doubtful, as in such a Subject may reasonably be expected; but in general, have been much more probably interpreted in another Sense, as it would be easy to shew, if this were a proper Place for such Disquisition. Insufficient Grounds these surely, for the Belief of a Thing in its Nature thus marvellous.

IT may well be stiled *marvellous*, since the very Possibility of this admired Art hath been, with much Appearance, at least of Reason, called in Question.

IT hath been observed, that musical Tones proceed in a certain known Proportion, and at fixed Intervals; which enableth us to represent them by Signs; and thus to communicate the Knowledge of them to the Experienced, by Inspection: Whereas, in Speech, the Tones proceed

[a] Reflexions sur la Poesie, la Peinture, & la Musique. To. iii.

proceed not in any known Proportion, but are indefinite, and vary in numberless Degrees, all which cannot be marked, as the Skilful in Harmony say, by the Sounds of any musical Instrument; how then can they be recorded, or communicated in the same Manner?

BUT whatever may have been the Case among the Antients, for that is rather Matter now of Curiosity than Use; whether the Fact be even possible or not; this we may assert, and it is sufficient to our present Purpose, that with regard to the Elocution we now treat of, that of the Pulpit, the Scheme is altogether chimerical.

FOR suppose all the Tones of Speech to be thus marked, in some such Way as the Notes are in Musick; whom do you propose to benefit thereby? The Young and Unexperienced, who may by this Help learn mechanically to pronounce justly. But still the Labour of learning all these Marks must be very great; that of being able at first Sight to hit exactly the true Value of each, must be next to insuperable, the Labour indeed of a long Life: Where then is its Utility? Doth not this Scheme overthrow itself? You devise an Art useful to the Young and Unexperienced; which, if at all useful, can be so only in old Age.

AND would this Utility, if real, recompence the Pains of acquiring? Consider, in the Case of one who is to preach the Gospel, is all the Time necessary for the more important Acquisition of Knowledge in Things divine and human,

human, to be given up to this immenſe Toil of meer Pronunciation?

OR laſtly, waving theſe Objections, granting the Scheme to be practicable, that Time and Labour may be afforded, ſtill we aſk, What may be learned by theſe Signs or Notes? The Seaſons of raiſing or lowering the Voice, the Emphaſis and Cadences. But how ſmall a Part do theſe make? It is the Warmth, the Vehemence, the natural Earneſtneſs joined to Variety in the Orator, which form the Excellence of Pronunciation, which alone have mighty Influence on the Heart and Mind of the Hearer.

THUS, among an infinite Number of Tones, a Miſtake in one may alter the Senſe of a Paſſage, and cauſe much Confuſion: Can Skill ſo nice and complicated be conveyed mechanically to one ignorant of, or inattentive to the Senſe? Or ſuppoſe it conveyed, will this Man therefore ſpeak well? Muſt not the Features, Air, Motion, whole Perſon correſpond with the Diſcourſe? Hence Silence, Attention, Sympathy in the Audience. Without theſe, Exactneſs of Tone is dull, dead Juſtneſs. Words are Inſtruments; Soul only can act on Soul; and this is diffuſed through the whole Man. Say then that you may communicate juſtly ever-varying Tones; what avails it? Can your Notes communicate alſo Knowledge, Vivacity, Ardour? Can they infuſe a Soul?

WHEREFORE, leaving all ſuch refined and viſionary Projects, let us return to our firſt Plan.

" Obſerve

"Observe Nature well: Trace her from her "simplest Elements up through every higher "and more complex Form; and adhere to her "as closely as you can, with proper Consider- "ation of Circumstances, of Subject, Place, "and Audience."

THE second Part of Pronunciation was said to be *Gesture* or *Action*. *Cicero* and *Quintilian* have left scarcely any Thing to be added on this Subject. They direct the Speaker, not to stand altogether still and without Action, which is lifeless and unaffecting. Yet not to use immoderate Motion, because light and unbecoming. Not to loll and lean, as arguing Indifference, and want of Respect to your Audience. Not to use extravagant, or theatrical Gestures. To avoid all Grimace and Distortion. They take Notice of the due Position of the Head, the Disposition of the Features, the Motion of the Eyes, and more especially of the Hands, which you should not toss about, not raise too high, nor suffer to hang loosely down. Particularly, *Cicero* recommends in the strongest Manner Modesty; a Virtue, without which he thinks there never was a great Orator: And mentions, in the Person of *Crassus*, what was true of himself; that he never began to plead without turning pale, and even trembling [*b*].

OTHER Precepts there are, which I need not recite, as you may with more Profit consult the Originals. And besides, we may remark

[*b*] De Oratore. Lib. 1.

mark of all Rules in this Matter, that they help you to avoid Faults, rather than assist in doing well; which also will be performed much better by a well-judging Friend, than by the wisest Rules; and such therefore you should by no Means fail to consult.

BUT there is one general Observation, which if we would consider it well, and keep ever in our Minds, ready to be applied on all Occasions, would, if I be not deceived, answer the End proposed by these and the like Rules, more fully. It may be traced out in this following Manner.

NATURE, we know, hath adapted to the Sentiments and Passions their proper Look: She hath farther, as we have just now seen, fitted to them their several Tones of Voice: And we are now to observe, that she hath in the same Manner appropriated to each its own *Gesture*. Anger, Fear, Love, Hatred, Admiration, Astonishment, express themselves immediately, by involuntary Changes in the Features, in the Attitude of the Body, in the Motions of its several Parts, of the Head, the Eyes, and principally of the Hand, the Weapon of the Orator, as one aptly names it, not less clearly, than by the Sound of the Voice. The Constancy and Universality of which Expression it is, that makes some Degree of Action necessary, wherever the Matter of the Discourse is interesting; because, in such Cases, it is natural, it is always expected; the Want of it therefore disappoints, offends: You cannot be deemed sincere

sincere without it, and will not for that Reason obtain Belief, scarcely Attention.

THIS indeed is more variable from Custom, than are the Tones of the Voice. The Inhabitants, for Instance, of warmer Climates, use more Action than those of the colder; our Neighbours on the Continent more than we: Which Difference, we should in speaking have Regard to; because universal Custom is to be considered as Nature. There is not therefore required among us, the same Variety in Gesture as in Pronunciation; nor is it an Article of equal Importance,—although by no Means to be neglected.

ONE Thing let me add farther: A scrupulous Adherence to Rules, the Meditating and Practising beforehand Gestures, and affixing to each Period or Member of each, its peculiar one, is, I believe, however recommended, very prejudicial. For the Effort used in recollecting and applying these rightly, according to the pre-established Purpose, employeth the Mind, distracteth greatly its Attention, and must embarrass the Delivery: And the Consequence will be, that you shall become, through this divided Care, faulty in speaking, and affected in Action.

THE better Way is, "After some general "Care in observing what is graceful, what "unbecoming; make yourself perfect Master "of what you are to say, and of the Manner "in which you are to pronounce it: This "done, leave your Action to Nature. She will

" will faithfully attend, and accompany your
" Sentiments and Words as they flow, with
" aptly-correfponding Geftures.

ONE Limitation add:—There are few who do not in their younger Years contract fome Aukwardnefs or Ungracefulnefs of Manner, which groweth imperceptibly, and becometh confirmed by Habit. This we fhould ever be fufpicious of, and confult fome well-judging Friend concerning it. When we have been informed of any fuch, we fhould endeavour to retain always during the Time of fpeaking fo much Attention to Gefture, as may be fufficient to guard againft this ill Cuftom, ever ready to return upon us.

THUS to comprize in few Words this Article: "You fhould employ Gefture; Nature
" and Truth require it. Suit it to the receiv-
" ed Cuftom; that is Nature with you. Much
" Study herein is hurtful; only correct faulty
" Habits. Beware of taking Models from the
" Stage; they fit not the Gravity of this Place
" and Subject. Lean to the moderate Side:
" Too much Gefture in our Climate is offen-
" fively Faulty; too little, but Imperfection."

THE Conclufion of the Whole is this: The great Endeavour of every one who preaches the Gofpel, fhould be, to acquire, with his Audience, *Authority*. It is not to be expected, that all fhould arrive near to Perfection in the feveral Articles treated of, in folid Reafoning, good Compofition, true Ornaments; neither can the Bulk of Mankind diftinguifh nicely in thefe these Points: But this *Authority*, if obtained, will make up abundantly for whatever may be wanting in your Genius, or defective in their Conceptions. It sets every Thing you say in a favourable Light, hiding Imperfections, and doubling the Value of what is good. It giveth Spirit to your Diction, Force to your Arguments, Strength and Weight to your Advice. It rendereth you beloved and reverenced, and by Means thereof, useful; indeed, a publick Blessing.

How then shall we obtain this so valuable Authority? Ye may be assured of it by a reasonable Attention to what hath been delivered: "By establishing a Belief, that you are possest "of a competent Degree of Knowledge, of "perfect Sincerity, of Diligence. By com-"posing your Discourses with due Care; by "exact Attention in the right Choice of Sub-"jects; disposing them with clear Method; "treating them with close Reason, well mo-"derated Passion, and chaste Fancy; by ex-"pressing your Sense properly, with Perspi-"cuity and Shortness; and by delivering the "Whole with a natural, becoming Warmth "and Variety.

AND more especially, if you would do Good by Preaching, or maintain any Degree of this *Authority*, "Preserve a strict Conformity of "Manners to your Doctrines: Be what you "recommend."

LECTURE

LECTURE the Twenty-third.

Of modern LATIN POESY.

HAVING finiſhed the ſeveral Articles propoſed in the Beginning of theſe Lectures to be treated of, I had intended to have cloſed the whole Courſe with the preceding one: And it is a Reaſon of a particular Kind, which hath occaſioned the Addition of the preſent Diſcourſe. Some Things accidentally mentioned in the Series of the foregoing Lectures, have been thought liable to Objection, and, as I am farther informed, have even offended.

"IT is ſaid, that I have ſpoken with too "much Contempt of modern *Latin* Poeſy: I "have, it is urged, raſhly condemned At"tempts, ever held uſeful, recommended by "the Learned, and authoriſed by the Practice "of the moſt eminent Perſons; to an Excel"lence in which, ſome of the moſt diſtin"guiſhed Names in the Commonwealth of Letters owe their whole Splendor."

IT ſeems to me of Importance to clear up this Point: As the beſt Means to which, I ſhall deliver my Sentiments concerning it, as briefly as I can.

THE

THE Article which gave Rife to the Objection, was a Comparifon between the Writing of Verfe in one's own Tongue, and in a dead Language; wherein I did not hefitate to pronounce the former to be clearly preferable [a]: Which Decifion, however difpleafing it may be to fome, upon reconfidering the Affair, appeareth to me right.

IN poetical Performances, which are to be Works of Length and Care, (for I fpeak not of Trifles) you are to regard chiefly three Things:

How you may be moft ufeful. How you may moft generally pleafe. And in which Particular Kind you are moft likely to excel.

CONCERNING the two former of thefe, no Doubt can be entertained: A Poet in his native Language hath manifeftly the Advantage. If his Compofitions be fuch as are capable of giving Pleafure, or of being ufeful, they will produce thefe Effects more generally than the others, becaufe they are written in a Tongue univerfally fpoken and underftood; whereas the others are confined to the Few verfed in claffical Literature; and that to a certain Degree of Proficiency, lefs common, perhaps, than is ufually imagined.

THE People of *Syracufe*, after the Victory obtained over *Nicias*, fpared thofe among the *Athenian* Prifoners who could repeat Verfes of *Euripides*; for he was then alive, and his Works had not reached *Sicily*: A Proof, how

 fenfible

[a] See Lectures v, vi, xiii.

ſenſible even the common Sort were of the Beauty of his Tragedies.

THE *Italian* Peaſants in many Places have large Portions of *Arioſto* and [*b*] *Taſſo* by Heart, which they ſing or recite with a Kind of Rapture. And I have met with a Story relating to the former, that having fallen into the Power of noted Robbers, who were about to treat him with their uſual Violence, one of the Band having before accidentally ſeen him, diſcovered to the reſt his Name and Condition: Whereupon they diſmiſſed him with much Honour, in Return, ſaid they, for the Pleaſure he had given them by his Verſes. For, there is not any Rank of Men, in which ſome may not be found capable of reliſhing, and being delighted with a Work of true Genius. But no ſuch Effects as theſe above-mentioned, can happen with reſpect to the moſt excellent Poets in a dead Tongue: Nine Parts in ten of the Publick are ſhut out from them.

THE third Article it is, for which the Advocates of *Latin* Poeſy moſt earneſtly contend. "It is acknowledged, ſay they, that the *Ro*-"*mans* have left behind more perfect Models "of poetical Compoſition, than any ſince pro-"duced: How then are we moſt likely to ex-"cel? By following them as cloſely as we can. "Their Language alſo for Energy and Har-"mony is far ſuperior to every modern one; "the beſt among which are but Corruptions "of

[*b*] See ADDISON's Travels into *Italy*, under the Article of *Venice*.

"of it; an Advantage, that should determine "in its Favour the Choice of all Writers, who "are desirous to excel.

I SHALL not enter into the comparative Merit either of Writers or Language, a Point which would bear much Debate: Suppose for the present what is assumed, that the *Romans* are superior in both. My Doubts are these; Whether I may not imitate a good Model in a different Language? Whether I shall not imitate it better in this different Language, if I be much more skilled therein, than I could in that of the original Author? Whether, although the Language of the Model be much the finer, yet I shall not produce a Performance in this worse Language, but more familiar to me, better than in the other, better and less known. I cannot help thinking the Answer to these Points clear.

BUT whether these Arguments be strictly applicable to the Case before us, some have doubted, or affected to doubt. Yet how can we? Let a Person of the best Capacity study a modern Language with the utmost Application and Exactness, meerly in Books; let him compose a Poem in it; what innumerable Inelegancies and Improprieties would a skilful Native find therein? And this is precisely the Case of *Latin* Verses made at this Day; except that in the latter Case, there are no such Judges to detect the Errors; the Writers may escape Criticism, because the Readers are equally ignorant with themselves.

IT is agreed, that we know not at all the Pronunciation of antient *Rome:* Must we not then offend perpetually in Point of Harmony? It is not possible, that we should be acquainted with the precise Signification of Words, occurring but seldom in the few Books which now remain: And it is equally clear, that we cannot tell how the Signification of Words may be changed by their Union with others; which Ignorance must be a Source of great Improprieties. That very Disorder and Transposition peculiar to this Tongue, which seemeth to us arbitrary, had undoubtedly its Rules and Limits, which can be at best but faintly guessed at now. Writing therefore under these Disadvantages, we can proceed only by Conjecture; like one walking in dim Twilight, feeling out our Way, and chusing our Steps with much timorous Caution. We have a narrow Path chalked out for us by Authority, with many void Places and Chasms in it, in which we can at best but hobble and halt; whereas, a Poet should fly and soar, should subdue his Language to Enthusiasm, not creep its Slave.

THE Bulk of Mankind, whose Judgment ought to have great Weight in such Matters, hath determined accordingly. In all Countries, which are the Poets most highly celebrated, and read with universal Applause? Those who have written in the Dialect of their respective Countries. Thus all *Italians* have heard of *Ariosto* and *Tasso*; most read, all admire them: How few, comparatively, have any Knowledge

Knowledge of *Vida*, *Sannazar*, or *Fracastorio*, the best *Latin* Versifyers perhaps among the Moderns? Doth any *Frenchman* set the Fame of *Saint-Marthe*, *Santeüil* [b], or *Poligniac*, in Competition with that of *Corneille*, or *La Fontaine*? In our own Islands, can *Buchanan*, and all the Writers of the *Musæ Anglicanæ* put together, be compared with a *Shakespear*, a *Milton*, or a *Pope*?

At the same Time, I cannot agree with an admired *French* Writer, who remarks, and, if I remember rightly, repeats it as a favourite Observation, that because some of his Countrymen who have written well in *Latin* Verse, have not written in *French*, the former is therefore more easy: An Inference, it seems, not rightly drawn. To prove this, he should have shewn, that they had attempted the latter, and failed; which, I believe, does not appear to have been the Case in any Instance by him mentioned.

If we were to judge meerly from Reason, it should seem on the contrary, that a poetick Genius, in all Languages necessary to Excellence, if it appeared well in a dead Tongue, would exert itself with equal Vigour, and more Ease, in one known and familiar. Which Reasoning is also confirmed by Fact. *Sannazar* hath left in his *Arcadia*, *Italian* Verses justly esteemed. *Bembo* has written well in both Languages. *Ariosto* applied himself first, according

[b] *Voltaire*, *Siecle de Louis quatorze*, under the Article of *Santeuil*; and more particularly of *Poligniac*.

cording to the Fashion of the Age, to *Latin*, in which some of his Verses yet remain, pure and spirited: And it is known, that his Friend Cardinal *Bembo* thought so highly of his *Latin* Vein, that he earnestly exhorted him to write his Heroick Poem in that Language, which Advice he wisely and happily rejected. We have Cause to conclude, from *Milton*'s early Productions, that he would have equalled any *Latin* Writer of late Times, if he had not prudently preferred his native Tongue. To whom we may add *Cowley*, and *Addison*, especially the latter.

FROM all which my Inference is, that now, in these Days, as *Latin* poetical Compositions are the less excellent, so neither are they more easy; another Argument against applying to them Time and Genius, which might be more usefully employed.

IT would be easy to multiply Arguments; but they are not needful in a Point, according to my Apprehension, sufficiently clear: One, however, there is of a peculiar Nature, worthy of being mentioned.

IN every Undertaking of Moment which a Man engages in, he ought to intend and execute in such Manner, as to contribute, if it be possible, to the Advantage and Honour of his Country. This, it is true, in the Point before us, can be the Case of few; very few are qualified to improve a Language, or spread the Glory of a Country by poetical Compositions. Notwithstanding, the Intention, the Endeavour is right; and, in Disappointment, still it is a pleasing Reflexion, that one hath exerted his utmost Skill towards accomplishing a good Design.

I SHOULD not omit the Judgment of *Horace*, in a parallel Case, which is express:

"Atque ego cum Græcos facerem natus mare citrà
Versiculos; vetuit me tali voce Quirinus
Post mediam noctem visus, cum somnia vera:
In silvam non ligna feras insanius, ac si
Magnas Græcorum malis implere catervas."

AFTER this Preference given, as I imagine justly, to our native Tongue, the Question returns; "What? Are then *Latin* Compositions forbidden? Do you think that they should be discouraged and despised?" Herein it is, that I suppose a preceding Lecture to have been misunderstood. Few Words will suffice to explain my Opinion.

In former Mention made of this Matter, Works of Erudition and Science were excepted, which, for obvious Reasons, it may be prudent to compose in *Latin*. And it were to be wished, for general Utility, that these might be written with Clearness and Purity of Style, and, where the Subject admits, with Elegance: One of the best Treatises extant on the [*e*] Law of Nature, appears with great Disadvantage from the Uncouthness and Obscurity of the *Latin* Style. For this Reason it is fit, that all who

[*e*] Dr. CUMBERLAND

who mean to cultivate Letters, ſhould acquire a Skill of compoſing well in *Latin*; for which Purpoſe the making of Verſes in that Tongue is very uſeful: And therefore it is an Exerciſe much to be recommended to young Perſons. It is indeed the only Way, in which they are likely to obtain a full Knowledge of the Poets; a great, if not a neceſſary, Source of Elegance in every Language.

THIS Exerciſe is farther uſeful, as teaching the Force and Compaſs of the Tongue, and by this Means enabling them afterwards to vary at Will the Form of their Expreſſion.

BESIDES, this Exerciſe in riper Years will furniſh them with an Amuſement ſomewhat more than innocent, in ſome Sort uſeful, certainly polite.

MOREOVER, it may juſtly recommend thoſe who arrive at Excellence in it to Notice and Eſteem, as being a Proof of their Acquaintance with the beſt Authors, of their Diſcernment, and as Men love to ſpeak, of a *Claſſical Taſte*.

AND poſſibly, tho' in exceedingly rare Inſtances, this Talent may do Honour to a Country among Foreigners; which we are told was the Effect, the Peruſal of the *Muſæ Anglicanæ* had upon a famous *French* [a] Critick, who judged, that a Nation capable of producing ſuch *Latin* Poems, muſt have very fine Compoſitions in its own Language.

THESE are the chief Advantages which I can

[a] BOILEAU.

can recollect of writing in *Latin* Verse; and these rightly weighed point out the Degree of Esteem wherein it ought to be held : "A ne-"cessary Branch of early Education. After-"wards, a pleasing Amusement. An Ac-"complishment. And very rarely, if ever, a "Study or Business. Never contemptible: "And Praise worthy to a certain Degree."

I HOPE, that these Observations will be sufficient to answer the Objections made on this Head, or Suspicions entertained; probably from my having exprest my self on the Occasion, too shortly, or imperfectly.

ZEAL to justify myself, tempts me to produce yet a farther Proof, of another Kind; one fully decisive as to my own Opinion, but attended with some Hazard: This Zeal gets the better of Discretion so far as to make me own, that I have myself made more than one Attempt in this Way: And I believe, that the having taken Pains to perform well may be allowed a strong presumptive Proof, that the Performer disliketh not, nor despiseth the Art, or that Branch of it, in which he thus laboureth. Nay, I have been induced to go yet farther; and venture to lay before you the following *Latin* Composition; an Argument of my liking the Kind, however unable I may be to excel in it.

IRENE

IRENE

Carmen HISTORICUM.

Ad Præhonorabilem Vice-comitem BOYLE.

ROMANOS dum Musa modos, alienaque tentat
Regna, tremens, dubio passu, sub luce malignâ,
Heu! male dulciloqui numeros imitata Maronis,
Te BOYLÆE, vocat: Tibi non ignota sonat vox,
Quæ primis admota annis, mentique tenellæ,
Pieridum nitidos puerum te duxit in hortos;
Ergo adsis, dum fas nimirum, et blanda juventus
Crescentis vitæ semitam tibi floribus ornans,
Ridet adhuc, levibusque dat otia fallere nugis,
His saltem; quibus ipsa severo numine Pallas
Nempè docet juvenes altis proludere cæptis,
Sensim assurgentes. Teque ecce! volubilis ætas
Ad majora rapit; Sapientûm evolvere scripta,
Græcia quos peperit, quos artibus inclyta Roma,
Nec minor his, Britonûm, Phœbo carissima tellus:
Hinc regere eloquio populos, sanctumque senatum,
Consilioque gravi patriam fulcire labantem,
Atque novum claræ poteris decus addere stirpi.

Tu

Tu quoque florenti jam nunc gratulâris alumno
ALMA PARENS: Quin hujus et est mihi portio laudis.

JAM Scythiæ linquens hyemes, fluviosque perenni
Constrictos glacie, solique impervia regna,
Gens effræna virûm vastabat cladibus orbem
Attonitum. Non perpetuâ juga cana pruinâ,
Murorumque moræ, rapidos non æquora cursus
Oppositæve acies rumpunt. Orientis ab oris,
Occiduum ad Phæbum, quà littora Bosphorus urget
Perpetuo fremitu, dirâ cum strage procella
Intonat. Euxini fluctus et Caspia regna,
Caucaseæ rupes, vastique tremunt juga Tauri;
It supplex rutilas volvens Pactolus arenas.

QUINETIAM imperio tot quondam Græcia terras,
Tot populos complexa ruit. [b] Jam regia cingit
Mænia victor ovans: Tormentis ferrea grando
Funditur, et celsas quatiunt nova fulmina turres.
Murorum solidâ tandem compage solutâ,
Ingreditur, captâque ferox dominatur in urbe
Hostis; et in summis vexilla trementia muris
Auratas præbent vento diffundere Lunas.
Convellunt portas, et inundant strata viarum
Milite: Tum rapidas jactant ad culmina flammas;
Sævit atrox ignis, victorque incendia volvit
Cum strepitu, cælum & longè maria alta relucent.
Effusus furor hinc, et plena licentia ferro.

Sternitur

[b] Byzantii vel Constantinopolis.

Sternitur infælix populus discrimine nullo,
Infantes, canique patres, innuptaque Virgo,
Et gemitus tota morientûm personat urbe.

IPSE MAHUMMEDES fulgentibus arduus armis
Agmen agit, bello invictus, cæcumque tumultum
Dirigit, exacuens iras, et funera miscet;
Hunc Luctus, gelidusque Pavor comitantur euntem,
Et Lethum crudele; lavat vestigia sanguis.

NEC mora; Regales confestim turba penates
Aggreditur; rupto æratæ jam cardine valvæ
Dissiliunt, temeratque novus loca sacra tumultus:
Tum fragor armorum, tum fæminei ululatus
Ingeminare, minæque immistæ; it clamor ad auras.

AT Cæsar, fatis utcunque oppressus iniquis,
Cuncta videns amissa et ineluctabile numen,
Pugnat adhuc inter Primores, fidaque bello
Pectora, non dubiam quærens per vulnera mortem.
Hunc audentem animis, et adhuc vana arma moventem,
Hostis atrox cingit, mediisque in millibus unum
Claudit, et eversum sternit: tum multa pedum vis
Insilit, illiditque solo, calcatque, premitque
Exhalantem animam; non regia celsa gementi
Adgemit, exuperat misto clamore tumultus,
Et longè sævas voces vasta atria volvunt:
Concidit informi letho; pariterque vetustum
Imperium ruit, et ductum per sæcula regnum.

INTEREA

INTEREA trahitur magnâ comitante catervâ
Eximiâ virgo formâ, et florentibus annis;
Quam trepidam, dubioque ſequentem devìa paſſu,
Cum clamore trahunt captam, ſpolia ampla Tyranno.
Conſtitit Hæc cætu in medio, ſine more fluentes
Sparſa comas, lacrimiſque genas madefacta decoras:
Qualis ubi lucis portas Aurora recludit;
Quâ roſeos tollit vultus Dea, rore madeſcunt
Punicei flores, gemmataque prata renident.
STANT Proceres taciti; duruſque haſtilia miles
Inclinant, denſique inhiant et ſiñgula luſtrant,
Inſolitam ſpeciem ac divinæ munera formæ,
Ambroſiaſque comas, teneris rotantia nimbis
Lumina, marmoreumque premens ſuſpiria pectus.
Spectat inexpletùm, ſubito perculſus amore
Rex Aſiæ, figitque avidos in virgine vultus.
Tum fari hortatur quæ ſit; quo ſanguine creta;
Quid petat; et trepidam verbis ſolatur amicis.
[a] Ac veluti citharam doctus pulſare ſonantem,
Et liquido cantu ſuſpenſas ducere mentes,
Protinus haud voce ingenti ſacra ora reſolvit,
Dulcia ſed tenui flectens modulamina cantu
Proludit,

[a] Qual muſico gentil, prima che chiara
Altamentè la lingua al canto ſnodi;
All'harmonia gli animi d'altrui prepara
Con dolci ricercate, in baſſi modi:
Coſi coſtei, che ne la doglia amara
Già tutte non oblîa l'arti et le frodi;
Fà di ſoſpir breve concento in prima,
Per diſpor l'alma, in cui le voci imprima.
TASSO GIERUS—Canto 16, Stanza 43.

Proludit, ſenſimque illabitur intima corda:
Talis et hæc artis memor in diſcrimine ſummo
Fæmineæ, demiſſa caput, ſuſpiria ducit,
Et lacrymis faciles aditus ad pectora pandit;
Circumfuſa armis roſeo dein incipit ore.

O Rex, attonitum vaſto qui turbine mundum
Concutis invictus, patriaſque in mænia lunas
Erigis, invalidæ ſaltem miſerere puellæ,
Jam paſſæ mala dura, et adhuc graviora timentis.
Non humilis tamen, et plebeio ſanguine creta
Complector genua, illacrymans; ſed regibus orta
Sceptrigeris, quibus hæc olim pulcherrima tellus
Paruit, exultans meliori Græcia fato.
Ipſe etiam Cæſar qui funera multa ſuorum
Viderat heu! miſer, et miſerâ jam morte peremptus,
Me natam, caræ Genitricis nomine dictam
Irenen, in ſpem regni pater optimus alti
Eduxit; Nunc vincla ferunt contraria fata.
O Patria! O Genitor! Domus o per ſecula, terræ
Regnatrix! Vos templa dei, demiſſaque cælo
Religio! ergo omnes radice evertit ab ipſo,
Gens effuſa polo, atque æterni numinis ira.
Me tamen haud lethi facies, vibrataque terrent
Spicula; deſcendam læto jam funere ad imos
Caſta tamen, Manes, & digna parentibus umbra:
Quin reſera hoc gremium, vitamque abrumpe morantem.
Sed te per teneros ſenſit ſi pectus, amores,
Per dulces natos, caſti per fædera lecti,
Per majorum umbras oro, per quicquid ubique eſt
Sacrati, prohibe infandos a corpore tactus,
Neu mihi virgineos vis barbara polluat artus.

HÆC ait, et gemitus preſſit luctantia verba.

Stant

Stant proceres innixi haſtis, inſuetaque flexit
Corda dolor, lacrymæ manant invita per ora.
Non eadem Regi facies, non priſtina manſit
Durities; animum ſpecies præclara loquentis
Accendit, majorque afflictæ gratia formæ:
TUNC olli breviter: Quis te pulcherrima Virgo
Læderet, aut caſtum violaret vulnere corpus,
Crudelis? Non hæ nobis victoribus iræ:
Solve metus: Neu finge animo nos impia ferre
Sceptra, et inhumanis ſævos gaudere triumphis.
Gloria non mendax, non prædæ inſana cupido
Armatos in bella trahunt; aſt ardua juſſa
Divini *Vatis*, cælique ſuprema voluntas;
Exulet ut vetus impietas, ut fulgeat alte
Vera fides, iret magnis ſub legibus orbis.
Ipſe tibi, incenſus tantæ virtutis amore,
Munera magna feram, majoraque regna paternis
Subjiciam; preme ſingultus. His demere dictis
Æger amore ſtudet curas, ſolvitque timorem.
HANC Selymus, cui fæmineæ cuſtodia prædæ
Credita, deducit mæſtam in penetralia celſa,
Lætantes inter turmas, crepitantiaque arma.
IMPERII Rex inde gravi de pondere, canis
Cum patribus, quâ vi gentes frænare ſuperbas,
Quos bello vaſtare, Quibus dare jura ſubactis,
Conſulit; et regni ſurgentis lubrica firmat.
INTEREA ſummo, juſſu victoris, honore
Excipitur Virgo. Thalamis fulgentibus oſtro,
Auratis excelſa toris, et murice ſpreto,
Mæſta jacet: Sculptas onerant convivia menſas,
Nequicquam; vinum geminato ſpumat in auro.
Centum florentes formâ et juvenilibus annis,
Barbara quas acies regum de ſtirpe creatas

Sedibus

Sedibus abripuit crudeli ſorte paternis,
Circumſtant agiles Nymphæ; blandiſque miniſtrant
Officiis: Fundit dulci pars carmina voce;
Pars trěmulos docto percurrit pollice nervos;
Scilicet infixas ut poſſint fallere curas,
Exuat et lentos ſenſim mens ægra dolores.

IPSE ferox victor, durum cui pectus amore
Æſtuat, aſſiduis precibus faſtidia tendit
Vincere, nunc votis ſupplex, nunc lenitèr urgens
Blanditiis, ſimul et promiſſa ingentia miſcet,
Regalem exponens oculis longo ordine pompam.

QUID potuit Virgo infælix? Quâ rumpere tantas
Inſidias; quâ vi ſævis obſiſtere fatis?
Hinc regalis honos, menti quoque grata poteſtas
Fæmineæ, claruſque faventi marte tyrannus
Sollicitant; ſubitâ abſterrent proſtrata ruinâ
Indè paterna domus, miſeræ ſola ipſa ſuperſtes
Relliquiæ; et tepidi cognato ſanguine rivi.

AT natura trahens intùs, ſpes læta, Juventus
Flexilis, et tempus quod lenit acerba, labantem
Evicêre animum, fallaciſque ardor amoris
Dulcis inexpertæ. Qualis flos imbre gravatus
Labitur, et mæſtis moriens langueſcit in hortis;
At zephyro ſpirante levis ſe tollit ad auras,
Purpureos pandens læto ſub ſole colores:
Non ſecus Irenè luctu lacrymiſque fugatis,
Enituit: medios inter Regina triumphos
Incedit, niveam cingens diademate frontem,
Exultans umbrâ, tituliſque inflata ſuperbis.
Ah miſera! immitem teneris amplexibus hoſtem,
Immemor everſæ patriæ cæſique parentis,

Ergo

Ergo foves facilis, ſortiſque ignara futuræ?
JAM belli vox rauca ſilet. Non ærea cantu
Accendit tuba florentes ad prælia turmas;
Non undare cruor, non armis fulgere campos;
Mænia non tremere horribili concuſſa fragore
Aſper at exutâ molleſcit caſſide miles,
Regis ad exemplum, luxuque effrænis inerti
Laſcivit. Viridem pars lentè fuſa per herbam
Umbriferos inter ramos, et murmur aquarum,
Concentuſque avium, longis exhauſta periclis
Membra fovet, vetiti libantes pocula bacchi,
Inſtaurantque dapes: Pars cæco vulnere fixa
Haurit amans teneras curas, et blanda venena,
Captarum illecebris, et gratâ compede vincta.
QUALIS ubi rapido belli de turbine Mavors
Pulverulentus adhùc et fervens cæde recenti,
Victus amore, Cyprum quærens Paphioſque receſſus,
Cœleſtes petit amplexus, et dulcia furta:
Tum belli ſiluêre minæ; fremit Ira, Pavorque
Nequicquam, infrendet telo Mors ſæva repreſſo;
Candidaque effulget lætis Pax reddita terris.
SED non longa quies: Accendit priſtinus ardor
Corda virûm, et turpi pudet indulſiſſe veterno:
Extimulat Pietas atrox; ſimul alta priorum
Gloria geſtarum; atque angens ſatiata libido.
Ergo indignantes luxu fregiſſe vigorem,
Arma fremunt omnes, et mollia vincula rumpunt.
PRETEREA vulgus non cæco murmure regem
Incuſat, quem nunc pudet heu! muliercula victum
Detinet amplexu indigno; dum colligit hoſtis
Diſperſas acies, et bellum ſponte minatur,
Hæc agitant, gliſcitque truci violentia turbæ.

SENSERAT insolito misceri castra tumultu
Mustapha, quem claro virtus insignis honore
Evexit, Regique dedit fulgere secundum
Imperio: Metuens igitur ne serperet ultrà
Tanta mali labes, sumantque incendia vires,
Præcipitare moras statuit, regemque requirit:
Atque ita sublimem compellat voce tyrannum.
O decus heroum, summi sate sanguine Vatis,
Quem tellus devicta tremit, quà flavus Hydaspes
Gurgite fumanti tepidos secat aureus agros,
Threicias longe ad hyemes Hebrumque nivalem;
Sit fas vera loqui, sinceraque promere dicta,
Asperiora licet; vestræ res aspera poscunt.
QUICQUID sol oriens lustrat, terras ubi nunquam
Romani fulsêre aquilæ, devicimus armis:
Nunc quoque tot ducibus, tot quondam læta triumphis
Græcia vasta tremit, regnique vetusta superbi
Fumat adhuc sedes, spumatque cruore recenti.
Unde quies igitur? Belli cur fulmina cessant?
Deterior bello nos luxus fregit. Ad arma
En! iterum densæ excusso torpore catervæ
Conveniunt, hastasque minaci murmure vibrant,
Concussisque fremunt clypeis, regemque reposcunt.
" Cur medio exclamant, languet Victoria cursu?
" Cur torpent dextræ, et cessat Bellona tonare?
" Et nunc attoniti repetitis cladibus hostes
" Exhaustas reparant vires. En! agmina cogunt,
" Auratasque cruces iterum dant fulgere ventis.
" Quid Rex interea, sævâ quem strage cruentum

" Horruerant

" Horruerant toties, qui Græco ſanguine tinxit
" Flumina, et evertît fumantes fulmine muros?
" Imbelles fovet amplexus, inhoneſtaq; carpit
" Gaudia, et ingentes fœdo ſpes rumpit amore.
Scilicet hæc mandant divini oracula Vatis?
Sic Proavi meruêre? Fidem ſic protegis armis?
Surge, age, molle jugum collo excute, clarus ut olim
Egredere, O noſtrum decus. En! horrentia ferro
Millia multa vocant, ingens clamore remugit
Boſphorus, armorumque relucet fulgure cœlum.

Exarsit Victor monitis; excuſſus amoris
Torpor abit, rurſumque animis fremit arduus arma:
[a] Sic bellator equus, quem mollis inertia pugnæ
Detinet oblitum, per paſcua læta vagantes
Inter equas, mulcetque ſolutum blanda cupido;
Arma crepent ſi fortè, tubæ vel acuta ſonet vox,
Igne recaleſcit ſolito; tremit, arrigit aures,
Scintillatque oculis; reſonant hinnitibus arva.

Tunc breviter; Cum lux reſerabit craſtina cœlum,
Agmina dic coeant inſtructis cuncta maniplis,
Atque forum repleant; ſolium ſublime locetur;
Ipſe

[a] ῾ως δ'ότε τὶς ςάτος ἵππος ἀκοςήσας ἔπι φατνὴ, &c.
Hom. Ili. lib. 6.
Quem locum imitatus eſt Virgilius, & ferme æquavit; Torquatus quoq;
Taſſus uti ſolet, elegantèr. Gierus. Canto 16, Stanz. 28.
Qual feroce deſtrier, ch' al faticoſo
Onor de l' arme vincitor ſia tolto, &c.

Ipſe adero, et vanos pellam ratione timores.
Dixerat. Hic Regis properans mandata faceſſit.
POSTERA cœruleos fluctus Aurora reliquit,
Pallidaque emergens extinxit ſidera Titan,
Cum tuba clara canit: Tunc agmina denſa coire
Cernere erat, juſtiſque forum ſtipare maniplis;
Frænatis in equis, inter quos limite longo
Ductores volitant, auroque oſtroque decori:
Pondere terra gemit; per templa domoſq; coruſcat
Ænea lux, longoque illuſtrat fulgure cœlum:
Mille tremunt vexilla, ſinuſque ad flamina pandunt
Purpureos, curvæ diſcurrunt aere lunæ.
Stat circum inſtructus Miles, pacataque vibrat
Tela manu; ferri tremulus nitor exit ad auras
Concuſſi, dum turba fremens movet ordine denſo:
Qualis ubi primum jubar extulit ætherius Sol,
Mane novo, ſummum leviter cum flamina ſtringunt
Oceanum, criſpantur aquæ; mox tollitur, altùm
Magnâ mole fremens; Albeſcunt cærula ſpumis.
INCERTI, quæ cauſa vocat, quidve inſtet agendum,
Suſpenſis dubitant animis, quæruntq; paventque,
Arrecti ad vanos ſtrepitus; hinc corpore vaſto
Fluctuat hùc illùc inclinans turba, viciſſim
Pulſaque, et impellens, motuque reciproca vibrat.
AST ubi, cum magno Princeps clangore tubarum
Arduus ingreditur, multoque ſatellite cinctus,
Hùc

Hùc omnes tendunt, oculisque et mentibus
hærent:
Haud secus alma ceres, gravidis quæ nutat
aristis
Collis apricus ubi aut fœlix uligine campus
Semina læta fovet, dum vespertinus oberrat
Aer et incerto variantur cardine venti,
Huc levis àtque illuc fluitat, quá spiritus urget
Mobilis; at dubio si tandem regnet olympo
Eurusve, Zephyrusve, aut imbribus humidus
Auster,
Hæc sequitur facilis victorem, huic aurea culmos
Flectit, et unanimi procumbit messe supina.

EXCELSUM in medio solium supereminet,
amplis
Porrectum spatiis, multoque insternitur ostro;
Considet hic ingens Victor; simul inclyta regum
GræcorumSoboles, cui splendida murice et auro
Vestis et insignis gemmarum luce coruscat;
At velo caput abdiderat, vultusque decoros.
Tum vero cecidit sonus omnis, ut alta silet nox.
Tandem consurgens clarâ Rex voce profatur.

AUDIVI, nec me latuêrunt murmura vestra
Questusque insani, Miles; me nempe prioris
Oblitum decoris, me religionis avitæ
Immemorem, fœdo languere cupidine captum.
Scilicet hæc merui? Me siccine nôstis, iniqua
Pectora, qui totum laceravi cædibus orbem
Christicolam, qui tantum evertî sedibus imis
Imperium? Ecquando segnem me, aut forte
morantem,
Vel cupidum vitæ tranquilla et tuta sequentem
Vidîstis, dum pugna furit? Vos testor: An ultro
Incendentem

Incendentem animos, medioque in turbine belli
Pulvere consperfum, multoque cruore rubentem?
Quis fluvios innare ferox, quis mænia primus
Scandere, per densos hostes, per tela, per ignes,
Stridentesque globos, et sæva tonitrua ferro;
Atque triumphantes muris infigere Lunas?
Hæc mea laus; sileam quid enim, quod Græcia, quod Sol
Testatur, quod adhuc in pectore multa cicatrix?
Dextera, nec magis hâc, ditavit manibus umbras.

CESSAVI fateor; belli vox rauca parumper
Conticuit; dedimus nos corpora lassa quieti.—
Usque adeone nocet, post tot discrimina rerum,
Vel ludis animum, vel membra fovere sopore?
Nec venit in mentem quæ sit conditio vitæ
Mortalis, quàm fessa malis infractaque, poscat
Alternas mens ægra vices, et dulce levamen?

INSUPER audite, atque animis hæc figite dicta.
Rex sum, non titulos jactans et inania sceptra;
Haud vestrûm est igitur scrutari pectora regis,
Sensusque arcanos; sed contrà horrore vereri
Sancto perculsos: Vestrûm est parere, jubebo:
Mors premet invitos; Est omne rebellio murmur.

QUID tamen admisi facinus? quæ tanta peregi?
(Ut loquar ex æquo.) Quid enim? Male-cautus amabam.
Esto: novum crimen vos primi fingitis. Ergò
Rex, Juvenis, Victor nunquam sine crimine amabit?
Nil mos, nil leges, pietas nil tale profatur.
Infe Mahummedes, qui sancta oracula cœlo
Deduxit

Deduxit puramque fidem mortalibus ægris,
Divinus vates; cum bellum pace mutavit,
Otia fœmineo vacuus consumpsit amore.
Quid pretii sperat super ignea sidera virtus?
Quem sequimur finem? Perfunctis munere vitæ
Egregiis Deus ipse viris quæ dona rependet?
Scilicet insignes præstanti copore nymphas,
Atque immortali florentes vere juventæ,
Halantes per agros, ad aquarum murmura blanda,
Concentus inter volucrum, viridante sub umbrâ,
Amplecti dabit; et viventes omne per ævum
Carpere perpetuâ semper nova gaudia flammâ.

HUJUS at erroris, (si me tamen abstulit error,)
Quæ mihi causa fuit; Quæ discite, qualis origo,
Compede quâ teneor: Sic enim sint ferrea vobis
Corda licet, spero tamen ignoscetis amanti,
Cernentes faciem, quæ me pulcherrima vicit
Ætheriis similem, et radiantia lumina flammis.
Aspicite: atque meum si fas, reprendite crimen.

HÆC fatus, velum detraxit ab ore puellæ.
Qualis ubi spissâ dudum Sol conditus umbrâ,
Aureus emergit, tandem caligine pulsâ,
Splendidior; ridet diffuso lumine cœlum.
Non aliter posito velamine, regia proles
Extulit os roseum, solioque refulsit ab alto.
Attonitæ stupuêre acies, avidosque tuendo
Defixæ pascunt oculos, tacitæque pererrant
Quam faciem! quali cum majestate venustam!
Atque genas divæ similes; ac lactea colla;
Perque humeros crines, et eburnea pectora, sparsos.

INDE

INDE repentino cum primum erepta ſtupore
Libera mens rediit, tollunt ad ſidera plauſus
Sponte ſuâ, dignamq; fatentur crimine formam.
CONSTITIT, atque diu trux agmina circum-
ſpexit,
Terribiles volvens oculos, tum murmura dextrâ
Compeſcens, torvo ſic addidit ore, Tyrannus.
JAM ſatis eſt; ficto me crimine ſolvitis: Illam
Quis non victricem agnoſceret? Æthere talem
Ipſe ingens Vates vix credam amplectitur ulnis.
Es fateor mihi jure tuo cariſſima, vultu
Æmula Cœlicolis, animi neque dotibus impar
IRENE, mea lux, regum certiſſima proles:
Non radii ſolis, non vitæ carior ipſe
Spiritus hic, non qui nutrit præcordia ſanguis;
Eſt tamen his radiis, eſt vitâ carior ipſâ
Gloria, et invidiâ tandem laus bellica major:
Nec frangent animum molles ne fingite, curæ.
Quid quod amem? tamen et Rex ſum, Bellator,
& Heros:
Forſan amantem ætas, imbellem haud poſtera,
tradet.
Fracta meas iterum plorabit Græcia vires,
Occiduique orbis dominatrix, impia Roma:
Ecce! incenſa ruunt delubra, cruceſque profanæ,
Et ſimulacrorum fractus reſonabit humi grex.
QUIN hæc accipite, et veſtrum cognoſcite
Regem.
Audebit quicunque meos reprendere mores,
Immemorem carpens famæ, luxuque ſolutum,
Quid carâ pro laude geram, quid vindice dextrâ
Molior,

Molior, aſpiciat: — " Meque inde tremiſcite
cuncti."

Hæc ait, et gladium diſtringens, impulit ictu
In collum Irenes. Cadis heu! pulcherrima,
dextrâ
Quâ minime decuit, ſævæ data victima famæ:
Fœlix, ſi patriis jacuiſſes caſta ruinis,
Nec tibi barbarici placuiſſent fœdera lecti!
Nam mutilus ſubitâ truncus procumbit humi vi,
Singultanſq; tremenſq; cruorem tramite multo
Purpureis ſtillans rivis: Caput exilit altè
Avulſum, longo rapiturque volubile tractu.

Coelestes, Illi fœdos jam ſanguine, vultus,
Pallenteſque genas, extinctaque lumina cernunt,
Attoniti; exangueſque metu: labefacta per oſſa
Horror iit. Siluêre diu: Mox undique triſtis
Prorupit gemitus, perque agmina vaſta cucurrit.
Rex abit, infrendens gravitèr, viſumque relinquit.

The END.